James S. Bosco
*University of California, Santa Cruz*

William F. Gustafson
*San Jose State University*

# Measurement and Evaluation in Physical Education, Fitness, and Sports

PRENTICE-HALL, INC., Englewood Cliffs, New Jersey 07632

*Library of Congress Cataloging in Publication Data*

Bosco, James S.
  Measurement and evaluation in physical education,
fitness, and sports.

  Includes bibliographies and index.
  1. Physical fitness—Testing. 2. Sports—Ability
testing. I. Gustafson, William F. II. Title.
GV436.B54  1982      613.7'1      82-13204
ISBN 0-13-568352-1

Cover design by Ray Lundgren
Manufacturing buyer: Harry P. Baisley

Printed in the United States of America

10  9  8  7  6  5  4  3  2  1


ISBN 0-13-568352-1


Prentice-Hall International, Inc., *London*
Prentice-Hall of Australia Pty. Limited, *Sydney*
Editora Prentice-Hall do Brasil, Ltda., *Rio de Janeiro*
Prentice-Hall
Prentice-Hall of India Private Limited, *New Delhi*
Prentice-Hall of Japan, Inc., *Tokyo*
Prentice-Hall of Southeast Asia Pte. Ltd., *Singapore*
Whitehall Books Limited, *Wellington, New Zealand*

# CONTENTS

## CHAPTER FIVE
## TESTS OF "SPECIFIC" MOTOR ABILITIES:
## FLEXIBILITY, AGILITY, AND BALANCE  *105*

## CHAPTER SIX
## TESTS OF "SPECIFIC" MOTOR ABILITIES:
## CARDIOVASCULAR ENDURANCE  *125*

## CHAPTER SEVEN
## TESTS OF GENERAL MOTOR ABILITY  *143*

## CHAPTER EIGHT
## SPORTS SKILLS TESTS: INDIVIDUAL-PARTICIPANT
## SPORTS  *158*

## CHAPTER NINE
## SPORTS SKILLS TESTS: DUAL-PARTICIPANT
## SPORTS  *199*

## CHAPTER TEN
## SPORTS SKILLS TESTS: MULTIPLE-PARTICIPANT
## SPORTS  *227*

# PREFACE

Why another textbook in measurement and evaluation? The market has been literally flooded almost yearly with either new texts on the topics or with revisions of earlier texts. What would prompt two presumably rational professors to offer still another text? The expected response, of course, is that the authors have attempted to treat the content differently than has been the case in almost all other instances.

In what way does this textbook attempt to be different? First, the authors have not only confined their discussion of tests primarily to descriptive materials but have also attempted to critique many of these tests. In some sections, exception has been taken to many time-honored beliefs attributed to authorities in measurement and evaluation.

The authors have been around long enough to realize that others will critique their critiques. It is their judgment that this is most desirable. In fact, one of the major purposes of the text is to encourage critical thinking on the part of the reader. Even if some of the authors' theories or points of view are in error, if they serve to create intensified examination of the issues, then the time and effort expended in the preparation of the manuscript will have been justified.

The chapter on marking, for example, takes some rather definite positions on a variety of concerns. It discusses the meaning of marks; their uses and abuses; ways in which some order may be brought to the marking process; and the obligation of instructors in marking to their students, the students' parents, their schools, and to society in general.

The chapter on social appraisal attempts to explode some of the beliefs about the social value of participation in physical education. One of these is the "article of faith" that participation in physical education, per se, will contribute positively to one's social adjustment, development, or efficiency. Also examined is the question of whether physical education, as a discipline, has any responsibility for the social nurture of its students. Or, perhaps, the question should be phrased to ask whether physical education has greater responsibility than any other discipline. The answer to either question is based, in part at least, upon various considerations, including that of a definition or description of what is meant by terms such as social development.

Some of the orthodox views associated with test construction, revision, and evaluation are challenged. Some alternate suggestions are provided for the effective treatment of these concerns. Less attention is accorded to forms of examinations and more attention to effective use of examinations and to interpretations of test scores.

Another fairly novel approach has been taken to the evaluation of various tests of physical status or performance. Objection is made to the broad use of composite tests designed ostensibly to appraise what appear to be relatively specific qualities such as physical fitness. Instead, it is advanced that testing should be limited in most instances to qualities that are specific, indeed. Thus, tests of motor abilities are subdivided under headings such as strength, power, and balance. Where subscores of qualities such as these are summed in one or another way, it is possible, perhaps even likely, that several subjects will attain like scores even though their specific capabilities are quite diverse. Composite tests, therefore, may obscure the distinct needs or capabilities of students.

Still, it is recognized that there may be justification for the use of some composite tests. In either instance, if norms are available and of sufficient value to be included in the text, they will be provided in both the usual English units as well as in their metric equivalents. It is believed that this is the first time that metric equivalents for American tests have been published. As a consequence, the norms will be useful immediately in many foreign countries and will retain their value as this and other countries continue to adopt the metric system.

The chapter on applications and interpretations of statistics makes little in the way of claims to novelty and innovation. It is a fairly standard treatment of statistics that are commonly used by physical educators or that appear in the professional journals that are of primary interest to physical educators. More comprehensive treatments are found in numerous textbooks confined solely to statistics and even to several measurement books authored by physical education specialists. It is believed, however, that the chapter will prove useful to those readers who wish to have a handy guide to statistical formulas and tables. Explanations, although not comprehensive, do attempt to clarify those circumstances under which a particular statistic is appropriate for use. Very little space is given, on the other hand, to the underlying theoretical bases.

The section on accessing computers is an attempt at a compromise between

# CHAPTER ONE
# WHY TEST?

There are numerous reasons why physical educators should employ testing in their programs. They may be categorized in many different ways. For the purpose of this discussion, although not necessarily in order of importance, the reasons for testing have been divided into nine reasonably discrete categories: 1) classification of students; 2) diagnosis of student needs and weaknesses; 3) evaluation of instruction; 4) evaluation of program; 5) marking; 6) motivation; 7) instruction; 8) prediction; and 9) research.

## CLASSIFICATION OF STUDENTS

In order that instruction may be facilitated, it is often desirable to subdivide students into at least three instructional levels, for example, beginning, intermediate, and advanced. If students are heterogeneously classified, it is difficult to gear the instruction so that it will not be too difficult for the least experienced or least talented students or too easy, and insufficiently challenging, for the best students. On the other hand, if students are homogeneously grouped into beginning, intermediate, and advanced sections of a beginning badminton section, for example, the ranges of abilities found within any of the groups will be much smaller; hence, the instruction can be more appropriate for each particular level. In utilizing such a grouping procedure, it is expected that upon completion of a beginning section of a particular activity, the students will have had ample opportunity to acquire necessary skills and knowledges that will permit them to function effectively on the intermediate level and to qualify subsequently for the advanced level. For most of the typical activities offered in a secondary school physical education program, there are several appropriate tests that can be used for classification purposes. Care must be taken to assure that the test employed is valid, reliable, and appropriate to the skill level (see Chapter 3). Or, if the teachers wish, they can use their subjective judgment, based upon careful observation of students participating in the activity, in order to determine appropriate levels of classification.

## DIAGNOSIS OF STUDENT NEEDS AND WEAKNESSES

Tests may also be used to diagnose student weaknesses or needs. For example, a test of badminton playing ability may reveal an inability of the student to perform or execute certain basic strokes. One of these might be the deep-clear stroke. Noting this in the test, the instructor then can provide appropriate drills and instruction for the student in order to provide for the development or improvement of this particular stroke. A strength test may reveal that some students are weak in the shoulder girdle or in some other muscle group. The instructor can again insure that these particular students will have an appropriate program of developmental exercise of the shoulder girdle in order to develop satisfactory strength in this area.

## EVALUATION OF INSTRUCTION

Often, instructors wonder whether they are successful in presenting subject material to their students; they would like to have some device to assure themselves that their instruction is satisfactory. One of the means by which one can ascertain instructional effectiveness would be to test the levels of ability of students after instruction. Instructors would then compare their group test scores with those of other instructors who had administered tests to other sections. If the student groups could be assumed to have been of equal ability at the beginning, then it might be reasonable to also assume that those instructors whose classes demonstrate greater ability at the conclusion of the activity have been more effective as instructors.

It must be recognized, of course, that other factors could conceivably enter into the picture. Effectiveness of instruction would not be the sole determinant of playing ability at the conclusion of an activity. However, upon repeated testing with a number of groups, if the groups of a particular instructor are, in terms of playing ability, consistently superior to those of another instructor, the conclusion could well be drawn that the first of the two instructors is more effective. Such testing will also reveal certain areas of the instruction that may not be as effective as other areas. For example, a knowledge test in badminton might reveal that students have satisfactorily learned the rules but have not fully grasped some of the concepts involved in doubles strategy. Information of this sort, gained from testing, could then be utilized by the instructor in planning the content of subsequent courses in badminton. The instructor would make every effort to make clear the strategies of doubles play and to question students more frequently to determine whether they are grasping the essentials of this phase of the game.

## EVALUATION OF PROGRAM

Skills and knowledge tests may be administered at the beginning of a block of activity in order to determine past knowledge and abilities acquired by students. This information will help instructors determine the point at which to begin instruction. For example, if students are totally unaware of the rules and play procedures, instructors may begin with this phase of instruction. If students have a fairly thorough knowledge of the rules, this aspect would not have to be emphasized, and more advanced phases of the game could be pursued. Similarly, if it were observed through testing that students in a beginning section of badminton had had no previous background (i.e., did not know how to hold the racket, how to serve, the wrist action in executing the various strokes), then instruction would begin at the most basic stage.

## MARKING (GRADING)

One of the most important reasons for testing is to reveal students' performance levels, or, in other words, to ascertain the degree of achievement of program objectives by each student. This is not to suggest that test scores should be the sole determinant of student performance, but that they would be among the criteria utilized in determining a student's mark. In determining the degree to which students have acquired knowledge, written tests are probably one of the more efficient forms for evaluating student achievement. Such is not necessarily the case in evaluating achievement in terms of playing ability or of teamwork. Various tests might be used to determine how well a student can perform; quite often, however, an instructor will want to evaluate the student subjectively, not in an artificial testing situation but as the game is being played. Assuming instructors are experts, i.e., they have a thorough knowledge of the activities they teach, there is certainly no reason why they should hesitate to use their expert judgment, subjective in part though it may be, to evaluate student achievement. Marking procedures will be discussed more thoroughly in Chapter 13.

## MOTIVATION

It has been noted widely that if teachers notify their students that a test is to be given at some future date, this notification tends to motivate students to prepare for the test so that they may compare more favorably with other students when tested. It is recognized, of course, that all students are not motivated equally; but testing serves as a very useful motivational device and tends to encourage students to try harder to increase their levels of performance and their breadth and depth of knowledge.

## INSTRUCTIONAL DEVICE

Tests serve as very useful instructional devices. If students are permitted to observe other students as they take a badminton skills test, they may learn how they can perform better. They may observe and learn from the errors and successes of those who precede them. Also, at the conclusion of a test, if the instructor reviews the test, the students are given an additional opportunity to learn. If errors are pointed out to students when reviewing tests, it is interesting to note that students tend to reduce these errors on a second testing. When tests are returned to students and they note correct answers to questions answered incorrectly, this form of review can be a valuable aid in the learning process.

## PREDICTION

Because of the scarcity of tests that predict present and future performance levels, this type of testing is seldom used. More research is needed in this area of testing. The surface has only been scratched, and coaching of teams in various sports might be improved if coaches were able to predict which students will be among the better future performers. For example, freshmen, upon entrance into high school, may be among those late in maturing physically. In some sports, they may be too small to make freshman teams. If there were available a valid test that would predict whether they have the potential to develop into excellent performers in later school years, then it would be to the coach's advantage to know this. As a result, students would have an opportunity to develop the requisite skills during the freshman year, even though they are withheld from competition. Students who are more mature upon entrance to high school may tend to dominate freshman teams, even though their long-range potential may be of a lower order.

Another aspect of this question is the prediction of performance on a given day. A baseball coach would not wish to use the best pitcher if he or she knew that on the scheduled day the pitcher, for some reason, would have an off day. Under these circumstances, it would be wiser to withhold this pitcher and to substitute another of somewhat lower overall potential. It is likely, on the subsequent day, that the pitcher originally scheduled might be predicted to perform at his or her normal level. A basketball coach could use such predictive tests to determine which of several players, of relatively comparable ability, to start in a given game.

## RESEARCH

Research is a continuous, steadily increasing activity of physical educators. Tests may be utilized to determine which of two methods of instruction is better. Tests may also be used to determine which kind of student is likely to be a better performer in a given activity. Much important research can be conducted even by the teacher who has but an elementary knowledge of research procedures.

Underlying much of the research in physical education are tests of important skills that provide comparisons of instructional methods, procedures, and techniques.

Test results, if retained over a period of years, may provide historians and other investigators with opportunities to compare such results in terms of trends, evaluation of progress, or identification of changes in emphasis and philosophy.

# CHAPTER TWO
# APPLICATIONS AND INTERPRETATIONS OF STATISTICS

A persistent problem confronting teachers, including physical educators, is that of organizing, synthesizing, analyzing, and interpreting a variety of numerical data including measurements of dimensions, tallies of performances, and test scores. Prior to solving the problem identified above, it is necessary for a decision to be made as to the kinds of information that are desired by teachers. Do they wish to know the extremes of performances, the score that typifies the performance of the group as a whole, the manner in which the scores are distributed, how a group compares with other groups, or the probability that a group is representative of the unobserved population from which it was selected? Further, the statistics that are selected to provide the desired information cannot be chosen haphazardly. They depend for their appropriateness upon the manner in which a group has been formed, upon the nature of the larger group (population) of which the smaller group (sample) is a part, upon the kind of score (continuous, discrete, or dichotomous), and upon the distribution of the scores. Errors in selecting the statistics appropriate for a given set of conditions may lead to misinterpretation of the meaning of the data.

In the remainder of this chapter, several ends will be sought: 1) to provide understandable definitions for the statistical and parametrical terms included in this presentation; 2) to illustrate with a variety of examples means for appropriately interpreting these terms; 3) to provide examples of methods of statistical computation; and 4) a description of the applications and limitations of each of the statistics included for discussion. It is recognized that the material treated in this chapter is largely elementary in nature and is insufficient in scope or depth to satisfy the demands of the sophisticated research worker. On the other hand, the material is sufficiently comprehensive to provide one with the understanding and tools that are typically required.

The remaining sections are organized into three major statistical divisions: 1) descriptive; 2) comparative; and 3) inferential. Most of the discussion involving the second division, comparative statistics, will be treated under division three, inferential statistics, since it is the latter that gives meaning to the former. Several illustrative examples involving statistical computation will be provided in the chapter so that the reader may conveniently compare theory and application.

Before beginning the discussion of the three divisions of statistics, two terms, statistic and parameter, should be defined. A *parameter* is any measure of a population (a population includes every member of a defined group). Often it is not convenient or even possible to attempt to obtain parametric measurements. Instead, samples of the population are taken (in any one of a number of different ways), and their measurements, known as *statistics*, serve as estimates—of varying degrees of reliability—of their respective parameters.

## AN ILLUSTRATIVE PROBLEM

As an illustrative problem, let's assume that a teacher has collected a set of test scores (Table 2-1) for a group of 30 pupils. What kinds of information about pupil

TABLE 2-1   Scores Earned by Thirty Pupils on a Knowledge Examination

| PUPIL | SCORE | PUPIL | SCORE | PUPIL | SCORE |
|---|---|---|---|---|---|
| 1 | 14 | 11 | 42 | 21 | 99 |
| 2 | 32 | 12 | 73 | 22 | 96 |
| 3 | 36 | 13 | 23 | 23 | 92 |
| 4 | 49 | 14 | 43 | 24 | 85 |
| 5 | 46 | 15 | 59 | 25 | 77 |
| 6 | 28 | 16 | 72 | 26 | 68 |
| 7 | 100 | 17 | 83 | 27 | 57 |
| 8 | 62 | 18 | 90 | 28 | 45 |
| 9 | 17 | 19 | 96 | 29 | 31 |
| 10 | 64 | 20 | 99 | 30 | 16 |

performance can the teacher glean from these scores? Among the possibilities are the two extreme scores (the high and low scores) achieved on the test, the score that would be most representative of the group's performance, and the distribution of the scores. It might also be desired to compare these scores with scores achieved by the same group on a similar test taken earlier to see if improvement has taken place or to compare the scores made by this group with scores made by a second group on the same test.

Unfortunately, it is unwieldy to attempt to answer these questions in an orderly progression if the three statistical divisions are to be treated in largely independent fashion. Hence, the discussion will begin with various descriptive statistics and will progress into comparative and inferential statistics.

## DESCRIPTIVE STATISTICS

Three subdivisions of descriptive statistics will be treated. These are composed of measures of central tendency, measures of variability, and standard scores.

### Measures of Central Tendency

A measure of central tendency is a single score that provides an indication of the general performance of the group. Three measures of central tendency, mean, median, and mode, are used commonly. The question confronting the teacher is "which of these measures of central tendency will provide the best indication of the group's performance?" The answer depends upon several factors. One of these is the size of the group; a second, and often more influencing, is the manner in which scores are distributed. Each of the three measures will be examined in turn, including the methods by which they may be computed or otherwise determined. A final section will discuss their applications and limitations.

*The mean* $(\overline{X})$. If the scores (the symbol for a given score is $X$) in Table 2-1 were considered to be positions along a scale, the mean would be that point about which the scale would be in algebraic balance.

Figure 2.1 shows a group of scores distributed along a scale. The scores far-

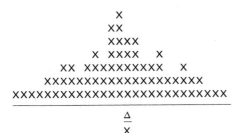

**FIGURE 2.1**  The distribution of scores (*X*) on a scale about their mean ($\bar{X}$).

thest to the left represent the lowest scores and those farthest to the right the highest. If more than one *X* appears in a given vertical position, it signifies that those *X*s all achieved the same score. The fulcrum (the triangle about which the scores are distributed) represents the mean ($\bar{X}$), if the scores are balanced about the fulcrum. If the scores are not balanced, then the fulcrum would have to be moved until balance is attained if the fulcrum and the mean are to coincide.

How is the mean computed? The most direct method is to obtain the sum of the scores ($\Sigma X$) and to divide this sum by the number (*N*) of scores in the distribution:

$$\bar{X} = \frac{\Sigma X}{N} \tag{1}$$

Hence, the computation of the mean of the scores in Table 2-1 would then be

$$\bar{X} = \frac{1794}{30} = 59.8$$

A second and somewhat indirect method involves the estimation of the mean and the subsequent determination of the mean deviation of the scores from this estimated mean ($\widetilde{X}$). The formula for this indirect method is:

$$\bar{X} = \widetilde{X} + \left(\frac{\Sigma x}{N}\right) \tag{2}$$

in which *x* is the deviation of each score from $\widetilde{X}$.

Here is an example of this method, using the first 10 scores in Table 2-1 and an estimated mean of 50:*

| Subject | Score | Deviation (*x*) | |
|---|---|---|---|
| | | + | − |
| 1 | 14 | | 36 |
| 2 | 32 | | 18 |

*The choice of an estimated mean of 50 is purely arbitrary. The closer the estimate is to the true mean, the easier the calculations will be.

|    |     |    |    |
|----|-----|----|----|
| 3  | 36  |    | 14 |
| 4  | 49  |    | 1  |
| 5  | 46  |    | 4  |
| 6  | 28  |    | 22 |
| 7  | 100 | 50 |    |
| 8  | 62  | 12 |    |
| 9  | 17  |    | 33 |
| 10 | 64  | 14 |    |

$$\Sigma x = +\widetilde{7}6 - 128 = -52$$

Substituting this value into formula (2), the mean may then be computed:

$$\bar{X} = 50 + \left(\frac{-52}{10}\right)$$

$$= 50 + (-5.2)$$

$$= 44.8$$

This compares precisely with the true mean of the first 10 scores as calculated with formula (1):

$$\bar{X} = \frac{x}{N} = \frac{448}{10} = 44.8$$

The reader may ask at this point: "Why would anyone want to employ this apparently laborious and indirect method in preference to the direct method?" The answer is that normally one would not. However, the indirect method is presented for two related reasons: 1) to establish the validity of the indirect method and 2) to provide the rationale for the use of a similar method in the treatment of grouped data. We shall now turn to the question of the grouping of data.

Time may be saved in the computation of a variety of statistics, particularly if samples are large in size, by grouping data into a series of categories, each category contributing scores within its particular domain. This is accomplished by establishing a number of categories or intervals of the same size ($i$ denotes interval size) and then placing each score in its appropriate interval. It is usually recommended that the number of intervals be not less than 10 or more than 20, with the number of intervals increasing as $N$ increases. If $N = 100$, for example, 13 intervals is about right. In the sample problem, 10 intervals will group the data adequately since $N$ is only 30. The next question is: "How large should each interval be?" This may be determined by subtracting the lowest score from the highest score (defined as the *range* of scores) and dividing this difference by the number of intervals desired. Thus:

$$i = \frac{100 - 14}{10} = \frac{86}{10} = 8.6$$

representative of half of the distribution of scores, i.e., $Mdn = .50N$. In the series of six scores given,

$$.50\,N = .50 \cdot 6 = 3$$

and the median would be identified as the third score from the bottom of the distribution, namely 6. Although simple inspection would indicate that the first of the two methods provides the more precise representation of the middle score, there are compelling arguments in favor of the second method. First, as $N$ increases, the difference in the values produced by the two methods becomes smaller and disappears if $N$ attains infinity ($\infty$).* Second, in later computations involving the assumption of an infinite body of scores, the second method provides a more convenient arrangement for computing the median.

Returning to the scores in Table 2-1, the median may now be computed. Both methods will be illustrated for the ungrouped and the grouped sets of data. For the ungrouped data, it is first necessary to arrange the scores in ascending order −14, 16, 17, 23, 28, 31, 32, 36, 42, 43, 45, 46, 49, 57, 59, 62, 64, 68, 72, 73, 77, 83, 85, 90, 92, 96, 99, 99, 100. In the first method, the median would lie at the point midway between the fifteenth and the sixteenth scores from the bottom of the distribution. Thus, the median would lie midway between 59 and 62 and would equal 60.5. With the second method, the median is equal to $.50N$ or the fifteenth score from the bottom of the distribution, which is 59.

Utilizing the first method with the grouped data in Table 2-2, the case† sought is 15.5. The interval in which this case falls may be determined by referring to the cumulative-frequency column. In this column, it may be observed that there are 13 cases in the 5 lowest intervals (as evidenced by the number 13 in the cf column of the fifth interval from the bottom). Since there are 4 additional cases in the sixth interval, i.e., through the seventeenth case, case 15.5 must lie within this interval. The solution at this point involves the application of a simple proportion in order to convert case 15.5 into its corresponding raw-score value ($X$ value). Case 15.5 lies 2.5 cases into the interval and, since the interval contains 4 cases ($f = 4$), case 15.5 is at a point 2.5/4 of the way into the interval. The size of the interval ($i$) is 9 (in terms of raw-score value), and, hence, 2.5/4 of 9 will produce the raw-score distance above the lower limit of the interval that case 15.5 will fall. This product, 5.625, must be added to the lower limit, 55.5, in order to provide the $X$ value (61.125) that corresponds to case 15.5.††

With method two, the solution is identical except that the case sought is now 15 ($.50 \cdot 30$) instead of 15.5:

---

*Much of statistical theory is based upon the assumption of infinite scores, even though infinity is never attained except in theory. However, failure to attain infinity does not limit the soundness of the assumption.

†The term "case" is used herein to distinguish the rank of a score from its raw-score value.

††Case 15.5 corresponds graphically to 61.125 on the $X$ scale. Case 15.0 corresponds graphically to 60.0 on the $X$ scale.

$$\text{Median} = \left( \frac{\text{case sought} - \text{cf of next lowest interval}}{f \text{ of interval in which case sought lies}} \cdot i \right) + LL_i \qquad (4)$$

in which

$LL_i$ = Lower limit of the interval containing the case sought.

The solution then becomes:

$$Mdn = \left( \frac{15 - 13}{4} \cdot 9 \right) + 55.5$$

$$= 4.5 + 55.5 = 60.0$$

The graphic representation of the solution that illustrates the relationship between a score's rank and its raw score value appears in Figure 2.2.

It might be pointed out that even though the size of the group ($N$ = 30) is not large, the difference in the values computed for the median using the two methods is relatively small. Since method two eliminates the need for interpolation between the two middle scores (with its potential for error), it is the method recommended.

*The mode* (Mo). By definition, the mode is the score that appears most frequently in an ungrouped distribution and is the midpoint of the interval with the greatest frequency if the scores are arranged in a frequency distribution.

No computation is required in the determination of the mode for either grouped or ungrouped data, as simple inspection of the scores or of the frequency distribution will provide the score value of the mode.

It is possible, or even likely if $N$ is quite small, that more than one mode will appear for a given set of scores. If this occurs, no attempt should be made to determine an "average mode" through interpolation or other methods.

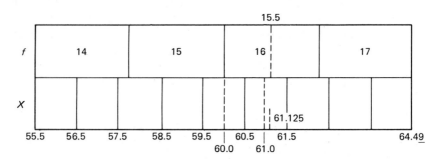

**FIGURE 2.2  Graphic representation of a single interval in terms of cases (f) within the interval and the corresponding X values.**

**Applications and Limitations of
Measures of Central Tendency**

The final resolution as to which of the three measures, mean, median, or mode, will represent most appropriately the central tendency of a set of scores will be governed by several factors, including the size of the group, the nature of the distribution, and whether subsequent statistical use is intended.

In general, each of the three measures becomes more reliable as group size increases. In the circumstance of a small group, the median is less likely to be affected by unusual or extreme distributions. In fact, for certain kinds of data, such as income, the influence of extreme values, particularly at the high end of the scale, may serve to radically distort the mean. Hence, official government reports of family or individual income are summarized in terms of median values in order to minimize the otherwise undue effect of the tremendously large income of a relatively small percentage of the population. Thus, if one person in one hundred had an income of $100,000 per year, its effect would be to raise the mean income of the group approximately $1,000 above the mean that would result if that person were not in the group. The effect of the $100,000 income on the median income of the group, on the other hand, would be no greater than if it were but one dollar more than the next highest income.

In some investigations, it is not desirable or feasible to ignore the full effect of an extreme value. The example of baseball averages will serve as an example to illustrate the point. If a baseball team produces 162 home runs in a 162-game schedule, and even if one player accounts for 50 of these, it may still be said that the *team* may be expected to produce an *average* (mean) of one home run per game. This is *not* to say that, if a team were limited to nine men per game, each man would be expected to deliver one home run every nine games that he plays.

Seldom are there data for which the mode is the best measure of central tendency. If *N* is very large, the mode will provide a fairly accurate *estimate* of central tendency at a glance. There are several special cases, such as typical mammalian gestation periods, for which the mode might well be the most appropriate measure of central tendency.

The final consideration, further statistical application, precludes the median and the mode, since neither utilizes the full effect of each score in its computation. A fuller understanding of the rationale underlying this decision should become apparent to the reader as other statistics are discussed.

**Measures of Variability**

From the foregoing examples, the teacher now has several insights into the nature of the group's performance. However, many groups of varying individual performances could produce very similar group measures of central tendency. What other kinds of information about the group performance might one wish to derive from the set of scores available? Certainly, there would be interest in knowing the extremes of the group's performance. It would also be useful to observe how the scores are distributed about the mean. Both of the above are measures of variability.

Following are a number of measures of variability that will provide the information that may be desired:

*Range* (R). The range is the most easily computed measure of variability but, correspondingly, it is also the least revealing measure of the distribution of group performances. It is determined quite simply by subtracting the lowest score in the set of scores from the highest. Thus, in the original example, the high score is 100, the low score is 14, and the range is 86. Although the range gives the teacher an idea of the extreme differences in performance, it must be cautioned that most knowledge of 28 of the 30 scores in the distribution is lacking. A similar group of 30 could have an identical range (14-100), could even have the same mean (59.8), and yet differ markedly insofar as the individual performances of all but the two extreme performances are concerned.

Are there other measures of variability that will provide additional evidence of the distribution of performances? Quite expectedly there are, and they are treated in order of their increasing complexity and utility.

*The mean deviation* (MD). In a set of scores such as the 30 in the example, most if not all of the individual scores deviate from (i.e., are removed from) the mean to some degree. The mean deviation indicates how much the scores, on the average, deviate from the mean. The degree to which each score deviates from the mean is, of course, the difference, $x$, between that score and the mean $(X - \bar{X})$. Once the individual deviations of the scores from the mean are computed, they are then summed. This sum must be divided by the number of scores in the group $(N)$ to produce the mean deviation:

$$MD = \frac{\Sigma x}{N} \tag{5}$$

Utilizing the scores from Table 2-1, the procedure for the computation of the mean deviation would be as shown in Table 2-3.

To repeat, the interpretation of the *MD* of approximately 23.97 is that this is the *average* distance in score points that the scores are removed (deviate) from the mean. And, from this value, the teacher becomes aware that the scores are of necessity not clustered, at least in any large degree, about the mean.

Next, we will investigate a still more precise measure of the manner in which the scores are clustered about the mean.

*The standard deviation* (s). The standard deviation is computed by a method that is an extension of that employed in the computation of the mean deviation. Each score's deviation $(x)$ from the mean is squared, and these squared values are summed $(\Sigma x^2)$ and then divided by $N$. The square root of this quotient is then extracted to produce the standard deviation:

**TABLE 2-3**  Deviations, Deviations Squared, and Mean Deviations for Scores in Table 2-1

| PUPIL | $X$ | $x$ ($\overline{X}$ = 59.8) | $x^2$ (FOR LATER USE) | |
|---|---|---|---|---|
| 1 | 14 | 45.8 | 2097.64 | |
| 2 | 32 | 27.8 | 772.84 | |
| 3 | 36 | 23.8 | 566.44 | |
| 4 | 49 | 10.8 | 116.64 | $MD = \dfrac{\Sigma x}{N}$ |
| 5 | 46 | 13.8 | 190.44 | |
| 6 | 28 | 31.8 | 1011.24 | |
| 7 | 100 | 40.2 | 1616.04 | |
| 8 | 62 | 2.2 | 4.84 | $= \dfrac{719.0}{30}$ |
| 9 | 17 | 42.8 | 1831.84 | |
| 10 | 64 | 4.2 | 17.64 | |
| 11 | 42 | 17.8 | 316.84 | $= 23.97$ |
| 12 | 73 | 13.2 | 174.24 | |
| 13 | 23 | 36.8 | 1354.24 | |
| 14 | 43 | 16.8 | 282.24 | |
| 15 | 59 | .8 | .64 | |
| 16 | 72 | 12.2 | 148.84 | |
| 17 | 83 | 23.2 | 538.24 | |
| 18 | 90 | 30.2 | 912.04 | |
| 19 | 96 | 36.2 | 1310.44 | |
| 20 | 99 | 39.2 | 1536.64 | |
| 21 | 99 | 39.2 | 1536.64 | |
| 22 | 96 | 36.2 | 1310.44 | |
| 23 | 92 | 32.2 | 1036.84 | |
| 24 | 85 | 25.2 | 635.04 | |
| 25 | 77 | 17.2 | 295.84 | |
| 26 | 68 | 8.2 | 67.24 | |
| 27 | 57 | 2.8 | 7.84 | |
| 28 | 45 | 14.8 | 219.04 | |
| 29 | 31 | 28.8 | 829.44 | |
| 30 | 16 | 43.8 | 1918.44 | |
| | | $\Sigma x$ = 719.0 | $\Sigma x^2$ = 22656.80 | |

$$s = \sqrt{\frac{\Sigma x^2}{N}} \qquad\qquad (6)$$

The scope of this section precludes the derivation of the foregoing formula and the rationale underlying the derivation. The reader may be assured, however, of its recognized validity.

Returning to the sample problem, the sum of the squared values equals 22656.80 and, when substituted into formula (6), produces a standard deviation of:

$$s = \sqrt{\frac{22,656.80}{30}}$$

$$= \sqrt{755.2267}$$

$$= 27.48$$

A simpler means of estimating the standard deviation involves the use of the frequency distribution (Table 2-2). The method involves the creation of an additional column that is the product of the $fd$ and $d$ columns ($fd^2$). This column is *not* the square of the values in the $fd$ column, a mistake that the unfamiliar may inadvertently make. The method utilizing the necessary expansion of Table 2-2 is shown in Table 2-4, in which $fd^2 = d \times fd$.

The formula for computing the standard deviation from a frequency distribution involves a modification of formula (6):

$$s = i \sqrt{\frac{\Sigma fd^2}{N} - \left(\frac{\Sigma fd}{N}\right)^2} \qquad (7)$$

The value for the sample problem would be:

$$= 9 \sqrt{\frac{305}{30} - \left(\frac{27}{30}\right)^2} = 9\sqrt{10.17 - .81}$$

$$= 9\sqrt{9.36} = 9 \cdot 3.059$$

$$= 27.531 = 27.53$$

Several explanations are in order at this point. It can be readily noted that the difference between the standard deviations computed with the two methods is very slight, and generally this is to be expected. Only in cases of extremely unusual distributions are somewhat larger differences likely to appear, and it should be mentioned that the distribution in the sample problem is quite different from most

**TABLE 2-4  Frequency Distribution for Scores Contained in Table 2-2**

| $i$ | $cf$ | $f$ | $d$ | $fd$ | $fd^2$ |
|---|---|---|---|---|---|
| 91.5–100.49 | 30 | 6 | +5 | +30 | +150 |
| 82.5–91.49 | 24 | 3 | +4 | +12 | + 48 |
| 73.5–82.49 | 21 | 1 | +3 | + 3 | + 9 |
| 64.5–73.49 | 20 | 3 | +2 | + 6 | + 12 |
| 55.5–64.49 | 17 | 4 | +1 | + 4 | + 4 |
| 46.5–55.49 | 13 | 1 | 0 | +55 / −28 | 0 |
| 37.5–46.49 | 12 | 4 | −1 | − 4 | + 4 |
| 28.5–37.49 | 8 | 3 | −2 | − 6 | + 12 |
| 19.5–28.49 | 5 | 2 | −3 | − 6 | + 18 |
| 10.5–19.49 | 3 | 3 | −4 | −12 | + 48 |
|  | $N = 30$ |  |  | $\Sigma fd = +27$ | $\Sigma fd^2 = 305$ |

distributions due primarily to chance (theories concerned with chance distributions will be discussed in the next section) and is not the most typical. At this point, the relative ease of computation of the standard deviation when the scores are grouped serves as a partial justification of grouping.

However, with the advent of the hand calculator, it is more economical in terms of time to use an alternate formula not requiring the calculation of the scores' deviations from the mean:

$$s = \frac{1}{N}\sqrt{N\Sigma X^2 - (\Sigma X)^2} \tag{7a}$$

Using the same scores as above, the calculation looks like this:

$$s = \frac{1}{30}\sqrt{30 \cdot 129938 - (1794)^2}$$

$$s = \frac{1}{30}\sqrt{3,898,140 - 3,218,436}$$

$$s = \frac{1}{30}\sqrt{679,704}$$

$$s = \frac{1}{30} \cdot 824.44163 = 27.48$$

What does it mean if the standard deviation of a distribution is equal to 27.48 (or to 27.53)? In distributions due to chance alone (called normal distributions), 68.26% of the cases in the distribution will lie within the limits of $-1s$ to $+1s$ about the mean. Thus, if 27.48 is respectively subtracted from and added to the mean of 59.8, the resulting limits (32.32 to 87.28) will be expected to include approximately 68.26% of the cases in the distribution. In the sample problem, 16 of the 30 cases (53.33%) fall within the limits, considerably fewer than the 20 or 21 cases that were expected. The large discrepancy is due to the unusual distribution (7 cases of 90 or higher). Most distributions, even if not approaching normal, will produce standard deviations that include close to 68.26% of the cases between $-1s$ and $+1s$.

### Normal Distributions

Much of what follows in this section is related to the concept of normal distributions. A distribution of characteristics such as test scores is termed "normal" if the distribution conforms to certain specifications: 1) the distribution is symmetrical; 2) the mean, median, and mode coincide; 3) 68.26% of the scores will lie between $+1.0s$ and $-1.0s$, 95.44% of the scores will lie between $+2.0s$ and $-2.0s$, etc.; and 4) the frequencies of scores decrease the farther they deviate from the mean.

At this point, a word of caution is in order. A curve that reflects a normal distribution is a theoretical curve and is based upon the assumption that the distribution contains an infinite number of scores. Since the distributions typically confronting teachers are anything but infinite in size, the latter should not be astonished to observe that these distributions tend to vary in one or more ways from the expected normalcy.

The underlying assumption upon which normal distribution theory is based is that the distribution has resulted from chance occurrences.† Again, it must be acknowledged that test scores, whether of physical or intellectual endeavors, are seldom a result exclusively or primarily of chance. Regardless of these departures from the theoretical base upon which normal distributions are supposed to depend, the theory may still be applied to test scores as though they conformed to normal and with infrequent errors of importance appearing. This is to say that most, but not all, collections of test scores tend to be distributed in a fashion approximating normal. For these collections, within the limits ±1.0s, will usually be found about two-thirds of the scores (a reasonable approximation of 68.26%). The farther scores deviate from the mean, the greater the probable corresponding deviation from normal theory largely as a consequence of the fewer scores contained in the extremes of the distribution with their greater susceptibility to chance aberration.

Figure 2.3 illustrates the properties of the normal probability curve.

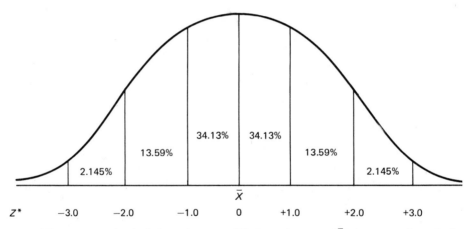

*Z represents the deviation of a score ($X$) from the mean ($\bar{X}$) in terms of standard deviation units. Thus:

$$Z = \frac{X - \bar{X}}{s}$$

**FIGURE 2.3  Normal Probability Curve.**

†An example of a chance occurrence is the tossing of a coin. If the tosser has no control over whether the landing will be head or tail, the probability is that, given a *large* number of tosses, 50% will be heads and 50% tails. If, for example, the coin is tossed 10 times, the probability is greater that 5 heads and 5 tails will result than for any other combination. But, in any given 10 tosses, other combinations will result including an occasional 10 heads (or 10 tails). The other possible combinations, in fact, will tend to be distributed in a normal fashion.

### Scale Scores

Scores such as the mean of 59.8 in the sample problem often may not lend themselves to ready comparisons with other statistics. For example, if one were asked to make a judgment as to which of two performances, a high jump of 6 feet (1.83 m) or a long jump of 20 feet (6.01 m) is better, it likely would involve some pondering before a guess, reasoned or otherwise, would be hazarded. By the same token, it may be unwise to assume that a student who earns a 79 on a test and then an 85 on a subsequent test in the same course has necessarily improved his/her performance. It is possible that he/she has, but it is also possible that the second test was relatively easier and that the increase in score does not necessarily reflect correspondingly higher levels of achievement. A further example of a similar kind may more clearly illustrate the point. If a golfer takes 79 strokes on a certain golf course and the next day takes 85 strokes on another course, is it safe to assume that the latter score necessarily represents a poorer round of golf? As any experienced golfer will testify, the difficulty of the course (which is not always reflected in the course's published par score) plays a very important role in the golfer's score.

The question then becomes, "How may *unlike* scores be compared in terms of level of accomplishment?" The answer lies in a series of processes by which raw-score values may be converted to comparable scale values based upon typical group performances. The form of these scale scores varies somewhat but all scale-score systems possess the attribute of facilitating comparisons between unlike scores. Nearly all derive their scale scores through mathematical processes that utilize a measure of central tendency, usually the mean, as the reference value.

*1. Percentiles and percentile ranks.* A percentile rank $(P)$ is defined as the percentage of scores in a distribution that lie at or below a given score point. Thus, the sixtieth percentile (termed a percentile rank) is the point in the distribution at and below which 60 percent of the scores fall. The $X$ value, known as the percentile, that corresponds to the sixtieth percentile may be determined in one of several ways.

For ungrouped (Table 2-1) or grouped (Table 2-2) data, it is first necessary to determine which of the scores in the distribution represents that score at and below which 60 percent of the scores lie. This may be computed readily by multiplying the percentile rank under consideration by the number of scores in the distribution ($.60 \times 30 = 18$).

For the ungrouped scores, the percentile that corresponds to this percentile rank of 60, i.e., the eighteenth score from the bottom of the distribution, has a raw-score value of 68 as determined by simple inspection if the scores have been placed in rank order from low to high.

For the grouped scores, it should be noted that the eighteenth score lies in the seventh interval from the bottom ($d = +2$). The *cf* column reveals that 17 scores lie in the six lowest intervals. Hence, the eighteenth score is the first of the three scores ($f = 3$) in the seventh interval, i.e., the eighteenth score lies at a point one-third of the distance into the interval. But what does one-third of the interval distance represent in terms of raw-score value? Since the total number of score points included within each interval is nine, one-third of nine is three. This value must be added to the raw-score value that represents the lower limit of the interval to determine the percentile of 60 (64.5 + 3.0 = 67.5). As with examples of statistics treated earlier, the $X$ values are quite close for the ungrouped and grouped scores.

The formula for converting percentile ranks into percentiles is

$$X = \left[ \frac{(P \cdot N) - cf_{i-1}}{f_i} \cdot i \right] + LL_i \tag{8}$$

in which

$X$ = Percentile
$P$ = Percentile rank
$N$ = Sample size
$cf_{i-1}$ = Cumulative frequency of the interval below that containing the percentile rank
$f_i$ = Frequency of the interval containing the percentile rank
$i$ = Range of the interval
$LL_i$ = Lower limit of the interval containing the percentile rank

A third method of computing the raw-score value that corresponds to the 60th percentile, in which the sample data are projected as though the sample contained a large number of scores, will be treated later in the chapter.

2. *Standard (Z) scores.* A standard score represents the deviation of a score ($X$) from the mean in terms of standard deviation units. If $X$, for example, were 87.28 (the sum of the sample mean, 59.8 and the sample standard deviation, 27.48), its corresponding $Z$-score would be +1.0, i.e., 87.28 is one standard deviation above the mean:

$$\frac{87.28 - 59.8}{27.48} = +1.0$$

If we return to the earlier example, the sixtieth percentile was equal to 68 for the ungrouped scores. The $Z$-score that corresponds to 68 would be computed utilizing the formula

$$Z = \frac{X - \bar{X}}{s} \tag{9}$$

$$Z = \frac{68 - 59.8}{27.48} = \frac{8.2}{27.48} = 0.298 = 0.30$$

For the grouped scores, the solution is the same except that the grouped values of $X$, $\overline{X}$, and $s$ are substituted into the formula:

$$Z = \frac{67.5 - 59.1}{27.53} = \frac{8.4}{27.53} = 0.305 = 0.31$$

At this point, the relationships among $X$, $Z$, and $P$ will be discussed in terms of projections of small-sample values to larger populations. Earlier in this chapter, mention was made of one of the basic properties of a normal distribution, namely, within the limits of $-1.0s$ to $1.0s$ deviations about the mean, 68.26% of the scores would be expected to fall. Table 2-5 provides the percentage of scores that would

**TABLE 2-5**  Percentage Parts of the Total Area Under the Normal Curve Corresponding to Distances on the Base Line Between the Mean and Successive Points from the Mean in Units of Standard Deviation ($Z$)

| Z | 0.00 | 0.01 | 0.02 | 0.03 | 0.04 | 0.05 | 0.06 | 0.07 | 0.08 | 0.09 |
|---|------|------|------|------|------|------|------|------|------|------|
| 0.0 | .0000 | .0040 | .0080 | .0120 | .0160 | .0199 | .0239 | .0279 | .0319 | .0359 |
| 0.1 | .0398 | .0438 | .0478 | .0517 | .0557 | .0596 | .0636 | .0675 | .0714 | .0753 |
| 0.2 | .0793 | .0832 | .0871 | .0910 | .0948 | .0987 | .1026 | .1064 | .1103 | .1141 |
| 0.3 | .1179 | .1217 | .1255 | .1293 | .1331 | .1368 | .1406 | .1443 | .1480 | .1517 |
| 0.4 | .1554 | .1591 | .1628 | .1664 | .1700 | .1736 | .1772 | .1808 | .1844 | .1879 |
| 0.5 | .1915 | .1950 | .1985 | .2019 | .2054 | .2088 | .2123 | .2157 | .2190 | .2224 |
| 0.6 | .2257 | .2291 | .2324 | .2357 | .2389 | .2422 | .2454 | .2486 | .2517 | .2549 |
| 0.7 | .2580 | .2611 | .2642 | .2673 | .2704 | .2734 | .2764 | .2794 | .2823 | .2852 |
| 0.8 | .2881 | .2910 | .2939 | .2967 | .2995 | .3023 | .3051 | .3078 | .3106 | .3133 |
| 0.9 | .3159 | .3186 | .3212 | .3238 | .3264 | .3289 | .3315 | .3340 | .3365 | .3389 |
| 1.0 | .3413 | .3438 | .3461 | .3485 | .3508 | .3531 | .3554 | .3577 | .3599 | .3621 |
| 1.1 | .3643 | .3665 | .3686 | .3708 | .3729 | .3749 | .3770 | .3790 | .3810 | .3830 |
| 1.2 | .3849 | .3869 | .3888 | .3907 | .3925 | .3944 | .3962 | .3980 | .3997 | .4015 |
| 1.3 | .4032 | .4049 | .4066 | .4082 | .4099 | .4115 | .4131 | .4147 | .4162 | .4177 |
| 1.4 | .4192 | .4207 | .4222 | .4236 | .4251 | .4265 | .4279 | .4292 | .4306 | .4319 |
| 1.5 | .4332 | .4345 | .4357 | .4370 | .4382 | .4394 | .4406 | .4418 | .4429 | .4441 |
| 1.6 | .4452 | .4463 | .4474 | .4484 | .4495 | .4505 | .4515 | .4525 | .4535 | .4545 |
| 1.7 | .4554 | .4564 | .4573 | .4582 | .4591 | .4599 | .4608 | .4616 | .4625 | .4633 |
| 1.8 | .4641 | .4649 | .4656 | .4664 | .4671 | .4678 | .4686 | .4693 | .4699 | .4706 |
| 1.9 | .4713 | .4719 | .4726 | .4732 | .4738 | .4744 | .4750 | .4756 | .4761 | .4767 |
| 2.0 | .4772 | .4778 | .4783 | .4788 | .4793 | .4798 | .4803 | .4808 | .4813 | .4817 |
| 2.1 | .4821 | .4826 | .4830 | .4834 | .4838 | .4842 | .4846 | .4850 | .4854 | .4857 |
| 2.2 | .4861 | .4864 | .4868 | .4871 | .4875 | .4878 | .4881 | .4884 | .4887 | .4890 |
| 2.3 | .4893 | .4896 | .4898 | .4901 | .4904 | .4906 | .4909 | .4911 | .4913 | .4916 |
| 2.4 | .4918 | .4920 | .4922 | .4925 | .4927 | .4929 | .4931 | .4932 | .4934 | .4936 |
| 2.5 | .4938 | .4940 | .4941 | .4943 | .4945 | .4946 | .4948 | .4949 | .4951 | .4952 |
| 2.6 | .4953 | .4955 | .4956 | .4957 | .4959 | .4960 | .4961 | .4962 | .4963 | .4964 |
| 2.7 | .4965 | .4966 | .4967 | .4968 | .4969 | .4970 | .4971 | .4972 | .4973 | .4974 |
| 2.8 | .4974 | .4975 | .4976 | .4977 | .4977 | .4978 | .4979 | .4979 | .4980 | .4981 |
| 2.9 | .4981 | .4982 | .4982 | .4983 | .4984 | .4984 | .4985 | .4985 | .4986 | .4986 |
| 3.0 | .4987 | .4987 | .4987 | .4988 | .4988 | .4989 | .4989 | .4989 | .4990 | .4990 |

Source: Sheehan, 1921, p. 258 (adapted). Reprinted with permission.

be expected to fall between the mean and any point in the distribution in terms of its standard ($Z$) score.

Thus, for the grouped-scores data, the percentage of scores of a large sample (assumed to be normally distributed) expected to fall between the mean ($Z = 0$) and $Z = .31$ is found from Table 2-5 to be 12.17%. The corresponding percentile rank would then be equal to 62.17, since 50% of the cases in the distribution are assumed to lie below the mean.

If, on the other hand, it was desired to ascertain the $X$ value that would correspond to the sixtieth percentile with the assumption that the sample is large and distributed in terms of normal probability, it would be necessary to refer to Table 2-5 for the $Z$-score that corresponds to the sixtieth percentile. It may be noted that Table 2-5 does not contain percentage values as large as 60. This is because both values, percentages, and $Z$-scores are, in terms of their respective percentages or distances, above or below the mean. The sixtieth percentile is 10% above the mean (in a normal probability distribution, the mean and median coincide and, thus, the mean coincides with the fiftieth percentile). Two values, 9.87% and 10.26%, may be found in the table, but not 10.00%. This is because the $Z$-score that corresponds to 10.00% would be represented in terms of thousandths, a precision not available in Table 2-5. Which of the two values, 9.87% or 10.26%, better represents 10.00%? Somewhat arbitrarily, it is recommended that the value closer to 10.00%, 9.87%, be selected. Its corresponding $Z$-score is found to be 0.25. To convert this $Z$-score into a percentile ($X$), it is necessary to transpose formula (9):

$$X = \bar{X} + (Z \cdot s) \tag{10}$$
$$X = 59.1 + (.25 \cdot 27.53)$$
$$= 59.1 + 6.88$$
$$= 65.98$$

It becomes apparent that this method of converting $X$ to $P$ (or $P$ to $X$) always involves the necessity of computing or otherwise determining the $Z$-score as the intermediate step.

Before concluding this section, an example is given in which the score for which a percentile rank is sought lies below the mean. If it is desired to determine the percentile rank of a score of 28, for example, careful attention must be paid to the mathematical signs of negative and positive:

$$Z = \frac{X - \bar{X}}{s}$$
$$= \frac{28 - 59.1}{27.53}$$
$$= \frac{-21.1}{27.53}$$
$$= -0.77$$

The percentage value in Table 2-5 corresponding to a $Z$-score of -.77 is -27.94, the negative sign denoting that this value is 27.94% *below* the mean. Thus, since 50% of the scores fall below the mean and 27.94% of these are between the mean and a score of 28 (converted to a $Z$-score of -0.77), the difference between these two percentages (50.00 - 27.94), 22.51, represents the percentile rank of a score of 28.

Each of the foregoing scale scores has certain inherent limitations. In small samples particularly, two equidistant percentile ranks, e.g., $P_{25}$ to $P_{35}$ and $P_{65}$ to $P_{75}$, are unlikely to reflect similarly equidistant raw-score values. The percentiles corresponding to the four percentile ranks, using the grouped-scores technique, are (to the nearest tenth) 36.0, 43.1, 72.0, and 87.0. The difference between the first pair of percentiles is found to be 7.1 whereas that between the second pair is 15.0, certainly not equal values.

$Z$-scores, although not beset with the difficulty of the percentile ranks, are often looked upon with disfavor because, theoretically, half of the scores in any distribution are necessarily negative. In addition, to be meaningful, they must be carried out to at least one and preferably to two decimal places.

Three scales, the T-scale, sigma-scale, and Hull-scale have been devised to eliminate the weaknesses of the two preceding scales, although each, in its turn, has one or more limitations. The advantage of these scales is that a scale score of 50 (rather than 0 for the $Z$-scale) is arbitrarily assigned to represent the mean raw-score value. By so doing, negative scale scores are effectively eliminated without creating any distortion of the scale scores.

T-*scores*. The $T$-scale is so organized that each ten points on the scale represent the equivalent of one standard deviation. Thus, utilizing the grouped-data values for the mean, 59.1, and for the standard deviation, 27.5, a $T$-score of 50 would correspond to a raw score of 59.1. A $T$-score of 60 would correspond to a raw score of 86.6 (59.1 + 27.5) and a $T$-score of 40 to 31.6 (59.1 - 27.5).

*Sigma-scores*. The principle of the sigma-scale is identical to that of the $T$-scale, except that each ten points on the scale represent the equivalent of .6 standard deviation. A sigma-score of 50 would correspond to a raw score of 59.1 (the mean), as with the $T$-scale. A sigma-score of 60, however, corresponds to a raw score of 75.6 (59.1 + .6 · 27.5 = 59.1 + 16.5), and a sigma-score of 40 to a raw score of 42.6 (59.1 - 16.5).

*Hull-scores*. Hull-scores are a further variation of $T$- and sigma-scores, in which each ten points on the scale represent .7 standard deviation. Again, the scale score of 50 is identical for all three scales ($\overline{X}$ = 59.1), but a Hull-score of 60 corresponds to a raw score of 78.4 (59.1 + .7 · 27.5), and a Hull-score of 40 corresponds to 39.8.

A comparison of the three scales appears in Table 2-6.

The weakness of the three scales is apparent—failure to utilize the entire range of the scale, particularly in the instance of the T-scale, and more so if the distribu-

TABLE 2-6   X Scores to Nearest Tenth Corresponding to Sigma-Scale, Hull-Scale, and T-Scale Scores

| SCALE SCORES | | X FOR SIGMA | X FOR HULL | X FOR T |
|---|---|---|---|---|
| 100 | | | | |
| 90 | | | | |
| 80 | | 108.3 | 117.0 | |
| 70 | | 91.9 | 97.7 | 114.1 |
| 60 | | 75.6 | 78.4 | 86.6 |
| 50 | Mean | 59.1 | 59.1 | 59.1 |
| 40 | | 42.6 | 39.8 | 31.6 |
| 30 | | 26.3 | 20.5 | 4.1 |
| 20 | | 9.9 | 1.2 | |
| 10 | | | | |
| 0 | | | | |

tion is sharply skewed. Regardless, these, like all standard scores, do permit a rational means of comparing and otherwise treating scores of a dissimilar nature.

Formulae for converting X-scores to scale scores are:

$$\text{T-score} = 50 + 10\left(\frac{X - \bar{X}}{s}\right) \tag{11}$$

$$\text{Hull-score} = 50 + 10\left(\frac{X - \bar{X}}{.7s}\right) \tag{12}$$

$$\text{Sigma-score} = 50 + 10\left(\frac{X - \bar{X}}{.6s}\right) \tag{13}$$

Formulae for converting scale scores to X-scores are:

$$\text{For T-scores} \quad X = \bar{X} + s\left(\frac{\text{T-score} - 50}{10}\right) \tag{14}$$

$$\text{For Hull-scores} \quad X = \bar{X} + .7s\left(\frac{\text{Hull-score} - 50}{10}\right) \tag{15}$$

$$\text{For Sigma-scores} \quad X = \bar{X} + .6s\left(\frac{\text{Sigma-score} - 50}{10}\right) \tag{16}$$

## COMPARATIVE STATISTICS

Comparative statistics are of two types: 1) a comparison of two descriptive statistics represented by the difference between the two; and 2) a comparison of scores of a single group in two or more tasks. The former type may be illustrated by the difference in mean scores obtained by two separate groups on a given test or by a single group on two administrations of a single test. The interpretation of these differences is uncertain without the assistance of inferential statistics and, as such, will not be treated until later in the chapter.

The latter type is represented by the relationship appearing to exist between the two performances. This relationship is termed *correlation* and is represented by a coefficient whose value ranges from +1.00, perfect positive relationship, through 0.00, no apparent relationship, to -1.00, perfect negative relationship. A positive relationship results if an increase (or decrease) of score on one performance is likely to be accompanied by an increase (or decrease) of score on the second performance. The higher the coefficient of correlation, the more likely that the scores on the two performances will increase (or decrease) in corresponding fashion. Put another way, the higher the coefficient of correlation between two variables, the greater the probability of successfully predicting performance in one variable from knowledge of performance in the other variable.

Correspondingly, a high negative coefficient between two variables signifies that as performance in one variable increases, performance in the other is also likely to decrease. In summary, the sign preceding the coefficient simply indicates whether the relationship is direct (+) or inverse (-).

A variety of statistical methods is available for computing coefficients of correlation. The method to be used depends upon the number of variables under consideration, the type of variable, the number of subjects involved, and whether a graphic plot of the relationship reveals one that is essentially rectilinear (straight-line) or curvilinear (curved-line).

### Rank-Difference Method

This method is employed for two variables if the number of subjects is small (small, in this context, is usually taken to be 30 or fewer subjects). A rank $(1 \ldots N)$ is assigned sequentially for each of the subjects for each of the variables with a rank of 1.0 assigned for the best performance, a rank of 2.0 for the next best performance, through a rank of $N$ for the poorest performance. The difference between the performance ranks $(RD)$ is computed for each subject (signs are of no consequence and are omitted); these differences are individually squared $(RD)^2$ and then summed. The coefficient of correlation, $r'$, is then computed by means of this formula:

$$r' = 1 - \frac{6\Sigma(RD)^2}{N(N^2 - 1)} \qquad (17)$$

Table 2-7 provides an example of the process by which the coefficient, $r'$, is computed.

The highest score in pull-ups (15 achieved by subject 5) is assigned the rank of 1.0. The next highest score (14 achieved by subject 8) is assigned the rank of 2.0 and so on through the lowest score (3 achieved by subject 4), which is assigned the

**TABLE 2-7  Coefficient of Correlation, $r'$, Utilizing the Rank-Difference Method**

| SUBJECT | PULL-UPS SCORE | PUSH-UPS SCORE | PULL-UPS RANK | PUSH-UPS RANK | RD | $(RD)^2$ |
|---|---|---|---|---|---|---|
| 1 | 9 | 16 | 6.0 | 7.5 | 1.5 | 2.25 |
| 2 | 6 | 16 | 9.0 | 7.5 | 1.5 | 2.25 |
| 3 | 13 | 24 | 3.0 | 2.0 | 1.0 | 1.00 |
| 4 | 3 | 7 | 10.0 | 10.0 | 0.0 | 0.00 |
| 5 | 17 | 25 | 1.0 | 1.0 | 0.0 | 0.00 |
| 6 | 9 | 14 | 6.0 | 9.0 | 3.0 | 9.00 |
| 7 | 8 | 17 | 8.0 | 6.0 | 2.0 | 4.00 |
| 8 | 14 | 20 | 2.0 | 4.0 | 2.0 | 4.00 |
| 9 | 12 | 18 | 4.0 | 5.0 | 1.0 | 1.00 |
| 10 | 9 | 23 | 6.0 | 3.0 | 3.0 | 9.00 |

$$\Sigma (RD)^2 = 32.50$$

$$r' = 1 - \frac{6\,(32.50)}{10\,(100 - 1)}$$

$$= 1 - \frac{195}{990}$$

$$= 1 - .20 = +0.80$$

rank of 10. In those instances in which two or more subjects achieve equal scores, e.g., subjects 1 and 2 each completed 16 push-ups, the mean of the ranks included for these subjects is assigned to each, i.e., subjects 1 and 2 tied for seventh and eighth places, and each is assigned the mean rank 7.5:

$$\left(\frac{7 + 8}{2} = \frac{15}{2} = 7.5\right)$$

A further example is found in the instance of the pull-up scores. Subjects 1, 6, and 10 tied for places 5, 6, and 7. The mean of these three places:

$$\left(\frac{5 + 6 + 7}{3} = \frac{18}{3} = 6\right)$$

is assigned to each of the tied subjects.

Certain checks may be employed to help insure the accuracy of the computations. One of these is that the number of values ending in .25 in the $(RD)^2$ column must always be even. If an odd number of .25 values is found, an error has been made in the assignment of the ranks, in determining the difference between rank values, or in squaring the $RD$ values. A second check is that the computed coefficient, $r'$, must lie within the range +1.0 to –1.0.

If, in Table 2-7, the best-performing subject in pull-ups is also the best in push-ups, the second best in pull-ups is the second best in push-ups, and so on down to the poorest in pull-ups is also the poorest in push-ups, it would be noted that the ranks for each of the subjects on the two tasks would correspond. This would result in the $RD$ and the $(RD)^2$ columns containing only zeroes. Thus, the sum of $(RD)^2$ would also be 0.00 as would the formula's fraction numerator and $r' = 1 - 0.00 = +1.00$.

If the reverse were the case (the best-performing subject in pull-ups was the worst-performing subject in pushups and the worst-performing subject in pull-ups was the best in push-ups and similarly for each of the subjects, i.e., second best pull-ups and second worst push-ups, etc.), it would be observed that the rank-difference value for each of the two most extreme subjects would be equal to $N - 1$ (for data in Table 2-7, $10 - 1 = 9$). For each of the next two most extreme subjects, the $RD$ would be $N - 3 = 7$ and so on. A generalized formula for determining the sum of $(RD)^2$ for perfectly inverse relationships follows.

For an even number of subjects:

$$\Sigma RD^2 = 2[(N-1)^2 + (N-3)^2 + (N-5)^2 + \ldots (N - (N-1))^2] \tag{18}$$

For 10 subjects:

$$\Sigma RD^2 = 2[(10-1)^2 + (10-3)^2 + (10-5)^2 + (10-7)^2 + (10-9)^2]$$
$$= 2(81 + 49 + 25 + 9 + 1)$$
$$= 2(165) = 330$$

When 330 is multiplied by 6 (formula 17) the numerator becomes 1980. The denominator for 10 subjects (from Table 2-7) is 990 which yields a quotient of 2 and $r' = 1 - 2 = -1.00$, a perfect negative (inverse) relationship.

For an odd number of subjects, formula 18 requires modification only in the last factor:

$$RD^2 = 2[(N-1)^2 + (N-3)^2 + (N-5)^2 + \ldots + (N-N)^2] \tag{19}$$

A convenient means for squaring $RD$ values ending in .5 is available. The square of any value ending in .5 will always end in .25. The value to the left of the decimal in the squared factor will always equal the product of the numeral(s) to the left of the decimal in the $RD$ value and that numeral plus one. If, for example, the square of 7.5 is desired, it will be found to be 56.25 [$7(7 + 1) = 56$, for the value to the left of the decimal and 25 to the right of the decimal]. This short cut, it should be cautioned, may only be employed in *squaring* values ending in .5.

### Product-Moment Method
### with Ungrouped Scores.

This method tends to be more precise in determining the coefficient of correlation between two variables but, because it is more time-consuming, is usually reserved in its application to paired scores in excess of $N = 30$. The data contained in Table 2-7 will be utilized to illustrate the steps in this method. First, the means of the pull-ups and of the push-ups must be computed. The mean of the pull-ups is found to be 10(100/10), and the mean of the push-ups is 18(180/10). Second, the deviation, $d_x$, of each pull-up score from the pull-up mean must be determined as must the deviation, $d_y$, of each push-up score from the push-up mean. Third, the square ($d_x^2$ and $d_y^2$) for each deviation must be computed. Fourth, the product, $d_x d_y$, for each pair of deviations must be entered as either a + or - value. Table 2-8 illustrates the method to this point.

The formula for determining $r$ is then:

$$r = \frac{\Sigma d_x d_y}{\sqrt{\Sigma d_x^2 \cdot \Sigma d_y^2}} \tag{20}$$

$$= \frac{163}{\sqrt{150 \cdot 260}} = \frac{163}{\sqrt{39{,}000}}$$

$$= \frac{163}{197.48} = +0.825 = +0.83$$

**TABLE 2-8** Calculation of Coefficient Correlation Utilizing Product-Moment Method with Ungrouped Scores

| SUBJECT | PULL-UPS SCORE | PUSH-UPS SCORE | $d_x$ | $d_y$ | $d_x^2$ | $d_y^2$ | $d_x d_y$ + | $d_x d_y$ − | $d_x d_y$ 0 |
|---|---|---|---|---|---|---|---|---|---|
| 1 | 9 | 16 | −1 | −2 | 1 | 4 | 2 | | |
| 2 | 6 | 16 | −4 | −2 | 16 | 4 | 8 | | |
| 3 | 13 | 24 | +3 | +6 | 9 | 36 | 18 | | |
| 4 | 3 | 7 | −7 | −11 | 49 | 121 | 77 | | |
| 5 | 17 | 25 | +7 | +7 | 49 | 49 | 49 | | |
| 6 | 9 | 14 | −1 | −4 | 1 | 16 | 4 | | |
| 8 | 8 | 17 | −2 | −1 | 4 | 1 | 2 | | |
| 8 | 14 | 20 | +4 | +2 | 16 | 4 | 8 | | |
| 9 | 12 | 18 | +2 | 0 | 4 | 0 | | | 0 |
| 10 | 9 | 23 | −1 | +5 | 1 | 25 | | 5 | |
| | $\overline{X} = 10$ | $\overline{Y} = 18$ | | | $\Sigma d_x^2 = 150$ | $\Sigma d_y^2 = 260$ | $\Sigma + = 168$ | $\Sigma - = 5$ | 0 |

$$\Sigma d_x d_y = +163$$

A second method involves the formula:

$$r = \frac{N\Sigma XY - (\Sigma X)(\Sigma Y)}{\sqrt{[N\Sigma X^2 - (\Sigma X)^2][N\Sigma Y^2 - (\Sigma Y)^2]}} \tag{21}$$

Utilizing the same data as in prior examples, the solution follows:

|    | $X$ | $Y$ | $X^2$ | $Y^2$ | $XY$ |
|----|-----|-----|-------|-------|------|
| 1  | 9   | 16  | 81    | 256   | 144  |
| 2  | 6   | 16  | 36    | 256   | 96   |
| 3  | 13  | 24  | 169   | 576   | 312  |
| 4  | 3   | 7   | 9     | 49    | 21   |
| 5  | 17  | 25  | 289   | 625   | 425  |
| 6  | 9   | 14  | 81    | 196   | 126  |
| 7  | 8   | 17  | 64    | 289   | 136  |
| 8  | 14  | 20  | 196   | 400   | 280  |
| 9  | 12  | 18  | 144   | 324   | 216  |
| 10 | 9   | 23  | 81    | 529   | 207  |
| $\Sigma =$ | 100 | 180 | 1150 | 3500 | 1963 |

$$r = \frac{(10 \cdot 1963) - (100) \cdot (180)}{\sqrt{[10 \cdot 1150 - (100)^2][10 \cdot 3500 - (180)^2]}}$$

$$= \frac{19630 - 18000}{\sqrt{(11500 - 10000)(35000 - 32400)}} = \frac{1630}{\sqrt{(1500)(2600)}}$$

$$= \frac{1630}{1974.8417} = +0.825 = +0.83$$

Again, the widespread availability of pocket calculators makes this method considerably more appealing.

### Product-Moment Method
### with Grouped Scores.

If the number of pairs of scores is fairly large (e.g., more than 30), it is convenient to group the scores by means of a scattergram (a two-dimensional frequency distribution) in which one variable (in this instance pull-ups) is plotted along the $X$-axis while the other variable (e.g., push-ups) is plotted along the $Y$-axis (Table 2-9). Thus, for each subject, there is a single point (coordinate) that represents both $X$ (pull-up) and $Y$ (push-up) scores. The rules established in arranging a frequency distribution apply in developing the two scales of the scattergram. The number of intervals along each axis must be equal. For the sake of

**TABLE 2-9 Calculation of Correlation Coefficient Utilizing the Product-Moment Method for Grouped Data**

$X$: Pull-up Scores

$Y$: Push-up Scores

| | 3-5 | 6-8 | 9-11 | 12-14 | 15-17 | $f_y$ | $d_y$ | $fd_y$ | $fd_y^2$ | $\Sigma xy$* |
|---|---|---|---|---|---|---|---|---|---|---|
| 23-26 | | | | ✓ | ✓ | 2 | +2 | +4 | +8 | +6 |
| 19-22 | | | ✓ | ✓ | | 2 | +1 | +2 | +2 | +1 |
| 15-18 | | ✓✓ | ✓ | ✓ | | 4 | 0 | 0 | 0 | 0 |
| 11-14 | | | ✓ | | | 1 | -1 | -1 | +1 | 0 |
| 7-10 | ✓ | | | | | 1 | -2 | -2 | +4 | +4 |
| $f_x$ | +1 | +2 | +3 | +3 | +1 | $N$ = 10 | | $\Sigma$ = +3 | $\Sigma$ = +15 | $\Sigma$ = +11 |
| $d_x$ | -2 | -1 | 0 | +1 | +2 | | | | | |
| $fd_x$ | -2 | -2 | 0 | +3 | +2 | $\Sigma$ = +1 | | | | |
| $fd_x^2$ | +4 | +2 | 0 | +3 | +4 | $\Sigma$ = +13 | | | | |
| $\Sigma xy$** | +4 | 0 | 0 | +3 | +4 | $\Sigma$ = +11 | | | | |

*$\Sigma_{xy} = \Sigma(x \cdot d_x) \cdot d_y$
**$\Sigma_{xy} = \Sigma(y \cdot d_y) \cdot d_x$
*$\Sigma xy$ = **$\Sigma xy$ (must result in equal sums)

expediency and in spite of the small number of subjects, the data in Table 2-8 are used in the example solution using formula 22. The formula for computing $r$ is:

$$r = \frac{\frac{\Sigma xy}{N} - \left(\frac{\Sigma fd_x}{N} \cdot \frac{\Sigma fd_y}{N}\right)}{\sqrt{\frac{\Sigma fdx^2}{N} - \frac{(\Sigma fd_x)^2}{N}} \cdot \sqrt{\frac{\Sigma fdy^2}{N} - \frac{(\Sigma fdy)^2}{N}}} \tag{22}$$

$$r = \frac{\frac{11}{10} - \left(\frac{1}{10} \cdot \frac{3}{10}\right)}{\sqrt{\frac{13}{10} - \frac{(1)^2}{10}} \cdot \sqrt{\frac{15}{10} - \frac{(3)^2}{10}}}$$

$$r = \frac{1.10 - 0.03}{\sqrt{1.30 - 0.10} \cdot \sqrt{1.50 - 0.90}} = \frac{1.07}{1.136 \cdot 1.187}$$

$$r = 1.348 = +.79$$

It should be noted that whenever scores are grouped as in a frequency distribution, errors arise. This is particularly true if the number of scores is relatively small. As the number of scores increases, the probability of errors tending to be in a given direction only diminishes. It should be obvious, further, that if $\Sigma xy$ is a negative value, the resulting coefficient will be negative, indicating an inverse relationship between the variables.

### Comparisons among the Three Methods

The advantage of the Spearman rank-difference method is in its ease of computation. It is reasonably accurate in spite of the fact that the intervals between successive scores vary widely and that these interval variances are disregarded. The reader should observe, however, that the method is restricted to small samples.

The product-moment method with ungrouped scores does take into account the precise value of each score and, hence, is relatively immune to the chance errors that may influence the rank-difference method. On the other hand, if the mean of either of the variables is not a whole number, the computation in squaring the deviation of each score from the mean for the first method can become laborious. As $N$ increases, the time consumed can become greater than the gain in accuracy justifies. If a calculator is readily available, there is no computational problem, of course.

When $N$ is very large, the use of the scattergram in grouping scores is recommended if no calculator is available. This method does introduce small errors, but these tend to cancel out as $N$ increases. The method is not unduly time-consuming.

### Correlation Coefficient for
### Curvilinear Relationships

The preceding product-moment coefficients apply if the means of the columns and of the rows in the scattergram form lines that are straight or nearly so. If the plots of the means produce curved lines, an alternate method should be employed in order to avoid a possibly mistaken impression of the relationship that could result from the use of the product-moment method. Only on infrequent occasions do paired variables of a single group produce curved-line plots and, consequently, the method will not be illustrated here.

### Point Biserial Coefficient of Correlation

The preceding methods have assumed that each of the variables has been composed of continuous scores. Although, in fact, continuous scores are those that theoretically may be divided infinitely, e.g., heights, weights, times, etc., most scores that are discrete, e.g., number of push-ups or pull-ups, may be treated for statistical purposes as continuous variables.

But how are data analyzed if one of the variables does not lend itself to the property assumed in a continuous variable? For example, if scores of team candidates on a basketball skills test are to be compared to success in making the team, the latter variable presents but two possibilities—make or don't make the team. Thus, two kinds of variables, one continuous and one dichotomous, confront the investigator.

In order to determine the relationship in an investigation such as this, the point biserial correlation, $r_{bis}$, may be used, albeit with some caution:

$$r_{bis} = \sqrt{\frac{\frac{(\Sigma X_o)^2}{N_o} + \frac{(\Sigma X_1)^2}{N_1} - \frac{(\Sigma X)^2}{N}}{(\Sigma X_o^2 + \Sigma X_1^2) - \frac{(\Sigma X)^2}{N}}}$$

(23)

in which

$\Sigma X_o$ = $\Sigma$scores in group$_o$ (e.g., make the team)

$\Sigma X_1$ = $\Sigma$scores in group$_1$ (e.g., not make the team)

$\Sigma X$ = $\Sigma$scores in both groups

$N_o$ = number in group$_o$

$N_1$ = number in group$_1$

$N$ = number in both groups

If the first 10 scores contained in Table 2-1 are used for illustrative purposes to determine if they are related to success in making a given team, and if the first four subjects are the ones who make the team, the computation for the determination of $r_{bis}$ would be:

| SUCCESSFUL GROUP | | | UNSUCCESSFUL GROUP | | |
|---|---|---|---|---|---|
| Subject | $X_o$ | $X_o^2$ | Subject | $X_1$ | $X_1^2$ |
| 1 | 14 | 196 | 5 | 46 | 2116 |
| 2 | 32 | 1024 | 6 | 28 | 784 |
| 3 | 36 | 1296 | 7 | 100 | 10000 |
| 4 | 49 | 2401 | 8 | 62 | 3844 |
| $N_o = 4$  $\Sigma X_o = 131$  $\Sigma X_o^2 = 4917$ | | | 9 | 17 | 289 |
| $\bar{X}_o = 32.75$ | | | 10 | 64 | 4096 |
| | | | $N = 6$  $\Sigma X_1 = 317$  $\Sigma X_1^2 = 21129$ | | |
| | | | $\bar{X}_1 = 52.83$ | | |

$\Sigma X = 131 + 317 = 448$

$$r_{bis} = \sqrt{\frac{\frac{(131)^2}{4} + \frac{(317)^2}{6} - \frac{(448)^2}{10}}{(4917 + 21{,}129) - \frac{(448)^2}{10}}}$$

$$= \sqrt{\frac{4,290.25 + 16,748.17 - 20,070.4}{26,046 - 20,070.4}}$$

$$= \sqrt{\frac{968.02}{5965.60}} = \sqrt{0.162}$$

$$= \pm.40$$

The coefficient $r_{bis} = .40$ would suggest that there is, at best, a small positive or negative relationship between the test scores listed and success in making the team (both factors were arbitrarily assigned). Whether the relationship is positive or negative may be readily determined by comparing the means of the two groups. If the mean of the successful group (make the team) is higher than the mean of the unsuccessful group (not make the team), the relationship is positive. If the mean of the unsuccessful group is higher, the relationship is negative. In the preceding example, the mean (52.83) of the unsuccessful group is higher than the mean (32.75) of the successful group and, therefore, $r_{bis} = -.40$.

The word of caution involves the underlying assumption that the scores contained in Table 2-1 are relatively normally distributed.

A second method of determining $r_{bis}$ utilizes the formula:

$$r_{bis} = \frac{\bar{X}_p - \bar{X}_q}{s} \cdot \sqrt{pq} \tag{24}$$

in which

  $\bar{X}_p$ = Mean of the successful group

  $\bar{X}_q$ = Mean of the unsuccessful group

  $p$ = Proportion of the successful group to the total group

  $q$ = Proportion of the unsuccessful group to the total group

  $s = \sqrt{x^2/N}$

The solution to the preceding example would then be:

$$r_{bis} = \frac{32.75 - 52.83}{\sqrt{\dfrac{5975.60}{10}}} \cdot \sqrt{\frac{4}{10} \cdot \frac{6}{10}}$$

$$= \frac{-20.08}{\sqrt{597.56}} \cdot \sqrt{.4 \cdot .6}$$

$$= \frac{-20.08}{24.45} \cdot \sqrt{.24}$$

$$= -0.82 \cdot \pm.49$$

$$= \pm.40$$

| $X$ | $x$ | $x^2$ |
|------|-------|---------|
| 14 | −30.8 | 948.64 |
| 32 | −12.8 | 163.84 |
| 36 | − 8.8 | 77.44 |
| 49 | + 4.2 | 17.64 |
| 46 | + 1.2 | 1.44 |
| 28 | −16.8 | 282.24 |
| 100 | +55.2 | 3047.04 |
| 62 | +17.2 | 295.84 |
| 17 | −27.8 | 772.84 |
| 64 | +19.2 | 368.64 |

$N = 10 \quad \Sigma X = \overline{448} \quad \Sigma x = \overline{\quad 0.0} \quad \Sigma x^2 = \overline{5975.60}$

$$\bar{X} = \frac{448}{10} = 44.8$$

A further and more common application of $r_{bis}$ is in the computation of the discrimination index of objective test items. In this instance, the successful group is composed of those who respond correctly to an item whereas the unsuccessful group is composed of those who respond incorrectly. The continuous variable, $X$, is composed of the subjects' scores on the whole test. Unless a computer or calculator is available, the process of determining the discrimination index for each item is quite time-consuming but not necessarily prohibitive, since single computations for the continuous variable (if Formula 24 is employed) are applicable to the solution for each test item.

A method for estimating whether the relationship is significant, i.e., not due to chance, will be discussed later in this chapter.

**The phi coefficient of correlation ($r_\phi$).** Whereas $r_{bis}$ involved one continuous and one dichotomous variable, the phi coefficient, $r_\phi$, (tetrachoric) is designed for two dichotomous variables. Examples of applications would include hand dominance and sex (e.g., is there a relationship between whether one is left-handed or right-handed and whether one is male or female?) or the relationship between a team's winning or losing and whether it was playing at home or away from home. Continuous variables may be treated arbitrarily as dichotomous variables. Examples would include taller than 6 feet (1.83 m) or 6 feet (1.83 m) or shorter, and heavier than 150 pounds (68.04 kg) or 150 pounds (68.04 kg) or lighter. Such arbitrary treatment, however, is generally discouraged, since precision tends to be reduced.

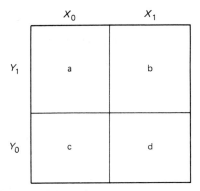

FIGURE 2.4 Example of a 2 × 2 Schematic.

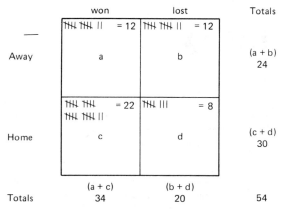

FIGURE 2.5 Example of a 2 × 2 Schematic (Actual Record).

The procedure for computing $r_\phi$ follows. A 2 × 2 schematic is drawn in which the four possibilities are represented by boxes (Figure 2.4).

If, for purposes of illustration, $X_0$ represents winning and $X_1$ represents losing, and $Y_0$ indicates a home game and $Y_1$ an away game, each box will contain the frequency of the particular combination. Figure 2.5 is based on the actual record of a major league baseball team during two months of play.

These coordinate values are then substituted into the formula

$$r_\phi = \frac{bc - ad}{\sqrt{(a + c)(b + d)(a + b)(c + d)}} \tag{25}$$

$$r_\phi = \frac{(12)(22) - (12)(8)}{\sqrt{(34)(20)(24)(30)}}$$

$$= \frac{264 - 96}{\sqrt{489,600}}$$

$$= \frac{168}{699.71}$$

$$= +.24$$

Thus, there appears to be a small positive relationship between winning and playing at home.

## INFERENTIAL STATISTICS

Statistics included in this section are directed toward a single concern: the probability that observed descriptions, differences, or relationships are due to chance influences. In the brief discussion of chance occurrences that appeared earlier in the chapter, it was noted that the probability ($P$) of a given toss of a coin resulting in a heads landing was 50% (.50). If $N$ coins are tossed simultaneously, the resulting probable frequencies for each of the possible combinations is represented by an algebraic expression termed the binomial expansion, $(H + T)^n$. Hence, if four coins are repeatedly tossed simultaneously, the expression becomes $(H + T)^4 = H^4 + 4H^3T + 6H^2T^2 + 4HT^3 + T^4$, i.e., if the four coins are tossed simultaneously 16 times, the probability is that the combination of four heads and no tails would occur once; of three heads and one tail, four times; of two heads and two tails, six times; of one head and three tails, four times; and of no heads and four tails, once. This is not to say that these frequencies would occur each time that four coins were tossed simultaneously 16 times, but rather that the probability of this distribution of combinations occurring is greater than for any other possible distribution. (The distributions least likely to occur are those of 16 consecutive combinations of either four heads and no tails or of no heads and four tails.) If the series of 16 tosses is repeated a large number of times, the proportion of combinations would be expected to approximate increasingly the 1, 4, 6, 4, 1 ratio.

### Standard Error of the Mean

If a random sample is selected from a larger, unobserved population, and the mean of the sample is computed, with how much confidence can it be assumed that the mean of the sample is representative of the mean of the population from which the sample was drawn? What are the factors that influence the reliability of the sample mean? If the scores contained in Table 2-1 comprised a sample drawn from a population of, say, 1,000 scores, what is the probability that the sample mean (59.8) approximates the true mean of all 1,000 scores? Before the procedure by which the probability may be computed is discussed, some further explanation of the general theory is in order.

If, after the mean of the sample has been computed, the 30 scores are replaced in the population of 1,000 and a new sample of 30 scores is selected randomly, would the mean of the new sample also be 59.8? The likelihood is that it would not, although it very likely would not be too different, either. If this process of replacement and reselection were repeated a large (theoretically an infinite) number of times, and the means of all the samples were placed along the abscissa (horizontal base line) of a distribution curve, it would be observed that the means would be distributed *normally* about the *true* mean of the 1,000 scores. Thus, 68.26% of the sample means would lie between ±1.0s of the true mean, 95.44% of the sample means would lie between ±2.0s of the true mean, and so on.

The above process, of course, would be uneconomical in terms of time. (Considerably less time would be involved in directly computing the true mean of the 1,000 scores; but what if the population contained 10,000 or 100,000 scores?) What factors influence the probability that a randomly selected sample's mean approximates the population mean? First, the probability is increased as the size of the sample becomes larger. If a single score comprised the sample, it might be an extreme score that would give a distorted impression of the characteristics of the population. If two scores comprised the sample, a slightly clearer impression of the population would be available. Thirty or more scores provide a reasonably accurate impression, particularly if the scores are not dispersed (spread out) too widely. This latter observation may be expressed as: "the smaller the standard deviation of the sample, the greater the probability that the sample mean is representative of the population mean." The degree, then, to which the sample mean is reliable as an estimate of the population is termed the *standard error* of the mean, $SE_{\bar{X}}$:

$$SE_{\bar{X}} = \frac{s}{\sqrt{N-1}} \quad * \tag{26}$$

For the scores contained in Table 2-1,

$$SE_{\bar{X}} = \frac{27.48}{\sqrt{30-1}} = \frac{27.48}{5.39} = 5.1$$

The interpretation of this statistic is that it may be predicted with a certain confidence that the mean of the population falls within the limits 59.8 ± 5.1. With what certain confidence? With the confidence that the prediction will be correct about two out of three times, i.e., 68.26 percent correct. If the confidence limits are extended to include two standard errors of the mean, 59.8 ± 10.2, the probability that the prediction is correct is increased to approximately 95 percent.

In the first instance, then, there is approximately a two-thirds probability that the population mean lies between 54.7 and 64.9 (59.8 ± 5.1). In the second instance, the probability is increased to about 95 percent† that the population mean lies within the limits 49.6-70.0. It follows, therefore, that the larger the standard error, the less reliable the sample mean is as a predictor of the population mean.

*Many references will express the denominator as $\sqrt{N}$. As $N$ increases, the effect of which of the two denominators is utilized diminishes in importance. For small samples, however, $\sqrt{N-1}$ will produce a larger $SE_{\bar{X}}$, and the probability of a false hypothesis, i.e., that $\bar{X}$ of the sample represents the $\bar{X}$ of the population being accepted, is reduced.

†If the table of normal probability is consulted it will be noted that 1.96 $SE_{\bar{X}}$ will establish the confidence limits within which precisely 95% of the time the mean of the population would be expected to lie.

### Differences Between Groups

The question may often arise as to whether the performance of one group on a test is superior to that of a second group (the size of the groups may be the same or they may be different depending upon how they are selected) on the same test. If the subjects in Table 2-1 are divided arbitrarily into two groups, with subjects 1-5 comprising group $X$ and subjects 6-10 comprising group $Y$, it is then possible to compute the respective group means and the differences between these means:

$$\bar{X} = \frac{177}{5} = 35.4 \qquad \bar{Y} = \frac{271}{5} = 54.2$$

The difference $(D)$ between the means (ignoring signs) is

$$D = 54.2 - 35.4 = 18.8$$

The question now becomes: "What is the probability that a difference of this magnitude resulted from chance variations in performance rather than from real differences in the groups' respective abilities to perform at the time the test was administered?" The answer depends upon several factors: 1) how the groups were selected—a single group taking the test at different times, two randomly selected groups, or two groups of paired subjects based upon a prior administration of the test and prior to the application of different methods of instruction that may account for the differences now observed; 2) the magnitude of the difference; 3) the size of the groups; and 4) the degree to which the scores in each group are dispersed. The probability that chance variations resulted in the observed difference varies directly with the dispersion (as measured by the groups' standard deviations) and indirectly with the magnitude of the difference and with the size of the groups.

The method by which the probability of chance influences may be determined involves the application of a t-test for which the general formula is

$$t = \frac{\bar{D}}{SE_{\bar{D}}} \tag{27}$$

in which $\bar{D}$ is the difference between the group means and $SE_{\bar{D}}$ is the standard error of the difference between the group means.

In all applications of the t-test discussed in this section, the method for determining $D$, i.e., the actual difference between the group means (often called the observed difference), is the same. The determination of the $SE_{\bar{D}}$ varies, however, depending upon the procedure used in selecting the groups and whether the groups are large or small in size.

Once the $t$ has been computed, it is necessary to refer to a table of $t$ to identify how large $t$ must be (for a given probability) before the assumption that there is no true difference in group performance (termed the null hypothesis) may be ruled out. Thus, if $t$ is sufficiently large, the probability that chance influences produced the difference observed is correspondingly small.

*The* t-*table*. The $t$-table (Table 2-10) is an adaptation of the table of normal probability. Whereas the table of normal probability is based upon the assumption of an infinite number of scores, the $t$-table takes into account the increasing probability of chance influences as $N$ decreases. Thus, as $N$ becomes smaller, the $t$-ratio needed to rule out chance as a factor becomes correspondingly larger.

To use the $t$-table, it is first necessary to compute the degrees of freedom* (d.f.). Then read across the row in which the computed d.f. lies until a $t$-value equal to or larger than the computed $t$-ratio is observed. At the top of the column in which this $t$-value lies will be found the probability ($P$) that chance was a factor.

It may be observed that when $N$ is as small as 30, the $t$-ratio required for $P$ = .05 is 2.042, a value only slightly larger than the $t$-ratio needed when $N = \infty$, 1.960.

How is the $t$-table read and interpreted? It will be seen that the table is composed of three kinds of data: 1) the $t$-values (located in the body of the table); 2) the probability levels (located in the row heading each of the $t$-value columns); and 3) the degrees of freedom (d.f.)—(located in the left-hand column). The latter term, degrees of freedom, introduces a new concept. If the example (two independent groups) introduced earlier in this section may serve as an illustration, it will be noted that each group contains 5 subjects. For a given group mean, the scores of 4 of these subjects may vary in an almost unlimited fashion. Once these 4 scores are obtained, however, the fifth score must assume a fixed value if the mean is not to be altered. Hence, the degrees of freedom of the group is $N - 1$ or 4. The same is true of the second group and, when considered together, the total degrees of freedom would equal $(N_1 - 1) + (N_2 - 1) = N_1 + N_2 - 2 = +8$. For a single group represented by two scores for each member or for paired groups, $d.f. = N - 1$ = 5 - 1 = 4. If the $t$-table is consulted, it will be apparent that $t$ must be at least 2.306 for 8 degrees of freedom if the probability that the difference observed is due to chance influences is to be no greater than 5%†, i.e., $P = .05$. For $P = .01$, $t$ must be at least 3.355.

*Computing* t *for small, correlated groups.* Two applications shall be considered: 1) subjects in the two groups have been paired by means of a pretest and, after the application of different treatments, e.g., training programs, a posttest is then administered to determine if one of the groups is now superior in performance; and 2) subjects comprise a single group with the paired scores representing pretest and posttest in an effort to determine the effect of a particular treatment. In

---

*For a single group or for matched groups, d.f. = $N - 1$. For two unmatched groups, d.f. = $N_1 + N_2 - 2$.

†Statisticians tend to agree that $P = .05$ is the minimum standard acceptable if chance is to be cautiously disregarded. The critical concern, however, would seem to be the risk involved in accepting a false hypothesis or in rejecting a true hypothesis. Risks in the space program, for example, must be reduced to an absolute minimum (i.e., a higher probability standard), whereas, for most other purposes, a less rigorous standard may be perfectly acceptable.

**TABLE 2-10  Table of t-values**

| d.f. | P = .8 | .6 | .5 | .4 | .3 | .2 | .1 | .05 | .02 | .01 | .001 |
|---|---|---|---|---|---|---|---|---|---|---|---|
| 1 | .325 | .727 | 1.000 | 1.376 | 1.963 | 3.078 | 6.314 | 12.706 | 31.821 | 63.657 | 636.619 |
| 2 | .289 | .617 | .816 | 1.061 | 1.386 | 1.886 | 2.920 | 4.303 | 6.965 | 9.925 | 31.598 |
| 3 | .277 | .584 | .765 | .978 | 1.250 | 1.638 | 2.353 | 3.182 | 4.541 | 5.841 | 12.941 |
| 4 | .271 | .569 | .741 | .941 | 1.190 | 1.533 | 2.132 | 2.776 | 3.747 | 4.604 | 8.610 |
| 5 | .267 | .559 | .727 | .920 | 1.156 | 1.476 | 2.015 | 2.571 | 3.365 | 4.032 | 6.859 |
| 6 | .265 | .553 | .718 | .906 | 1.134 | 1.440 | 1.943 | 2.447 | 3.143 | 3.707 | 5.959 |
| 7 | .263 | .549 | .711 | .896 | 1.119 | 1.415 | 1.895 | 2.365 | 2.998 | 3.499 | 5.405 |
| 8 | .262 | .546 | .706 | .889 | 1.108 | 1.397 | 1.860 | 2.306 | 2.896 | 3.355 | 5.041 |
| 9 | .261 | .543 | .703 | .883 | 1.100 | 1.383 | 1.833 | 2.262 | 2.821 | 3.250 | 4.781 |
| 10 | .260 | .542 | .700 | .879 | 1.093 | 1.372 | 1.812 | 2.228 | 2.746 | 3.169 | 4.587 |
| 11 | .260 | .540 | .697 | .876 | 1.088 | 1.363 | 1.796 | 2.201 | 2.718 | 3.106 | 4.437 |
| 12 | .259 | .539 | .695 | .873 | 1.083 | 1.356 | 1.782 | 2.179 | 2.681 | 3.055 | 4.318 |
| 13 | .259 | .538 | .694 | .870 | 1.079 | 1.350 | 1.771 | 2.160 | 2.650 | 3.012 | 4.221 |
| 14 | .258 | .537 | .692 | .868 | 1.076 | 1.345 | 1.761 | 2.145 | 2.624 | 2.977 | 4.140 |
| 15 | .258 | .536 | .691 | .866 | 1.074 | 1.341 | 1.753 | 2.131 | 2.602 | 2.947 | 4.073 |
| 16 | .258 | .535 | .690 | .865 | 1.071 | 1.337 | 1.746 | 2.120 | 2.583 | 2.921 | 4.015 |
| 17 | .257 | .534 | .689 | .863 | 1.069 | 1.333 | 1.740 | 2.110 | 2.567 | 2.898 | 3.965 |
| 18 | .257 | .534 | .688 | .862 | 1.067 | 1.330 | 1.734 | 2.101 | 2.552 | 2.878 | 3.922 |
| 19 | .257 | .533 | .688 | .861 | 1.066 | 1.328 | 1.729 | 2.093 | 2.539 | 2.861 | 3.883 |
| 20 | .257 | .533 | .687 | .860 | 1.064 | 1.325 | 1.725 | 2.086 | 2.528 | 2.845 | 3.850 |

| | | | | | | | | | | |
|---|---|---|---|---|---|---|---|---|---|---|
| 21 | .257 | .532 | .686 | .859 | 1.063 | 1.323 | 1.721 | 2.080 | 2.518 | 2.831 | 3.819 |
| 22 | .256 | .532 | .686 | .858 | 1.061 | 1.321 | 1.717 | 2.074 | 2.508 | 2.819 | 3.792 |
| 23 | .256 | .532 | .685 | .858 | 1.060 | 1.319 | 1.714 | 2.069 | 2.500 | 2.807 | 3.767 |
| 24 | .256 | .531 | .685 | .857 | 1.059 | 1.318 | 1.711 | 2.064 | 2.492 | 2.797 | 3.745 |
| 25 | .256 | .531 | .684 | .856 | 1.058 | 1.316 | 1.708 | 2.060 | 2.485 | 2.787 | 3.725 |
| 26 | .256 | .531 | .684 | .856 | 1.058 | 1.315 | 1.706 | 2.056 | 2.479 | 2.779 | 3.707 |
| 27 | .256 | .531 | .684 | .855 | 1.057 | 1.314 | 1.703 | 2.052 | 2.473 | 2.771 | 3.690 |
| 28 | .256 | .530 | .683 | .855 | 1.056 | 1.313 | 1.701 | 2.048 | 2.467 | 2.763 | 3.674 |
| 29 | .256 | .530 | .683 | .854 | 1.055 | 1.311 | 1.699 | 2.045 | 2.462 | 2.756 | 3.659 |
| 30 | .256 | .530 | .683 | .854 | 1.055 | 1.310 | 1.697 | 2.042 | 2.457 | 2.750 | 3.646 |
| 40 | .255 | .529 | .681 | .851 | 1.050 | 1.303 | 1.684 | 2.021 | 2.423 | 2.704 | 3.551 |
| 60 | .254 | .527 | .679 | .848 | 1.046 | 1.296 | 1.671 | 2.000 | 2.390 | 2.660 | 3.460 |
| 120 | .254 | .526 | .677 | .845 | 1.041 | 1.289 | 1.658 | 1.980 | 2.358 | 2.617 | 3.373 |
| $\infty$ | .253 | .524 | .674 | .842 | 1.036 | 1.282 | 1.645 | 1.960 | 2.326 | 2.576 | 3.291 |

Source: Fisher and Yates, 1974, p. 46.

either instance, the scores may be analyzed by means of a single method utilizing formula (27):

$$t = \frac{\bar{D}}{SE_{\bar{D}}}$$

in which

$$SE_{\bar{D}} = \sqrt{\left(\frac{\Sigma D^2}{N} - \bar{D}^2\right)\left(\frac{1}{N-1}\right)}$$

Utilizing the arbitrary division of scores into two groups, the calculation would be

| X | Y | D | $D^2$ |
|---|---|---|---|
| 14 | 28 | -14 | 196 |
| 32 | 100 | -68 | 4624 |
| 36 | 62 | -26 | 676 |
| 49 | 17 | +32 | 1024 |
| 46 | 64 | -18 | 324 |
| $\Sigma X = 177$ | $\Sigma Y = 271$ | $\Sigma D = -94$ | $\Sigma D^2 = 6844$ |
| $\bar{X} = 35.4$ | $\bar{Y} = 54.2$ | | |

$$t = \frac{35.4 - 54.2*}{\sqrt{\left[\dfrac{6844}{5} - (18.8)^2\right]\left[\dfrac{1}{5-1}\right]}}$$

$$= \frac{-18.8}{\sqrt{(1368.8 - 353.44)(.25)}}$$

$$= \frac{-18.8}{\sqrt{(1015.36)(.25)}} = \frac{-18.8}{\sqrt{253.84}}$$

$$= \frac{-18.8}{15.93} = -1.18$$

Consulting the $t$-table for 4 degrees of freedom ($N - 1$ for paired scores), it is seen that a $t$ of 2.776 is required for $P = .05$ and a $t$ of 4.604 is required for $P = .01$. Since the $t$ that was computed (-1.18) is less than 2.776, the null hypothesis (that there is no difference between the group means) must be accepted.

*The difference between means is equivalent to the mean difference, $\bar{D}$, which is equal to $\Sigma D/N = -94/5 = -18.8$. (Although a minus sign has been retained in the example, its only significance is to denote that $\bar{Y} > \bar{X}$.)

*Computing* t *for small, uncorrelated groups.* If the scores utilized in the preceding example may be assumed to represent two independent samples, another form of the basic formula must be used for determining the probability that the observed difference between means is due to chance:

$$t = \frac{\bar{D}}{SE_{\bar{D}}} = \frac{\bar{X} - \bar{Y}}{\sqrt{\left(\frac{\Sigma x^2 + \Sigma y^2}{N_x + N_y - 2}\right)\left(\frac{N_x + N_y}{N_x \cdot N_y}\right)}} \tag{28}$$

in which

$x$ = the deviation of each score in group $X$ from $\bar{X}$

$y$ = the deviation of each score in group $Y$ from $\bar{Y}$

($\bar{X}$ and $\bar{Y}$ have been rounded to one decimal for simplicity of computation.)

| $X$ | $x$ | $x^2$ | $Y$ | $y$ | $y^2$ |
|---|---|---|---|---|---|
| 14 | −21.4 | 457.96 | 28 | −26.2 | 686.44 |
| 32 | − 3.4 | 11.56 | 100 | +45.8 | 2097.64 |
| 36 | + 0.6 | .36 | 62 | + 7.8 | 60.84 |
| 49 | +13.6 | 184.96 | 17 | −37.2 | 1383.84 |
| 46 | +10.6 | 112.36 | 64 | + 9.8 | 96.04 |
| $X = 177$ | | $\Sigma x^2 = 767.20$ | $\Sigma Y = 271$ | | $\Sigma y^2 = 4324.80$ |
| $\bar{X} = 35.4$ | | | $\bar{Y} = 54.2$ | | |

$$t = \frac{35.4 - 54.2}{\sqrt{\left(\frac{767.2 + 4324.8}{5 + 5 - 2}\right)\left(\frac{5 + 5}{5 \cdot 5}\right)}}$$

$$= \frac{-18.8}{\sqrt{\left(\frac{5092}{8}\right)\left(\frac{10}{25}\right)}}$$

$$= \frac{-18.8}{\sqrt{(636.5)(.4)}} = \frac{-18.8}{\sqrt{254.6}}$$

$$= \frac{-18.8}{15.96} = -1.178$$

Consulting the *t*-table for 8 degrees of freedom ($N_1 + N_2 - 2$ for independent samples), it will be noted that a *t* of −1.178 is less than that needed for $P = .05$

(2.306). Therefore, the null hypothesis must again be accepted with approximately the same confidence as when the assumption was made that the groups were paired.

*Computing* t *for large, uncorrelated groups.* The scores in the previous examples will be used, with several assumptions, once again. Since the groups utilized before comprised *small* samples, an assumption (for purpose of illustration only) will be made that Group $X$ contains 125 subjects and that Group $Y$ contains 150 subjects. Further, it will be assumed that $\bar{X}$, $\bar{Y}$, $s_X$, and $s_Y$ are unaffected by the increase in Group $Ns$. The formula for computing $t$ is:

$$t = \frac{\bar{D}}{SE_{\bar{D}}} = \frac{\bar{X} - \bar{Y}}{\sqrt{SE_{\bar{X}}^2 + SE_{\bar{Y}}^2}} \tag{29}$$

$$1. \ SE_{\bar{X}} = \frac{s_X}{\sqrt{N-1}} = \frac{\sqrt{\dfrac{\Sigma x^2}{N}}}{\sqrt{N-1}} = \frac{\sqrt{\dfrac{767.2}{5}}}{\sqrt{125-1}} = \frac{\sqrt{153.44}}{\sqrt{124}}$$

$$= \frac{12.39}{11.14} = 1.11$$

$$2. \ SE_{\bar{Y}} = \frac{s_Y}{\sqrt{N-1}} = \frac{\sqrt{\dfrac{\Sigma y^2}{N}}}{\sqrt{N-1}} = \frac{\sqrt{\dfrac{4324.8}{5}}}{\sqrt{150-1}} = \frac{\sqrt{864.96}}{\sqrt{149}}$$

$$= \frac{29.41}{12.21} = 2.41$$

$$t = \frac{35.4 - 54.2}{\sqrt{(1.11)^2 + (2.41)^2}} = \frac{-18.8}{\sqrt{1.23 + 5.81}}$$

$$= \frac{-18.8}{\sqrt{7.04}} = \frac{-18.8}{2.65} = -7.09$$

With large samples, the table of normal probability may be used to determine the level of confidence. In order for $P = .05$, $t$ must be at least 1.96; for $P = .01$, $t$ must be at least 2.58. The computed $t$, $-709$, is well above 2.58 and the conclusion may be drawn that the difference between means is significant well beyond the 1 percent level of confidence and the null hypothesis may be rejected.

*Computing* t *for large, correlated groups.* Utilizing the data from the previous example, with the assumptions that Group $X$ represents pretest scores and Group $Y$ posttest scores and that the group is large rather than containing just 5 subjects, $t$ may be computed from the following formula:

$$t = \frac{\bar{D}}{SE_{\bar{D}}} = \frac{\bar{X} - \bar{Y}}{\sqrt{SE_{\bar{X}}^2 + SE_{\bar{Y}}^2 - (2r_{XY} \cdot SE_{\bar{X}} \cdot SE_{\bar{Y}})}} \quad\quad (30)$$

in which

$r_{XY}$ = coefficient of correlation between pretest and posttest scores.

All the data necessary are available, except for the determination of $r_{XY}$. On page 45, the equivalents of $d_x$, $d_y$, $d_x^2$, and $d_y^2$ are listed. Still to be computed is $\Sigma d_x d_y$. These values, respectively, are:

| Subject | $d_x$ | $d_y$ | $+$ $d_x d_y$ | $-$ |
|---------|-------|-------|---------------|-----|
| 1 | -21.4 | -26.2 | 560.68 | |
| 2 | - 3.4 | +45.8 | | 155.72 |
| 3 | + 0.6 | + 7.8 | 4.68 | |
| 4 | +13.6 | -37.2 | | 505.92 |
| 5 | +10.6 | + 9.8 | 103.88 | |

$$\Sigma d_x d_y = +669.24 \quad -661.64$$
$$= + \quad 7.60$$

From (20) it is possible to compute

$$r_{XY} = \frac{\Sigma d_x d_y}{\sqrt{\Sigma d_x^2 \cdot \Sigma d_y^2}} = \frac{7.60}{\sqrt{(767.2)(4324.8)}}$$

$$= \frac{7.60}{1821.53} = .004$$

Substituting this value of $r_{XY}$ into (30) will permit the calculation of $t$.

$$t = \frac{35.4 - 54.2}{\sqrt{(1.11)^2 + (2.41)^2 - (.008 \cdot 1.11 \cdot 2.41)}} = \frac{-18.8}{\sqrt{1.23 + 5.81 - 0.02}}$$

$$= \frac{-18.8}{\sqrt{7.02}} = \frac{-18.8}{2.65}$$

$$= -7.094$$

As in the prior example, a $t$ of -7.094 is well beyond the 2.58 needed for $P = .01$, and the null hypothesis may again be rejected.

### Analysis of Variance

The preceding section dealt with an analysis and interpretation of the difference between two means in which a $t$-ratio was computed. Often, it is desirable to be able to analyze and interpret differences among three or more group means. Analysis of variance permits such an undertaking. Whereas $t$-values are functions of group standard deviations, analysis of variance involves the computation of an $F$-ratio which, in turn, is a function of the variances* of the respective group distributions. As a consequence, the $F$-value may be shown to be equal to $t^2$ if just two groups are analyzed in which both of the methods are used.

If $k$ groups are treated as a single group, the total variance, $S_T{}^2$, may be computed. Further, the variance within each group, $S_W{}^2$, and the variance between groups, $S_B{}^2$, may also be computed. The relationship among these variances may be expressed as:

$$S_T{}^2 = S_W{}^2 + S_B{}^2 \qquad (31)$$

In order to maintain continuity with previous examples, the 30 scores from Table 2-1 will be divided into three groups: Group 1 (scores 1-10); Group 2 (scores 11-20); and Group 3 (scores 21-30). If there are observed differences among the means of the three groups, it will be desirable to calculate whether these differences are likely to be due to chance or whether they are the result of some treatment. If it may be assumed that all three groups were equal in the performance of a particular skill at the beginning of an instructional unit, and if each group receives a different method of instruction, it may be determined through the analysis of variance ($ANOVA$) which of the three methods of instruction is most effective.

The method for calculating the $F$-ratio involves nine steps if more than two groups are involved:

1. The score for each subject is squared.
2. The scores and their squares are summed for each group.

| GROUP 1 | | GROUP 2 | | GROUP 3 | |
|---|---|---|---|---|---|
| $X$ | $X^2$ | $X$ | $X^2$ | $X$ | $X^2$ |
| 14 | 196 | 42 | 1764 | 99 | 9801 |
| 32 | 1024 | 73 | 5329 | 96 | 9216 |
| 36 | 1296 | 23 | 529 | 92 | 8464 |
| 49 | 2401 | 43 | 1849 | 85 | 7225 |
| 46 | 2116 | 59 | 3481 | 77 | 5929 |
| 28 | 784 | 72 | 5184 | 68 | 4624 |
| 100 | 10000 | 83 | 6889 | 57 | 3249 |

*The standard deviation of a group of scores is equal to the square root of the scores' variance, $S^2$, i.e., $s = \sqrt{S^2}$ where $s^2 = \Sigma d^2/N$.

| | | | | | |
|---|---|---|---|---|---|
| 62 | 3844 | 90 | 8100 | 45 | 2025 |
| 17 | 289 | 96 | 9216 | 31 | 961 |
| 64 | 4096 | 99 | 9801 | 16 | 256 |

$\Sigma X_1 = 448$    $\Sigma X_1{}^2 = 26{,}046$    $\Sigma X_2 = 680$    $\Sigma X_2{}^2 = 52{,}142$    $\Sigma X_3 = 666$    $\Sigma X_3{}^2 = 51{,}750$

$\bar{X}_1 = 44.8$          $\bar{X}_2 = 68.0$          $\bar{X}_3 = 66.6$

3. Determine the total sum of the squares, $S_T{}^2$, for the three groups:

$$S_T{}^2 = (\Sigma X_1{}^2 + \Sigma X_2{}^2 + \Sigma X_3{}^2) - \frac{(\Sigma X_1 + \Sigma X_2 + \Sigma X_3)^2}{N_T} \tag{32}$$

$$= (26{,}046 + 52{,}142 + 51{,}750) - \frac{(448 + 680 + 666)^2}{30}$$

$$= 129{,}938 - 107{,}281.2$$

$$= 22{,}656.8$$

4. Determine the sum of the squares between means, $S_B{}^2$:

$$S_B{}^2 = \frac{(\Sigma X_1)^2}{N_1} + \frac{(\Sigma X_2)^2}{N_2} + \frac{(\Sigma X_3)^2}{N_3} - \frac{(\Sigma X_1 + \Sigma X_2 + \Sigma X_3)^2}{N_T} \tag{33}$$

$$= \frac{200704}{10} + \frac{462400}{10} + \frac{443556}{10} - 107{,}281.2 \text{ (from 3. above)}$$

$$= 110{,}666.0 - 107{,}281.2$$

$$= 3{,}384.8$$

5. $S_W{}^2 = S_T{}^2 - S_B{}^2$            (34)

$$= 22{,}656.8 - 3{,}384.8$$

$$= 19{,}272.0$$

6. Enter the values calculated in steps 4 and 5 in the summary below:

| VARIATION SOURCE | SUM OF SQUARES | d.f.* | MEAN SQUARE | F |
|---|---|---|---|---|
| $S_B{}^2$ | 3,384.8 | 2 | 1692.4 | |
| | | | | 2.37 |
| $S_W{}^2$ | 19,272.0 | 27 | 713.8 | |

*Degrees of freedom between groups is equal to k − 1 in which k is the number of groups. Degrees of freedom within groups is equal to N − k.

7. Compute the mean squares and place in the summary above:

$$\text{Mean Square} = \frac{\text{Sum of Squares}}{d.f.} \tag{35}$$

$$= \frac{3{,}384.8}{2} = 1692.4 \ (\text{for } S_B{}^2)$$

$$= \frac{19{,}272.0}{27} = 713.8 \ (\text{for } S_W{}^2)$$

8. Establish the $F$-ratio and compute $F$:

$$F = \frac{\text{Mean Square Between Group Means}}{\text{Mean Square Within Groups}}$$

$$= \frac{1692.4}{713.8} = 2.37 \tag{36}$$

9.   Consult the Table of $F$ (Table 2–11) for interpretation of the $F$ value that has been computed. For 2 degrees and 27 degrees of freedom, the $F$-values required for $P = .05$ and for $P = .01$ are 3.35 and 5.49, respectively. Since the computed $F$ of 2.37 is less than 3.35, the null hypothesis is accepted, i.e., there are no significant differences among the means of the three groups.

But what if, for example, the computed value of $F$ had equalled or exceeded 3.35 or 5.49? If such had occurred, it would have indicated that significant differences were likely to exist between two or more means. In order to determine for which pair(s) of means significant differences were obtained, it is necessary to employ the $S$-method as devised by Scheffé:[1]

Step A.   Calculate $t'$:

$$t = \sqrt{F(k-1)} \tag{37}$$

in which $F$ = value for $k - 1$ $d.f.$ in the numerator and for $k(N - 1)$ $d.f.$ in the denominator (See summary in step 6 above, and formula 36).

$$= \sqrt{3.35(3-1)} \ (\text{for } \alpha = .05)^*$$

$$= \sqrt{6.70}$$

$$= 2.59$$

Step B.   Calculate $t$ for every pair of group means:

*$\alpha$ represents the predetermined level of confidence at which a difference will be considered significant. In the example, $\alpha = .05$ was selected, but $\alpha = .01$ could have been selected if desired.

**TABLE 2-11**   Critical Values of *F*

| Degrees of Freedom for Lesser Mean Square | P | DEGREES OF FREEDOM FOR GREATER MEAN SQUARE | | | | | | | | | |
|---|---|---|---|---|---|---|---|---|---|---|---|
| | | 1 | 2 | 3 | 4 | 5 | 6 | 7 | 8 | 9 | 10 |
| 1 | (.05) | 161 | 200 | 216 | 225 | 230 | 234 | 237 | 239 | 241 | 242 |
| | (.01) | 4052 | 4999 | 5403 | 5625 | 5764 | 5859 | 5928 | 5981 | 6022 | 6056 |
| 2 | | 18.51 | 19.00 | 19.16 | 19.25 | 19.30 | 19.33 | 19.36 | 19.37 | 19.38 | 19.39 |
| | | 98.49 | 99.01 | 99.17 | 99.25 | 99.30 | 99.33 | 99.34 | 99.36 | 99.38 | 99.40 |
| 3 | | 10.13 | 9.55 | 9.28 | 9.12 | 9.01 | 8.94 | 8.88 | 8.84 | 8.81 | 8.78 |
| | | 34.12 | 30.81 | 29.46 | 28.71 | 28.24 | 27.91 | 27.67 | 27.49 | 27.34 | 27.23 |
| 4 | | 7.71 | 6.94 | 6.59 | 6.39 | 6.26 | 6.16 | 6.09 | 6.04 | 6.00 | 5.96 |
| | | 21.20 | 18.00 | 16.69 | 15.98 | 15.52 | 15.21 | 14.98 | 14.80 | 14.66 | 14.54 |
| 5 | | 6.61 | 5.79 | 5.41 | 5.19 | 5.05 | 4.95 | 4.88 | 4.82 | 4.78 | 4.74 |
| | | 16.26 | 13.27 | 12.06 | 11.39 | 10.97 | 10.67 | 10.45 | 10.27 | 10.15 | 10.05 |
| 6 | | 5.99 | 5.14 | 4.76 | 4.53 | 4.39 | 4.28 | 4.21 | 4.15 | 4.10 | 4.06 |
| | | 13.74 | 10.92 | 9.78 | 9.15 | 8.75 | 8.47 | 8.26 | 8.10 | 7.98 | 7.87 |
| 7 | | 5.59 | 4.74 | 4.35 | 4.12 | 3.97 | 3.87 | 3.79 | 3.73 | 3.68 | 3.63 |
| | | 12.25 | 9.55 | 8.45 | 7.85 | 7.46 | 7.19 | 7.00 | 6.84 | 6.71 | 6.62 |
| 8 | | 5.32 | 4.46 | 4.07 | 3.84 | 3.69 | 3.58 | 3.50 | 3.44 | 3.39 | 3.34 |
| | | 11.26 | 8.65 | 7.59 | 7.01 | 6.63 | 6.37 | 6.19 | 6.03 | 5.91 | 5.82 |
| 9 | | 5.12 | 4.26 | 3.86 | 3.63 | 3.48 | 3.37 | 3.29 | 3.23 | 3.18 | 3.13 |
| | | 10.56 | 8.02 | 6.99 | 6.42 | 6.06 | 5.80 | 5.62 | 5.47 | 5.35 | 5.26 |
| 10 | | 4.96 | 4.10 | 3.71 | 3.48 | 3.33 | 3.22 | 3.14 | 3.07 | 3.02 | 2.97 |
| | | 10.04 | 7.56 | 6.55 | 5.99 | 5.64 | 5.39 | 5.21 | 5.06 | 4.95 | 4.85 |
| 11 | | 4.84 | 3.98 | 3.59 | 3.36 | 3.20 | 3.09 | 3.01 | 2.95 | 2.90 | 2.86 |
| | | 9.65 | 7.20 | 6.22 | 5.67 | 5.32 | 5.07 | 4.88 | 4.74 | 4.63 | 4.54 |
| 12 | | 4.75 | 3.88 | 3.49 | 3.26 | 3.11 | 3.00 | 2.92 | 2.85 | 2.80 | 2.76 |
| | | 9.33 | 6.93 | 5.95 | 5.41 | 5.06 | 4.82 | 4.65 | 4.50 | 4.39 | 4.30 |
| 13 | | 4.67 | 3.80 | 3.41 | 3.18 | 3.02 | 2.92 | 2.84 | 2.77 | 2.72 | 2.67 |
| | | 9.07 | 6.70 | 5.74 | 5.20 | 4.86 | 4.62 | 4.44 | 4.30 | 4.19 | 4.10 |
| 14 | | 4.60 | 3.74 | 3.34 | 3.11 | 2.96 | 2.85 | 2.77 | 2.70 | 2.65 | 2.60 |
| | | 8.86 | 6.51 | 5.56 | 5.03 | 4.69 | 4.46 | 4.28 | 4.14 | 4.03 | 3.94 |
| 15 | | 4.54 | 3.68 | 3.29 | 3.06 | 2.90 | 2.79 | 2.70 | 2.64 | 2.59 | 2.55 |
| | | 8.68 | 6.36 | 5.42 | 4.89 | 4.56 | 4.32 | 4.14 | 4.00 | 3.89 | 3.80 |
| 16 | | 4.49 | 3.63 | 3.24 | 3.01 | 2.85 | 2.74 | 2.66 | 2.59 | 2.54 | 2.49 |
| | | 8.53 | 6.23 | 5.29 | 4.77 | 4.44 | 4.20 | 4.03 | 3.89 | 3.78 | 3.69 |
| 17 | | 4.45 | 3.59 | 3.20 | 2.96 | 2.81 | 2.70 | 2.62 | 2.55 | 2.50 | 2.45 |
| | | 8.40 | 6.11 | 5.18 | 4.67 | 4.34 | 4.10 | 3.93 | 3.79 | 3.68 | 3.59 |
| 18 | | 4.41 | 3.55 | 3.16 | 2.93 | 2.77 | 2.66 | 2.58 | 2.51 | 2.46 | 2.41 |
| | | 8.28 | 6.01 | 5.90 | 4.58 | 4.25 | 4.01 | 3.85 | 3.71 | 3.60 | 3.51 |

TABLE 2-11 (continued)

| Degrees of Freedom for Lesser Mean Square | P | DEGREES OF FREEDOM FOR GREATER MEAN SQUARE | | | | | | | | | |
|---|---|---|---|---|---|---|---|---|---|---|---|
| | | 1 | 2 | 3 | 4 | 5 | 6 | 7 | 8 | 9 | 10 |
| 19 | | 4.38 | 3.52 | 3.13 | 2.90 | 2.74 | 2.63 | 2.55 | 2.48 | 2.43 | 2.38 |
| | | 8.18 | 5.93 | 5.01 | 4.50 | 4.17 | 3.94 | 3.77 | 3.63 | 3.52 | 3.43 |
| 20 | | 4.35 | 3.49 | 3.10 | 2.87 | 2.71 | 2.60 | 2.52 | 2.45 | 2.40 | 2.35 |
| | | 8.10 | 5.85 | 4.94 | 4.43 | 4.10 | 3.87 | 3.71 | 3.56 | 3.45 | 3.37 |
| 21 | | 4.32 | 3.47 | 3.07 | 2.84 | 2.68 | 2.57 | 2.49 | 2.42 | 2.37 | 2.32 |
| | | 8.02 | 5.78 | 4.87 | 4.37 | 4.04 | 3.81 | 3.65 | 3.51 | 3.40 | 3.31 |
| 22 | | 4.30 | 3.44 | 3.05 | 2.82 | 2.66 | 2.55 | 2.47 | 2.40 | 2.35 | 2.30 |
| | | 7.94 | 5.72 | 4.82 | 4.31 | 3.99 | 3.76 | 3.59 | 3.45 | 3.35 | 3.26 |
| 23 | | 4.28 | 3.42 | 3.03 | 2.80 | 2.64 | 2.53 | 2.45 | 2.38 | 2.32 | 2.28 |
| | | 7.88 | 5.66 | 4.76 | 4.26 | 3.94 | 3.71 | 3.54 | 3.41 | 3.30 | 3.21 |
| 24 | | 4.26 | 3.40 | 3.01 | 2.78 | 2.62 | 2.51 | 2.43 | 2.36 | 2.30 | 2.26 |
| | | 7.82 | 5.61 | 4.72 | 4.22 | 3.90 | 3.67 | 3.50 | 3.36 | 3.25 | 3.17 |
| 25 | | 4.24 | 3.38 | 2.99 | 2.76 | 2.60 | 2.49 | 2.41 | 2.34 | 2.28 | 2.24 |
| | | 7.77 | 5.57 | 4.78 | 4.18 | 3.86 | 3.63 | 3.46 | 3.32 | 3.21 | 3.13 |
| 26 | | 4.22 | 3.37 | 2.89 | 2.74 | 2.59 | 2.47 | 2.39 | 2.32 | 2.27 | 2.22 |
| | | 7.72 | 5.53 | 4.64 | 4.14 | 3.82 | 3.59 | 3.42 | 3.29 | 3.17 | 3.09 |
| 27 | | 4.21 | 3.35 | 2.96 | 2.73 | 2.57 | 2.46 | 2.37 | 2.30 | 2.25 | 2.20 |
| | | 7.68 | 5.49 | 4.60 | 4.11 | 3.79 | 3.56 | 3.39 | 3.26 | 3.14 | 3.06 |
| 28 | | 4.20 | 3.34 | 2.95 | 2.71 | 2.56 | 2.44 | 2.36 | 2.29 | 3.24 | 2.19 |
| | | 7.64 | 5.45 | 4.57 | 4.07 | 3.76 | 3.53 | 3.36 | 3.23 | 3.11 | 3.03 |
| 29 | | 4.18 | 3.33 | 2.93 | 2.70 | 2.54 | 2.43 | 2.35 | 2.28 | 2.22 | 2.18 |
| | | 7.60 | 5.52 | 4.54 | 4.04 | 3.73 | 3.50 | 3.32 | 3.20 | 3.08 | 3.00 |
| 30 | | 4.17 | 3.32 | 2.92 | 2.69 | 2.53 | 2.42 | 2.34 | 2.27 | 2.21 | 2.16 |
| | | 7.56 | 5.39 | 4.51 | 4.02 | 3.70 | 3.47 | 3.30 | 3.17 | 3.06 | 2.98 |

Source: Sheehan, 1971, pp. 266–269 (adapted).

$$t = \frac{\bar{X}_1 - \bar{X}_2}{\sqrt{\dfrac{2MS_W}{N}} \text{ or } (SE_{\bar{D}})} \quad (\text{or } \bar{X}_1 - \bar{X}_3 ; \bar{X}_2 - \bar{X}_3 , \text{etc.})$$

(38)

in which

$MS_W$ = Mean square within groups
$N$ = Number within each group

Step C.   Calculate:

$$SE_{\bar{D}} = \sqrt{\frac{2(713.8)}{10}}$$

$$= \sqrt{142.76}$$

$$= 11.95$$

Step D.  Compute between-means $t$-ratios for each paired combination:

$$t = \frac{\bar{X}_1 - \bar{X}_2}{SE_{\bar{D}}} = \frac{44.8 - 68.0}{11.95} = \frac{-23.2}{11.95} = -1.94$$

$$t = \frac{\bar{X}_1 - \bar{X}_3}{SE_{\bar{D}}} = \frac{44.8 - 66.6}{11.95} = \frac{-21.8}{11.95} = -1.82$$

$$t = \frac{\bar{X}_2 - \bar{X}_3}{SE_{\bar{D}}} = \frac{68.0 - 66.6}{11.95} = \frac{1.4}{11.95} = .12$$

Step E.  Compare each $t$ with $t'$. (The signs indicate only which of two means is greater; only the absolute value is of concern in estimating significance.) Each $t$ that equals or exceeds $t'$ indicates that a significant difference (for a given $\alpha$) exists between the two means. If $\alpha = .01$ had been desired, $t'$ would have had to be recalculated with $F = 5.49$ (for 2 and 27 $d.f.$).

In the above example, no $t$ equalled or exceeded the value of $t'$ and, thus, the null hypothesis must be retained. The decision to retain, of course, is consistent with the determination made earlier with respect to $F$, i.e., that there were no significant differences among any of the means.

### Significance of Correlation Coefficients

When coefficients of correlation are computed, they are intended to represent the degree of relationship existing between two variables. If, before a coefficient is computed, the null hypothesis is assumed, i.e., that the variables are independent and, hence, that no relationship exists, how large must the coefficient be before the null hypothesis may be rejected with some reasonable confidence, i.e., before chance influences may be discounted? As might be expected, there is no single answer to the question. What may be said is that the greater the number of paired scores involved, the smaller the coefficient needs to be in order to reject the null hypothesis. The precise relationship between paired scores and the coefficient needed for the rejection of the null hypothesis is expressed in the formula

$$t = \frac{r\sqrt{N - 2}}{\sqrt{1 - r^2}} \qquad (39)$$

in which

$r$ (or $r'$) is the coefficient of correlation
$N$ is the number of paired scores

In the earlier example of 10 paired scores (Table 2-7) the rank-difference coefficient, $r'$, was computed to be .80. In order to estimate if this coefficient represents a relationship between the variables not due to chance, $t$ must be calculated.

$$t = \frac{.80\sqrt{10 - 2}}{\sqrt{1 - (.80)^2}} = \frac{.80\sqrt{8}}{\sqrt{1 - .64}}$$

$$= \frac{.80(2.83)}{\sqrt{.36}} = \frac{2.264}{.60}$$

$$= 3.77$$

If the $t$-table is now consulted for $N - 2$ d.f., it will be observed that $t$ must equal or exceed 2.306 and 3.355, respectively, if the null hypothesis is to be rejected $(P = .05)(P = .01)$. Since the computed $t$ of 3.77 exceeds 3.355, the null hypothesis may be rejected and the coefficient accepted as evidence that the variables are not independent.

*Significance of* $r_{bis}$. For this coefficient, a process similar to that employed in analysis of variance is utilized and an $F$-ratio established:

$$F = \frac{S_B^2}{MS_W} \tag{40}$$

in which

$S_B^2$ = Between groups variance
$MS_W$ = Mean square within groups

If reference is made to the computations for $r_{bis}$ made earlier, utilizing formula (31), $S_W^2$, necessary for calculating $MS_W$, is

$$S_W^2 = S_T^2 - S_B^2$$
$$= 5975.6 - 968.02$$
$$= 5007.6$$

and

$$MS_W = \frac{S_W^2}{d.f.} = \frac{5007.6}{10 - 2}$$

$$= \frac{5007.6}{8} = 625.95$$

and

$$F = \frac{968.02}{625.95} = 1.546$$

With 1 and 8 *d.f.*, 5.23 and 11.26 are needed for $P = .05$ and $P = .01$, respectively. Since the computed $F$ of 1.546 falls below the two values, the null hypothesis must be accepted at $P = .05$ and at $P = .01$.

*Significance of* $r_\phi$. Whether the null hypothesis is accepted or rejected in the case of $r_\phi$ depends upon the test of $\chi^2$ (Chi-square) in which

$$\chi^2 = Nr_\phi^2 \tag{41}$$
$$\chi^2 = (54)(.24)^2 = (54)(.0576)$$
$$= 3.11$$

Reference to the abridged $\chi^2$ table (Table 2-12) reveals that a $\chi^2$ of 3.11 with 1 *d.f.* is less than that needed for $P = .05$, and the null hypothesis is accepted.

**TABLE 2-12    Abridged Table of** $\chi^2$

| | | | | *P* | | | |
|---|---|---|---|---|---|---|---|
| | .90 | .50 | .30 | .10 | .05 | .02 | .01 |
| *d. f.* | | | | | | | |
| 1 | .0158 | .455 | 1.074 | 2.706 | 3.841 | 5.412 | 6.635 |
| 2 | .211 | 1.386 | 2.408 | 4.605 | 5.991 | 7.824 | 9.210 |
| 3 | .584 | 2.366 | 3.665 | 6.251 | 7.815 | 9.837 | 11.345 |
| 4 | 1.064 | 3.357 | 4.878 | 7.779 | 9.488 | 11.668 | 13.277 |
| 5 | 1.610 | 4.351 | 6.064 | 9.236 | 11.070 | 13.388 | 15.086 |
| 10 | 4.865 | 9.342 | 11.781 | 15.987 | 18.307 | 21.161 | 23.209 |
| 20 | 12.443 | 19.337 | 22.775 | 28.412 | 31.410 | 35.020 | 37.566 |
| 30 | 20.599 | 29.336 | 33.530 | 40.265 | 43.773 | 47.962 | 50.892 |

Source: Fisher and Yates, 1974, p. 47.

## ACCESSING THE ELECTRONIC COMPUTER

The electronic computer has for many years been in extensive use in colleges and universities. Yet, typical students in physical education have had little exposure to this rather amazing technology, unless they have been involved in a master's thesis or doctoral dissertation. With the advent of hand calculators (within the economic reach of most students) and microcomputers (within the economic reach of most primary and secondary school systems), familiarity with the use of the electronic computer should be expected of all students in higher education. Some would go so far as to say that, today, the general education of students is incomplete if it does not include a general understanding of, and familiarity with, the use of the electronic computer. Another interesting observation was made by Simon, who stated that the meaning attached to the verb "to know" has changed. In the past "to know" meant to have stored in one's memory, but, today, "knowing" implies having access to information rather than actual possession of it.[2]

The above may sound somewhat farfetched. Yet few would deny that the impact of computers on science has been revolutionary. Computers permit researchers to organize and access huge quantities of information. Operating at speeds of up to a trillionth of a second, computers shorten the time necessary for lengthy calculations and enable researchers to solve problems that were once considered beyond their capacity.[3]

Physical education undergraduate students appear to have an innate fear of the computer. This might be traced to the possibility that few have had exemplary experiences with mathematics at the secondary school level. Yet, most computer manuals stress the fact that the computer can be used successfully by those with little mathematical background.

The following discussion will deal with general information about computers and how to access a computer rather than with the inner workings of the machinery (hardware) or the writing of programs (software) for the computer. Since the reader of this book will probably be a student, researcher, or professional in the field, for the sake of brevity, the person who aspires to use a computer will henceforth be called the user.

### What the Computer Can Do[4]

The amazing array of tasks that can be accomplished by the electronic computer include the following:

*Data handling and synthesis.* The computer can greatly speed the statistical analysis of large amounts of data, seeking functional relationships and intercorrelations between a wide range of experimental variables.

*Equation solving.* Solution of complex algebraic, differential, polynomial, and matrix equations can be accomplished.

*Process simulation.* Physical or biological systems can be simulated to test the validity of current hypotheses describing their behavior.

*Data storage.* Vast quantities of data can be rapidly stored and retrieved, thereby offering possible solutions to problems created by the *knowledge explo-*

*sion.* Computers may be programmed to *learn* and to make a variety of logical decisions based on their acquired knowledge.

*Process control. On-line* computations of data and the information thus produced can be used as feedback to modify the rate of an ongoing physical or biological process.

*Construction of tables.* Mathematical, physical and biological, and other types of data in the form of tables can be printed accurately and in great detail.

*Design and instruction.* Computers have a role in the designing of equipment and the printing of instructions for its use.

*Large memory capacity.* The large memory capacity of modern computers can be used to provide translation, indexing, and cataloguing services.[5]

The typical user in physical education will most likely be concerned with the statistical analysis of research data and the construction and scoring of tests and surveys.

### Availability of Computers, Computer Languages, and Computer Programs

Computers can be found on most college campuses and, increasingly, in high schools and/or school-district administrative offices. They are used to service administrative functions such as record-keeping and/or instructionally related functions such as research and scoring of tests and surveys. At the outset, the user is often confused by the various acronyms associated with *manufacturers' names* for computers and "families" of computers, such as CDC 3150, CDC 3300, CYBER 174, CYBER 170–730, etc. Each of these computers may be able to handle one or more *computer languages* such as FORTRAN, BASIC, APL, PASCAL, COBOL, ALGOL, etc. These languages instruct the computer through the use of statements and commands organized as sentences and paragraphs. The barrage of acronyms continues with the addition of various *program packages* such as SPSS, BMDP, MINITAB, etc. These program "canned" packages instruct the computer to calculate the usual descriptive statistics such as frequency distributions, cross tabulations, and simple and partial correlations. Statistical program packages for larger computers might include analysis of variance, multiple regression, discriminant analysis, scatter diagrams, factor analysis, etc.

### Interaction with the Computer Expert

The novice user of the computer should seek advice from the computer operator and/or statistician at the earliest possible occasion. Assuming that the user is interested in the computer in connection with a research project, the following schedule is recommended:

1. The user should consult the computer expert *prior* to obtaining any data.

If possible, the computer expert should be included in planning of the research design in order to avoid the common and unhappy experience of obtaining data in a form unacceptable to the computer. At this point, the novice should be informed as to proper level of measurement, development of a research form, and the use of coding sheets— all of which will be discussed in this chapter.

2. The computer expert should again be consulted *prior* to the running of the statistical program. At this time, the novice user should receive instructions concerning keypunching, the layout (format) of the data, and features common to all computer programs, such as control language and system cards. These, too, will be discussed in this chapter. Also, at this time, the statistical technique suitable for the data should be agreed upon. It should be noted that the final decision is the responsibility of the user.

3. After the computer printout of the statistical analysis is obtained and studied by the user, a final meeting should be held between the user and computer expert. At this time, users should make certain that they have understood the computer program language and the mnemonics used in the printout, and that the agreed upon statistics have indeed been applied to the appropriate variables. Another source of possible confusion is the fact that comprehensive computer programs often print out additional statistical analyses not familiar to the user. Finally, if the computer expert is also a statistician, it would be wise to ascertain that the statistics are being interpreted properly.

### Preparation and Organization of Data for the Computer

*Level of measurement.*   The *measurement* of variables is the act of recording an observation and assigning a value or score to the observed phenomenon. Some variables have obvious numeric values, such as age. Others require an arbitrary coding scheme to identify various conditions, such as race or religion. The *level of measurement* determines the appropriate value assignment. Since each statistical technique is appropriate for data measured only at certain *levels*, and since the computer does not know what *level* of measurement underlies the numbers it receives, the importance of interfacing the *level of measurement* with the appropriate statistical procedure is emphasized.

Four *levels* of measurement are in common use:[6]

1. The *nominal* level of measurement is used as a label for a variable that has no inherent numeric value. In nominal measurement, numbers are used merely as symbols to facilitate analysis. For example, female may be designated as number one and male labeled number two.

2. The *ordinal* level of measurement requires that each variable have a unique position relative to the other values of the same variable; e.g., it is lower or higher than some other value, but the distance between the value positions is not known. An example is the common scales used in survey research in which numbers one through four are arbitrarily used to designate a continuum between strongly agree and strongly disagree.

3. The *interval* level of measurement defines the distances between values in terms of fixed and equal units. Interval measurement allows the study of differences between values but not their proportionate magnitudes. The zero point is not inherently defined by the measurement scheme. For example, temperature is measured at the interval level because the zero point is arbitrarily determined.

4. The *ratio* level of measurement has the same definition as the interval level except that the zero point *is* inherently defined by the measurement scheme. For example, it can be said that a 100-pound/kilogram person weighs twice as much as a 50-pound/kilogram person.

*Research forms.*    When collection of data is not automated, data are usually recorded on a research form or coding sheet designed especially for the study. An example of automated data collection is a situation where, through the use of electrodes and other sensors, physiological data are fed from a subject's body directly into a computer. Most often, however, data are collected on research forms, coding sheets, or optical scanner forms, examples of which are shown in Appendix A.

The following are suggested rules for designing a research form:[7]

1. Make an outline of all data to be collected.

2. Make a rough draft of the form. Include a space for indicating the card columns used for specific data on the form, preferably in the right-hand margin; this will simplify coding and keypunching, and the correct transfer of data to the assigned fields will be ensured. Consult a keypunch supervisor and/or statistician for suggestions. Revise the form and check with them again. When the form is completed and approved, have it printed for use.

3. On each form and each computer card, include a subject or case number that identifies each subject individually; this number is used to identify all data pertaining to one subject. Examples are predetermined subject sequence numbers, social security numbers, etc. The identification numbers make it possible to refer back to a form to check for errors. A sequence number on each data form or card allows for the cards to be placed in sequence by the computer should they be dropped or otherwise disordered.

4. Assign a number to *each* card if more than one form is involved, or if there is more than one card per case. This number identifies the data on the card.

5. Include explicit instructions at the beginning of each form, specifying how it should be filled out. If the form is misunderstood, the data may not be entered properly and the study may be useless. Forms that are filled out by subjects must be simple, easily understood, and ordered conveniently. See Appendix A for a combination research and coding form.

*Coding sheets.*    Coding sheets should be prepared with care to avoid common keypunch errors. If the decimal point location is the same for every case, it need not be punched, and plus signs need not be punched. Care should be taken to avoid ambiguity in the use of numbers, letters, and symbols. For example, the letter O may be written with a slash ($\emptyset$) to distinguish it from the number zero. Other number-letter pairs often confused are 1 and I, 2 and Z, 6 and G, 7 and T.

Always use numbers when coding information; i.e., assign numbers to represent race, sex, etc., so they can be included in computations. One column should be used for each digit in the number: 1-9, one column; 10-99, two columns; 100-999, three columns, etc. Additional columns are needed if decimal points or signs are used with numbers. See Appendix A for a typical IBM coding form.

*Optical scanner forms.* Optical scanner forms are ideal for recording data of a survey type and for grading of examinations of an objective type. The forms are usually filled out by the subjects themselves and can be fed directly into the computer, thereby eliminating the need for the user to transfer data from research or coding forms to computer cards. The computer can count the number of correct answers and weight the scores according to some predetermined formula. If norm-referenced data are desired, the computer can convert raw scores to standard scores and scale scores. Finally, the computer can transfer data from optical scanner forms directly onto computer cards, tapes, or disks.

*The computer card.* The most familiar method of data input into the computer is probably the common keypunch card. Using a cardpunch machine that resembles a typewriter, data information in the form of small rectangular holes is punched on a card in specific locations. The standard IBM card has 80 vertical columns and 12 horizontal rows. This gives 12 punching positions in each column. Each letter, symbol, or number is represented on the card by a specific combination of holes in one column. One or more punches in a single column represent a *character*. Ten of the 12 rows are numbered 0 to 9 and two are unnumbered. The last two rows are used for recording plus and minus signs or for recording alphabetic information. The standard IBM computer punch card is shown in Appendix A.

*The layout (format) of the data on the computer card.* Each variable must be located in the same columns on the data card for all cases. The layout of the data card is described by a format statement.

The word "format" refers to the arrangement of information on the data card. The format specifications tell the computer program which columns of the record to skip, which columns to group together as one number, and which columns to treat as numbers in a row.

A format specification indicates the size of the field (skipping data, entering data into the computer as a whole number, entering data into the computer as a whole number with two decimal digits, etc.). Each case is assumed to have the same format as other cases in the same analysis.

Each computer system requires a certain format that must be learned by the user. A sample of a format statement is included in the example of the control language instructions given below. The letter A represents the A-type format used only for variables that contain case-identification information, such as a subject's name, and are not used in computations. The letter F represents the F-type format used when all data input values are numbers to be used in subsequent computations.

A4 means that the A-type format is being used; that the first variable is informational, i.e., tells something about the subject; and that up to a maximum of four columns on the IBM card will be used, but that the numbers will not be used in any computations. 5F4.0 means that the F-type format is being used; that the next five variables will have a maximum of four digits each; and that there will be no decimals, i.e., the last digit will be a whole number. 3F4.1 means that the F-type format is being used, that the next three variables will have a maximum of four digits each, and that there will be a decimal point in front of the last digit.

*Control language.* Control language instructs the computer through the use of statements and commands organized as sentences and paragraphs. These instructions are keypunched on computer cards called control cards and are used to: 1) describe the data *input*; 2) name the *variables* and state missing value codes and upper and lower limits for the variables; 3) specify the statistical analysis to be made, such as *correlation*; 4) request optional results to be *printed*, if any; and 5) specify variables to be *plotted*, if any. The following sample taken from the BMDP computer programs[8] demonstrates some control language instructions:

| / Problem | Title is 'WERNER BLOOD CHEMISTRY DATA'. |
|---|---|
| / Input | Variables are 9. |
| | Format is '(A4,5F4.0,3F4.1)'. |
| / Variable | Names are ID, AGE, HEIGHT, WEIGHT, BRTHPILL, |
| | CHOLSTRL, ALBUMIN, CALCIUM, URIC ACID. |
| | Label is ID. |
| | Blanks are missing. |
| / Plot | *y* variables are CHOLSTRL, WEIGHT. |
| | *x* variables are AGE, HEIGHT. |
| / End | |

The above control language instructions specify: a *title* (Werner blood chemistry data) for the analysis; the number of *variables* in the data (9); the *format* (layout) of the data in a case; *names* for the 9 variables (ID is the name of the first variable, AGE the second, etc.); that the variable containing case *labels* (subject identification) is ID; that *blanks* are used for *missing* value codes; and pairs of variables to be plotted (CHOLSTRL against AGE, and WEIGHT against HEIGHT). Syntax and placement of punctuation are specific to the control language used and are a common source of user error.

*System cards.* When the control language is keypunched on the cards at a typical computer facility, three additional functions must be specified on cards called *system cards*. Users must: 1) identify themselves as legitimate users of the computer; 2) state the computer program to be used; and 3) state that the control language instructions for the program follow immediately.

If the computer is accessed from an outside terminal rather than the central processing unit, the same information is required, but the form of specifying is different. If the data input is on a magnetic disk or paper tape rather than computer cards, it is also necessary to describe the tape or disk to be used. At the end of the job, another system card is necessary to tell the computer that the job is finished.

The exact form of all system cards is specific for a particular computer facility. Before running a particular program in another facility, the appropriate system cards for that facility must be determined.

Much of the preceding information about computers was taken from the *Biomedical Computer Programs* (BMDP) manual.[9] The general intent of that statistical package was to service the needs of biological/physiological research. In recent years, however, there has been a marked increase in psychosocial research in physical education, physical fitness, and sports. A comprehensive statistical program package is available for the purpose of servicing the needs of social science research.

### The Statistical Package for the Social Sciences (SPSS)[10]

The Statistical Package for the Social Sciences (SPSS) is an integrated system of computer programs for the analysis of social science data. The system has been designed to provide users with a unified and comprehensive package enabling them to perform many different types of data analysis in a simple and convenient manner. SPSS allows a great deal of flexibility in the format of data. It provides the user with a comprehensive set of procedures for data transformation and file manipulations, and it offers the user a large number of statistical routines commonly used in the social sciences.

In addition to the usual descriptive statistics, simple frequency distributions, and crosstabulations, SPSS contains procedures for simple correlations (for both ordinal and interval data), partial correlations, multiple regression, and factor analysis. The data-management facilities can be used to modify a file of data permanently and can also be used in conjunction with any of the statistical procedures. These facilities enable the user to generate variable transformations; to recode variables; sample, select, or weight specified cases; and to add to or alter the data or the file-defining information. SPSS enables the user to perform analyses through the use of natural English language control statements and requires no programming experience on the part of the user. A brief overview of the SPSS process in included in Appendix B.

### Summarizing Comments

The first section of this chapter discussed the underlying concepts and gave computational examples of a number of descriptive and inferential statistics.

Throughout the section on the electronic computer, the process of accessing the computer, using prepackaged statistical programs, was emphasized. Most likely, the BMDP and the SPSS statistical packages described would handle any needs of the novice computer user. Certainly, all of the techniques discussed in the statistics section of this chapter are within the computational scope of BMDP, SPSS, and many other statistical packages.

It is safe to say that the novice computer user need not understand the inner workings of the computer machinery. Also, with the availability of so many "packaged" computer programs, it is probably safe to say that the successful computer user need not have an extensive mathematical background or the ability to create original computer programs. This is *not* to imply that, therefore, there is no need for the computer user to understand the statistical concepts discussed in the first section of this chapter. On the contrary! The final interpretation of the statistical analyses output by the computer is the responsibility of the user.

## BIBLIOGRAPHY

AFIFI, A.A., and S.P. AZEN, *Statistical Analysis, A Computer Oriented Approach.* New York: Academic Press, 1972.

BAUMGARTNER, TED R., and ANDREW S. JACKSON, *Measurement for Evaluation in Physical Education.* Boston: Houghton Mifflin Company, 1975.

*BMDP Biomedical Computer Programs, P. Series,* edited by W.J. Dixon. Berkeley: University of California Press, 1977.

ECKERT, HELEN M. *Practical Measurement of Physical Performance,* pp. 249–64. Philadelphia: Lea and Febiger, 1974.

HOGBEN, D., S. PEAVY, and R. VARNER, *Omnitag II, User's Reference Manual,* Technical Note 552. Washington: National Bureau of Standards, 1971.

KLECKA, W., N. NIE, and C.H. HULL, *SPSS Primer.* New York: McGraw-Hill, 1975.

KRAMER, WILLIAM D., "A Computerized System for Analyzing and Evaluating Performance Data in Physical Education." Unpublished doctoral dissertation. Bloomington: Indiana University, 1970.

MOLNAR, ANDERSON R., "The Next Great Crisis in American Education: Computer Literacy." *EDUCOM* 14 (Spring 1979), 2–6.

NIE, N., C.H. HULL, J. JENKINS, K. STERNBRENNER, and D. BENT, *SPSS, Statistical Package for the Social Sciences,* 2nd ed. New York: McGraw-Hill, 1975.

PHILLIPS, D., D. ALLEN and JAMES E. HORNAK, *Measurement and Evaluation in Physical Education.* New York: John Wiley, 1979.

RYAN, THOMAS A., JR., BRIAN L. JOINER, and BARBARA F. RYAN, *Minitab Student Handbook.* North Scituate, Mass.: Duxbury Press, 1976.

SERVICE, J., *SAS, A User's Guide to the Statistical Analysis System.* Raleigh: Student Supply Stores, North Carolina State University, 1972.

SCHEFFÉ, H., "Statistical Inference in the Non-Parametrics Case." *Annals of Mathematical Statistics,* 14 (1943), 305–32.

SHEPHARD, ROY J., *Men at Work: Applications of Ergonomics to Performance and Design.* Springfield: Chas. Thomas, 1974.

SIMON, HERBERT, "Designing Organizations for an Information Rich World." in *Computers, Communications, and the Public Interest,* edited by Martin Greenberger. Baltimore: The John Hopkins Press, 1971.

STEVENS, S.S., "On the Theory of Scales of Measurement." *Science,* 103 (June 1946), 677–80.

## SUGGESTED READINGS

BAUMGARTNER, TED A. and ANDREW S. JACKSON, *Measurement for Evaluation in Physical Education.* Boston: Houghton Mifflin Company, 1975.

BLALOCK, HUBERT M., *Social Statistics,* 2nd ed. New York: McGraw-Hill, 1972.

BLOMMERS, PAUL J. and E.F. LINDQUIST, *Elementary Statistical Methods in Psychology and Education.* Boston: Houghton Mifflin Company, 1960.

FERGUSON, GEORGE A., *Statistical Analysis in Psychology and Education,* 2nd ed. New York: McGraw-Hill, 1966.

GARRETT, HENRY E., *Statistics in Psychology and Education,* 5th ed. New York: Longman, Inc., 1959.

HAYS, WILLIAM L., *Basic Statistics.* Belmont: Brooks/Cole, 1967.

LINDQUIST, EVERET F., *Statistical Analysis in Educational Research.* Boston: Houghton Mifflin Company, 1940.

MINIUM, EDWARD W., *Statistical Reasoning in Psychology and Education.* New York: John Wiley, 1970.

SAFRIT, MARGARET J., *Evaluation in Physical Education.* Englewood Cliffs: Prentice-Hall, 1973.

SHEEHAN, THOMAS J., *An Introduction to the Evaluation of Measurement Data in Physical Education.* Reading: Addison-Wesley, 1971.

SMITH, G. MILTON, *A Simplified Guide to Statistics for Psychology and Education,* 3rd ed. New York: Holt, Rinehart and Winston, 1962.

WALKER, HELEN M. and JOSEPH LEV, *Elementary Statistical Methods,* 3rd ed. New York: Holt, Rinehart and Winston, 1969.

# CHAPTER THREE
# SELECTION AND CONSTRUCTION OF TESTS

In the selection of tests, it is important to keep in mind the purposes (Chapter 1) for which the tests are going to be used. Whereas the purposes are of major concern, among other factors to be considered are the length of the test, maturity of students, testing conditions, and type of scoring methods used. Each of these factors may, on occasion, limit the use of a particular test or suggest the need for a different kind of test.

For instance, if a test designed to measure one's understanding of a particular body of knowledge is too long, fatigue or boredom may occur, with their resultant effects upon the meaningfulness of the test scores. Conversely, if a test is too short, it may sample too narrow a selection of a student's total understanding of the subject, and chance might turn out to be the predominant factor in determining a student's score. It cannot be emphasized too strongly that unless a test discriminates well among the various levels of student understanding or performance, its potential uses disappear or are, at least, severely limited. At the same time, the test must be economical of time and money if it is to have practical value.

Other factors for which concern must be given are the maturity of the students (a college-level test would not be appropriate for elementary students), testing conditions (time of day; weather, court and/or field conditions), the health of students (one's performance is usually lessened if one is not well), and the variability of human performance (even when well, human beings tend not to reproduce precisely recent performances of even a day or less prior).

Scoring errors are a constant concern. Witness the differences in stopwatch times in sprint races even among experienced timers. Reaction time and perception, among a host of factors, vary a little or a lot from one person to another. Then, too, chance may influence a person's score on, say, a badminton serving test. They say that a miss is as good as a mile! Well, perhaps not in a serving test. Yet, a slight miss may be penalized as much as a greater miss, even though it is clear that the performances are not the same. Chance errors of this kind, of course, tend to even out, *provided* the number of trials is sufficient to permit the cream to rise to the top. There is also the possibility of variation in how a scorer perceives just where the bird landed. A bird that lands in the same spot on two trials may be credited with one score on one trial and with another score on the second trial, depending upon the ability and the attention of the scorer. Scorer partiality, if it exists, can also influence scores.


## CRITERIA FOR THE SELECTION
## OF TESTS

Four criteria should be considered in the selection of tests: validity, reliability, objectivity, and administrative usability. Of these, validity is most important. However, a discussion of validity is incomplete without an analysis of reliability, since a test cannot be considered valid unless it also possesses suitable reliability. Once concerns of validity and reliability have been satisfied, administrative usability is the next focus of attention, with objectivity important only if more than one judge or scorer is to be used. In physical tests, the practice of having students paired off so that one is scoring the performance of the partner is quite common and, in these settings, objectivity of the scorers assumes greater importance than for a written test that is to be scored only by the teacher or with a key.

### Validity

Validity is an estimate of the degree to which a test measures the factor or factors for which it was designed. Four ways of determining whether a test is valid have been employed, depending upon the nature of the test, the availability of acceptable criteria, and the particular use to which the test results will be subjected. These four are construct validity, content validity, concurrent validity, and predictive validity.

*Construct validity.* The underlying assumption of this form of validity is that good performers of a particular task (or sport) will score higher on the test than will poor performers. A key to this approach is in the adequacy of distinguishing between the good and the poor performers. Organized sports typically provide a convenient means for making the distinction, e.g., varsity versus junior varsity football players or beginner versus advanced swimmers.

Once the two groups have been identified, the test is administered to each member of the two groups. If the mean or means of the scores of the good performers are significantly higher than the mean or means of the scores of the poor performers, the test may be considered to possess construct validity.

*Content validity.* In some ways, content validity (often termed face validity) possesses characteristics similar to those of construct validity. The term is associated principally with reference to written tests in which the basic concern is that the test adequately samples the universe of subject matter from which the individual items have been drawn. If the universe of subject matter is fairly large, a circumstance found more often than not, then it becomes clear that a test consisting of a very few items is less likely to possess content validity than would be true of a longer test.

Regrettably, length of test in itself does not assure content validity. A test may be quite long and yet the items of which it is composed may be trivial in form or deal with trivial matters. Or the sophistication of the vocabulary may be beyond the capabilities of the subjects being tested. Some test constructors seem to delight in wording items so that they will confuse or mislead rather than clarify or direct. Such a practice is to be deplored, of course!

How does one write items that will serve the purpose for which they are intended? General instructions are provided in the chapter on knowledge testing, but one point should be stressed in the immediate context. If it is desired to construct a test (often called an instrument) for the measure of attitudes toward something, a typical approach would be to draft a large number of statements believed to represent the attitude in question in its various dimensions. These statements are then submitted to a panel of "experts," who are asked to state independently whether a statement represents a positive, neutral, or negative attitude toward the factor. Those statements for which agreement to a previously designated level (perhaps 80 percent) is obtained would then be retained in the pool of potential items to be used in the inventory. These items would then be subjected to item analysis to eliminate duplicate items among other concerns.

In sports, it is more difficult to directly establish content validity. It might seem, for example, that a basketball skills test consisting of shooting, passing, dribbling, and perhaps rebounding items would possess content validity. And yet it is well known, particularly in team sports, that some who appear to have all of the tools for stardom never seem to be able to put it all together in the heat of competition; it may also be that some of the exquisite skills often required in competition such as split-second reaction time may not lend themselves well to measurement in an individual testing situation.

But even in sports, some efforts can be made to establish content validity particularly with respect to singular skills. An example might be a serving test in badminton in which the standard of success is specifically defined, is subject to accurate assessment, and elicits concurrence among a group of experts. This form is called *logical validity* by some authorities.

*Concurrent validity.* This form of validation involves the correlation of scores achieved on the test with an external criterion. The criterion may be another test that has been determined valid, or it could be performance in or of the factor as determined in competition used in sports skills testing.

As is often the case, several caveats must be offered. In the first instance cited—the correlation of scores with those earned on a previously validated test— the critical concern is the means by which the original test was validated. Regardless of its validity coefficient, if the method of validation was flawed, then it should not be used as the criterion. One obvious flaw would be the criterion against which it was validated. An example might be the use of team members. Where this *might* be reasonably acceptable in events such as rowing, pairs skating, or ballroom dancing, it is not acceptable in baseball, soccer, volleyball, or even tennis doubles, since members of a team may differ markedly in their respective skills. Even stars such as Jabbar and Barry in basketball, Morgan and Ryan in baseball, and Simpson and Tarkenton in football possess quite dissimilar skills.

If experts are used to judge the respective talents of performers in a given activity for which a test is to be validated, several factors should be taken into account. First, a determination should be made of the agreement of the judges with respect to the factors that comprise good and poor performance; they must be able to rate performances accurately as the game is in progress. The intercorrelations of their ratings should be high if confidence is to be maintained in the criterion. Second, the judges should not be apprised of the subjects' test scores before they make their independent ratings of the subjects' game performances (by "independent" is meant that no judge influences another judge in any way). This is to guard against a judge's rating being influenced by knowledge of how a subject scored on the test. Finally, there is the number of judges. It should be obvious that if a group of judges agreed precisely every time, only one judge would be needed. But human error occurs even in the best of judges. When human error occurs, especially if it is substantial, its effect upon overall judges' ratings is less as the number of judges is greater. If the demands upon the judges are relatively light, one might be able to secure more judges. If the demand is heavy in terms of time or pressure, then it will be more difficult to obtain willing and able volunteers. An acceptable number of judges, for practical purposes then, would probably be between three and five.

In dual sports such as badminton, tennis, and other racket or court sports, a round-robin singles tournament is probably the best way to establish the criterion. If good performance is found in winners more than in losers, it can be concluded that the player who won the most games should be among those scoring highest on the test, and that one who won the fewest games should be among those scoring lowest on the test, if the test is to be considered valid. This, of course, is a simplistic illustration of the principle, and it is necessary to correlate performance in the tournament with test scores for all the subjects before the test's validity can be estimated. Here again, the greater the number of subjects, within reason, the greater the probability that the correlation coefficient will be a reliable estimate of the test's validity. Single- and double-elimination tournaments and ladder tournaments are less desirable than round-robin play, because there are too many ties in elimination tournaments and, in both elimination and ladder tournaments, not every player competes with every other player.

*Predictive validity.* Predictive validity is much the same as concurrent validity except that it is a measure of a test's ability to predict future performance. It is one thing to say that a person who scores highest on a valid tennis test is the best or, at least, among the best tennis players in the group. It is quite another to say that this same person will be the best tennis player at some future point in time. Little has been done in this country to attempt to identify potential All-Americans among the young, except via attempts to give the young ample opportunities to hone their skills and to gain the attention of others as they mature and as their success merits it.

There is evidence that many of the iron-curtain countries have begun to identify potential world-class athletes among the very young and to submit them to intensive training programs.[1] In the past three Olympic games, East Germany has won far more than its share of medals in a variety of sports, and credit has been given to its vast program of early identification and specialized training of youths. Whether programs of this sort are in the best interest of the individuals involved is more in the realm of ethics, psychology, and sociology and is probably not a proper topic for discussion in a measurement textbook. The writers personally have reservations about the use (or abuse) of people in this way but believe, on the other hand, that it is perfectly proper for scientists to continue their investigations into the development of instruments that may be used in predicting human potential in a complete spectrum of activities. A step-by-step procedure for developing these prediction equations is suggested at the end of this chapter.

Attempts at prediction have been used for some time in estimating potential for success in academic pursuits. For example, most colleges require applicants for admission to complete an aptitude test such as the S.A.T. Admission is then determined on the basis of a combination of test scores and grade-point averages. The lower an applicant's grade-point average, the higher his or her test score must be if admission is to be gained.

How well does the S.A.T. measure up as a predictor of academic success? Similarly, how well does the Graduate Record Examination predict success in graduate studies? In the many studies in which test scores have been correlated with grade-point averages, the coefficients generally have been positive but low. If, however, tetrachoric correlations are computed in which one dichotomy is established between those scoring above and below a given test score and the other dichotomy between those who are successful and those who are unsuccessful in their academic pursuits, fairly high coefficients may be obtained.[2]

### Reliability

Reliability refers to the degree to which a test consistently measures a given factor. This is not to say that the factor is necessarily the one that the test or other measurement instrument is thought to measure, i.e., a test may be reliable but not valid in the sense of measuring what it is thought to measure.

Earlier mention has been given to the consideration of scoring errors. A scoring error is one example of a broader concept termed measurement error. Measurement error is the difference between the observed score (e.g., what is read on the stopwatch) and the true score (the actual elapsed time of a runner between starter's gun and the crossing of the finish line). Thus, whatever the source of measurement error—inconsistent scoring or timing, inconsistent performance by the subject, inability of the instrument to measure consistently—it takes its toll of the reliability that may be calculated by one of several methods available.

*Test-retest method.* The coefficient calculated by this method, often termed the coefficient of stability, is derived from the correlation of scores obtained by subjects on two administrations of the test. Normally, if the stability of the instrument is of primary concern, the retest is administered soon after the initial testing period so as to minimize the effects of learning, practice, reflection on the task, diminution of skill, or other factors. Still, even immediate retesting does not rule out entirely the influence of all of these potential contaminants.

In order to minimize potential sources of error, it is prudent to make certain that the test conditions for the second administration are as nearly like those of the first test. If the test is conducted outdoors, factors to be taken into account include wind, condition of the field, time of day, and, for some tests, barometric pressure.

For events involving endurance, testers must be cognizant of the potential effect of varying levels of air pollution. Not to be ignored either is that the procedures for the second administration must be the same as for the first. Instructions should be standardized, warm-ups should be of the same kind and duration, and timing instruments and the timers should be the same.

*Alternate-form method.* An alternative method that may be used to obviate some of the concerns raised in the test-retest method is to administer two forms of the same test, equivalent in content and difficulty but different with respect to the specific items. The scores obtained on the two forms may then be correlated to estimate reliability, provided the equivalency of the two forms has been satisfactorily established. Curiously, much the same procedure is used in ascertaining the equivalency of the two forms, and, unless equivalency has been calculated from scores earned by large numbers of subjects, the potential for error is obvious.

This method is generally restricted to knowledge tests and other paper-and-pencil instruments. Tests involving physical performances seldom have a large enough pool of relevant items to permit the construction of alternate forms. Other forms of item analysis are also available in establishing the equivalency of paper-and-pencil instruments.

*Split-halves method.* In order to check the internal consistency of a paper-and-pencil instrument, the test may be divided into odd and even items. In effect, then, two separate tests have been established; one consisting of the odd items (items 1, 3, 5, etc.), and one consisting of the even items (items 2, 4, 6, etc.). Scores earned on the odd items are then correlated with those earned on the even items. The reliability estimate that results, however, is for a test of only half the length of the original test. And since it has been demonstrated that reliability tends to increase as the length of the test increases (if fatigue or boredom do not result), some means must be used to estimate the reliability for the full test. That method is the Spearman-Brown Prophecy formula subsequently described.

At times, the method used has been to subdivide a test into first and second halves. Although for certain analytical purposes, particularly with respect to internal consistency, this method may be useful, it presents some obvious perils in the estimation of reliability. Among these are fatigue and boredom, which would have an adverse effect upon second-half scores; practice or familiarity with the items, on the other hand, would tend to have a beneficial effect upon second-half scores. The assumption is made that these effects, if they are active, will not significantly displace the relative rank placement of scores of the subjects. In the instance of fatigue, in particular, the assumption may well prove false. Again, the variability of human performance is such that it is hazardous to assume that the potential contaminants would have similar effects upon the subjects and that they would operate along a similar time continuum.

The same procedure may be used with skills tests in which the odd and even trials are correlated.

*Spearman-Brown Prophecy formula.*    Regardless of whether an odd-even or a first-half–second-half approach is used, the reliability coefficient that is computed is, in fact, for a test or instrument of only half the length of the original test for which reliability is to be estimated. Since the length of the test, within typical test-length limits, affects the reliability, i.e., the shorter the test, the less reliable it tends to be, correction must be made for the halving of the original test in the computation of the coefficient. This may be accomplished by use of the Spearman-Brown Prophecy formula:

$$r_{wt} = \frac{2r_{ht}}{1 + r_{ht}}$$

in which

$r_{wt}$ = the reliability coefficient for the whole test

$r_{ht}$ = the reliability coefficient obtained when the split halves were correlated

Baumgartner[3] found, however, that, under certain conditions, the Spearman-Brown Prophecy formula tended to overestimate the test-retest reliability coefficient of the whole test.

*Intraclass correlation coefficient.*    This method involves the use of analysis of variance procedures and offers the advantage of permitting the identification of sources of variance. Although several ANOVA methods are available depending upon the particular needs of the test, the illustrative problem will be restricted to a simple one-way ANOVA design involving four subjects, with each subject completing three trials of the particular test.[4]

| SUBJECT | TRIAL 1 | TRIAL 2 | TRIAL 3 | TRIAL TOTAL $(X_T)$ |
|---------|---------|---------|---------|---------------------|
| A | 6 | 5 | 6 | 17 |
| B | 5 | 6 | 7 | 18 |
| C | 7 | 7 | 7 | 21 |
| D | 4 | 5 | 6 | 15 |

Step-by-step procedure:

1. $\Sigma X_T = 17 + 18 + 21 + 15 = 71$
2. $(\Sigma X_T)^2 = (71)^2 = 5041$
3. $\Sigma X^2 = 6^2 + 5^2 + 6^2 + 5^2 + 6^2 + 7^2 + 7^2 + 7^2 + 7^2 + 4^2 + 5^2 + 6^2$
   $= 36 + 25 + 36 + 25 + 36 + 49 + 49 + 49 + 49 + 16 + 25 + 36$
   $= 431$

**4.** $\Sigma X_T^2 = 17^2 + 18^2 + 21^2 + 15^2 = 1279$

**5.** $k$ (no. of trials) $\times N$ (no. of subjects) $= 3 \times 4 = 12$.

**6.** $S_B^2 + S_W^2 = S_T^2$

    **a.** $S_B^2 = \dfrac{\Sigma X_T^2}{k} - \dfrac{(\Sigma X_T)^2}{N \times k} = \dfrac{1279}{3} - \dfrac{5041}{12}$

       $= 426.33 - 420.08 = 6.25$

    **b.** $S_W^2 = \Sigma X^2 - \dfrac{\Sigma X_T^2}{k} = 431 - 426.33 = 4.67$

    **c.** $S_T^2 = \Sigma X^2 - \dfrac{(\Sigma X)^2}{k \times N} = 431 - \dfrac{5041}{12}$

       $= 431 - 420.08 = 10.92$

$S_B^2 + S_W^2 = 6.25 + 4.67 = 10.92$

**7.** Place the values in the summary table, as shown here.

| VARIANCE SOURCE | $s^2$ | d.f. | MS |
|---|---|---|---|
| Between Subjects | 6.25 | $(N-1) = 3$ | 2.08 |
| Within Subjects | 4.67 | $k(N-1) = 9$ | 0.52 |

$$R = \frac{MS_B - MS_W}{MS_B} = \frac{2.08 - .52}{2.08} = \frac{1.56}{2.08} = .75$$

### Objectivity

Objectivity is similar in nature to reliability, except that it applies to the consistency of agreement among scorers with respect to the quality or correctness of a performance. This is to say that scores assigned by different scorers for a group of subjects who have completed the same test will yield high reliability coefficients.

Certain measurements tend to be more objective than others. For instance, in knowledge tests, test questions of the true-false, multiple-choice, and matching types are objective in that, with a scoring key, it matters little who scores the test—the scores will be identical with rare exceptions. Essay or free-response items are less objective in that the scorer's judgment may enter markedly into the evaluation. Measurements such as jump heights or distances and archery scores tend to be quite objective; measurements of whether a tennis serve is in or out or whether a foot fault has been committed are somewhat less objective; and judgments of the relative merits of performances in diving, gymnastics, figure skating, and other activities in which form is an important factor often tend to reflect sizable disagreements.

If scorer judgment is important in determining a subject's performance, objectivity can be improved by subdividing the various elements of a correct response or performance and weighting these elements according to their importance. But even if this practice is observed, an experienced scorer is still necessary to ensure that the scores assigned to the elements are accurate measurements of the performance or the correctness of the response.

### Research Steps in Constructing and Validating Physical Performance Tests

If one wishes to construct a *new* test from beginning to end, the following list of steps is suggested:

1. Establish philosophically the traits or characteristics to be measured. Use a few experts in the field involved and one or more experts on test construction. Opposite each test item, list the trait tested and a popular interpretation of what is being measured.

2. Carefully prepare the testing specifications for each item, including exact instructions for giving and scoring each item.

3. Give the test to a population (sample) of subjects, preferably more than 200, with consideration given to the randomness, adequacy, and representativeness of the sample for the purpose at hand.

4. Consider the feasibility of an external validity criterion, so that the validation can be done against an "outside" criterion rather than the composite score on all items in the battery (internal criterion). However, correlating each item against the total score is one validity scheme.

5. After giving the test, arrange to retest the group to check on the routine experimental errors unless such reliability coefficients are well known from similar work under identical conditions. In a new test, a complete check would include retests for reliability and objectivity.

6. Study the physical accuracy of the measurements including, possibly, the mechanical calibration of the instruments used.

7. Compute the mean, standard deviation, range, and standard scores for each item and criterion; also, compute and construct a norm table that includes matched standard scores, percentiles, T-scores, and raw scores at increments of five standard scores from 0–100.* Use the categories of excellent, very good, above average, average, below average, poor, and very poor with approximately 15 standard scores in each classification.

8. Test each distribution for normality by matching the actual frequency polygon with a superimposed normal curve, and by the quantitative chi-square technique.

9. Determine all intercorrelations by correlating each item with each other item. Pearson scattergram correlations are preferred when the data are continuous and distributed normally. In the case of pass-fail test items versus a continuous,

---

*A table of equivalent percentile scores and standard scores is included in Appendix C.

quantitative criterion, the biserial correlations are indicated. In case of pass-fail test items versus a pass-fail criterion, tetrachoric correlations are indicated.

**10.** Compute the criterion correlations, i.e., each item is correlated against the composite total of the standard scores (internal validity criterion).

**11.** *Compute the net Beta weighting coefficients for each item indicating the relative net weighting for an optimum prediction of the validity criterion.

**12.** Compute a prediction equation to predict the validity criterion from each of the following types of scores: a) raw scores; b) deviation scores; and c) standard scores.

### BIBLIOGRAPHY

BAUMGARTNER, TED A., "The Application of the Spearman-Brown Prophecy Formula When Applied to Physical Performance Tests." *Research Quarterly,* 39 (December 1968), 847–856.

GUSTAFSON, WILLIAM F., "The Graduate Record Examination and the Advanced Physical Education Test as Predictors of Success in a Master's Degree Program," *70th Proceedings.* National College Physical Education Association for Men (1966), 96–98.

RAFFAELE, PAUL, "Chinese Train to be the World's Best Athletes." *Parade,* (July 23, 1977), pp. 14, 16.

SAFRIT, MARGARET J., ed., *Reliability Theory.* Washington: AAHPERD Publications, 1976.

*The multiple correlation techniques required for item 11 and the regression analysis required for item 12 are not covered in this text but can be found in most texts on statistics.

**CHAPTER FOUR**

# TESTS OF "SPECIFIC" MOTOR ABILITIES: STRENGTH, POWER, AND MUSCULAR ENDURANCE

## GENERAL INTRODUCTION ON
## MOTOR ABILITY TESTING

The authors of this text are aware of the general confusion among such terms as motor fitness, general motor fitness, physical fitness, organic fitness, physical capacity, motor ability, general motor ability, motor capacity, general motor capacity, motor educability, motor skills, general motor skills, motor achievement, general motor achievement, athletic ability, sports skills, etc., etc. Definitions for all of the above are as varied as the authors who suggest them. No attempt at definitions will be made here. The interested reader is referred to a few sources[1-5] that have attempted to define some of the terms as well as differentiate some of the nuances among them.

In the simplest practical sense, tests purported to measure motor ability may be classified into two principal groups: 1) those that purport to measure "general" or "all-around" ability by means of batteries of items selected from an assortment of choices and 2) those that purport to measure "specific" ability in particular performance areas. Thus, the following seven chapters will be organized to include selected tests of: 1) individual motor ability components; 2) general motor ability; and 3) sports skills.

The identification of motor ability (physical fitness) components has progressed from the arbitrary selection by early researchers to the use of factor analysis, a sophisticated statistical technique whereby principal components are "factored out" or identified from a matrix of intercorrelations.[6,7] Theoretically, the resulting factors do not correlate well with each other, i.e., each has a distinctive feature and each contributes an essential element of motor ability (physical fitness). Many factor analysis studies have appeared in the physical education literature over the years.[8] Whereas there is no general consensus on what the components of motor ability are, there appears to be little disagreement on three of them: muscular strength, muscular endurance, and cardiovascular endurance—sometimes called circulo-respiratory endurance.

The factors or components selected to represent general motor ability for this book were those that resulted from logical and factor analyses by Cureton,[9] which were further substantiated by Latham.[10] These included strength, power, muscular endurance, flexibility, agility, and balance. A seventh component, cardiovascular endurance (fitness), though not included in the above analyses, will be given special emphasis in Chapter 6.

Finally, it is understood (by use of quotation marks in the title of this chapter) that the above components are not scientifically pure; i.e., they can be further divided into subfactors. In addition, they may be correlated somewhat with each other, although most studies show that these correlations are generally very low. In spite of all this, the rationale for their use is simply that the complex of general motor ability can probably best be understood in terms of its components. Thus, representative tests on all of the above components follow.

## STRENGTH TESTING

It is probably safe to say that the systematic study of measurement and evaluation in American physical education began with the study of muscle size and strength at Amherst College about 1861. This period was reviewed substantially in the works of Seaver[11] and Bovard and Cozens.[12]

The first battery of strength tests was developed by Sargent, beginning with his study of Harvard students in 1880 and culminating with the publication of "Intercollegiate Strength Tests."[13] These tests included strength of the back and legs and of the right grips, pull-ups, push-ups, and vital capacity. Note that the battery included components other than strength as subsequently defined. Sargent continued his extensive work in this area and, in 1913, published a 20-year progress report.[14]

Many of the early "strength" tests used combinations of strength, muscular endurance, and even respiratory measures. Examples of these are the aforementioned "Intercollegiate Strength Tests" of Sargent and the Strength Index and Physical Fitness Index (P.F.I.) of Rogers.[15]

According to Hunsicker and Donnelly,[16] the forerunner of the spring dynamometers used by Sargent (variations of which are still in use today) was produced by Regnier, in France, in 1807. With this instrument, grip strength, pulling power of the arm muscles, and lifting power of the back muscles could be measured. In the same article, the authors described various other devices used by researchers in physical education and other fields to measure strength of muscle groups.

During World War II, in the Army Air Forces convalescent hospital physical conditioning service, cable-tension tests for measuring strength in orthopedic disabilities[17] were developed and subsequently perfected by Clarke[18] for use in physical education testing and research. This technique will be discussed later.

In recent years, with the increased interest in weight training and weight lifting, some so-called isotonic strength tests have appeared in the literature.[19,20] These tests are distinguished from isometric or static (no motion) strength tests by the fact that maximal weights are lifted *once* through a full range of motion. More recently, a new concept in strength testing called isokinetic strength[21] has been introduced. Isokinetic exercise employs a simple but unfamiliar physical principle of loading a dynamically contracting muscle and controlling the speed of the motion produced by the muscles throughout the full range of motion.

### Strength Defined

Strength may be defined as the muscular force utilized in the creation or prevention of movement. In the creation of movement, the force is isotonic (active) in nature, i.e., muscles shorten (concentric contraction) or lengthen (eccentric contraction) as they develop tension, and the force generated is directed toward overcoming a resistance, e.g., the mass of the body, if the body is to be moved, or some external object. In the prevention of movement, the force generated by the muscles, often called isometric or static strength, is utilized to resist and equalize the effect of internal or external forces, thereby preventing movement.

Strength emphasizes the capacity of the body or its segments to exert force. Ultimately, it is a complex human quality involving motivation, the number of muscle fibers that can be brought into the act, the efficiency of the levers involved in the act, the nutritive state of the muscle fibers at the moment of the act—brought together in a coordinated effort against a particular resistance. For the purpose of clarity, strength will be differentiated from other types of motor fitness in that speed, distance, and muscular endurance will *not* be primary considerations. Thus, isometric or static strength will be defined as the tension that a single muscle or muscle group can develop in a single maximum contraction against immovable resistance. Isotonic or dynamic strength will be defined as the maximum tension a single muscle or groups of muscles can develop in a *single* maximal contraction through the full range of motion of the part or parts being tested. Since, for all practical purposes, it is still impossible to measure the strength of a single muscle, all strength tests used in physical education are of the muscle-group type.

## ISOMETRIC OR STATIC
## STRENGTH TESTS

### Dynamometer Tests

As stated earlier, Hunsicker and Donnelly have summarized the numerous types of equipment used traditionally in measuring static strength. Although slightly different in design, all of the spring-steel dynamometers are based on the same principle, namely, deformation of a piece of steel in the form of a ring, ellipse, or coil, with the deformation of the metal being proportional to the force applied. A few of these instruments are shown in Figure 4.1.

*Equipment.* The instruments used in the tests described below are the hand and back and leg dynamometers.

*Description and administration of the hand (grip strength) dynamometer test.* The hand and the instrument should be dry. The subject puts some magnesium chalk on the hand. The tester sets the pointer to zero and places the dynamometer in the subject's hand, with the dial against the palm and the larger (concave) pressing edge in the "heel" of the palm. The subject squeezes sharply and steadily as possible, making certain that no part of the arm touches the body. Three trials are allowed with a one-minute rest between squeezes.

*Scoring.* The highest reading of the three squeezes is recorded in pounds or kilograms.

FIGURE 4.1 Instruments used to measure static strength; top—various hand dynamometers; bottom—a back and leg dynamometer.

*Description and administration of the back-strength dynamometer test.*  One
hand grips over and the other under the bar. The hands are spread the width of the
shoulders. The trunk is flexed only slightly forward (10-15 degrees) at the hips.
Excessive forward bend results in poor leverage and could cause lower back strain.
The body weight is balanced on the feet, which are placed about 6 inches (15.24 cm.)
apart. The knees are kept straight throughout the lift. The lift is steadily upward,
without jerking. The subject should not be allowed to lean backward on the heels.
At the end of the lift, the back should be almost straight. If not, reject the lift. If
any other deviations from proper procedure are noted, the test should be repeated.

*Scoring.*  The highest of two or three readings is recorded in pounds or
kilograms.

*Description and administration of the leg-strength dynamometer test.*  Two
common methods have been described in the literature. The older (without the belt)
method has been outlined by Rogers,[22] and the "newer" (with the belt) method
was discussed by Everts and Hathaway.[23] Only the belt method will be described here.

The feet are placed as in the back lift. The bar is held in the center (at the
level of the pubis) with both palms facing downward. The looped end of the belt is
placed in one end of the bar and the free end is wrapped around the hips and gluteal
muscles and then looped around the opposite end of the bar; when the subject lifts,
the force of the bar will hold the free end of the belt securely against the subject's
body. It is recommended that the knees be flexed between 115 and 125 degrees.[24]
The subject's knees should be nearly straight at the end of the lift. The chain is adjusted until a maximum lift is obtained.

*Scoring.*  The highest of two or three readings is recorded in pounds or
kilograms.

*Reliability and validity.*  Rogers[25] reported test-retest reliabilities of .92, .90,
.88, and .86 for right grip, left grip, back strength, and leg strength, respectively.
Metheny[26] reported objectivity coefficients for right grip strength of .95 for boys
and girls between the ages of 2-6 years. Cureton[27] published reliabilities of .92,
.90, .91, and .82 for right hand, left hand, back strength, and leg strength, respectively. The subjects were 72 boys ages 7-13. Finally, Fleishman[28] reported a reliability coefficient of .91 for boys and girls ages 13-18. There seems to be little
argument in the literature that the dynamometer strength tests are acceptably
reliable.

Since it is generally agreed that it is impossible to measure the "absolute"
strength of the body, experimental attempts to validate strength as a fundamental
physical component have followed four major lines: 1) correlation of individual
strength tests with batteries of strength tests; 2) correlations with general motor
ability or athletic ability tests; 3) correlations with physique; and 4) correlations
with health tests. A number of these validity schemes have been summarized by
Cureton,[29] Cureton and Larson,[30] Fleishman,[31] and McCloy.[32]

*Normative information.*   Norms for right grip, left grip, back and leg strength, total strength, and strength/weight were published in Cureton,[33] who measured 106 male college freshmen in 1945. Again, in 1964, Cureton[34] published a series of norm tables using the above measures on young boys, ages 7-13. Also, in 1964, after measuring thousands of young boys and girls, ages 13-18, Fleishman[35] published a set of norms for hand-grip strength.

*Comments.*   Confusion abounds in the area of strength testing in physical education. This is due largely to the failure of authors to distinguish between static and isotonic strength, power, and muscular endurance events and the common practice of combining all of the above into "strength indices" or batteries. Only static strength tests using dynamometers have been discussed in the foregoing section.

Extreme caution should be taken in the use of published norm tables. Authors do not always note the type of hand dynamometer used, nor is it always clear whether the leg-strength test has been conducted with or without the use of a belt.

### Cable-Tensiometer Strength Tests

*Equipment.*   Tensiometer; goniometer or large protractor for placing body parts at proper angles; chain, cable, and strap attachments for securing body parts to an immovable object such as a wall or table (Figures 4.2 and 4.3).

**FIGURE 4.2   The tensiometer.**

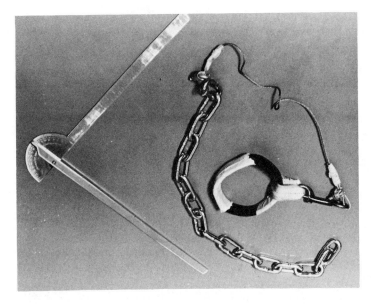

**FIGURE 4.3** Left—the pulling apparatus; right—the goniometer.

*Description and administration.* The tests were originated during World War II and were intended initially to measure the strength of muscles involved in war-related orthopedic disabilities. The tests have since been used to measure normal individuals as well as champion athletes. Thirty-eight such tests were developed, including those for movements of the finger, thumb, wrist, elbow, shoulder, neck, trunk, hip, knee and ankle.[36] The subject, after being positioned for a specific test, pulls on a light cable. Cable tension is determined by measuring the force applied to a riser, causing an offset in a cable stretched taut between two sectors.

### Overall Directions for Tensiometer Testing

Prepare the tensiometer by mounting the correct riser for the size of cable used (manufacturer supplies these directions). Place the subject in the correct position for the joint movement to be tested. Mount the cable-pulling apparatus assembly and place it around the subject's limb. Adjust the slide so that the pulling strap is snug. Tighten the cable to a taut position by moving the adjuster bar or chain. Open the trigger of the tensiometer and pass the cable between the two sectors and the riser. Instruct the subject to pull on the cable and make as strong an effort as possible. Carefully observe the pointer during the pull, visually noting its high point. Use of the brake rod usually causes inaccuracies.

*Scoring.* Take the reading on the dial of the tensiometer. Convert the reading into pounds or kilograms on the calibration chart attached to the inside cover of the tensiometer case.

Complete directions for use of the tensiometer, as well as specific measurement of 28 of the original 38 movements, have been published by Clarke.[37, 38]

*Reliability and validity.* Clarke[39] reported high objectivity coefficients between .92 and .97 for 22 of the tests mentioned above and between .84 and .90 for the remaining six tests. These coefficients were obtained from 64 male college students tested independently by two testers.

Validation of the tensiometer tests have followed along the same lines as the dynamometer tests discussed earlier, namely: 1) intercorrelations between individual test items and batteries of test items; 2) internal validation schemes composed of multiple correlations between small and large batteries of test items (Table 4-1); 3) correlations between tensiometer strength tests and other published motor ability tests; and 4) correlations between tensiometer tests and other published tests of athletic ability. Many of the above are discussed adequately by Clarke.[40]

*Normative information.* An extensive project was conducted at the University of Oregon where 25 cable-tension strength tests were administered to 72 boys and 72 girls at each of four school levels. In each instance, batteries of three tests each were selected by multiple correlation procedures; the correlations ranged between .92 and .96.

The process developed by Rogers[41] (which included height and weight) was followed in order to arrive at a desirable base for test norms. Two battery scores were obtained for the two sexes at various school levels:

Strength Composite (SC): Gross strength score, obtained by adding the 3 strength tests in each battery
Strength Quotient (SQ): Relative Strength Score, derived from the following formula:

$$SQ = \frac{\text{Achieved } SC}{\text{Normal } SC} \: X \: 100$$

The ultimate goal achieved was the construction of strength test batteries with norms for each sex at the upper elementary, junior high, senior high and college levels. A manual is available describing and illustrating the test batteries and presenting the norms.[42]

*Comments.* The cable tensiometer strength tests are probably the most reliable static strength tests in common use. The evaluation of "total-body" musculature probably does not require testing of a large number of muscle groups as it has been demonstrated repeatedly that a small number of properly selected tests will reflect the "total" musculature as reflected in measurement of at least 38 body movements. Such batteries, with norms, are available for both boys and girls. However, in developing the strength of the "total" musculature for physical fitness or

TABLE 4-1  Distribution of Strength Tests Among the Several Batteries as Determined by Multiple Correlations*

| STRENGTH TESTS | UPPER ELEM. SCHOOL | | JUNIOR HIGH SCHOOL | | SENIOR HIGH SCHOOL | | COLLEGE | |
|---|---|---|---|---|---|---|---|---|
| | BOYS | GIRLS | BOYS | GIRLS | BOYS | GIRLS | MEN | WOMEN |
| Shoulder Extension | 1 | 1 | 1 | 1 | 1 | | | |
| Shoulder Flexion | | | | | | 3 | 2 | |
| Shoulder Adduction | | | | | | | | 1 |
| Trunk Extension | 2 | | | 4 | | | | |
| Trunk Flexion | | 2 | | | | | | |
| Hip Extension | | 3 | | 3 | | | | |
| Hip Flexion | | | | | | 2 | 3 | 3 |
| Hip Adduction | | | 3 | | | | | |
| Hip Inward Rotation | | | | 2 | | | | |
| Knee Extension | 3 | | 2 | | 3 | 4 | | 4 |
| Knee Flexion | | 4 | | | | 1 | | |
| Ankle Plantar Flexion | | | | | 2 | | 1 | 2 |
| R | .98 | .96 | .97 | .97 | .96 | .96 | .94 | .97 |

*Numbers in table refer to the order in which the strength tests appeared in the multiple correlation.

Source:  Clarke, 1973, Series 3, No. 1., p.6.

sports training purposes, involvement of all large-muscle groups is necessary since, apparently, there exists a pronounced specificity of strength among the various muscle groups.

## ISOTONIC STRENGTH TESTS

As mentioned earlier, these tests are distinguished from static tests by the fact that some motion is present. Berger[43] developed the use of 1-RM (the maximum load a person can raise only once) as a means for evaluating strength improvement. He later used the same principle for the purpose of classifying students in weightlifting classes on the basis of strength.[44] Tests were given 174 male college students to determine the 1-RM for the following weight training lifts: curl, upright rowing, deep knee bend, sit-up, military press, bench press and back hyperextension. Total strength was the sum of the 1-RM loads of all lifts. Only the military press will be discussed here.

### The Military Press

*Equipment.* A weight bar 5 feet or 6 feet (1.52 m or 1.83 m) in length, and enough weight plates to be more than sufficient for the strongest subject.

*Description and administration.*[45]    The bar is raised to the chest, there is a pause and the "get set" position is assumed. The feet are 14–16 inches (35.56–40.64 cm) apart and parallel, knees locked, head up, eyes focused slightly upward and ahead, elbows in at the sides, and the bar resting across the upper chest and shoulders. A deep breath is taken and the hip, thigh and abdominal muscles are contracted simultaneously. The bar is lifted overhead vigorously, elbows locked. Throughout the movement, the knees are locked, the feet are flat, and no excessive bending of the back is permitted; i.e., the upright position should be maintained. For safety purposes, this test may also be performed by having two assistants place the bar in the subject's hands at the front chest position, then having the subject raise the weight. In any event, two assistants should remain ready to catch the barbell at all times during the trial. The weight should be held steady for a count of three to demonstrate control, after which it is lowered to the floor by the assistants.

*Scoring.*    The greatest weight lifted once properly is recorded. A second or third trial may be permitted but fatigue becomes a factor with repeated trials.

*Reliability and validity.*    Berger did not report test-retest reliability coefficients in either of the two studies mentioned above. However, Johnson and Nelson[46] did report reliabilities ranging from .91 to .99 for the following isotonic strength tests: pull-up, dip, bench squat, sit-up, bench press, and standing vertical arm press test. The latter test, which is similar to the military press described above, had a reliability of .98.

**TABLE 4-2  Table to Predict Various Repetitions Maximum from One Lifting Bout**

| 1-RM* 100.0% | 2-RM 97.4% | 3-RM 94.9% | 4-RM 92.4% | 5-RM 89.8% | 6-RM 87.6% | 7-RM 85.5% | 8-RM 83.3% | 9-RM 81.1% | 10-RM 78.9% |
|---|---|---|---|---|---|---|---|---|---|
| 20.0 | 19.5 | 19.0 | 18.5 | 18.0 | 17.5 | 17.1 | 16.7 | 16.2 | 15.8 |
| 25.0 | 24.4 | 23.7 | 23.1 | 22.5 | 21.9 | 21.4 | 20.8 | 20.3 | 19.7 |
| 30.0 | 29.2 | 28.5 | 27.7 | 26.9 | 27.3 | 25.7 | 25.0 | 24.3 | 23.7 |
| 35.0 | 34.1 | 33.2 | 32.3 | 31.4 | 30.7 | 29.9 | 29.2 | 28.4 | 27.6 |
| 40.0 | 39.0 | 38.0 | 37.0 | 35.9 | 35.0 | 34.2 | 33.3 | 32.4 | 31.6 |
| 45.0 | 43.8 | 42.7 | 41.6 | 40.4 | 39.4 | 38.5 | 37.5 | 36.5 | 35.5 |
| 50.0 | 48.7 | 47.5 | 46.2 | 44.9 | 43.8 | 42.8 | 41.7 | 40.6 | 39.5 |
| 55.0 | 53.6 | 52.2 | 50.8 | 49.4 | 48.2 | 47.0 | 45.8 | 44.6 | 43.4 |
| 60.0 | 58.4 | 46.9 | 55.4 | 42.9 | 42.6 | 51.3 | 50.0 | 48.7 | 47.3 |
| 65.0 | 63.3 | 61.7 | 60.1 | 58.4 | 56.9 | 55.6 | 54.1 | 52.7 | 51.3 |
| 70.0 | 68.2 | 66.4 | 64.7 | 62.9 | 61.3 | 59.9 | 58.3 | 56.8 | 55.2 |
| 75.0 | 63.1 | 61.2 | 69.2 | 67.3 | 64.7 | 63.1 | 61.4 | 60.8 | 49.2 |
| 80.0 | 77.9 | 75.9 | 73.9 | 71.8 | 70.1 | 68.4 | 66.6 | 64.9 | 63.1 |
| 85.0 | 82.8 | 80.7 | 78.5 | 76.3 | 74.5 | 72.7 | 70.8 | 68.9 | 67.1 |
| 90.0 | 87.7 | 85.4 | 83.2 | 80.8 | 78.8 | 77.0 | 75.0 | 73.0 | 71.0 |
| 95.0 | 92.5 | 90.2 | 87.8 | 85.3 | 83.2 | 81.2 | 79.1 | 77.0 | 75.0 |
| 100.0 | 97.4 | 94.9 | 92.4 | 89.8 | 87.6 | 85.5 | 83.3 | 81.2 | 78.9 |
| 105.0 | 102.3 | 99.6 | 97.0 | 94.3 | 92.0 | 89.8 | 87.5 | 85.2 | 82.8 |
| 110.0 | 107.1 | 104.4 | 101.6 | 98.8 | 96.4 | 94.1 | 91.6 | 89.2 | 86.8 |
| 115.0 | 112.0 | 109.1 | 106.3 | 103.3 | 100.7 | 98.3 | 95.8 | 93.3 | 90.7 |
| 120.0 | 116.9 | 113.9 | 110.9 | 107.8 | 105.1 | 102.6 | 100.0 | 97.3 | 94.7 |
| 125.0 | 121.8 | 118.6 | 115.5 | 112.3 | 108.5 | 105.8 | 104.1 | 101.4 | 97.6 |
| 130.0 | 126.6 | 123.4 | 120.1 | 116.7 | 113.9 | 111.2 | 108.3 | 105.4 | 102.6 |
| 135.0 | 131.5 | 128.1 | 124.7 | 121.2 | 118.3 | 115.4 | 112.5 | 109.5 | 106.5 |
| 130.0 | 126.6 | 123.4 | 120.1 | 116.7 | 113.9 | 111.2 | 108.3 | 105.4 | 102.6 |
| 135.0 | 131.5 | 128.1 | 124.7 | 121.2 | 118.3 | 115.4 | 112.5 | 109.5 | 106.5 |
| 140.0 | 136.4 | 132.9 | 129.4 | 125.7 | 122.6 | 119.7 | 116.6 | 113.5 | 110.5 |
| 145.0 | 141.2 | 137.6 | 134.0 | 130.2 | 127.0 | 124.0 | 120.8 | 117.6 | 114.4 |
| 150.0 | 146.1 | 142.4 | 138.6 | 134.7 | 131.4 | 128.3 | 125.0 | 121.7 | 118.4 |

TABLE 4-2 (continued)

| 1-RM* 100.0% | 2-RM 97.4% | 3-RM 94.9% | 4-RM 92.4% | 5-RM 89.8% | 6-RM 87.6% | 7-RM 85.5% | 8-RM 83.3% | 9-RM 81.1% | 10-RM 78.9% |
|---|---|---|---|---|---|---|---|---|---|
| 155.0 | 151.0 | 147.1 | 143.2 | 139.2 | 135.8 | 132.5 | 129.1 | 125.7 | 122.3 |
| 160.0 | 155.8 | 151.8 | 147.8 | 143.7 | 140.2 | 136.8 | 133.3 | 129.8 | 126.2 |
| 165.0 | 160.7 | 156.6 | 152.5 | 148.2 | 144.5 | 141.1 | 137.4 | 133.8 | 130.2 |
| 170.0 | 165.6 | 161.3 | 147.1 | 142.7 | 148.9 | 145.4 | 141.6 | 137.9 | 134.1 |
| 175.0 | 170.5 | 166.1 | 161.7 | 157.2 | 153.3 | 149.6 | 145.8 | 141.9 | 138.1 |
| 180.0 | 175.3 | 170.8 | 166.3 | 161.6 | 157.7 | 153.9 | 149.9 | 146.0 | 142.0 |
| 185.0 | 180.3 | 175.6 | 170.9 | 166.1 | 162.1 | 158.2 | 154.1 | 150.0 | 146.0 |
| 190.0 | 185.1 | 180.3 | 165.6 | 170.6 | 166.4 | 162.5 | 153.3 | 154.1 | 149.9 |
| 195.0 | 189.9 | 185.1 | 180.2 | 175.1 | 170.8 | 166.7 | 162.4 | 158.1 | 153.9 |
| 200.0 | 194.8 | 189.8 | 184.8 | 179.6 | 175.2 | 171.0 | 166.6 | 162.2 | 157.8 |

(N = 94)

*1–RM = one maximum lift

Source: Berger, 1961, pp. 108–10, 117.

Johnson and Nelson claimed face validity for their tests. Berger[47] used the multiple correlation method to determine internal validity by correlating combinations of test items with a test criterion (total strength, i.e., sum of seven isotonic strength tests). A combination of military press, upright rowing and back hyperextension lifts correlated .96 with the test criterion. Military press alone correlated .87 with the test criterion suggesting that, for practical purposes, in the classification of students in a weight training class, only military press need be used.

*Normative information.*    Johnson and Nelson[48] have published norm tables for college men and women for six isotonic strength tests based on body weight.

Berger[49] has published a table for college men to predict various repetitions (2-RM to 10-RM) from one lifting bout (1-RM) (Table 4–2).

*Comments.*    The isotonic strength tests appear to have high reliability. Their major value is in measuring a certain type of strength in a nonlaboratory setting. Their major applications appear to be in relation to weight training classes for the purposes of classifying students or measuring strength improvement.

## TESTS OF POWER

Power is a function of force and time (power = work/time) and is defined as the rate of performing work (work = force × distance). Since work is the product of force and the distance over which the force is applied, power is that product divided by the time during which the force is applied. Thus, if two individuals of equal height, weight, and leg strength were to perform vertical jumps, the one who could apply force downward against the floor more rapidly would have a faster upward reaction, would achieve the higher vertical jump, and would have the more powerful legs.

Many physical performances in sport demand power of the participant. Little is known about the complex physiological processes and factors that influence the speed and strength of contraction of muscles; but it is well known that strength of muscles may be increased through the medium of exercises performed against resistance. Hence, appropriate programs of resistive exercises can increase a performer's power by increasing muscular strength in order that additional force may be produced.

In physical education literature, much confusion surrounds the measurement of power. This is due to the fact that early researchers tended to use the all-inclusive term "strength" to identify not only dynamometer (static) strength but also items that are more appropriately termed power and muscular endurance events. The problem is further compounded by the fact that most of the traditional power events such as the vertical jump and standing broad jump have been measured in distance traversed (inches or feet, centimeters or meters) rather than in work (force × distance) or power (work/time) units. Still another problem has been the inclusion of speed items, such as the 60-yard (54.86-meter) dash, among power tests. The so-called speed tests usually measure time needed to traverse a certain distance or distance/ time (average velocity) and are, therefore, inadequate measures of power. That is not to say that speed and power are not related. A number of studies have demonstrated this relationship.[50,51] Johnson and Nelson[52] have attempted to shed light on the problem by delineating between "athletic"-power events and work-power events.

Events of "athletic" power would include the traditional power events such as: 1) those expressed in terms of propelling the body through space (vertical jump, standing long jump, etc.) and 2) those propelling an object through space (softball throw, shot put, medicine ball throw, etc.). The factors of force and velocity are not measured in these tests, i.e., only the resultant distance is recorded.

Work-power events are those resulting in a score reflecting work (force × distance) or power (work/time). Only a few of the above tests will be discussed here.

## TESTS OF "ATHLETIC" POWER

### Vertical Jump Test (Jump and Reach)

Variations of the vertical jump test abound in the literature. Those used by Sargent,[53,54] Phillips,[55] and Fleishman[56] are but a few. Some of the variations have been summarized by Van Dalen.[57] The test described here is basically that used by Bookwalter.[58]

*Equipment.* A plywood board 2 feet × 5 feet (60.96 cm by 152.40 cm), painted flat black with five yellow lines one inch (2.54 cm) apart extending across the width of the board and numbered from 70 to 139, bottom to top. The board is attached firmly to the wall, preferably 6 inches (15.24 cm) from the wall, with the lines parallel to the floor and the bottom edge of the board exactly 70 inches (177.80 cm) above the floor. Chalk for the fingertips is required.

*Description and administration.* Chalk is placed on the fingertips of the dominant hand, the subject faces the board, reaches to a maximum height without lifting the heels, and marks the maximum height to the fingertips. The fingertips are rechalked and, with the dominant side to the wall, a jump is made straight upward and another mark made at the top of the jump with the same hand used in measuring the reaching height. No run or preliminary hop is allowed. The subject may bend the knees and swing the arms preparatory to the jump.

*Scoring.* The score to be recorded is the difference between the reaching height and the jumping height. Three trials are allowed and scored to the nearest quarter inch (.64 cm).

*Reliability and validity.* Reliability coefficients have been published by many authors. Glencross[59] reported a test-retest reliability of .92, using 85 male college students; Fleishman,[60] using 201 male college students averaging 18 years of age, reported a coefficient of .90. Cureton,[61] on the other hand, reported a coefficient of only .78 for 74 young boys ages 7–13.

Face or content validity are most often claimed for the vertical jump test. However, some attempts have been made to validate the vertical jump against external criteria. McCloy,[62] in a series of studies, correlated the vertical jump against a battery of four track events and reported validity coefficients ranging from .65 to .93 for men and boys and .60 to .88 for girls. On the basis of these and other studies, he concluded that the vertical jump could be used as a prediction of track and field abilities, especially when combined with age and size or with some measure of strength.

More recently, Glencross,[63] using 85 male college students, reported a validity coefficient of .73 when the vertical jump was correlated against a battery of four power tests measured with the power lever,[64] a simple pulley device that permits the measurement of the average horsepower developed in a variety of single "explosive" movements.

*Normative information.*    Norm tables for the jump and reach are available for elementary and junior high school boys and girls[65] and for high school and college women.[66] Those norms are based on height-weight class divisions. Other norms have been published by Cureton[67] (boys, 7–13 years) and by Johnson and Nelson[68] (boys and men, 9–34 years; girls and women, 9–34 years).

*Comments.*    The vertical jump is a reliable, practical test for measuring "athletic" power of the lower extremities. The test appears to be more reliable for college-age men than for young boys. The construct validity is high, but more work needs to be done to determine its validity against mechanical tests of power. Since so many variations of the vertical jump test are found in the literature, care must be taken when using published norms for local comparison.

### Standing Broad Jump (Long Jump) Test

One of the happy circumstances surrounding the use of the standing broad jump is the fact that few variations exist. These variations are usually minor in nature. The test discussed below is that used as part of the AAHPER Youth Fitness Test.[69]

*Equipment.*    A mat; floor or outdoor jumping pit; tape measure.

*Description and administration.*    The subject stands with feet several inches (or centimeters) apart and toes just behind the takeoff line. Preparatory to jumping, the arms are swung backward and the knees bent. The jump is done by extending the knees and swinging the arms forward simultaneously. Measurement is taken from the takeoff line to the heel or part of the body that touches the floor nearest the takeoff line.

*Scoring.* The score is the best of the three trials in feet and inches (meters and centimeters) to the nearest inch (centimeter).

*Reliability and validity.* The AAHPER Test Manual mentioned above did not report reliability coefficients. However, reliabilities for this test may be obtained from a number of sources. Glencross[70] reported a test-retest reliability of .96 using 85 male college students; Fleishman,[71] using 201 male college students averaging 19 years of age, reported a coefficient of .90.

Face or construct validity are most often claimed for the standing broad jump test. In combination with chins and push-ups, this test correlated .82, with a 12-item criterion composed of strength, velocity, motor ability, and endurance factors.[72] Glencross[73] reported a validity coefficient of .75 between standing broad jump and a battery of four power tests measured with the power lever mentioned previously.

*Normative information.* Norms for the standing broad jump test abound in the literature, since this factor is often included, in combination with other items, in typical motor ability test batteries. Norms for high school girls were included in the study by Powell and Howe.[74] Fleishman[75] published norms for boys and girls, ages 13–18, and AAHPER[76] has norms for girls and boys ages 9–17.

*Comments.* The standing broad jump is a reliable and practical test of "athletic" power of the lower extremities. The construct validity is high, but more research is needed to determine its validity against true tests of power. It correlates reasonably well with vertical jump and, therefore, should probably not be included in the same battery. Additional sources of "athletic"-power tests may be found in the previously cited works of Neilson and Cozens (1934), Cozens, Cubberly, and Neilson (1939), and Fleishman (1964).

## WORK-POWER TESTS

Rather complex power tests have been devised for the lower extremity[77] and the upper extremity.[78] Practical modifications thereof will be presented.

### Modified Vertical Power Jump Test

*Equipment.* A vertical jump board as described earlier; magnesium carbonate chalk for the fingers; a weight scale.

*Description and administration.* The body weight is taken and the subject stands sideways to the jump board with the preferred arm extended above the head and next to the board. The other arm is placed behind the back and, while the subject stands on tiptoe, the height of the extended finger is noted on the board. A full squat position is assumed while a straight back and original position of the arms are maintained. When stationary and balanced, the subject jumps upward, and the maximum height of the jump is marked on the jump board by means of the chalked fingertips.

*Scoring.* The distance between the starting height and the maximum height jumped is recorded. The best of three jumps recorded to the nearest one quarter inch (.64 cm) is then converted to work in terms of foot pounds (kilogram meters) by this formula:

$$\text{work} = \frac{\text{body weight lbs (kg)} \times \text{distance jumped ins (cm)}}{12\ (30.48)}$$

*Reliability and validity.* The test-retest reliability, using a random sample of 80 male college students, was .97; the validity coefficient, using the original vertical power jump test as the criterion, was .98.

*Normative Information.* No norms were published in the original study. However, Johnson and Nelson[79] published norms, based on between 100 and 125 cases, for college men and women and high school girls.

*Comments.* The modified vertical power jump is a reliable, valid, and practical test of power of the lower extremities. It eliminates the necessity of measuring the height of the center of gravity as required in the original test, and it also eliminates extraneous movements common in other vertical jump tests.

### The Vertical Arm Pull Test

Johnson[80] recognized the need for a power test for the upper extremity. In the original study, he measured the time factor required in pure power tests by photographing the height of the pull with an 8-mm camera. The test described below is a modification of the original test.

*Equipment.* A climbing rope; marking tape; tape measure; weight scale.

*Description and administration.* Body weight is taken, and the subject assumes a sitting position on a bench 15 inches (38.10 cm) from the floor.
The rope is grasped as high as possible without raising the buttocks. The hand of the preferred arm should be placed just above the opposite hand. The tester places a piece of masking tape around the rope just above the uppermost hand. The performer pulls as hard as possible (feet do not touch the floor), reaches as high as possible, and grasps the rope until the tester can again place a piece of masking tape above the uppermost hand.

*Scoring.* The distance between the starting tape and the finish tape is recorded.

The best of three trial recorded to the nearest one-quarter inch (.64 cm) is then converted to work in terms of foot-pounds (kilogram-meters) by the formula:

$$\frac{\text{foot-pounds}}{\text{(kilogram-meters)}} = \frac{\text{distance of pull in inches (cm)} \times \text{body wt in lbs (kg)}}{12(30.48)}$$

*Reliability and validity.* The test-retest reliability, using 160 male college students, was .94; the validity coefficient using the original power test (that included the time measurement) was .76.

*Normative information.* No norms were included in the original study. In another publication, the author[81] did present norms, based on between 150 and 200 cases, for college men and high school boys.

*Comments.* The vertical arm-pull test is a reliable and practical test of power of the upper extremities. It eliminates the necessity of photographing the arm pull as required in the original test. More work needs to be done on the validity of the test. For example, it might be validated against the Glencross power lever previously described.


## TESTS OF MUSCULAR ENDURANCE

Although related to strength in the sense of the presence of force and resistance, muscular endurance involves the ability of a group of muscles to repeat continuously a performance requiring a relatively high level of muscular force (isotonic dynamic endurance) or to maintain a position (isometric or static endurance) against a force that is counteracting it. In isotonic or dynamic endurance, the greater the frequency or the longer the duration of the repetitions, the greater the endurance. Hence, in the example of a pull-up, sufficient force in the form of isotonic strength (discussed previously) must be available to overcome the body's mass in the first execution. If subsequent executions are to be achieved, endurance (resistance to fatigue) of the muscles is now involved. This resistance to fatigue is a function of the total available force of the involved muscles, of the ability of the cardiovascular system to nourish the muscles with oxygen, and of the muscle's internal chemistry both aerobic and anaerobic.

It must be emphasized here that circulatory-respiratory factors are involved only minimally in isotonic endurance tests since these tests are characterized by a high degree of muscular tension over a relatively short period of time. Thus, muscular endurance tests tax the endurance of the skeletal muscles and should not be confused with the cardiovascular endurance tests which tax circulatory-respiratory systems to a much greater extent.

In isometric or static tests of muscular endurance, one continuous muscular contraction is maintained rather than a series of repetitive bouts. Thus, no movement is involved and the underlying muscle chemistry is basically anaerobic.

Historically, the testing of muscular endurance has been plagued (as in the testing of muscular power) by the fact that early researchers (and some relatively recent ones) have used the term "strength" to include all of what we are now differentiating as strength, power, or muscular endurance tests. To the novice student of measurement and evaluation, we can only urge caution and express sympathy. Table 4-3[82] is included to highlight the problem.

## ISOTONIC (DYNAMIC) MUSCULAR ENDURANCE TESTS

These practical tests are most numerous and have probably been the most extensively used by physical educators in schools and in physical fitness testing programs. They require little, if any, special equipment and are included in most motor ability test batteries. Only a few of the more common ones will be described in greater detail below.

### Pull-ups (Chin-ups)

Several variations of the pull-up test occur in the literature. Some controversy exists as to whether the palms forward (overhand) or backward (reverse) grip should be used. Although some research[83] has shown that individuals tend to average from one to two pull-ups more using the palms backward (facing the performer) grip, many tests use the palms forward approach. Such a test, taken from the AAHPER battery,[84] is described.

*Equipment.* A metal or wooden bar approximately 1½ inches (3.81 cm) in diameter. The bar should be placed high enough so that the arms can be extended fully and the feet will clear the floor.

*Description and administration.* The palms-forward (overhand) grip is assumed, and the body is lowered to a full stationary hang (arms and body fully extended). The body is raised until the chin is placed over the bar. The body is lowered to a full hang, as in the starting position, and the act is repeated as often as possible. Body swinging, knee raising, or leg kicking are not permitted.

*Scoring.* The number completed properly to the nearest whole number is recorded. One fair trial is allowed.

*Reliability and validity.* Although the AAHPERD did not report the reliability of its test, a number of authors have published reliability coefficients. Cureton[85] reported test-retest reliabilities of .89, .96, and .70 for college men (N = 119), high school boys (N = 60), and young boys[86] (N = 74), respectively. Fleishman[87] reported a reliability of .93 for 201 young men.

Face or content validity is usually claimed for the pull-up test. Cureton,[88] however, reported an internal validity coefficient of .64 between pull-ups and a

**TABLE 4-3  Historical Analysis of Arm and Shoulder Girdle Musculature Tests***

| DATE | TEST OR BATTERY | TEST ITEM | STATED TO TEST: |
|---|---|---|---|
| 1897 | Intercollegiate Strength Tests—men (Sargent, 1897) | dips on parallel bars | strength of triceps and chest |
| 1926 | Rogers Strength Inventory and Physical Fitness Inventory—boys and girls (Rogers, 1926) | boys: dips and pull-ups girls: stool push-ups and ring pull-ups | upper arm and shoulder girdle strength |
| 1931 | McCloy's Strength Index—boys and girls (McCloy, 1931) | chins and dips (with weights) | total strength |
| 1935 | Wendler's Total Strength Index—boys and girls (Wendler, 1935) | dynamometer | total strength (47 muscle groups tested) |
| 1936 | Anderson's Weighted Strength Tests for Girls (Anderson, 1936) | ring pull-ups and dips | strength |
| 1940 | Cozens' Muscular Strength Test—boys (Cozens, 1940) | push-ups, chins, and dips | total strength (combined with back strength and leg lift) |
| 1940 | Larson's Muscular Strength Test—boys (Larson, 1940) | chins and dips | total strength (combined with vertical jump) |
| 1943 | Navy Standard Physical Fitness Test—men (U.S. Navy, 1943) | push-ups and pull-ups | strength and endurance of extensor muscles of arm and shoulder girdle |
| 1944 | WAC Physical Fitness Rating—women (WAC Dept., 1944) | knee or full dips | physical fitness |
| 1945 | Motor Fitness Tests for High School Girls (O'Connor, 1945) | kneeling push-ups | endurance |
| 1945 | NSWA Physical Performance Test—High School Girls (Metheny, 1945) | push-ups or pull-ups (modified) | physical performance |
| 1946 | Army-Air Force Physical Fitness Test—men (U.S. Govt., 1946) | chinning | physical fitness |
| 1947 | Adult Indoor Motor Efficiency Classification Test Without Apparatus (18 item)—men and women (Cureton, 1947) | man lift, extended press-up (forearm for women) | strength |
| | | push-ups (knee-type for women), straddle chinning | endurance |
| 1947 | Illinois Motor Fitness Inventory (14 item)—college men (Cureton, 1947) | chinning, dips, barbell lift, extended press-up | endurance strength |
| 1947 | The JCR Test (Phillips, 1947) | chinning | total ability of individual in fundamental skills (combined with vertical jump) |

96

**TABLE 4-3 (continued)**

| DATE | TEST OR BATTERY | TEST ITEM | STATED TO TEST: |
|------|-----------------|-----------|-----------------|
| 1948 | U.S. Office of Education Physical Fitness Tests— high school girls (U.S. Office of Ed., 1948) | push-ups | arm strength |
| 1950 | Oregon Motor Fitness Test— high school boys and girls (Clarke, 1950) | boys: pull-ups girls: modified pull-ups | motor fitness |
| 1957 | AAHPER Youth Fitness Tests— boys and girls, grades 5–12 (AAHPER, 1957) | boys: pull-ups girls: modified pull-ups | arm and shoulder strength |
| 1958 | Indiana Physical Fitness Tests— boys and girls (State of Indiana, 1958) | boys: straddle chins and push-ups, girls: knee push-ups | arm and shoulder girdle strength and endurance |
| 1958 | New York State Physical Fitness Test—boys and girls, grades 4–12 (State of N.Y., 1958) | boys: bar pull-ups girls: modified pull-ups | strength |
| 1959 | Scott Push and Pull Test— women (Scott, 1959) | manuometer | static strength of arm and shoulder girdle |
| 1961 | North Carolina Fitness Test— boys and girls, grades 9–12 (State of N.C., 1961) | boys: pull-ups girls: modified pull-ups | arm and shoulder girdle strength, endurance and speed |
| 1962 | Purdue Motor Fitness Test Batteries for Senior High School Girls—(Arnett, 1962) | bench push-ups modified pull-ups | motor fitness |
| 1965 | Grossmont College Physical Fitness Test—men and women, junior college (Grossmont P.E. Dept., 1965) | men: pull-ups women: bent-arm hang | arm and shoulder strength |
| 1966 | Physical Performance Test for California—high school boys and girls (Cal. Board of Ed., 1966) | boys: pull-ups girls: knee push-ups | muscular strength and endurance |

*Note: Although many of the above tests include a number of motor ability components, only arm and shoulder girdle items have been included in this table. After having read the sections on strength, power, and muscular endurance, the reader is challenged to reclassify the above items in terms of the definitions used herein.

Source: Diridon, 1967.

large battery of 28 predominantly muscular endurance events; Fleishman[89] reported a correlation of .81 between pull-ups and a muscular endurance factor (obtained through factor analysis) that he unfortunately called dynamic strength.

*Normative information.* Numerous sets of norms are available in the literature, since pull-ups are often included in batteries of motor ability tests, especially for men and boys. Larson[90] and Cureton[91] published norms for college men, whereas Cureton[92] and the AAHPERD[93] presented norms for young boys ages 7-12 and 9-17, respectively. Fleishman[94] and the State of California[95] published norms for boys and girls ages 12-18 and 10-18, respectively.

*Comments.* The pull-up test is practical and reliable, and one of the more valid tests for measuring isotonic muscular endurance of the arms and shoulder girdle in young men and boys. It should probably not be used at this time for young women and girls. Apparently, in the past, such a large proportion of them were unable to do one pull-up that normative comparison is rendered meaningless statistically.

### Sit-Ups (Bent-Knee)

A number of variations of this test appear in the literature. Some examples are ankles held down; knees held down; feet free; hands laced behind head; hands laced behind neck; touch both elbows to knees; touch elbow to opposite knee; raise straight up to 90°; perform to limit; perform maximum number in 30 seconds; perform maximum number in 60 seconds; and so on. The one chosen for further description is that used in the AAHPER Youth Fitness Test,[96] since it will probably enjoy greater use nationally.

*Equipment.* A mat or dry turf; stopwatch.

*Description and administration.* The subject lies on the back with knees bent, feet on the floor, and heels between 10-12 inches (25.40 cm-30.48 cm) from the buttocks. The fingers are clasped behind the neck and the elbows placed flat on the floor. The feet are held in place by a partner. The abdominal muscles are tightened, head and elbows brought forward, and the elbows touched to the knees. The subject returns to the starting position and repeats the exercise.

*Scoring.* The number of correctly completed sit-ups in 60 seconds is recorded. One fair trial is allowed.

*Reliability and validity.* The AAHPERD did not report the reliability of the above test. Cureton[97] reported a reliability coefficient of only .70 for college men using a feet-free, knees-straight, all-out test. Fleishman[98] reported a reliability of only .72 for young men using a knees-held, knees-straight, 30-second limit test. Reliabilities as high as .94 were reported by Johnson and Nelson[99] using a bent-knee, elbow-cross-over test of college men and women.

Face validity is often accepted for the sit-up test. Few attempts have been made to validate sit-ups against larger batteries of muscular endurance tests. Validity coefficients of only .39 and .31 were reported by Cureton[100] and Fleishman[101] in the studies cited above. These low validities were probably due to the relatively low reliabilities also found in the same studies.

*Normative information.*  Johnson and Nelson[102] presented norms for college men and women, and the AAHPERD[103] has published norms for boys and girls ages 9-17. The new AAHPERD Health-Related Physical Fitness Test[104] also includes norms for the sit-up test for ages 6-17.

*Comments.*  The sit-up test (knees bent) is a practical test of muscular endurance of the abdominal musculature. More research is needed on the reliability of this test. Lack of validity may be due simply to the fact that the sit-up test is usually correlated against tests of the arms and shoulder girdle, and that the endurance of the abdominals simply does not correlate highly with the endurance of the muscles of the arms and shoulder girdle. Other sources of isotonic muscular endurance tests appear in the works of Cureton (1945) and Fleishman (1964).

## ISOMETRIC (STATIC) MUSCULAR ENDURANCE TESTS

As mentioned previously, this type of test involves one contraction held continuously. It differs from isometric strength in that it includes a time factor, and the weight or resistance held is usually submaximal. Johnson and Nelson[105] discussed variations of this type of test, which they called "repetitive static tests of muscular endurance." These tests will not be discussed here, however.

### Flexed Arm Hang

This test has come into more common use recently due largely to the fact that, on the average, young women and girls have been found to have difficulty in performing the regular pull-up. The test used by the AAHPERD[106] has been selected for further description.

*Equipment.*  A horizontal bar approximately 1½ inches (3.80 cm) in diameter; stopwatch.

*Description and administration.*  The height of the bar is adjusted approximately equal to the standing height. The body is raised off the floor to a position at which the chin is above the bar, the elbows are flexed, and the chest is close to the bar (assistants are used if necessary). The position is held as long as possible. The watch is started as soon as the hanging position is assumed. The watch is stopped; 1) when the chin strikes the bar; 2) when the head tilts backward to keep the chin above the bar; or 3) when the chin falls below the bar.

*Scoring.*  The length of time the proper position is held is recorded to the nearest second.

*Reliability and validity.*  The AAHPERD did not report the reliability of its test. Johnson and Nelson[107] mentioned reliabilities as high as .90 but did not cite the sources. Fleishman[108] reported a test-retest reliability coefficient of .77, using 200 young men as subjects. However, this test varied slightly from the AAHPERD test in that the bar was held at eyebrow level rather than at chin level.

Face validity is normally claimed for this test. Some attempts have been made at internal validation of this test against a battery of tests composed mostly of isotonic muscular endurance items. Interestingly, the validity coefficient was a reasonably high .73.[109] In a similar type of study, Cureton[110] reported a relatively low validity coefficient of .49 for a variation of the test (arms fully extended). However, the reliability of his test was also low (.59).

*Normative information.*   Norms for flexed arm hand for girls ages 9-17 were published by the AAHPERD.[111] Cureton[112] published norms for young college men for the straight arm hang variation.

*Comments.*   The flexed arm hang is a practical test of isometric endurance of the arm and shoulder girdle musculature. The test is particularly suited for young women and girls. More research needs to be done on the reliability and validity of this test.

### Hold Half Push-Up

This test was one of four static endurance tests studied by Fleishman.[113]

*Equipment.*   Floor or mat; stopwatch.

*Description and administration.*   The standard push-up position is assumed on the floor: legs and feet together, hands beside the chest, fingers pointed forward. The hands are spread far enough away from the body so that 90° angles can be formed between the forearm and the floor and between the forearm and the upper arm when the subject pushes up. The subject then pushes up to the above position with back, legs, neck, and head remaining in a straight line. The correct position is practiced once, then held as long as possible.

*Scoring.*   The number of seconds the position is maintained correctly is recorded.

*Reliability and validity.*   The reliability of this test was .85, using 201 college-age men as subjects.[114] The internal validity coefficient was .68 when the test was validated against a large battery of isometric and isotonic muscular endurance tests.[115]

*Normative information.*   No norms were published for this test, but a table may be readily constructed using the reported mean of 39.54 seconds and standard deviation (21.98 seconds).

*Comments.* This is a practical and reliable test for measuring static endurance of the arm and shoulder girdle musculature. The test may be utilized for both sexes. Face validity may be claimed for this test, but more study is needed on validation against a battery of static endurance tests of the arms and shoulder girdle musculature. Other sources for isometric muscular endurance tests appear in the works of Cureton (1945) and Fleishman (1964).

## BIBLIOGRAPHY

AAHPERD, *Measurement and Evaluation Materials in Health, Physical Education and Recreation.* Washington: AAHPERD Publications, 1950.

AAHPERD, *Youth Fitness Test Manual.* Washington: AAHPERD Publications, 1957.

AAHPERD. *Health-Related Physical Fitness Test Manual.* Washington: AAHPERD Publications, 1980.

ANDERSON, THERESA W., "Weighted Strength Tests for the Prediction of Athletic Ability in High School Girls." *Research Quarterly,* 7 (March 1936), 136–42.

ARNETT, CHAPPELLE, "The Motor Fitness Test Batteries for Senior High School Girls." *Research Quarterly,* 33 (October 1962), 323–28.

BERGER, RICHARD A., "Classification of Students on the Basis of Strength." *Research Quarterly,* 34 (December 1963), 514–15.

____. "Determination of the Resistance Load for 1-RM and 10-RM." *Journal of the Association for Physical and Mental Rehabilitation,* 15 (July-August 1961), 108–10; 117.

BOOKWALTER, KARL W. and CAROLYN W. BOOKWALTER, "A Measure of Motor Fitness for College." *Bulletin of the School of Education,* Indiana University, Vol. 19, No. 2 (March 1943).

BOOKWALTER, KARL W., "Test Manual for Indiana University Motor Fitness Indices for High School and College Men." *Research Quarterly,* 14 (December 1943), 356–65.

BOVARD, J.F. and F.W. COZENS. *Tests and Measurements in Physical Education,* 2nd ed. Philadelphia: W.B. Saunders Co., 1938.

BROCK, JOHN, WALTER A. COX and ERASTUS W. PENNOCK, "Motor Fitness." *Research Quarterly,* Supplement, 12 (May 1941), 407–15.

CALIFORNIA STATE BOARD OF EDUCATION, *The Physical Performance Test for California.* Sacramento: State Board of Education, 1966.

CALIFORNIA STATE DEPARTMENT OF EDUCATION, *The Physical Performance Test for California,* revised, Sacramento: State Board of Education, 1971.

CARPENTER, AILEEN, "A Study of the Angles of Measurement of the Leg Lift." *Research Quarterly,* 9 (October 1938), 70–72.

CLARKE, H. HARRISON, *Application of Measurement to Health and Physical Education,* 2nd ed. Englewood Cliffs, N.J.: Prentice-Hall, Inc., 1950.

____. *Cable Tension Strength Tests.* Springfield, Mass.: Stuart E. Murphy, 1953.

____, and DAVID H. CLARKE, *Developmental and Adapted Physical Education.* Englewood Cliffs, N.J.: Prentice-Hall, Inc., 1963.

CLARKE H. HARRISON, *Muscular Strength and Endurance in Man.* Englewood Cliffs, N.J.: Prentice-Hall, Inc., 1966.

____. "Objective Strength Tests of Affected Muscle Groups Involved in Orthopedic Disabilities." *Research Quarterly,* 19 (May 1948), 113–47.

_____. editor, *Physical Fitness Research Digest,* Series 3, No. 1. Washington: President's Council on Physical Fitness and Sports, January, 1973.

_____, and RICHARD A. MUNROE,  *Test Manual: Oregon Cable-Tension Strength Batteries for Boys and Girls from Fourth Grade Through College.* Eugene: Microform Publications in Health, Physical Education and Recreation, University of Oregon, 1970.

COZENS, FREDERICK W., HAZEL J. CUBBERLY and N.P. NEILSON,  *Achievement Scales in Physical Education Activities for Secondary School Girls and College Women.* New York: A.S. Barnes and Co., 1939.

COZENS, F.W.,  "Strength Tests as Measures of General Athletic Ability in College Men." *Research Quarterly,* 11 (March 1940), 45–52.

CURETON, THOMAS K.,  *Endurance of Young Men.* Washington: Society for Research in Child Development, National Research Council, 1945.

_____. "Improving the Physical Fitness of Youth." *Monographs of the Society for Research in Child Development,* Serial No. 95, Vol. 29, No. 4, 1964.

_____. *Physical Fitness Appraisal and Guidance.* St. Louis: C.V. Mosby Co., 1947.

_____, and LEONARD A. LARSON,  "Strength as an Approach to Physical Fitness." *Research Quarterly,* Supplement, 12 (May 1941), 391–406.

DeWITT, R.T.,  "A Comparative Study of Three Types of Chinning Tests." *Research Quarterly,* 15 (October 1944), 240–48.

DIRIDON, MARY ANN,  "A Study of Methods of Testing Arm and Shoulder Girdle Musculature Capacity with an Emphasis on the Bent-Knee Push-up and Bent-Arm Hang Tests for High School Girls." Unpublished student project, San Jose State College, San Jose, California, 1967.

EVERTS, EDGAR W. and GORDON J. HATHAWAY,  "The Use of the Belt to Measure Leg Strength Improves the Administration of Physical Tests." *Research Quarterly,* 9 (October 1938), 62–69.

FLEISHMAN, EDWIN A.,  *The Structure and Measurement of Physical Fitness.* Englewood Cliffs, N.J.: Prentice-Hall, Inc., 1964.

_____. *Examiner's Manual for the Basic Fitness Tests.* Englewood Cliffs, N.J.: Prentice-Hall, Inc., 1964.

FRUCHTER, B.,  *Introduction to Factor Analysis.* Princeton, N.J.: D. Van Nostrand Co., Inc., 1954.

GLENCROSS, D.J.,  "The Nature of the Vertical Jump Test and the Standing Broad Jump." *Research Quarterly,* 37 (October 1966), 353–59.

_____. "The Power Lever: An Instrument for Measuring Muscle Power." *Research Quarterly,* 37 (May 1966), 202–10.

GRAY, R.K., K.B. START and D.J. GLENCROSS,  "A Test of Leg Power." *Research Quarterly,* 33 (March 1962), 44–50.

GROSSMONT COLLEGE PHYSICAL EDUCATION DEPARTMENT, "Grossmont College Physical Fitness Testing Program." Unpublished material, Grossmont College, La Mesa, California, 1965.

HARMON, H.,  *Modern Factor Analysis.* Chicago: University of Chicago Press, 1960.

HISLOP, HELEN and JAMES J. PERRINE,  "The Isokinetic Concept of Exercise," *Journal of the American Physical Therapy Association,* 47 (February 1967), 114–17.

HUNSICKER, PAUL A. and RICHARD L. DONNELLY,  "Instruments to Measure Strength." *Research Quarterly,* 26 (December 1955), 408–20.

HUNSICKER, PAUL and GUY G. REIFF,  *Youth Fitness Manual,* revised ed. Washington: AAHPERD Publications, 1976.

JOHNSON, BARRY L.,  "Establishment of a Vertical Arm-pull Test (Work)." *Research Quarterly,* 40 (March 1969), 237–39.

____, and JACK K. NELSON, *Practical Measurements for Evaluation in Physical Education.* Minneapolis: Burgess Publishing Co., 1969.

LARSON, LEONARD A., "A Factor Analysis of Motor Ability Variables and Tests, with Tests for College Men." *Research Quarterly,* 12 (October 1941), 499–517.

____. "A Factor and Validity Analysis of Strength Variables and Tests with a Combination of Chinning, Dipping and Vertical Jump." *Research Quarterly,* 11 (December 1940), 82–96.

LATHAM, DARRELL, "Factor Analysis of the Illinois 14-Item Motor Fitness Screen Test." Unpublished master's thesis. Champaign: University of Illinois, 1945.

McCLOY, C.H., "A New Method of Scoring Chinning and Dipping." *Research Quarterly,* 2 (December 1931), 132–43.

____. *Tests and Measurement in Health and Physical Education.* New York: F.S. Crofts and Co., 1946.

METHENY, ELEANOR, "Breathing Capacity and Grip Strength of Pre-School Children." *University of Iowa Studies in Child Welfare,* 18 (1940), 114–15.

____. "Physical Performance Levels for High School Girls." *Journal of Health, Physical Education and Recreation,* 16 (June 1945), 308–11.

NEILSON, N.P. and FREDERICK W. COZENS, *Achievement Scales in Physical Education Activities for Boys and Girls in Elementary and Junior High Schools.* Sacramento: California State Department of Education, 1934.

O'CONNOR, MARY and T.K. CURETON, "Motor Fitness Tests for High School Girls." *Research Quarterly,* 16 (December 1945), 302–14.

O'SHEA, JOHN P., *Scientific Principles and Methods of Strength Fitness.* Reading: Addison-Wesley Publishing Co., 1969.

PEARSON, GEORGE B. and JACQUELINE K. WHALIN, *Reference Index of the Research Quarterly (1930–1960).* San Diego: All American Productions and Publishers, 1964.

PHILLIPS, B.E., "The JCR Test." *Research Quarterly,* 18 (March 1947), 12–19.

POWELL, ELIZABETH and E.C. HOWE, "Motor Ability Tests for High School Girls." *Research Quarterly,* 10 (December 1939), 81–88.

RARICK, G. LAWRENCE, "An Analysis of the Speed Factor in Simple Athletic Activities." *Research Quarterly,* 8 (December 1937), 89–105.

ROGERS, FREDERICK RAND, *Physical Capacity Tests in the Administration of Physical Education.* New York: Bureau of Publications, Teachers College, Columbia University, Contributions to Education, No. 173, 1925.

____. *Physical Capacity Tests in the Administration of Physical Education.* New York: Bureau of Publications, Teachers College, Columbia University, 1926.

SARGENT, D.A., "Intercollegiate Strength Tests." *American Physical Education Review,* 2 (December 1897), 216.

____. "The Physical Test of A Man." *American Physical Education Review,* 26 (April 1921), 188–94.

____. "Twenty Years of Progress in Efficiency Testing." *American Physical Education Review,* 18 (October 1913), 452.

SARGENT, L.W., "Some Observations in the Sargent Test of Neuromuscular Efficiency." *American Physical Education Review,* 29 (1924), 47–56.

SCOTT, M. GLADYS and ESTHER FRENCH, *Measurement and Evaluation in Physical Education.* Dubuque, Iowa: Wm. C. Brown Co., 1959.

SEAVER, J.W., *Anthropometry and Physical Education.* New Haven: A.O. Dorman Co., 1896.

START, K.B., R.K. GRAY, D.J. GLENCROSS and A. WALSH, "A Factorial Investigation of Power, Speed, Isometric Strength and Anthropometric

Measures in the Lower Limb." *Research Quarterly,* 37 (December 1966), 553–59.

STATE OF INDIANA, *High School Physical Education Course of Study.* Bulletin No. 222, Department of Public Instruction, Indianapolis, Indiana, 1958.

STATE OF NEW YORK, *The New York State Physical Fitness Test—A Manual for Teachers of Physical Education and Recreation.* 1958.

STATE OF NORTH CAROLINA, *North Carolina Fitness Test.* 1961.

U.S. GOVERNMENT PRINTING OFFICE, *U.S. Army Basic Field Manual FM 21-20.* Washington: Physical Training, 1946.

U.S. NAVY, *Physical Fitness Manual for the USN.* Bureau of Naval Personnel, Training Division Physical Section, 1943.

U.S. OFFICE OF EDUCATION, "Physical Performance Levels for High School Girls." *Reprint Education for Victory,* Washington: Federal Security Agency (May 1948).

VAN DALEN, D.B., "New Studies in the Sargent Jump." *Research Quarterly,* 11 (May 1940), 112–15.

"WAC PHYSICAL FITNESS RATING." *Training Circular* No. 40. Washington: WAC Department, U.S. Government Printing Office, 1944.

WENDLER, A.J., "An Analytical Study of Strength Tests Using the Universal Dynamometer." *Research Quarterly,* Supplement, 6 (October, 1935), 31–85.

**CHAPTER FIVE**

# TESTS OF "SPECIFIC" MOTOR ABILITIES: FLEXIBILITY, AGILITY, AND BALANCE

## TESTS OF FLEXIBILITY

Flexibility, often referred to as suppleness, is usually defined as the measure of the range of the motion of body parts about their joints, attainable without undue strain to those joints and their muscular attachments. Most tests of flexibility have been of two types: 1) range of motion about a single joint and 2) degree of twist or bend of the body or its parts involving the flexibility or extensibility of two or more joints. Examples of sports movements that require or are enhanced by flexibility of body parts are back handsprings and "splits" in gymnastics, dolphin stroke in swimming, high hurdling in track, and competitive diving.

Early flexibility testing consisted of single-joint evaluation in which some form of goniometry was used. Moore[1] reported that goniometry had been practiced since the turn of the century. Numerous types of goniometers have been devised since that time. (See Figure 4.3) The goniometer consists of a 180° protractor with two extended arms, usually 15 inches (38.1 cm) in length. The stationary arm is fixed to the zero point of the protractor whereas the other arm is movable. A winged nut at the center point at which the two arms meet may be tightened when a measurement is desired. The center point of the goniometer is placed over the geometric center of the joint to be measured, and the two body segments about the joint to be measured form the two legs of the angle recorded on the protractor. A comprehensive review of the literature on flexibility was published by Wiechec and Krusen,[2] who discussed the problems of measurement, nomenclature, and the need for standardization of norms used in the clinical setting.

More recently, a device called the flexometer was devised by Leighton[3] to measure range of motion of the trunk, neck, and extremities (Figure 5.1). Even more recently, an electrogoniometer (ELGON)[4,5,6] has been devised for recording angles in joints during various body movements.

As the development and maintenance of general body flexibility has been accepted as a physical education function, practical tests of gross flexibility, rather than tests for individual joints, have been emphasized. These tests, in general, do not require special or expensive equipment. A few will be described briefly.

## THE CURETON FLEXIBILITY TESTS

This battery of four tests of gross flexibility was first described by Cureton in 1941.[7] The subjects are allowed to warm up thoroughly before taking any of the tests.

### Trunk Flexion Forward

*Equipment.* Sliding wood caliper or measuring stick.

*Description and administration.* The subject sits on a flat surface, legs 18 inches (45.72 cm) apart, hands interlaced behind the neck. The forehead is bent

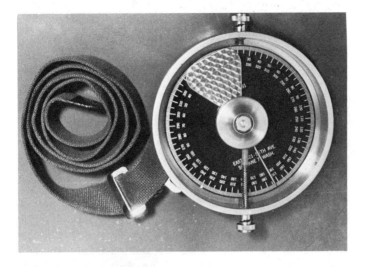

FIGURE 5.1   The flexometer.

slowly forward and downward as far as possible. The knees are kept straight by an assistant.

*Scoring.*   The distance is measured in inches (or centimeters) from the forehead to the surface. The best of three trials is recorded. For this and the following three tests, the subject must remain in position at least two seconds.

### Trunk Extension Backward

*Equipment.*   Sliding wood caliper or measuring stick.

*Description and administration.*   The subject lies in a prone (face down) position on a flat surface, hands interlaced behind the neck. The hips are held firmly to the surface by an assistant straddling the legs and pressing forward and downward on the buttocks. The subject lifts the head and chest slowly and backward as far as possible.

*Scoring.*   The distance is measured in inches (or centimeters) from the chin to the surface.

### Shoulder Flexibility

*Equipment.*   A sliding wood caliper or measuring stick; a small round wooden rod 24 inches (60.96 cm) in length.

*Description and administration.* The subject lies in a prone position on a flat surface, the chin touching the floor, and the arms extended forward shoulder-width apart. The rod is grasped and the elbows and wrists kept straight. The rod is raised the maximum distance possible from the floor.

*Scoring.* The distance is measured in inches (or centimeters) from the underside of the rod to the surface.

### Average Ankle Flexibility

*Equipment.* Paper; long pencil; ruler; solid ⅜-inch (9.5 mm) thick plywood board 18 inches × 18 inches (45.72 cm × 45.72 cm); protractor; compass.

*Description and administration.* The subject sits on a flat surface, keeping the legs flat on the surface. A board is placed vertically against the outside edge of a foot, with a piece of paper between the board and the foot. A pencil held horizontally traces the top of the foot at maximum flexion and maximum extension. The lines are drawn long enough to intersect and points are marked with a compass on each line 2 inches (5.08 cm) from the point of intersection. The legs of the angle are formed by drawing a line from the point of intersection to the 2-inch (5.08 cm) points.

*Scoring.* The angle is measured with a protractor and the right and left ankles are averaged.

*Reliability and validity.* Cureton[8] reported test-retest reliability coefficients of .95, .71, .85, and .72 for college men for trunk flexion, trunk extension, shoulder flexibility, and ankle flexibility, respectively. For the same tests in young boys ages 7–13 he reported coefficients of .87, .76, .70, and .55, respectively.[9]

Face validity is usually claimed for most flexibility tests, since it is generally agreed that little relationship exists among them, (i.e., the degree of flexibility in various joints of the same individual may differ greatly). An internal validity study by Cureton,[10] using an average T-score for the four flexibility tests as the test criterion, indicated that no single test had superiority in predicting performance in all four. In the same study, validity coefficients of .77–.88 for trunk extension, .29–.64 for trunk flexion, .23–.64 for shoulder flexibility, and .16–.38 for ankle flexibility indicated that the tests may have some validity in differentiating between expert and ordinary swimmers.

*Normative information.* Norms for all four tests for college men[11] and for young boys[12] (trunk flexion and trunk extension only) were published by Cureton. Norms for college men and women for trunk extension and shoulder and ankle flexibility were also published by Johnson and Nelson,[13] using slight variations in test administration and scoring.

*Comments.* The Cureton tests are practical and reasonably reliable tests of gross flexibility. One criticism of the tests is the failure to take into consideration the length of the trunk in the tests of flexion and extension of the trunk and the length of the arms in the shoulder flexibility test. This would cast doubt on the value of the use of his norms for making individual comparisons. However, the tests would still have value for assessing improvements in flexibility due to participation in physical fitness and sports programs when the subject is his or her own control. The norms published by Johnson and Nelson may be of more general value since they did include trunk and arm length in their scoring system.

### Wells and Dillon Sit and Reach Test[14]

This test is a modification of the Standing Bend and Reach Test described by Scott and French.[15] The modification was made to eliminate the fear of falling, a common criticism of the latter test.

*Equipment.* A platform scale; two small benches; a rubber mat 4 feet (1.22 m) square. The platform scale consists of a piece of plywood 8 inches X 24 inches (20.32 cm X 60.96 cm) with lines drawn horizontally (the short way) at half-inch (1.27 cm) intervals. A center line is marked zero, with plus and minus scales drawn on each side of the zero line. The support for the platform scale consists of an elongated plus sign made of 11-inch (27.94 cm) boards placed on their edges, a cross board, and a stem board. The platform (horizontal) scale is attached to the upper edges of the support in such a way that when the subject is seated on the floor, with the feet against the cross board, the zero line coincides with the near surface of this board and the minus values are toward the subject. The two benches are placed side by side on their sides about 12 inches (30.48 cm) apart, with their legs against the wall. The platform scale is placed between the benches with the cross board braced against them. The rubber matting is spread on the floor in front of and partially under the scale.

*Description and administration.* The subject sits on the rubber matting, legs separated enough to straddle the stem board, with feet pressed firmly against the cross board. The subject bobs forward four times and holds the position of maximum reach on the fourth movement. The knees must remain straight.

*Scoring.* The score is taken to the nearest half-inch (1.27 cm) of maximum reach. If the hands reach unevenly, the hand reaching the shorter distance determines the score.

*Reliability and validity.* The odd-even method of reliability was used, in which the sum of the first and third trials was correlated with the sum of the second and fourth trials. A reliability coefficient of .98 was reported, using 100 college women as subjects.

A validity coefficient of .90 was reported, using the Scott and French Standing Bend and Reach Test as the criterion.

*Normative information.* No norms were published by the authors, although means and standard deviations were reported. Norms for college men and women have been published by Johnson and Nelson, who used a slight modification of the test.[16] The new AAHPERD Health-Related Physical Fitness Test[17] also includes norms for a sit and reach test for ages 6–17.

*Comments.* The Wells and Dillon Test is a practical and reliable test of back and leg flexibility. The use of the raised platform scale is criticized, however, since extremely flexible individuals would be hindered by it from bending all the way to the floor. The Johnson and Nelson Sit and Reach Test overcame that problem by placing the measuring scale on the floor.

### The Fleishman Extent Flexibility (Twist and Touch) Test[18]

This test was one of six flexibility tests in an extensive factor analysis study of physical fitness components. The purpose of the test was to measure trunk rotation.

*Equipment.* A measuring scale is drawn on a wall. The scale is 30 inches (76.2 cm) long and is marked off in half-inch (1.27 cm) intervals from 0–30 inches (0–76.2 cm). The scale should be sufficiently wide to accommodate differences in heights of subjects. A line is drawn on the floor, perpendicular to the wall and in line with the 12-inch (30.48 cm) mark on the scale.

*Description and administration.* A right-handed subject stands with the left side toward the wall, toes touching the line on the floor, and feet together and perpendicular to the line. The subject stands far enough from the wall so that he or she can just touch the wall with the left fist when the arm is held horizontally from the shoulder. The feet are kept in place and the right arm is extended to the side (abducted) to shoulder height. The palm faces downward, with fingers extended and together. The wrist is kept straight. The subject twists clockwise as far as possible, so that the scale on the wall is touched with the right hand while an assistant assures that the subject's right foot remains in place.

*Scoring.* One practice trial is given and the second trial is scored to the nearest inch (or centimeter) at the farthest point reached. The position must be held at least two seconds.

*Reliability and validity.* A test-retest reliability of .90 was reported for this test. An internal validity coefficient of .49 was reported, using a factor called "extent flexibility" as the test criterion.

*Normative information.* Percentile norms, by age group, were published for boys and girls ages 13–18.[19]

*Comments.* Although the test as described was practical and reliable, it obviously does not measure only trunk rotation. The test includes shoulder flexibility (horizontal abduction) as well.

### The Leighton Flexometer Tests[20]

Through the development of the flexometer,* Leighton has contributed probably the most comprehensive method of measuring the range of motion of various joints of the body including the trunk, head and neck, and extremities. Nineteen separate joint-range-of-motion tests may be made with the flexometer, for a total of 30 when the joints of both right and left extremities are included. All 30 tests are described in the original article and will not be discussed here.

*Equipment.* A flexometer. This instrument consists of a weighted 360° dial and a weighted indicator arm, each of which operates independently of the other. The influence of gravity and the positioning of the extremity move both the dial and the indicator arm to the proper position for recording the joint angle (Figure 5.1).

*Description and administration.* The following general procedure applies for all joint movements.

The flexometer is secured to the extremity with a one-inch (2.54 cm) webbed strap. When testing, the dial is locked at the starting position and the indicator arm remains free. The joint being measured is then moved through its full range. The indicator arm is locked at the completion of the joint movement.

*Scoring.* The difference in degrees between the locked dial at the starting position and the indicator arm at the completion of the movement is the actual range of motion through which the movement was performed.

*Reliability and validity.* Test-retest reliability coefficients for 120 boys ranged from .91 to .99 for all tests. Face validity was claimed for the tests based upon the now recognized specificity of individual joint movements.

*Normative information.* No norms were published in the original study, but means and standard deviations for a group of 40 sixteen-year-old boys, for all tests, were reported. Rating scales based on 100 sixteen-year-old boys were included in a dissertation by Forbes.[21]

*Comments.* The Leighton flexometer tests are simple, practical, and reliable tests of joint movements. Only the expense of the flexometer precludes its more widespread use in the typical school situation.

*The flexometer may be purchased from J.A. Preston Corporation, 71 Fifth Ave., New York, N.Y. 10003.

## TESTS OF AGILITY

Agility refers to the controlled ability to change position and direction rapidly and accurately. Two conditions exist under which the ability of the performer may be influenced diversely: 1) a reaction, of a known type and in a known direction, to a stimulus that is anticipated (e.g., a sprinter reacting to the starting gun); and 2) a reaction, of an undetermined type and in an unknown direction, to a set of stimuli that may vary widely and, hence, be somewhat unpredictable: for example, a defensive halfback reacting to the changes in speed or direction of a pass receiver. Reactions of the performer under the second condition are inevitably slower and initially less precise, since the body is usually in a position that restricts rapid maximum reactions in almost all directions.

Agility items are of three main types: 1) change of direction in running; 2) change of body position; and 3) changes of direction of body parts. Examples of these types are, respectively, maze or dodge runs, squat thrusts, and various items demanding change of position of the hands or feet.

Terminology is particularly confusing in this area, since various authors use the terms coordination and dynamic balance synonymously with agility. There is also considerable disagreement in the literature as to the extent to which agility can be considered a "pure" component of motor ability. In a factor analysis study of 20 "agility" items, Jennett[22] identified at least six factors. These included reaction time, speed, strength, balance, change of direction, and change of position. All but two, strength and balance, can be subsumed under the definition we have used for agility, and these two have been treated as separate or specific motor abilities in this text.

The few tests selected for brief review are predominantly tests of change of direction and position. These particular kinds of tests are in more common use in the field and are quite practical to administer.

### Illinois Agility Run[23]

The test is representative of the many dodge-run tests that have appeared in the literature over the years. It is recommended that the test be taken barefooted and practiced at least once slowly and once rapidly.

*Equipment.* Four chairs; stopwatch.

*Description and administration.* A diagram of the floor markings for the test are shown in Figure 5.2. The test is started from a prone position, hands at the sides of the chest and on the starting line. At the command, "go," the subject jumps to the feet and sprints 30 feet (9.14 m), stops and reverses (at least one foot must touch or cross line), and sprints back toward the starting line. A left turn is made around the first chair, followed by a zig-zag around each chair. A right turn is made around the fourth chair, followed by a zig-zag around each chair toward the starting line. A left turn is made around the first chair, followed by a 30-foot (9.14 m)

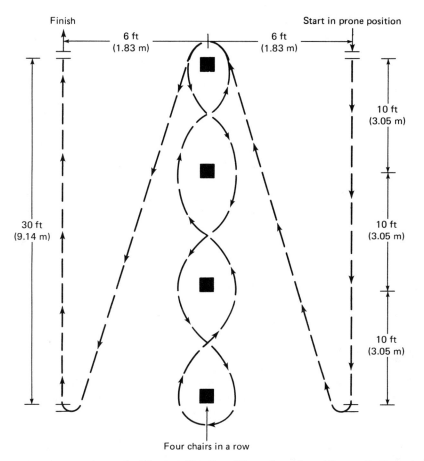

Finish

Start in prone position

6 ft
(1.83 m)

6 ft
(1.83 m)

10 ft
(3.05 m)

10 ft
(3.05 m)

30 ft
(9.14 m)

10 ft
(3.05 m)

Four chairs in a row

**FIGURE 5.2  Diagram for Illinois Agility Run. (Reproduced from Thomas K. Cureton,** *Physical Fitness of Champion Athletes.* **Urbana: University of Illinois Press, 1951, p. 68.)**

sprint. A stop and reverse is repeated as above, and the subject runs full speed across the finish line.

*Scoring.* The subject's chest is timed even with the finish line to the nearest half second. If time permits, the best of three trials should be used for best reliability.

*Reliability and validity.* The test was devised originally for use with young men ages 17–26. Cureton did not publish reliability coefficients for this age group. However, Sterling[24] reported a coefficient of .92 for this age group, and O'Connor[25] obtained the same coefficient for high school girls. In later work Cureton[26] reported a coefficient of .77 for young boys ages 7–13. For boys in grades 7–9, Gates and Sheffield[27] reported a coefficient of .97 for a similar dodge-run test.

Validity work is lacking on this test. In a factor analysis study, it ranked third in measuring a 5-item agility factor and correlated .33 with a 30-item battery composed of strength, balance, agility, flexibility, power, and endurance items.[28] O'Connor[29] obtained a .46 validity coefficient with a similar battery composed of 19 items.

*Normative information.* Cureton[30] published standard score tables for young men ages 17-25 and for young boys ages 7-13.[31] O'Connor [32] presented tables for high school girls.

*Comments.* This is a practical and reliable test of agility, involving change of direction and running. It is easy to administer, adaptable for both sexes and most age groups, and fun to take. However, more work needs to be done to determine the relative validity of this particular test as a measure of agility, even though Mc-Cloy[33] reported a validity coefficient of .82 for a similar type test against a 16-item agility battery.

### Burpee Test[34, 35]

This test has been attributed to Burpee, although it had been used as a calisthenic exercise for many years before he advocated its use, and was known as the four-count squat thrust.

*Equipment.* Stopwatch.

*Description and administration.* From a straight-standing position, the subject moves to a squat-rest position, to a front-leaning-rest position, back to a squat-rest, and finally returns to the straight-standing position.

*Scoring.* One completed four-part performance is scored as one point. The final score is the total number of performances and fractions thereof completed in ten seconds. Scores for a partial performance are as follows: one-quarter for touching the hands to the floor; one-half for thrusting the legs backward; and three-quarters for returning to a squat-rest position with the hands still on the floor.

*Reliability and validity.* Test-retest reliability coefficients of .85 and .92 have been reported for high school girls[36] and junior high school boys,[37] respectively.
The study on high school girls revealed an internal validity coefficient of .46 between the Burpee test and a 19-item criterion consisting of a number of motor ability components. The study on junior high boys revealed internal validity coefficients of .48 to .63 between the Burpee test and a criterion composed of 16 agility items.

*Normative information.* Norms are available for elementary school boys and girls,[38] although the norms for high school girls are high compared to those reported by O'Connor.[39] Norms for college men and women were published by Johnson and Nelson,[40] who used a slightly different scoring technique.

*Comments.*    This is a practical and reliable test of agility involving change of position but no running. It is easy to administer, applicable to both sexes, and fun to take. Its validity does not appear to be as high as common agility tests that include running.

### Boomerang Run (Right)[41]

This was one of 16 agility items investigated in the original study.

*Equipment.*    One chair or similar object for the center point; 4 Indian clubs or similar objects for the outside points; stopwatch; marking tape.

*Description and administration.*    The center point is placed 17 feet (5.18 m) from the starting line. One Indian club is placed 15 feet (4.57 m) on each side of the center point. At the command "Go," the subject runs to the center point, makes a quarter turn right, and completes the course as shown in Figure 5.3.

*Scoring.*    The score is the time taken to complete the course to the nearest tenth of a second.

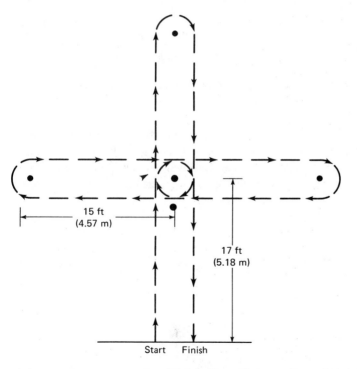

FIGURE 5.3    Boomerang Test (Right)—Floor Markings. (Reproduced from Donald D. Gates and R. P. Sheffield, "Tests of Change of Direction as Measurements of Different Kinds of Motor Ability in Boys of the Seventh, Eighth and Ninth Grades." *Res. Quart.*, 11 (October, 1940), 136–74.)

*Reliability and validity.* Gates and Sheffield[42] reported a test-retest reliability coefficient of .92 for junior high boys, and Sierakowski[43] gave the same coefficient for high school girls.

Sierakowski also reported an internal validity coefficient of .72 for girls, using the sum of T-scores for a 15-item agility battery as the test criterion. Gates and Sheffield reported validity coefficients ranging from .78 to .87 for junior high boys, using a similar 16-item battery.

*Normative information.* The original authors did not publish norms for this test. However, Johnson and Nelson[44] presented norms for junior high boys (grades 7-8).

*Comments.* This is a practical, reliable, and reasonably valid test of agility that includes running. Like most tests of agility, it is easy to administer, inexpensive, applicable to both sexes, and fun to take.

### Gates-Sheffield Agility Batteries[45]

Few batteries of agility tests have been developed, and these have been validated predominantly for small and select samples of the population. In this study the subjects were boys from grades 7-9. A 16-item agility battery was subjected to regression analysis in order to arrive at a representative small battery.

*Equipment.* Nine chairs or similar objects; 6 Indian clubs or similar objects; stopwatch; marking tape.

*Description and administration.* Of the 16 items studied originally, six were included in a series of three, 3-item batteries. The description in the original paper of each of the six items (including floor diagrams) will not be repeated here. These include the 40-yard (36.58 m) maze, zig-zag side step, zig-zag run, loop-the-loop, boomerang right, and 30-foot (9.14 m) shuttle run.

*Scoring.* Each of the six tests is scored by determining, to the nearest tenth of a second, the time it takes to complete each test. Tables are provided for converting raw scores to T-scores. The final three test batteries and regression coefficients were as shown here.

Seventh grade boys:

agility = .771 × 40-yd (36.58 m) maze run (T-score)
  + .409 × zig-zag side step (T-score)
  + .205 × 30-ft (9.14 m) shuttle run (T-score)

Eighth grade boys:

agility = .389 × loop-the-loop (T-score)
+ .449 × 30-ft (9.14 m) shuttle run (T-score)
+ .528 × zig-zag side step (T-score)

Ninth grade boys:

agility = .397 × zig-zag run (T-score)
+ .460 × boomerang, right (T-score)
+ .453 × 30-ft (9.14 m) shuttle run (T-score)

*Reliability and validity.*   Test-retest reliability coefficients for the six items ranged from .91 to .97.

The internal validity coefficients for each of the six items against the 16-item agility criterion ranged from .73 to .92. Three additional validity schemes were employed. The first was correlation of the sum of the T-scores (total T-score) against agility, i.e., scores obtained from the regression equations. The coefficient obtained was .86. The second was correlation of total T-scores against an external criterion consisting of a subjective judgment (one judge) of games ability versus agility. The coefficient obtained was .80. The third was multiple correlation of each of the three batteries against the 16-item criterion. The coefficients obtained were .96, .95, and .92 for the seventh, eighth, and ninth grade batteries, respectively.

*Normative information.*   No norms were published in the original paper. However, since the sum of the weighted scores in each battery constitutes a total score (in standard scores), a T-score of 50 would be average, and deviations higher or lower would be indications of above or below average performance, respectively.

*Comments.*   These batteries of agility tests are practical, reliable, and valid. They are easy to administer, applicable to both sexes, and fun to take. If time permits, the batteries are recommended over individual test items, even though there is probably some overlap, since intercorrelations among all 6 items used in the batteries ranged from .56 to .82.

## TESTS OF BALANCE

"Static balance" involves the ability to maintain the body's center of gravity over the center of its supporting base. Two main factors determine the degree of stability (balance) of a body: 1) the larger the area of the base, the greater the range of stability; and 2) the closer the center of gravity of the body is positioned over the center of the base (in terms of both horizontal and vertical distance), the greater is the degree of stability. Ability to maintain static balance is critical in such activities as gymnastics balancing (hand balances, head balances, etc.) and in defensive positions in wrestling.

Similarly critical is the ability to disturb momentarily the body's balance in a controlled movement (often referred to as "dynamic balance") that is immediately followed by the recovery of a similar or dissimilar position of balance (e.g., dismounting from gymnastics apparatus, running, a series of movements in floor exercises in gymnastics, and offensive movements in wrestling). Thus, all human motion is generated by the disturbance of the body's balance, and motion largely ceases when the body's stability is regained and maintained.

For practical purposes, balance is considered here as a "specific" component of motor ability. However, it probably results from complex combinations of kinesthetic (sensory and motor) responses, visual responses, and semicircular canal function. Muscular strength is a factor in some tests of balance.

A few representative tests are selected for brief review because of their practicality. Other tests requiring more expensive and/or complex equipment are also available.[46,47]

### Bass Stick Test of Static Balance (Lengthwise)[48]

This test is also performed with the supporting foot crosswise on the balance stick. Except for the obvious difference, the crosswise test is administered identically to the lengthwise test.

*Equipment.*  Several wooden sticks 1 inch $\times$ 1 inch $\times$ 12 inches (2.54 cm $\times$ 2.54 cm $\times$ 30.48 cm); a watch with a second hand; adhesive tape to secure the sticks to the floor.

*Description and administration.*  At the word "Ready," the subject places the supporting foot lengthwise on the balance stick, i.e., with the long axis of the foot parallel to the long axis of the stick. At the word "Go," the subject raises the free foot (eyes open) and holds this position as long as possible to a maximum of 60 counts. The timer counts aloud one count per second. A trial is terminated if: 1) either the heel or toe of the supporting foot touches the floor; 2) the free foot touches the floor; or 3) balance is maintained for 60 counts. No more than three practice trials are recommended.

*Scoring.*  The score of the test is the sum of the times for six official trials of the test.

*Reliability and validity.*  A reliability coefficient of .86 was obtained on a sample of 270 college women. Years later, Fleishman[49] obtained a coefficient of .82 on a slight modification of the test.

Three validity schemes were presented in the original paper: 1) correlation (.50) of the test with a subjective rating (one judge) of rhythmic ability; 2) correlation (.50) with a subjective rating (one judge) of general motor ability; and 3) factor analysis in which the test correlated .45 with a battery of balance tests involving use of visual cues. Years later, Fleishman[50] obtained a coefficient of .64 between a slight modification of this test and a very similar balance battery.

*Normative information.* No norms were published in the original paper. Since that time, however, Johnson and Nelson,[51] using a slight modification of the test, published T-score norms for college men and women. Fleishman,[52] also using a slight modification of the test, presented norms for boys and girls ages 13–18.

*Comments.* This is a practical, reasonably reliable, and valid test of static balance. It is easy to administer and adaptable to both sexes and various age groups. With sufficient sticks, a large number of subjects can be tested simultaneously.

The number of trials can probably be decreased from six without seriously compromising the test's reliability.

### The Stork Stand[53] (Static Balance)

*Equipment.* One stopwatch or watch with a second hand.

*Description and administration.* The performer stands on the dominant foot, places the other foot flat on the medial (inside) aspect of the supporting knee (heel on knee), and places the hands on the hips.

At the signal "Now," the performer raises the heel of the supporting foot and maintains balance as long as possible without moving the ball of the supporting foot or letting its heel touch the floor.

*Scoring.* Three trials are given. Time is counted in seconds from the time the heel is raised to the time the balance is lost or the hands are removed from the hips. The highest of the three scores is recorded to the nearest second.

*Reliability and validity.* A test-retest reliability coefficient of .87 was reported for the best of three trials given on different days.

No validity study was attempted. Face validity was claimed by the authors.

*Normative information.* T-score norm tables were included for college men and women.

*Comments.* This is a most practical and reasonably reliable test of static balance. It is easy to administer and adaptable to both sexes and various age groups. If time is a factor, subjects may be tested in pairs by having one person perform and the other note the seconds as they are called aloud by the timer.

This test needs to be studied as to its relative ability to measure static balance, i.e., it should be correlated against a battery of other tests purported to measure static balance. Finally, norms are needed for school-age groups other than college students.

### The Springfield Beam-Walking Test[54]

This is an example of a "dynamic" balance test, according to our definitions.

*Equipment.* The test utilizes 9 hardwood beams 4½ inches (11.43 cm) high and 10 feet (3.05 m) long, but with varying widths for walking surfaces of 4, 3½, 3, 2½, 2, 1½, 1, ½ and ¼ inches (10.16, 8.89, 7.62, 6.35, 5.08, 3.81, 2.54, 1.27, and .64 centimeters). Short cross pieces are needed to keep the beams steady. A simple foot-measuring board is used to classify all subjects into six categories of foot length (shoes on), ranging from those having foot lengths between 7 and 8 inches (17.78 cm and 20.32 cm) to those between 12 and 13 inches (30.48 and 33.02 cm). Six starting points are painted in different colors on the sides of the beam, such that if ten heel-to-toe steps are taken, the subject will finish the tenth step at the end of the beam.

*Description and administration.* A standardized practice is recommended. The subject is placed at the starting point on the beam according to shoe length, so that he or she could walk a maximum of ten steps from the starting point to the end of the beam. The subject attempts to walk ten steps in heel-to-toe fashion and with hands on hips. Subjects who fall off or drop their hands from the hips before completing the ten steps are allowed to continue from that point until they fall off or drop the hands a second time. The second "fall-off" terminates the trial on that particular beam.

*Scoring.* The walking surfaces of the beams are marked in quarter lengths. Since different people start at six different places, depending on shoe length, there are six different color markings of quarter lengths. Thus, the score of a person on a particular beam is the score value of the segment of the beam in which the second fall-off occurs. Since the maximum score on each beam is four quarters (points) and there are nine beams, the maximum score on the entire test (one trial) is 36 points. In the original study, for reliability purposes, the average of six trials was used as the final score.

*Reliability and validity.* Reliability coefficients were obtained by correlating the three odd trial scores against the three even trial scores. This was done on samples of 30 boys each for each year of age from years 5–18. Coefficients ranged from .75 to .89.

No validity work was reported in the original paper, although the author cited the works of others who correlated modifications of this test with other balance tests. The "validity" coefficients were generally very low.

*Normative information.*   No norms appeared in the original paper. However, the author published for each age group (5-18 years) means, standard deviations, medians, and first and third quartiles from which standard score and percentile tables could be constructed easily.

*Comments.*   This appears to be a practical and reliable test of dynamic balance. Attempts should be made to determine if the number of trials could be shortened without compromising the reliability of the test. The validity of the test needs to be explored more fully. Norms should be developed for various age groups and for both sexes.

### Bass Test of Dynamic Balance[55]

*Equipment.*   Stopwatches; tape measure; chalk. An oil cloth pattern may be made or lines may be painted on the floor according to Figure 5.4.

*Description and administration.*   The subject stands with the right foot in the starting circle and leaps—not steps—into the first circle with the left foot, then leaps from circle to circle, alternating the feet. The subject lands on the ball of the foot and does not touch the heel to the floor. The following are considered "errors" and each error counts one penalty point every time it occurs: 1) touching the heel to the floor; 2) moving or hopping on the supporting foot while in the circle; 3) touching the floor outside a circle with the supporting foot; and 4) touching the floor with the free foot or any other part of the body. The timer counts the seconds (up to five seconds) aloud, beginning the count as the performer lands in a circle. If the performer leaps to the next circle before the count of five, the count is restarted. If more than five seconds is taken in a circle, the extra time is deducted from the total time. The instructor follows the performer closely and counts the errors silently and cumulatively.

*Scoring.*   A total of five trials is given. Three practices are allowed and the score of the better of the next two trials is the official score. The final score is the total time plus 50, minus three times the total errors. Thus, the greater the time and the fewer the errors, the better the score. The person scoring total time (from start to finish) stands to the side of circle 10 and counts the seconds aloud. The person scoring errors stands to the side and back as the performer progresses through the test.

*Reliability and validity.*   A high reliability coefficient of .95 was obtained, using college women as subjects.
   Three different validity schemes were used: 1) correlation (.34-.75) with tests of static balance; 2) correlation (.74) with subjective judgment (one judge) of rhythm ability; and 3) correlation (.69) with subjective judgment (one judge) of general motor ability.

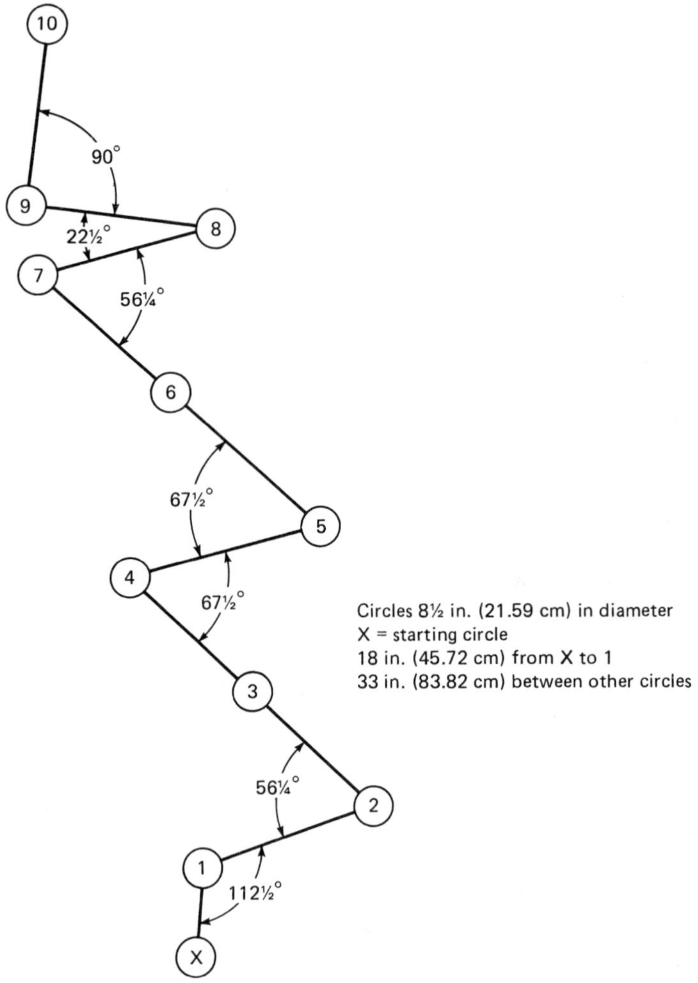
10
90°
9
22½°
8
7
56¼°
6
67½°
5
4
67½°
3
56¼°
2
1
112½°
X
Circles 8½ in. (21.59 cm) in diameter
X = starting circle
18 in. (45.72 cm) from X to 1
33 in. (83.82 cm) between other circles

**FIGURE 5.4 Diagram for Bass Dynamic-Balance Test Pattern. (Reproduced from Ruth I. Bass, "An Analysis of the Components of Tests of Semicircular Canal Function and of Static and Dynamic Balance,"** ***Res. Quart.*****, 10 (May, 1939), 33–52.)**

*Normative information.* No norms were included in the original study. However, Johnson and Nelson,[56] using a modified version of the Bass Test, published T-scale norms for college men and women.

*Comments.* This is a practical and reliable test of dynamic balance. It is easy to administer and adaptable to both sexes and various age groups. More work needs to be done on the validity of this test. It should be correlated against a battery of other tests purported to measure dynamic balance. Norms are needed for various age groups.

AAHPERD, Health Related Physical Fitness Test Manual. Washington: AAHPERD Publications, 1980.

ADRIAN, MARLENE, CHARLES M. TIPTON and PETER V. KARPOVICH, *Electrogoniometer Manual.* Springfield, Mass: Springfield College, 1965.

BASS, RUTH I. "An Analysis of the Components of Tests of Semicircular Canal Function and of Static and Dynamic Balance." *Research Quarterly,* 10 (May 1939), 33–52.

BURPEE, ROYAL H. "Differentiation in Physical Education." *Journal of Physical Education,* 18 (March 1931), 130–36.

____. *Seven Quickly Administered Tests of Physical Capacity.* New York: Bureau of Publications, Columbia University, 1940.

COLLINS, VIVIAN D. and EUGENE C. HOWE. "A Preliminary Selection of Tests of Fitness." *American Physical Education Review,* 29 (December 1924), 563–71.

CURETON, THOMAS K. "Flexibility as an Aspect of Physical Fitness." *Research Quarterly,* Supplement, 12 (May 1941), 381–90.

____. "Improving the Physical Fitness of Youth." *Monographs of the Society for Research in Child Development,* Serial No. 95, 29, No. 4, 1964.

____. *Physical Fitness Appraisal and Guidance.* St. Louis: C.V. Mosby Co., 1947.

____. *Physical Fitness of Champion Athletes.* Urbana: University of Illinois Press, 1951.

____. *Physical Fitness Workbook.* St Louis: The C.V. Mosby Co., 1947.

____, LYLE WELSER and W.F. HUFFMAN, "A Short Test for Predicting Motor Fitness." *Research Quarterly,* 16 (May 1945), 106–19.

FLEISHMAN, EDWIN A. *The Structure and Measurement of Physical Fitness.* Englewood Cliffs: Prentice-Hall, Inc., 1964.

FORBES, JOSEPH M. "Characteristics of Flexibility in Boys." Unpublished doctoral dissertation, University of Oregon, 1950.

GATES, DONALD D. and R.P. SHEFFIELD. "Tests of Change of Direction as Measurements of Different Kinds of Motor Ability in Boys of the Seventh, Eighth and Ninth Grades." *Research Quarterly,* 11 (October 1940), 136–74.

JENNETT, CLAIR. "An Investigation of Tests of Agility." Unpublished doctoral dissertation State University of Iowa, 1959.

JOHNSON, BARRY L. and JACK K. NELSON. *Practical Measurements for Evaluation in Physical Education.* Minneapolis: Burgess Publishing Co., 1969.

KARPOVICH, P.V. and G.P. KARPOVICH. "Electrogoniometer: A New Device for Study of Joints in Action." *Federation Proceedings,* Part 1, 18 (March 1959), 79.

KARPOVICH, PETER V. *Physiology of Muscular Activity,* 6th ed. Philadelphia: W.B. Saunders Co., 1967.

LEIGHTON, JACK R. "An Instrument and Technic for the Measurement of Range of Joint Motion." *Archives of Physical Medicine and Rehabilitation,* 36 (September 1955), 571–78.

McCLOY, C.H. and NORMA D. YOUNG. *Tests and Measurements in Health and Physical Education,* 3rd ed. New York: Appleton-Century-Crofts, Inc., 1954.

MOORE, MARGARET L. "The Measurement of Joint Motion: Introductory Review of the Literature." *Physical Therapy Review,* 29 (June 1949), 281.

MUMBY, J. HUGH. "Kinesthetic Acuity and Balance Related to Wrestling Ability." *Research Quarterly,* 24 (October 1953), 327–34.

O'CONNOR, MARY F. and THOMAS K. CURETON. "Motor Fitness Tests for High School Girls." *Research Quarterly,* 16 (December 1945), 302–14.

SCOTT, M. GLADYS and ESTHER FRENCH. *Measurement and Evaluation in Physical Education.* Dubuque, Iowa: Wm. C. Brown Co., 1959.

SEASHORE, HAROLD G. "The Development of a Beam-Walking Test and Its Use in Measuring Development of Balance in Children." *Research Quarterly,* 18 (December 1947), 246–59.

SIERAKOWSKI, FRANCES. "A Study of Change-of-Direction Tests for High School Girls." Unpublished master's thesis, State University of Iowa, 1940.

STERLING, LEROY F. "Effect of Badminton on Physical Fitness." Unpublished master's thesis, University of Illinois, 1955.

WELLS, KATHARINE F. and EVELYN K. DILLON. "The Sit and Reach—A Test of Back and Leg Flexibility." *Research Quarterly,* 23 (March 1952), 115–18.

WIECHEC, F.J. and F.H. KRUSEN. "A New Method of Joint Measurement and a Review of the Literature." *American Journal of Surgery,* 43 (1939), 3.

# CHAPTER SIX
# TESTS OF "SPECIFIC" MOTOR ABILITIES: CARDIOVASCULAR ENDURANCE

A cursory study of the history of cardiovascular endurance tests shows that the first tests used extensively in the field of physical education were predominantly postural tests, i.e., tests that measured the effects of mild exercise or changes in body position (lying, sitting, standing, etc.) upon heart rate and/or blood pressure. Among these tests were the Crampton Blood Ptosis Test,[1,2] the Foster Test,[3] the Schneider Test,[4] the McCurdy Condition Test,[5] and the McCurdy-Larson Test of Organic Efficiency.[6] It is interesting to note that, with few exceptions, these early tests were devised by medical doctors and physiologists rather than practicing physical educators.

It soon became apparent that although these types of tests had merit in distinguishing the pathological from the "normal," i.e., they were valid medical screening tools, they showed little promise in assessing the relative cardiovascular condition of the vast majority of "healthy" young people in the schools.

In response to the above problem, as well as the need to assess the cardiovascular condition of people in the military during World War II, we began to see the development of a series of tests that demanded considerably more involvement of the cardio-respiratory mechanisms. Among these were the Tuttle Pulse-Ratio Test,[7] The Harvard Step Test,[8] and the Carlson Fatigue Curve Test.[9] Numerous variations of the "postural" and step tests are discussed and analyzed in Cureton's book[10] and in the thesis by Dorothy Mae Hart.[11]

With the easier availability of such equipment as treadmills and bicycle ergometers and an increased interest in distinguishing between the cardiovascular condition of "normals" and high-level athletes, we saw the rapid development of maximal and submaximal tests. Among these were the Cureton All-Out Treadmill Test,[12] the Balke Treadmill Test,[13] and the Rhyming Test.[14] In recent years, a number of variations of the maximal and submaximal tests have been published.[15,16,17]

With the advent of electrocardiography, heartography, ballistocardiography, and telemetry, cardiovascular testing has reached a point of complexity that takes it well beyond the scope of this text and the typical school situation.

Finally, before attempting to describe a few of the more practical tests, a distinction must be made between the so-called "postural" tests defined earlier and the tests of cardiovascular endurance. In this text, cardiovascular endurance is characterized by moderate contractions of large muscle groups for relatively long periods of time, during which submaximal or maximal adjustments of the circulatory-respiratory systems to the activity are necessary, as in stepping, swimming, running, cycling, rowing, etc.

This aspect of physical appraisal is extremely complex, when one considers the various elements involved, e.g., the heart, lungs, major blood vessels, the capillary system, and the oxygen and nutrient-carrying capacity of the blood. Typically, measurements of these elements include heart rate; stroke volume of the heart; systolic and diastolic blood pressure; and oxygen utilization taken in the resting state, during exercise, during recovery after exercise, and in numerous combinations.

## "POSTURAL" TESTS

### The Schneider Test

This test is included as an example of the "postural" tests mentioned earlier. It was published by E.C. Schneider in 1920[18] after a careful analysis of the available evidence on the significance of a number of cardiovascular measurements such as: 1) pulse rates in the lying and standing positions; 2) changes in pulse rate from lying to standing position; 3) maximum pulse rate after a standard exercise of stepping up and down on an 18-inch (45.72 cm) bench five times in 15 seconds; 4) changes in pulse rate from the standing position to the rate immediately after exercise; 5) time for the pulse to return to the standing normal rate after a standard 15-second exercise; and 6) change in systolic blood pressure from the lying to standing position.

The Cureton modification of the Schneider test has been selected for further description.[19]

*Equipment.* A 20-inch (50.80 cm) bench; a table or bed; stethoscope; sphygmomanometer; stop watch.

*Description and administration.* 1. The subject rests in the supine position for five minutes or more. If the pulse is more than 70 after five minutes' rest, the rest in the horizontal position should continue for another five minutes at least and the pulse then retaken. The low pulse should be inserted on the Schneider Score Sheet (Table 6–1).

2. The lying systolic blood pressure is taken with a sphygmomanometer.

3. The lying diastolic blood pressure is taken in similar manner, reading the sound at the fourth phase when a change is noted in sound from sharp and clear to muffled sounds. This is somewhat higher on the scale than when the sounds disappear.

4. The standing systolic blood pressure is taken with precautions that the subject is standing on both feet and is in a relaxed state. A word to the subject is helpful as a reminder to stand easily on both feet and to relax.

5. The standing diastolic blood pressure is also taken, similarly to lying diastolic.

6. The standard step-up is demonstrated as one step up and down in 3 seconds or five times in 15 seconds. The subject is asked to step up five times at that rate. The pulse is counted immediately after for 15 seconds and noted on the data sheet as (16 × 4 = 64).

7. Thirty seconds after the exercise, the pulse is again counted for 15 seconds. This is recorded quickly on the data sheet and compared with the standing pulse. If it is higher than the standing pulse, another count is taken beginning 60 seconds after exercise. If this is still higher than the standing pulse, another count is taken at 90 seconds and 120 seconds. On the count equal to or lower than the standing pulse, the procedure is stopped and that pulse is placed in the corresponding time space of the data sheet.

*Scoring.* Place the data at the top of the scoring sheet shown in Table 6-1. Each of the sections—A, B, C, D, E and F—is scored as follows:

**1.** Section A is scored for reclining pulse rate. The appropriate pulse rate interval is circled, as are the equivalent points.

**2.** Section C is scored in like manner for the standing pulse rate.

**3.** Section B is scored on the same line as circled previously for the lying pulse rate. It is important to stay on this same line, as the amount of change is traced from left to right to section B. The amount of change from lying to standing pulse must be subtracted and matched with the headings of section B. The points earned are circled in the body of section B.

**4.** Section D is scored in similar manner to section B. It is important to stay on the same line as was used in scoring the standing pulse rate. The horizontal line is traced from section C to section D horizontally across the page from left to right. The amount of pulse rise from the standing rate to the rate after exercise is noted by subtraction, and this amount is matched with the headings in section D. The points earned are encircled in the body of section D.

**5.** The return of pulse rate to the standing normal is now scored, using section E. The time for the pulse to return to the standing normal is noted and matched with section E. The points earned are encircled.

**6.** The Schneider Index is obtained by adding up the points encircled in each of the six sections. This result is placed in the space provided.

*Reliability and validity.* It is well known that, in addition to exercise, "normal" pulse rate and blood pressure are influenced by age, sex, diurnal changes, season and climate, altitude, air and water movements, loss of sleep, respiration, metabolic activity, changes in body posture, digestion, and emotional factors, just to name a few. Unless these are relatively controlled in test-retest situations, reliability coefficients are apt to be low. In a study of more than 800 male college students, Cureton[20] reported reliability coefficients ranging from .58 to .91 for each separate item and .86 for the entire Schneider Index. McFarland and Huddleston[21] reported reliabilities as high as .89. Apparently, the test is reliable when administered by experienced examiners under identical conditions.

Although today the test is not considered a test of cardiovascular endurance, some attempts have been made to validate it against endurance variables. Espenschade[22] reported a validity coefficient of .78 for 53 college women between the Schneider Index and a relatively mild endurance test of running up and down a flight of twelve steps five times. Henry and Herbig,[23] using college men as subjects, reported a validity coefficient of only .44 between the Schneider Test and the 880-yard (804.6 m) run. Cureton[24] reported a coefficient of .71 between the Schneider Index and a battery of four endurance runs.

*Normative information.* Norms based on over 800 young college men, for each component of the Schneider Test and the total Schneider Index, can be found

**TABLE 6-1  Schneider Index Test—Score Sheet (Cureton Modification)**

Name _____  Date _____  Schneider Index _____

### OBSERVATIONS

Lying Position:        Pulse Rate _____  Systolic BP _____  Diastolic BP _____
Standing Position:     Pulse Rate _____  Systolic BP _____  Diastolic BP _____
STEP EXERCISE (5 steps—chair 20″ high); Pulse Rate Immediately After Exercise _____
Pulse Rate After Exercise:   30 sec _____   60 sec _____   90 sec _____   120 _____

### SCORING TABLE

A. Reclining Pulse Rate

B. Pulse Rate Increase on Standing

| Rate | Points | 0–10 | 11–18 | 19–26 | 27–34 | 35–42 |
|------|--------|------|-------|-------|-------|-------|
| 41–50   | 4  | 4 | 4  | 3  | 2  | 1  |
| 51–60   | 3  | 3 | 3  | 2  | 1  | 0  |
| 61–70   | 3  | 3 | 2  | 1  | 0  | -1 |
| 71–80   | 2  | 3 | 2  | 0  | -1 | -2 |
| 81–90   | 1  | 2 | 1  | -1 | -2 | -3 |
| 91–100  | 0  | 1 | 0  | -2 | -3 | -3 |
| 101–110 | -1 | 0 | -1 | -3 | -3 | -3 |

C. Standing Pulse Rate

D. Pulse Rate Increase Immediately After Exercise

| Rate | Points | 0–10 | 11–20 | 21–30 | 31–40 | 41–50 |
|------|--------|------|-------|-------|-------|-------|
| 51–60   | 4  | 4 | 4  | 3  | 2  | 1  |
| 61–70   | 3  | 3 | 3  | 2  | 1  | 0  |
| 71–80   | 3  | 3 | 2  | 1  | 0  | 0  |
| 81–90   | 2  | 3 | 2  | 1  | 0  | -1 |
| 91–100  | 1  | 2 | 1  | 0  | -1 | -2 |
| 101–110 | 1  | 1 | 0  | -1 | -2 | -3 |
| 111–120 | 0  | 1 | -1 | -2 | -3 | -3 |
| 121–130 | 0  | 0 | -2 | -3 | -3 | -3 |
| 131–140 | -1 | 0 | -3 | -3 | -3 | -3 |

E. Return of Pulse Rate to Standing
   Normal After Exercise

| Seconds | Points |
|---------|--------|
| 0–30   | 3  |
| 31–60  | 2  |
| 61–90  | 1  |
| 91–120 | 0  |
| AFTER 120 | |
| 2–10 beats | |
| above normal | -1 |
| AFTER 120 | |
| 11–30 beats | |
| above normal | -2 |

F. Standing Systolic BP Compared
   with Reclining Systolic BP

| Change in Millimeters | Points |
|-----------------------|--------|
| Rise 30 and more    | -2 |
| Rise 20 to 30       | -1 |
| Rise 16 to 20       | 0  |
| Rise 11 to 15       | 1  |
| Rise of 6 to 10     | 2  |
| No change greater than 5 | 3 |
| Fall of 6 to 10     | 2  |
| Fall of 11 to 15    | 1  |
| Fall of 16 to 20    | 0  |
| Fall of 21 to 25    | -1 |
| Fall of 26 and more | -2 |

Source: University of Illinois (Champaign) Physical Fitness Laboratory Materials.

in Cureton's work.[25] Norms for the same variables are also available for young boys ages 7-17.[26] Caution must be observed in using the latter, however, since low reliability coefficients ranging from .37 to .72 were reported for this age group.

*Comments.*    The Schneider Test is reliable when administered under standardized conditions by experienced examiners. Although some attempts have been made to validate it against cardiovascular endurance items, it should probably be used in the schools as a medical screening test or as a test for older persons suspected of cardiovascular deficiency.

## CARDIOVASCULAR ENDURANCE TESTS: SUBMAXIMAL

### Tuttle Pulse-Ratio Test

As early as 1911, Collis and Pembrey[27] introduced the concept of a practical 1-minute pulse-ratio test. Subsequently, many variations of this concept appeared in the literature, notably that of Campbell,[28] who introduced stepping onto a 13-inch (33.02 cm) stool for 3 minutes at 24 steps per minute and counting the pulse rate for 2 minutes after the exercise. Tuttle picked up on the theme and, after a series of revisions[29,30] that included exercise ranging from 18-50 steps per minute on a 13-inch (33.02 cm) stool, he reverted back to the simplified pulse-ratio test described below.[31] This test correlated .90 with the steps necessary to obtain a 2.5 pulse-ratio as originally described by Tuttle.

*Equipment.*    13-inch (33.02 cm) stool; stopwatch.

*Description and administration.*    The sitting pulse count is taken for one minute. The subject steps up and down on the stool for one minute at the rate of 30 complete step-ups per minute. There are four counts to one complete step-up. The subject sits down immediately after exercise and the pulse rate is taken continuously for 2 minutes.

*Scoring.*    The 2-minute pulse count divided by the 1-minute resting pulse count is the pulse-ratio.

*Reliability and validity.*    Henry and Farmer[32] reported a reliability coefficient of .78 for the pulse-ratio test. In a study using 105 women ages 17-23, Phillips, et al.,[33] found test-retest coefficients of .85, .84, and .77 for resting heart rate, heart rate after exercise, and pulse-ratio, respectively. They felt that .77 was not sufficiently high to justify its use for college women. They also recognized a fallacy in the pulse-ratio test in that it had a tendency to favor those with higher resting heart rates.

Flanagan[34] reported a validity coefficient of -.89 between pulse-ratio and a ratio between times in two sprinting events—220-yard (201.17 m) and 60-yard (54.86 m) sprints. This relatively high correlation was questioned by Henry and Kleeberger,[35] who replicated the study and found correlations of only -.46 when speed was held constant and -.42 when speed and body weight were held constant. This is probably a moot point, since neither the 60-yard (54.86 m) nor the 220-yard (201.17 m) sprint would be considered tests of cardiovascular endurance by modern exercise physiologists.

*Normative information.*   Cureton[36] published norms for the simplified pulse-ratio test using 53 college-age male subjects. He also reported norms based on between 96 and 116 males, 26 to 60 years of age, for pulse ratios after workloads of 12, 18, 24, 30, and 36 steps per minute.[37] However, in the latter work, he used a 16-18 inch (40.64 cm to 45.72 cm) bench.

*Comments.*   The simplified pulse-ratio test is a practical but only moderately reliable and valid test of cardiovascular endurance. Whereas the test is probably of little value by itself in predicting higher levels of cardiovascular endurance, it would have value in distinguishing between those with normal vs. deficient cardiovascular systems, or as part of a battery of tests. The test is sensitive to training, however, and could be used to reflect cardiovascular improvements due to various training programs.

### The Harvard Step Test and Modifications

It is probably safe to say that the Harvard Step Test or modifications thereof have been the most widely used cardiovascular endurance tests in physical education. The original test was devised by Brouha and associates[38] in 1943. This test and a few modifications are described here.

### The Harvard Step Test

*Equipment.*   20-inch (50.80 cm) bench; stopwatch; metronome (optional).

*Description and administration.*   At the signal "Up," the subject places one foot on the platform; steps up, placing both feet fully on the platform; straightens the legs and back; and immediately steps down again, one foot at a time. The pace is counted by the tester: up-up-down-down, the command "Up" coming every 2 seconds. The subject should lead off and step down with the same foot each time. The tester begins keeping the time as soon as the subject starts. The exercise is continued for 5 minutes unless the subject stops because of fatigue or exhaustion. The subject sits down immediately upon cessation of exercise and, after noting the duration of exercise, the tester records the pulse from 1-1½, 2-2½ and 3-3½ minutes after exercise; i.e., the first pulse count is not taken until the subject has rested for 1 minute.

*Scoring.*   The three half-minute pulse counts are summed and then multiplied by two. The duration of exercise in seconds is multiplied by 100. The Index is obtained by the following formula:

$$\text{Fitness Index} = \frac{\text{Duration of exercise period in seconds} \times 100}{2 \times \text{sum of pulse counts after exercise}}$$

For those who could not complete the 5-minute test, Brouha proposed the following scoring scheme:

| Duration | Score |
| --- | --- |
| less than 2 minutes | 25 |
| from   2–3    " | 38 |
| "    3–3½  " | 48 |
| "    3½–4   " | 52 |
| "    4–4½  " | 55 |
| "    4½–5   " | 59 |

Also included in the original article is a table from which the score could be obtained directly from the sum of the three pulse counts for those who finished the entire 5 minutes of exercise.

*Reliability and validity.*    Reliability coefficients were not reported for the original test. Cureton, however, reported reliabilities ranging from .73 to .86 for various groups of college-age men.[39]

Although validity coefficients were not published by Brouha, he did present evidence that the test differentiated between trained and untrained people. Attempts at validating this test have produced rather negligible results. One of the problems has been that early researchers[40] tended to employ strength or muscular endurance items as validating test criteria rather than submaximal or maximal tests of cardiovascular endurance. Most notable of these was the study by Cureton,[41] who reported correlations ranging from .002 to .31 between the step test and 27 predominantly *muscular endurance* items. Interestingly, the highest correlation was with the mile run which, on a logical basis, came closest to being a cardiovascular endurance event. The validity coefficient between the step test and the entire battery of 27 tests was only .27.

*Normative information.*    Brouha's original norms based on thousands of young men were as follows:

| | | |
| --- | --- | --- |
| below  55 | — | poor condition |
| from   55–64 | — | low average |
| from   65–79 | — | high average |
| from   80–89 | — | good |
| above  90 | — | excellent |

Norms for the sum of three pulse counts (young men) were also published by Cureton.[42]

*Comments.* The original Harvard Step Test is a practical test of cardiovascular endurance. It can be used to distinguish between the trained and the untrained and as an indicator of improvement resulting from participation in endurance training programs. One of its features is that large numbers can be tested simultaneously.

The reliability of the test is probably adequate for relatively trained young men, but one of the less strenuous modifications should be used for the untrained and older subject.

### Harvard Step Test—Short Form

A rapid form for scoring the Harvard Step Test was developed based on the duration of exercise and a single pulse count taken from 1–1½ minutes after exercise.[43] The scoring formula is:

$$\text{Index} = \frac{\text{Duration of exercise in seconds} \times 100}{5.5 \times \text{pulse count 1–1½ minutes after exercise}}$$

The score obtained is interpreted as follows:

below 50    —    poor
50–80       —    average
above 80    —    good

A handy scoring table can be found in Mathews' book.[44]

### Gallagher and Brouha Modification
### (High School Boys).[45]

The Harvard Step Test was modified for use with boys 12–18 years of age. Boys with a surface area (based on height and weight) less than 1.85 use an 18-inch (45.72 cm) bench; those with a surface area of 1.85 or more use a 20-inch (50.80 cm) bench. A nomogram for determining body surface area is included in the article. The time of work has been reduced to 4 minutes for both groups. The sequence of pulse counts and the formula for scoring are similar to those used originally for college men. Also included is a table from which the score can be obtained directly from the sum of the 3 pulse counts for those who finish the entire 4 minutes of exercise. The score obtained is interpreted as follows:

50 or less    —    very poor
51–60         —    poor
61–70         —    fair
71–80         —    good
81–90         —    excellent
91 or more    —    superior

### The Clarke Modification (College Women)[46]

The height of the bench is reduced to 18 inches (45.72 cm) and the duration of exercise is four minutes. The sequence for pulse counts and the formula for scoring are the same as the original Harvard Step Test. The physical fitness index can be obtained directly from a nomogram included in the article. The 6-category classification for interpreting college men's scores is also used for college women.

### Brouha and Ball Modification (Elementary School Boys and Girls)[47]

The height of the bench is reduced to 14 inches (35.56 cm) for boys and girls under 12 years of age. Children 7 years old or under exercise for 2 minutes. Those from 8-12 years exercise for 3 minutes. The sequence of the pulse counts and the formula for scoring are the same as for college men. The scores are interpreted as follows:

| AGE | AVERAGE SCORE | |
|---|---|---|
| 7 years or less | 40 | — above, good; below, poor |
| 7–10 | 57 | —    ”       ”       ”       ” |
| 10–12 | 61 | —    ”       ”       ”       ” |

### Skubic and Hodgkins Modification (Girls and Women)[48]

The basic procedures are followed as were described for the Harvard Step Test, except that: 1) the bench is 18 inches (45.72 cm) rather than 20 inches (50.80 cm); 2) the sequence is 24 steps per minute rather than 30; 3) the duration of exercise is 3 minutes rather than 5, and 4) only one pulse count is taken (1–1½ minutes after exercise). The same procedures as the Harvard Step Test apply to those who cannot complete the entire 3 minutes; i.e., 1 minute after exercise the time is noted and the pulse is counted for 30 seconds.

The score is determined as follows:

$$\text{Cardiovascular Efficiency Score} = \frac{\text{No. of seconds completed} \times 100}{\text{recovery pulse} \times 5.6}$$

Norms for junior and senior high school girls[49] and for college women[50] have been published. It should be noted that this test has a test-retest reliability of .82.

Although validity coefficients were not reported, this test differentiated successfully among sedentary, active, and well-trained subjects.

## CARDIOVASCULAR ENDURANCE
## TESTS: MAXIMAL

Historically, the sequence of the development of tests of cardiovascular endurance is a logical one. The early, so-called postural tests tended to distinguish between the "normal" and "pathological," whereas the later step tests attempted to measure relative levels of cardiovascular fitness of "normal" individuals. It was only a matter of time before the normal curve of human cardiovascular capacity would be completed, i.e., tests would be developed to distinguish between "normals" and top endurance athletes.

Following World War II, we saw increased interest in the development of "all-out" tests of cardiovascular endurance. These tests are impractical for use in typical school situations or community physical fitness programs, since they require expensive laboratory facilities such as treadmills and bicycle ergometers as well as highly trained technicians. A few of these tests are mentioned briefly in the next pages, since more and more schools and colleges are installing human performance laboratories not only for the purpose of studying high-level athletes but also for the monitoring of adults in physical fitness and cardiac rehabilitation programs. Three main methods have been used for producing standard workloads: running on a treadmill; pedalling on a bicycle ergometer; and stepping on a bench.

### The "All-Out" Treadmill Run

Cureton[51,52] described a treadmill run at 7 m.p.h. with an 8.6% grade that would bring most ordinary subjects to maximal oxygen intake values, and the same test at 10 mph or 13.5 mph that would bring most top endurance athletes to maximum. Basically, the tests consists of: 1) a 5-minute quiet sitting metabolism test; 2) 5 minutes of warm-up practice on the treadmill, including 30 seconds of hard running; and 3) all-out run to exhaustion for time, with all expired air metered, collected, and analyzed during the run and for 15 minutes after the run. Heart rate is recorded continuously by means of an electrocardiograph.

Reliability coefficients for tests on young boys for several oxygen intake variables can be found in the study by Brown,[53] and means and standard deviations for young men for run time and a number of oxygen intake variables may be found in Sterling's work.[54]

The disadvantages of this type of test are obvious: They are time-consuming; they require expensive equipment; several laboratory assistants are needed; they cause tensing up of inexperienced subjects due to fear of falling; etc. This test is probably most valuable for testing trained endurance athletes.

### The Balke Treadmill Test[55]

This test is based on the assumption that when, during a given exercise, a subject's heart rate reaches 180 beats per minute, cardiovascular capacity has been reached. Basically, the test consists of having a subject walk on a treadmill at a constant speed while the heart rate is measured each minute. At the end of 1 minute, the slope of the treadmill is increased to a 2% grade; at the end of each succeeding minute, the slope is increased by 1% until the heart rate reaches 180 beats per minute.

Balke suggested the following rating system for his test:

| MINUTES TO REACH HEART RATE OF 180 | CLASSIFICATION |
|---|---|
| 12–below | very poor |
| 13–14 | poor |
| 15–16 | fair |
| 17 | average |
| 18–19 | good |
| 20–21 | very good |
| 22–above | excellent |

Norms for performance time for college males were also published by Howell and Associates.[56]

Little is known of the reliability of this test. Alderman,[57] using young men, studied the test-retest reliability of individual responses to graded exercise on a bicycle ergometer rather than the treadmill. He found that the reliability increased to .89 up to 160 heart beats per minute and tapered off thereafter.

The advantages of the Balke Test over an all-out run are obvious. All that is needed is a treadmill, stopwatch, and electrocardiograph for measuring heart rate. Apprehension is decreased by use of walking rather than running, and the necessity of gas analysis is eliminated. The test is applicable for young "normals" as well as older subjects.

### The Kasch Step Test of Maximal Work Capacity

Seldom has the step test been used as a device for inducing maximum work. Kasch and associates[58,59] described such a test. It makes use of a 12-inch (30.48 cm) padded bench and consists basically of the following: 1) a 5–7 minute warm-up on the 12-inch (30.48 cm) bench, increasing the heart rate to 140–180 beats per minute or 80% of maximum; 2) a 10-minute rest period; 3) a stepping rate that starts at 24 steps per minute and is increased by 3 steps each 2–3 minutes until maximum is reached (maximum step rates usually range between 37–60); and 4) collection of expired air during the last 3–4 minutes of exercise. (This is analyzed later to determine oxygen intake capacity).

The obvious advantage of this test is the substitution of an inexpensive bench for expensive treadmills or bicycle ergometers. It does, however, necessitate collecting and analyzing gas samples and associated mathematical computations. The test is relatively safe and is easily applicable for young "normals" and older subjects.

## SUBMAXIMAL TESTS FOR PREDICTION OF MAXIMAL CARDIOVASCULAR ENDURANCE

In recent years a series of submaximal tests that purport to predict maximal cardio-vascular endurance have appeared. Some of these are scaled-down versions of the Balke test described earlier. For example, Billings and associates[60] found that the time required to reach a heart rate of only 150 beats yielded information sufficiently comparable to Balke's maximal test. A few of the more practical tests will be described briefly here.

### The Åstrand Submaximal Test[61]

This test is based on the assumption that, provided the workload is not too heavy, respiration and circulation will increase during the first few minutes of exercise and then attain a steady state. For most people, this steady state will be reached at a heart rate of between 130 and 160 beats per minute. This bicycle ergometer test consists mainly of the following: 1) a workload is predetermined based on age, sex, and general condition (trained or untrained); 2) the subject is seated such that when the front part of the foot is on the pedal, the knee is slightly bent in the lowest position, i.e., with the front of the knee directly over the tip of the foot; 3) the subject pedals at 50 rpm and the heart rate is recorded every minute, preferably during the last 15-20 seconds of each working minute; and 4) the mean value of the heart rate at the fifth and sixth minutes of exercise is designated as the working pulse for the load in question. If the difference between the last two heart rates exceeds 5 beats per minute, the test should be prolonged one or more minutes until a constant level is reached.

Suggestions for predetermined workloads; tables for prediction of maximum oxygen intake based on age, sex and body weight; and norm tables by age group and sex can be found in the previously cited source. These have been determined from work done on the Monark bicycle ergometer.[62]

This test is particularly applicable for adult fitness programs. It considers the effect of a particular training program when the pulse response in the same individual is compared before and after the program and the subject serves as his or her own control.

### The Ohio State University Step Test[63]

This test is based on the assumption that the time it takes for the heart rate to reach 150 beats per minute is indicative of the individual's (young man 18 years or older) cardiovascular capacity for maximal work.

*Equipment.* A split-level bench, 15 inches (38.10 cm) high on one level, 20 inches (50.80 cm) on the other, with an adjustable hand bar; metronome; stopwatch.

*Description and administration.*  The test consists of three continuous phases: 1) six bouts or "innings" at 24 steps per minute on the 15-inch (38.10 cm) bench; 2) six innings at 30 steps per minute, also on the 15-inch (38.10 cm) bench; and 3) six innings at 30 steps per minute on the 20-inch (50.80 cm) bench for a total of 18 innings. Each inning is 50 seconds in duration and is divided into a 30-second exercise period and a 20-second rest period. Heart rate is taken for 10 seconds during each rest period, beginning with the fifth second and ending with the fifteenth. Thus, the subject has 5 seconds to get set for the next inning of exercise. The test is terminated when the subject's heart rate reaches 25 beats in any 10-second pulse-counting period (150 beats per minute). At the end of the sixth inning, after the 10-second pulse count has been obtained, the cadence is increased to 30 steps per minute. At the end of the twelfth inning, after the 10-second pulse count has been obtained, the subject is told to move over to the 20-inch (50.80 cm) bench and the 30 steps per minute cadence is maintained for the remainder of the test. If completed, the entire test is 15 minutes in duration.

*Scoring.*  The subject's score is the inning in which the heart rate reaches 150 beats per minute, i.e., the inning in which a heart rate of 25 beats is recorded during any 10-second pulse-counting period. The subject's score is 18, if all 18 innings of exercise are completed.

*Reliability and validity.*  The author reported a test-retest reliability of .94. When validated against the Balke test described earlier, the validity coefficient was also .94.

*Normative information.*  The author did not publish norms, but he did report the following means and standard deviations for males in various age groups, from which norms can be calculated easily:

| AGE GROUP | MEAN INNINGS | STANDARD DEVIATION |
| --- | --- | --- |
| 19–29 | 12.4 | 4.7 |
| 30–40 | 13.0 | 4.0 |
| 41–56 | 11.8 | 3.4 |

*Comments.*  This submaximal test appears to be reliable and valid for predicting cardiovascular capacity for maximal exercise. It is safe and has the obvious advantage of not requiring expensive equipment. Since the workload is increased gradually, it can be used for both unfit and highly trained individuals.

### The 12-Minute Run-Walk Test[64]

By the 1960s, the measurement of cardiovascular fitness had become almost synonymous with the measurement of maximum oxygen capacity. Since the latter required special expertise and expensive equipment, it was impractical for testing large numbers of people. Thus, the search was on for a practical field test that would correlate highly with maximum oxygen intake capacity. As early as 1963, Balke[65] proposed a 15-minute run-walk test. Considerable interest has also centered on the 9-minute run-walk, 1-mile (1.61 km) run-walk, and 1.5-mile (2.42 km) run tests reported by Jackson.[66] But the 12-minute run-walk test proposed by Cooper[67,68] has probably enjoyed the most widespread popularity and generated the most research activity.

*Equipment.* All that is needed is a stopwatch, a starting device (whistle), and an accurately measured track or running area.

*Description and administration.* The subjects stretch and warm up, then assemble behind a starting line. At the whistle, they run and/or walk as far as possible in 12 minutes. After their scores are posted, they should be given sufficient time to cool down.

Since some would have a tendency to exhaust themselves too quickly, they should be given some instruction and practice in pacing before the test is administered.

*Scoring.* The score is the distance in miles (kilometers) covered in 12 minutes. If the running surface is marked in yards, the conversion factor is 1760 yards = 1 mile. If the running surface is marked in meters, the conversion factor is 1000 meters = 1 kilometer.

*Reliability and validity.* Apparently, Cooper did not report a reliability coefficient for his test in 1968. Other studies have reported coefficients ranging from .75[69] to .94.[70] A summary of a number of reliability coefficients reported in the literature can be found in Safrit.[71]

Validity coefficients for this test correlated against maximum oxygen intake capacity abound in the literature. These range from .34[72] to .90.[73] Cooper[74] also reported a validity coefficient of .90 on the original test performed on 115 males, ages 17-52. A summary of a number of validity coefficients reported in the literature can also be found in Safrit.[75]

*Normative information.* Norms for both sexes and for age groups ranging from 13-60 years and older are shown in Safrit.[76] Norms for boys and girls (grades 5-8) can be found in Clarke.[77]

*Comments.* The 12-minute run-walk test is simple, practical, and inexpensive. A large number of subjects can be tested simultaneously. It can be used with most age groups and for both sexes.

There is general agreement that the test is reliable, although it probably is not as reliable for female as for male subjects. This may be due to the possibility that females have less experience in pacing than males. In any event, practice in pacing should be conducted before testing of subjects of both sexes.

There is some question of the test's predictive validity using maximum oxygen intake capacity as the external criterion. Few researchers have been able to obtain the high validity coefficient (.90) reported by Cooper. This might be due to the differences in homogeneity (in age) of groups of subjects used in various studies. Most studies have used relatively homogeneous groups, whereas Cooper's subjects ranged from 17-52 years of age.

### BIBLIOGRAPHY

ALDERMAN, RICHARD B. "Reliability of Individual Differences in the 180 Heart Rate Response Test in Bicycle Ergometer Work." *Research Quarterly,* 37 (October 1966), 429-31.

ÅSTRAND, P.O. and KAARE RODAHL. *Textbook of Work Physiology.* New York: McGraw-Hill Book Co., 1970.

BALKE, B. "A Simple Test for the Assessment of Physical Fitness." CARI Report, Civil Aeromedical Research Institute, Aviation Agency, Oklahoma City, 1963.

BAUMGARTNER, TED A. and ANDREW S. JACKSON. *Measurement for Evaluation in Physical Education.* Boston: Houghton-Mifflin Company, 1975.

BILLINGS, CHARLES E., J. TOMASHEFSKI, E.T. CARTER, and W. ASHE. "Measurement of Human Capacity For Aerobic Muscular Work." *Journal of Applied Physiology,* 15 (September 1960), 1001-1006.

BOOKWALTER, KARL W. "A Study of the Brouha Step Test." *The Physical Educator,* 5 (May 1948), 55.

BROUHA, L. and M.V. BALL. *Canadian Red Cross Society's School Meal Study.* Toronto: University of Toronto Press, 1952.

BROUHA, LUCIEN. "The Step Test: A Simple Method of Measuring Physical Fitness for Muscular Work in Young Men." *Research Quarterly,* 14 (March 1943), 32-36.

BROWN, STANLEY, "Factors Influencing Improvement in the Oxygen Intake of Young Boys." Unpublished doctoral dissertation, University of Illinois, 1960.

CAMPBELL, J.M.H. "The Pulse Rate after Exercise in Health and Disease." *Guy's Hospital Reports,* 77 (1917), 184-215.

CARLSON, H.C. "Fatigue Curve Test." *Research Quarterly,* 16 (October 1945), 169-75.

CLARKE, H. HARRISON. *Application of Measurement to Health and Physical Education,* 5th ed. Englewood Cliffs, N.J.: Prentice-Hall, Inc., 1976.

____. "A Functional Physical Fitness Test for College Women." *Journal of Health and Physical Education,* 14 (September 1943), 358-9.

COLLIS, E.L. and M.S. PEMBREY. "Observations Upon the Effects of Warm Humid Atmospheres in Man." *Journal of Physiology,* 43 (1911), 11.

COOPER, KENNETH H. "A Means of Assessing Maximum Oxygen Intake." *Journal of the American Medical Association,* 203 (1968), 201-4.

____. *The Aerobics Way.* New York: M. Evans and Company, 1977.

____. *The New Aerobics.* New York: Bantam Books, 1970.

CRAMPTON, C.W. "The Blood Ptosis Test and its use in Experimental Work in Hygiene." *Proceedings of the Society for Experimental Biology and Medicine,* 12 (1915), 119.

____. "A Test of Condition: A Preliminary Report." *Medical News,* 87 (September 1905), 529-35.

CURETON, THOMAS K., *Endurance of Young Men.* Washington: Society for Research in Child Development, National Research Council, 1945.

____. *Improving the Physical Fitness of Youth.* Monographs of the Society for Research in Child Development, Serial No. 95, Vol. 29, No. 4, 1964.

_____. *Physical Fitness Appraisal and Guidance.* St Louis: C.V. Mosby Co., 1947.

_____. *Physical Fitness of Champion Athletes.* Urbana: University of Illinois Press, 1951.

_____. *The Physiological Effects of Exercise Programs on Adults.* Springfield, Il: Charles C. Thomas Co., 1969.

DOOLITTLE, R.L. and ROLLIN BIGBEE. "The Twelve-Minute Run-Walk: A Test of Cardiorespiratory Fitness of Adolescent Boys." *Research Quarterly,* 39 (1968), 491–95.

DOOLITTLE, R.L., J.C. DOMINIC, and J. DOOLITTLE. "The Reliability of Selected Cardio-Respiratory Endurance Field Tests with Adolescent Female Populations." *American Corrective Therapy Journal,* 23 (1969), 135–38.

ESPENSCHADE, ANNA. "A Study of the Factors of Physical Endurance." *Research Quarterly,* Supplement, 9 (March 1938), 11–12.

FLANAGAN, K. "The Pulse Ratio Test as a Measure of Athletic Endurance in Sprint Running." *Research Quarterly,* 6 (October 1935), 46–50.

FOSTER, W.I. "A Test of Physical Efficiency." *American Physical Education Review,* 19 (December 1914), 632–36.

GALLAGHER, J.R. and L. BROUHA. "A Simple Method of Testing the Physical Fitness of Boys." *Research Quarterly,* 14 (March 1943), 23–30.

GUTIN, B., R.K. FOGLE, and K. STEWART. "Relationship among Submaximal Heart Rate, Aerobic Power, and Running Performance in Children." *Research Quarterly,* 47 (1976), 536–39.

HART, DOROTHY MAE. "A History of Cardiovascular Testing of Normal Subjects." Unpublished master's thesis, University of Illinois, 1946.

HENRY, F. and W. HERBIG. "The Correlations of Various Functional Tests of the Cardio-Circulatory System with Changes in Athletic Conditions of Distance Runners." *Research Quarterly,* 13 (May 1942), 185–200.

HENRY, FRANKLIN M. and DANIEL FARMER. "Functional Tests II: The Reliability of the Pulse Ratio Test." *Research Quarterly,* 9 (May 1938), 81–87.

HENRY, FRANKLIN M. and FRANK L. KLEEBERGER, "The Validity of the Pulse Ratio Test of Cardiac Efficiency." *Research Quarterly,* 9 (March 1938), 32–46.

HODGKINS, JEAN and VERA SKUBIC. "Cardiovascular Efficiency Test Scores for College Women in the United States." *Research Quarterly,* 34 (December 1963), 454–61.

HOWELL, MAXWELL L., et al. "Progressive Treadmill Test Norms for College Males." *Research Quarterly,* 35 (October 1954), 322–25.

JACKSON, ANDREW S. "Technical Report 1: Normative Study of the Texas Physical Fitness Motor Ability Test." Mimeographed material from Governor's Commission on Physical Fitness, Austin, 1974.

JESSUP, GEORGE T., HOMER TOLSON and JAMES W. TERRY. "Prediction of Maximal Oxygen Intake Capacity from Åstrand-Rhyming Test, 12-minute Run and Anthropometric Variables Using Stepwise Multiple Regression." Paper read at AAHPER Convention, Minneapolis, 1973.

JOHNSON, R.E. and S. ROBINSON. "Selection of Men for Physical Work in Hot Weather." Appendix I, CMR, OSRD, Report 16, Harvard Fatigue Laboratory, 1943.

KASCH, F.W., et al., "A Comparison of Maximum Oxygen Uptake by Treadmill and Step Test." *Journal of Applied Physiology,* 21 (July 1966), 1387–88.

_____. "Maximum Work Capacity in Middle-Aged Males by a Step Test Method." *Journal of Sports Medicine* 5 (December 1965), 198–202.

KURUSZ, ROBERT L. "Construction of the Ohio State University Cardiovascular Fitness Test." Unpublished doctoral dissertation, The Ohio State University, September, 1967.

MATHEWS, DONALD K. *Measurement in Physical Education,* 3rd ed. Philadelphia: W.B. Saunders Co., 1968.

McCURDY, J.H. and L.A. LARSON. "Measurement of Organic Efficiency for Prediction of Physical Condition." *Research Quarterly,* Supplement, 6 (May 1935), 11–41.

McCURDY, J.H. *Physiology of Exercise,* 1st ed. Philadelphia: Lea and Febiger, 1924.

McFARLAND, R.A. and J.H. HUDDLESTON. "Neurocirculatory Reactions in the Psychoneuroses Studied by the Schneider Method." *American Journal Psychiatry,* 93 (November 1936), 567–99.

PHILLIPS, MARJORIE, ELOISE RIDDER, and HELEN YEAKEL. "Further Data on the Pulse Ratio Test." *Research Quarterly,* 14 (December 1943), 425–29.

RHYMING, IRMA. "A Modified Harvard Step Test for the Evaluation of Physical Fitness." *Arbeitsphysiologie,* 15 (1954), 235–50.

SAFRIT, MARGARET J. *Evaluation in Physical Education,* 2nd ed. Englewood Cliffs, N.J.: Prentice-Hall, Inc., 1981.

SCHNEIDER, E.C. "A Cardiovascular Rating as a Measure of Physical Fitness and Efficiency." *Journal of the American Medical Association,* 74 (May 1920), 1507.

SKUBIC, VERA and JEAN HODGKINS. "Cardiovascular Efficiency Test for Girls and Women." *Research Quarterly,* 34 (May 1963), 191–98.

____. "Cardiovascular Efficiency Test Scores for Junior and Senior High School Girls in the United States." *Research Quarterly,* 35 (May 1964), 184–92.

STERLING, LEROY F. "A Factoral Analysis of Cardiovascular Variables." Unpublished doctoral dissertation, University of Illinois, 1960.

TRUETT, JEANNE T., HERBERT BENSON, and BRUNO BALKE. "On the Practicability of Submaximal Exercise Testing." *Journal of Chronic Disease,* 19 (1966), 711–15.

TUTTLE, W.W. and GEORGE WELLS. "The Response of the Normal Heart to Exercises of Graded Intensity." *Arbeitsphysiologie,* 4 (1931), 519–26.

TUTTLE, W.W. and R.E. DICKINSON. "A Simplification of the Pulse-Ratio Technique for Rating Physical Efficiency and Present Conditions." *Research Quarterly,* 9 (May 1938), 73–81.

TUTTLE, W.W. "The Use of the Pulse Ratio Test for Rating Physical Efficiency." *Research Quarterly,* 2 (1931), 5–17.

# CHAPTER SEVEN
# TESTS OF GENERAL MOTOR ABILITY

Literally hundreds of motor ability tests are available when one considers the professional literature; the efforts of the states and the federal government, military organizations, private and semiprivate sports organizations; and the efforts of individual schools, colleges, and universities. A small list of 25 is included in Table 4-3. A longer list of 69 may be found in the manual written by McCollum and McCorkle,[1] who categorized the tests by source (nearly all secondary), sex, and school or age level. Only a small representative sample of the tests will be briefly reviewed.

For years, writers of measurement books in physical education have been stymied in their attempts to systematically and consistently categorize the various motor ability tests. Some tests purport to measure motor educability, i.e., the facility with which an individual is able to learn *new* motor "skills."[2,3,4,5]

Others attempt to measure *motor capacity*, i.e., an individual's innate *potential* for performance of motor "skills." Most claim the measurement of *general motor ability,* i.e., the efficiency with which a person performs motor tests at the time of testing.

No attempt to categorize tests in terms of these definitions will be made here. Instead, all tests will be deemed tests of *general* motor ability, defined as tests composed of two or more specific components identified and discussed in Chapters 4, 5, and 6, namely, strength, power, agility, flexibility, balance, muscular endurance, and cardiovascular endurance.

The tests we will review were selected, in most cases, according to the following criteria: common usage; practicality; some attention to reliability and statistical validity; and availability of norms. Because of space limitation, a slightly different format will be used in this chapter. Unlike Chapters 4 through 6, description and administration of tests will not be given. Instead, an attempt will be made to identify the "specific" components being measured, according to the definitions used in the cited chapters.

### Carpenter Motor Ability Test[6,7]

*Sex and age.* Boys and girls, grades 1, 2, and 3.

*Equipment.* Mat; 4-pound (1.81 kg) shot; measuring tape; weight scale.

*Items tested.* Broad jump; shot put; body weight.

*Motor ability components tested.* Power.

*Scoring.* Two multiple regression equations for predicting general motor ability were developed:

girls: standing broad jump + 1.5 shot put + .05 weight

boys: standing broad jump + 2.5 shot put + .5 weight

*Reliability and validity.* No reliability coefficients were reported, but other authors have reported coefficients as high as .96 for the standing broad jump. Using a battery of items as the test criterion, internal validity coefficients of .84 and .82 were reported for boys and girls, respectively.

*Normative information.* Norms for the above equations were not developed, but a Physical Efficiency Index was devised utilizing a second set of equations and McCloy's Classification Index,[8] (10 × age) + weight, for elementary school children. Norms for the latter are available for both boys and girls (Carpenter, October, 1942).

*Comments.* Although this test purports to measure general motor ability, it is obvious that the major items tested are the power events defined in Chapter 4. The inclusion of additional components of motor ability would be desirable.

### The Illinois Motor Fitness Test[9]

*Sex and age.* Young men, ages 15-25.

*Equipment.* Chinning bar; stopwatch.

*Items tested.* Sitting tucks; pull-ups; one-mile (1.61 km) run.

*Motor ability components tested.* Muscular endurance; cardiovascular endurance.

*Scoring.* Methods for obtaining raw scores for each test item were included with descriptions of the test items. Tables for converting raw scores to product scores were included in the original publication, but a more comprehensive, revised version is shown in Table 7-1. The test is scored by circling the raw score of each item. The adjacent product score is the weighted score, i.e., the standard score times the weighting coefficient. To arrive at the final score, the sum of the three product scores is taken.

*Reliability and validity.* For various groups of young men, test-retest reliability coefficients were reported for sitting tucks (.90-.92), chins (.89-.95), and mile (1.16 km) run (.80-.89).

An extensive validity and factor analysis was made using 28 predominantly muscular endurance items. Through the use of multiple regression and prediction equations, it was possible to derive three items that would be highly predictive of all 28. Using all 28 items as the internal validity criterion, validity coefficients of .60, .65, and .71 were reported for sitting tucks, chins, and mile (1.61 km) run, respectively. The three combined gave a multiple correlation (predictive value) of .88 with all 28 items.

**TABLE 7-1  University of Illinois Motor Fitness Test Scoring Tables**

PRODUCT TABLE*

| STANDARD SCORE | SITTING TUCKS (.401) | | CHINNING THE BAR (.366) | | MILE (1.61 km.) RUN (.411) | | TOTAL PRODUCT | PERCENTILE SCORES |
|---|---|---|---|---|---|---|---|---|
| | RAW SCORE | PRODUCT | RAW SCORE | PRODUCT | RAW SCORE | PRODUCT | | |
| 100 | 115 | 40.1 | 22.5 | 36.5 | 4:35 | 41.1 | 117.8 | 99.87 |
| 98 | 112 | 39.0 | 22.0 | 35.5 | 4:40 | 40.0 | 114.5 | |
| 96 | 110 | 38.0 | 21.5 | 35.0 | 4:45 | 39.0 | 112.0 | |
| 94 | 108 | 37.5 | 21.0 | 34.0 | 4:50 | 38.5 | 110.0 | |
| 92 | 106 | 37.0 | 20.5 | 33.5 | 4:55 | 38.0 | 108.5 | |
| 90 | 104 | 36.0 | 20.0 | 33.0 | 5:00 | 37.0 | 106.0 | 99.18 |
| 88 | 102 | 35.0 | 19.5 | 32.0 | 5:05 | 36.0 | 103.0 | |
| 86 | 100 | 34.0 | 19.0 | 31.0 | 5:10 | 35.0 | 100.0 | |
| 84 | 97 | 33.5 | 18.5 | 30.5 | 5:15 | 34.5 | 98.5 | |
| 82 | 95 | 33.0 | 18.0 | 30.0 | 5:20 | 35.0 | 97.0 | |
| 80 | 93 | 32.0 | 17.5 | 29.0 | 5:25 | 33.0 | 94.0 | 96.40 |
| 78 | 91 | 31.0 | 17.0 | 28.5 | 5:30 | 32.0 | 91.5 | |
| 76 | 89 | 30.0 | 16.5 | 28.0 | 5:35 | 31.0 | 89.0 | |
| 74 | 87 | 29.5 | 16.0 | 27.0 | 5:40 | 30.0 | 86.5 | |
| 72 | 85 | 29.0 | 15.5 | 26.0 | 5:45 | 29.5 | 84.5 | |
| 70 | 82 | 28.0 | 15.0 | 25.5 | 5:50 | 29.0 | 82.5 | 83.4 |
| 68 | 80 | 27.0 | 14.5 | 25.0 | 5:55 | 28.0 | 80.0 | |
| 66 | 78 | 26.0 | 14.0 | 24.0 | 6:00 | 27.0 | 78.0 | |
| 64 | 76 | 25.5 | 13.5 | 23.0 | 6:05 | 26.0 | 74.5 | |
| 62 | 74 | 25.0 | 13.0 | 22.5 | 6:10 | 25.0 | 72.5 | |
| 60 | 72 | 24.0 | 12.5 | 22.0 | 6:15 | 24.5 | 70.5 | 72.6 |
| 58 | 70 | 23.0 | 12.0 | 21.0 | 6:20 | 24.0 | 68.0 | |
| 56 | 67 | 22.0 | 11.5 | 20.5 | 6:25 | 23.0 | 65.5 | |
| 54 | 65 | 21.5 | 11.0 | 20.0 | 6:30 | 22.0 | 63.5 | |
| 52 | 63 | 21.0 | 10.5 | 19.0 | 6:35 | 21.0 | 61.0 | |

| | | | | | | | | Product* |
|---|---|---|---|---|---|---|---|---|
| 50 | 61 | 20.0 | 10.0 | 18.0 | 6:40 | 20.0 | 58.0 | 50.0 |
| 48 | 59 | 19.0 | 9.5 | 17.5 | 6:45 | 19.5 | 55.5 | |
| 46 | 57 | 18.0 | 9.0 | 17.0 | 6:50 | 19.0 | 54.0 | |
| 44 | 55 | 17.5 | 8.5 | 16.0 | 6:55 | 18.0 | 51.5 | |
| 42 | 52 | 17.0 | 8.0 | 15.0 | 7:00 | 17.0 | 49.0 | |
| 40 | 50 | 16.0 | 7.5 | 14.5 | 7:05 | 16.0 | 46.5 | 27.4 |
| 38 | 48 | 15.0 | 7.0 | 14.0 | 7:10 | 15.5 | 44.5 | |
| 36 | 46 | 14.0 | 6.5 | 13.0 | 7:15 | 15.0 | 42.0 | |
| 34 | 44 | 13.5 | 6.0 | 12.0 | 7:20 | 14.0 | 39.5 | |
| 32 | 42 | 13.0 | 5.5 | 11.5 | 7:25 | 13.0 | 37.5 | |
| 30 | 40 | 12.0 | 5.0 | 11.0 | 7:30 | 12.0 | 35.0 | 11.5 |
| 28 | 37 | 11.0 | 4.5 | 10.0 | 7:35 | 11.0 | 32.5 | |
| 26 | 35 | 10.0 | 4.0 | 9.5 | 7:40 | 10.5 | 30.0 | |
| 24 | 33 | 9.5 | 3.5 | 9.0 | 7:45 | 10.0 | 28.0 | |
| 22 | 31 | 9.0 | 3.0 | 8.0 | 7:50 | 9.0 | 26.0 | |
| 20 | 29 | 8.0 | 3.0 | 7.0 | 7:55 | 8.0 | 23.0 | 3.6 |
| 18 | 27 | 7.0 | 2.5 | 6.5 | 8:00 | 7.0 | 20.5 | |
| 16 | 25 | 6.0 | 2.0 | 6.0 | 8:05 | 6.5 | 18.5 | |
| 14 | 22 | 5.5 | 2.0 | 5.0 | 8:10 | 6.0 | 16.5 | |
| 12 | 20 | 5.0 | 1.5 | 4.0 | 7:15 | 5.0 | 14.0 | |
| 10 | 18 | 4.0 | 1.5 | 3.5 | 8:20 | 4.0 | 11.5 | .82 |
| 8 | 16 | 3.0 | 1.0 | 3.0 | 8:25 | 3.0 | 9.0 | |
| 6 | 12 | 2.0 | 1.0 | 2.0 | 8:30 | 2.0 | 6.0 | |
| 4 | 8 | 1.5 | 0.5 | 1.5 | 8:35 | 1.5 | 4.5 | |
| 2 | 4 | 1.0 | 0.5 | 1.0 | 8:40 | 1.0 | 3.0 | |
| 0 | 0 | 0.0 | 0.0 | 0.0 | 8:45 | 1.0 | 0.0 | |
| M = 61 | | | M = 10 | | M = 6:40 | | | |
| s = 17.9 | | | s = 3.53 | | s = :39.2 | | | |
| N = 1046 | | | N = 1061 | | N = 491 | | | |

*Product is the result of standard scores multiplied by the weighting coefficient.

Source: Cureton, 1960.

*Normative information.* Standard score and percentile tables for each of the three test items as well as the sum of the three items are included in Table 7-1.

*Comments.* The three items included in this test are practical and reliable. Since most of the items included in the original battery of 28 were of the muscular endurance type, it may be said that this is a valid test of muscular endurance (as measured by all 28). Based on the definitions given in Chapter 4, it is debatable as to whether the mile (1.61 km) run should be classified as a muscular or cardio-vascular endurance item. For this text, the mile (1.61 km) run is considered a cardiovascular item.

### Barrow Motor Ability Test[10]

*Sex and age.* Junior and senior high school boys; college men.

*Equipment.* Measuring tape; softballs; stopwatch; 5 standards or obstacles; basketball; 6-pound (2.72 kg) medicine ball; whistle.

*Items tested.* Standing broad jump; softball throw; zig-zag run; wall pass; medicine ball put; 60-yard (54.86 m) dash.

*Motor ability components tested.* Muscular endurance; power; agility; speed.

*Scoring.* The author provides the following regression equation for determining the total General Motor Ability Test score:

GMAS = 2.2 (standing broad jump) + 1.6 (softball throw)
+ 1.6 (zig-zag run) + 1.3 (wall pass) + 1.2 (medicine ball put)
+ 60-yard (54.86 m) dash.

*Reliability and validity.* Test-retest reliability coefficients for the six items ranged from .79 to .92. From an original battery of 29 items administered to 222 college men, two smaller test batteries were developed, using multiple correlation and regression equation techniques. The 6-item test consists of the aforementioned items. The 3-item test consists of standing broad jump, zig-zag run, and medicine ball put. Internal validity coefficients were .95 and .92 for the 6-item and 3-item tests, respectively.

*Normative information.* Norms are available for college men for total score in the 6-item test and each individual item in the 3-item test. Norms are also available for junior and senior high school boys by age (ages 7-11) for each item in the 3-item test.

*Comments.* The individual test items were reasonably reliable and the two test batteries were quite valid. Since so little validity is lost using the 3-item battery, it is recommended if time is limited. The inclusion of both a balance and a flexibility item and the exclusion of the wall pass test might have made this a more comprehensive test.

### Fleishman Physical Fitness Test Battery[11,12]

*Sex and age.* Boys and girls 14–18 years of age, with some norms for boys and girls 12–13 years of age.

*Equipment.* Stopwatch; hand grip dynamometer; horizontal bar; tape measure; softballs; 24-inch (60.96 cm) length of rope; wooden balance rail 1½ inches (3.81 cm) high, ¾-inch (1.91 cm) wide, and 24 inches (60.96 cm) long, mounted on a base board.

*Items tested.* Extent flexibility; dynamic flexibility; shuttle run; softball throw; hand grip; pull-ups; leg lifts; cable jump; balance; 600-yard (548.64 m) run-walk.

*Motor ability components tested.* Flexibility; agility; power; strength; muscular endurance; cardiovascular endurance.

*Scoring.* Methods for scoring each of the 10 items in the battery are included with the description of each test item. Tables are included for converting raw scores to percentiles. In order to obtain an overall Fitness Index (FI), a table is also provided for converting percentiles to standard scores. The Fitness Index is obtained simply by adding the total index points, i.e., summing the standard scores. If fewer than 10 tests are given, the Fitness Index is obtained as follows:

$$FI = \frac{\text{total index points}}{\text{number of tests given} \times 10}$$

*Reliability and validity.* Test-retest reliability coefficients for the 10 items ranged from .70 to .93. The validity scheme made use of the factor analysis statistical technique. From an original battery of 85 test items, nine "basic fitness factors" were identified and named. The single test item that correlated most highly (i.e., best measured a particular factor) was singled out for the final test battery. Thus, with the exception of the softball throw, each item in the final test battery was most valid in measuring a particular "basic fitness factor."

*Normative information.* Norms are included for boys and girls for each of the 10 items and for the overall Fitness Index.

*Comments.* This test is a result of one of the most thorough and comprehensive studies of motor ability components available in the literature. In some instances, as many as 20,000 cases were measured. The items are practical to administer and require very little and inexpensive equipment. However, the large number of items in the final battery probably precludes its popular use in the field. It is our belief that the battery, upon further analysis, could be condensed to five or six items without serious omission of "basic fitness factors."

### Scott Motor Ability Test[13,14,15]

*Sex and age.*   High school girls; college women.

*Equipment.*   Basketballs; measuring tape; chalk or marking tape; stopwatch; whistle; vertical standard; 6-foot (1.83 m) cross bar made of light material; two supports for the cross bar.

*Items tested.*   Basketball throw; dash (4 seconds); wall pass; broad jump; obstacle race.

*Motor ability components tested.*   Power; speed; muscular endurance; agility.

*Scoring.*   Methods of determining raw scores are included with descriptions of each item. Regression equations are provided for computing composite scores of two separate test batteries as follows:

Test Battery 1 score = .7 (basketball throw) + 2.0 (dash)
+ 1.0 (wall pass) + .5 (broad jump)

Test Battery 2 score = 2.0 (basketball throw) + 1.4 (broad jump)
− (obstacle race)

*Reliability and validity.*   Test-retest reliability coefficients for each of the five items ranged from .62 to .91. The overall validity criterion made use of a composite of three external criteria. These included: 1) subjective ratings of sports ability; 2) skill items common to sports; and 3) scores on the McCloy General Motor Ability Test for Girls.[16,17] The validity coefficients were .91 and .87 for the 4-item and 3-item batteries, respectively.

*Normative information.*   Standard score tables (T-scales) are available for each test item and for the composite scores for each test battery for college women and high school girls.[18]

*Comments.*   This is one of the few tests of this type in the literature that used external criteria for validity purposes. The validity coefficients were quite high, even though two of the items (dash and wall pass) had low reliabilities (.62). These two items were omitted, however, in the three-item battery.

### Rogers Physical Fitness Index[19,20]

*Sex and age.*  Both sexes, ages 8-38.

*Equipment.*  Hand grip dynamometer; back and leg dynamometer; horizontal bar; parallel bars; magnesium carbonate chalk; wet spirometer; wooden mouth pieces.

*Items tested.*  Age; height; weight; right and left hand grip; back and leg lift; pull-ups; dips on parallel bars; lung capacity.

*Motor ability components tested.*  Strength; muscular endurance.

*Scoring.*  Methods of scoring individual test items are included with descriptions of the test items. The following three formulas are used for determining the final Physical Fitness Index (PFI):

a) arm strength = dips + pull-ups $\dfrac{\text{weight (lbs)}}{10}$ + height (in.) - 60

b) strength index = arm strength + grip strength (lbs) + back and leg lifts (lbs) + lung capacity (cc)

c) PFI = $\dfrac{\text{achieved strength index}}{\text{normal strength index}} \times 100$

Normal strength index can be obtained from tables published by the original author and can also be found in Mathews' book.[21]

*Reliability and validity.*  Test-retest reliability coefficients of the test items ranged from .86 to .97.

Validity coefficients were not presented in the original study, although subsequent attempts[22] have been made to validate this test in light of: 1) theoretical relationships; 2) significance of changes in strength; 3) experimental evidence; and 4) representative case studies of low PFI's.

*Normative information.*  Physical Fitness Index norms are included for boys and girls ages 8-18 with an average PFI being 100, the lower quartile commencing at 85 and the upper quartile at 115.

*Comments.*  This test has been utilized widely, particularly in the eastern United States, for screening and classifying students and for research purposes. The validity of the test and its norming procedures have been subjected to much criticism.[23] The inclusion of lung capacity has come in for particular criticism. The administration of the test is considered by many to be time-consuming unless several dynamometers and skilled testers are available. A number of recommended revisions of this test are available.[24,25,26]

### Phillips JCR Test[27]

*Sex and age.*   Men 18–45 years of age.

*Equipment.*   Chinning bar; vertical jump board or wall markings; magnesium carbonate chalk; stopwatch; 2 wooden bankboards, 12 inches (30.48 cm) wide, and secured to the floor and set at 40° angles to it.

*Items tested.*   Pull-ups; vertical jump; shuttle run.

*Motor ability components tested.*   Power; muscular endurance; agility.

*Scoring.*   Methods for obtaining raw scores on individual test items are included with descriptions of the test items. Also available is a table for obtaining a composite score of the three items. This final score is obtained by converting raw scores to standard scores and summing the standard scores.

*Reliability and validity.*   Reliability coefficients for the individual test items ranged from .80 to .92 and from .81 to .95 on two different groups of men, whereas coefficients for the composite JCR score were .91 and .94 for the same groups, respectively.

Internal validity coefficients of .81 and .90 were obtained for a 25-item and a 19-item battery, respectively. Lower coefficients (.66 and .78) were obtained when the test was validated against external criteria—the Army Air Force Motor Fitness Test[28] and an obstacle course, respectively.

*Normative information.*   Norms based on 3,783 cases are presented in the original reference.

*Comments.*   Aside from the fact that it lacks a cardiovascular component, the JCR test appears to be a practical, reasonably reliable, and valid test of general motor ability for men. The fact that original data were obtained from a highly select group of men (military officers and trainees) might raise questions as to use of the test in typical high schools and colleges today. Because of this, it is recommended that local norms be constructed whenever possible.

### Larson Dynamic Strength Test[29]

*Sex and age.*   High school and college males.

*Equipment.*   Horizontal bar; parallel bars; vertical jump board or wall markings; chalk for the hands.

*Items tested.*   Pull-ups; dips; vertical jump.

*Motor ability components tested.*   Power; muscular endurance.

*Scoring.*   Methods for obtaining raw scores for individual test items are included with descriptions of test items. By means of a scoring table, the raw scores are converted into weighted standard scores. The three weighted scores are summed to obtain a total (composite) score.

*Reliability and validity.*   Reliability coefficients were not presented in the original study, but Cureton[30] has reported coefficients of .89 and .90 for pull-ups and dips, respectively, whereas Glencross[31] has shown a coefficient of .92 for the vertical jump.

An internal validity coefficient of .82 was obtained when the three items were correlated against a 15-item composite motor ability criterion. Similar results were obtained for college and high school samples.

*Normative information.*   No norms were published in the original study. However, in a later publication, a classification index with five categories ranging from very poor to excellent was provided as a basis for interpreting the total score.[32] Cureton[33] has provided norms for this test based on 2,600 college men, and Bookwalter [34] has prepared achievement scales for secondary school boys as well as college men.

*Comments.*   This test contains many of the positive characteristics and shortcomings of the preceding JCR test. Because original data were taken from "typical" college and high school students rather than military officers, it might be more applicable to modern school populations than the JCR Test. Although it is classified as a "strength" test, it measures power and muscular endurance according to the definitions used in this text.

### Newton Motor Ability Test[35]

*Sex and age.*   High school girls.

*Equipment.*   Lined gymnasium mat for broad jump; ten standards 15 inches (38.10 cm) high; five cross pieces (sticks) to place on standards; one Indian club or similar object; a 4-foot (1.22 m) high table or standard; a top bell; stopwatch.

*Items tested.*   Broad jump; hurdle; scramble.

*Motor ability components tested.*  Power; agility.

*Scoring.*  Methods for obtaining raw scores for each test item are included with descriptions of each item. A table is included for converting raw scores to un-weighted "point" scores. The final motor ability score is the sum of the three un-weighted point scores.

*Reliability and validity.*  Reliability coefficients were not included in the original reference. However, in an earlier report,[36] coefficients of .89 and .80 were reported for the broad jump and hurdles, respectively.

Among the validity schemes employed were: 1) external criterion—a subjective rating by a jury of competent judges and 2) internal criterion—a score based on 18 motor ability items. Validity coefficients for the 3-item battery were .73 and .91 for criteria 1 and 2, respectively.

*Normative information.*  A motor ability achievement scale with five categories ranging from inferior to superior was provided as a basis for interpreting the overall motor ability score.

*Comments.*  This test is practical and economical of time and expense. It also appears to be reasonably reliable and valid. However, it should be noted that although correlated .91 with an 18-item battery, the final 3-item battery measures only two of the seven components of motor ability identified in Chapter 4.

### AAHPER Youth Fitness Test
### (1976 Revision)[37]

*Sex and age.*  Boys and girls ages 9–17.

*Equipment.*  Horizontal bar; two blocks of wood, 2 inches × 2 inches × 4 inches (5.08 cm × 5.08 cm × 10.16 cm); 2 stopwatches or 1 split-second timer; tape measure.

*Items tested.*  Pull-ups (boys); flexed-arm hang (girls); shuttle run (boys and girls); standing long jump (boys and girls); 50-yard (45.72 m) dash (boys and girls); 600-yard (548.64 m) run (boys and girls).

*Motor ability components tested.*  Muscular endurance; power; agility; speed; cardiovascular endurance.

*Scoring.*  Methods for obtaining raw scores for individual test items are included with the descriptions of the items. Tables are available for converting raw scores directly to percentile scores. No statistical scheme has been developed to arrive at a composite score, i.e., a total score for all six items.

*Reliability and validity.*   No attempt was made by the developers of this test to determine the reliability of the test items. The authors were satisfied that the reliability of the items had been substantiated satisfactorily by other researchers.

No attempt was made to validate this test either internally (as part of a larger battery of tests) or externally (against other subjective or objective tests of general motor ability). Therefore, face validity of the items was accepted. However, inter-correlations among the test items were low, indicating little overlap of motor ability components.

*Normative information.*   Separate percentile tables for all items were included for boys and girls ages 9–17. These tables were based on a nationwide sample of 8,500 boys and girls in grades 5–12. Combined percentile tables for boys and girls ages 9–17 were also included for sit-ups, shuttle run, standing long-jump, 50-yard (45.72 m) dash, and 600-yard (548.64 m) run.

Finally, because of the current national interest in cardiovascular fitness, percentile tables for boys and girls 13 years and older were included for the 9-minute run, 12-minute run, one-mile (1.61 km) run and 1½-mile (2.41 km) run. However, these norms were based on data from the Texas Physical Fitness Motor Ability Test.[38]

*Comments.*   Unlike most of the previous tests reviewed in this chapter, the AAHPER Youth Fitness Test, from its very inception, has not been subjected to the usual requirements of good test construction, namely, statistical reliability, validity and multiple correlations, regression equations, or factor analysis.

It is given emphasis in this book because it represents the first attempt by the physical education profession to establish national norms. The original test battery was developed in 1957, and revised editions were published in 1965 and 1975. It is estimated that the test has been administered to millions of youngsters in the United States* and abroad.

Finally, the test does appear to fulfill the original criteria established by a special committee of the AAHPER Research Council: 1) The test items should be reasonably familiar; 2) the tests should require little or no equipment; 3) the tests could be administered to the entire age ranges of grades 5–12; and 4) the tests could be given to both boys and girls.

## BIBLIOGRAPHY

BARROW, HAROLD M. "Test of Motor Ability for College Men." *Research Quarterly*, 25 (October 1954), 253–60.
BOOKWALTER, K.W. "Achievement Scales in Strength Tests for Secondary

---

*For example, note the extensive use of this test in the Tecumseh, Michigan experiment reported by Henry J. Montoye in *An Introduction to Measurement in Physical Education*, p. 349.

School Boys and College Men." *Physical Educator,* 11 (February, 1942), 130-51.

CARPENTER, AILEEN. "Strength Testing in the First Three Grades." *Research Quarterly,* 13 (October 1942), 328-35.

_____. "The Measurements of General Motor Capacity and General Motor Ability in the First Three Grades." *Research Quarterly,* 13 (December 1942), 444-65.

CLARKE, H. HARRISON. *Application of Measurement to Health and Physical Education,* 2nd ed. New York: Prentice-Hall, Inc., 1950.

_____ and GAVIN H. CARTER. "Oregon Simplification of the Strength and Physical Fitness Indices for Upper Elementary Junior High and Senior High School Boys." *Research Quarterly,* 30 (March 1959), 3-10.

CURETON, THOMAS K. *Endurance of Young Men.* Washington: National Research Council Society for Research in Child Development, 1945.

_____. *Physical Fitness Appraisal and Guidance.* St. Louis: The C.V. Mosby Co., 1947.

_____. *Physical Fitness of Champion Athletes.* Urbana: University of Illinois Press, 1951.

FLEISHMAN, EDWIN A., *Examiner's Manual for the Basic Fitness Tests.* Englewood Cliffs, N.J.: Prentice-Hall, Inc., 1964.

_____. *The Structure and Measurement of Physical Fitness.* Englewood Cliffs, N.J.: Prentice-Hall, Inc., 1964.

HATLESTAD, LUCILLE. "Motor Educability Tests for Women College Students." *Research Quarterly,* 13 (March 1942), 10-15.

HUNSICKER, PAUL and GUY G. REIFF, *AAHPER Youth Fitness Test Manual* (Revised edition). Washington: AAHPERD Publications, 1976.

LARSON, LEONARD A. "A Factor and Validity Analysis of Strength Variables and Tests with a Test Combination of Chinning, Dipping and Vertical Jump." *Research Quarterly,* 11 (December 1940), 82-96.

LARSON, LEONARD A. and R.D. YOCOM. *Measurement and Evaluation in Physical Education, Health and Recreation Education.* St. Louis: C.V. Mosby Co., 1951.

LARSON, LEONARD A. "Some Findings Resulting from the Army Air Forces Physical Training Program." *Research Quarterly,* 17 (May 1946), 144-64.

MATHEWS, DONALD K. *Measurement in Physical Education,* 3rd ed. Philadelphia: W.B. Saunders Co., 1968.

McCLOY, C.H. "An Analytical Study of the Stunt Type Test as a Measure of Motor Educability." *Research Quarterly,* 8 (October 1937), 26-55.

_____. "The Measurement of General Motor Capacity and General Motor Ability." *Research Quarterly,* Supplement. 5 (March 1934), 46-61.

_____. *Tests and Measurements in Health and Physical Education.* New York: F.S. Crofts & Co., 1946.

_____ and NORMA D. YOUNG. *Tests and Measurement in Health and Physical Education,* 3rd ed. New York: Appleton-Century-Crofts, Inc., 1954.

McCOLLUM, ROBERT H. and RICHARD B. McCORKLE. *Measurement and Evaluation: A Laboratory Manual.* Boston: Allyn and Bacon, 1971.

METHENY, ELEANOR. "Studies of the Johnson Test as a Test of Motor Educability." *Research Quarterly,* 9 (December 1938), 105-14.

MONTOYE, HENRY J. *An Introduction to Measurement in Physical Education.* Boston: Allyn and Bacon, 1978.

PHILIPS, B.E. "The JCR Test." *Research Quarterly,* 18 (March 1947), 12-29.

POWELL, ELIZABETH and E.C. HOWE. "Motor Ability Tests for High School Girls." *Research Quarterly,* 10 (December 1939), 81-88.

ROGERS, FREDERICK RAND. *Physical Capacity Tests in the Administration of*

*Physical Education.* New York: Bureau of Publications, Teachers College, Columbia University, 1926.

SCOTT, M. GLADYS. "The Assessment of Motor Abilities of College Women Through Objective Tests." *Research Quarterly,* 10 (October 1939), 63–83.

SCOTT, M. GLADYS and ESTHER FRENCH. *Measurement and Evaluation in Physical Education.* Dubuque, Iowa: Wm. C. Brown Co., 1959.

SCOTT, M. GLADYS. "Motor Ability Tests for College Women." *Research Quarterly,* 14 (December 1943), 402–5.

SEYMOUR, EMORY W., "Follow-up Study on Simplifications of the Strength and Physical Fitness Indices." *Research Quarterly,* Part I, 31 (May 1960), 208–16.

TEXAS GOVERNOR'S COMMISSION ON PHYSICAL FITNESS. *Physical Fitness Motor Ability Test.* Austin: The Commission, 1973.

"WELLESLEY COLLEGE STUDIES IN HYGIENE AND PHYSICAL EDUCATION." *Research Quarterly,* Supplement, 9 (March 1939), 49–56.

**CHAPTER EIGHT**
# SPORTS SKILLS TESTS: INDIVIDUAL-PARTICIPANT SPORTS

One area of testing with which the typical student of physical education can readily identify involves the testing of ability in specific sports such as badminton, basketball, tennis, etc. Consequently, Chapters 8 through 10 will attempt a comprehensive identification of individual, dual, and team sports tests, respectively.

It may be argued that most sports skills tests, when analyzed critically, could also be classified into the seven "specific" motor ability components discussed in Chapters 4 through 7. A cursory review of the tests discussed in those chapters will show, however, that the emphasis was on fundamental or gross "big muscle" movements or held positions requiring very little learning or skill. In Chapters 8 through 10, it will be shown that, generally, sports skills are comprised of more complex, coordinated, or specialized abilities associated with particular sports such as a tennis serve, a baseball throw for accuracy, a golf drive, dribbling a basketball, etc.

Before discussing specific tests, it seems desirable to review those technical and practical qualities, discussed in Chapter 3, considered essential in the construction or selection of good sports skills tests in general.

## CRITERIA FOR CONSTRUCTING OR SELECTING SPORTS SKILLS TESTS

### Validity

A good test has validity, i.e., it measures what it purports to measure. Ordinarily, this is accomplished by correlating scores on the test with some external or internal performance criterion.

*External criterion.* The test scores are correlated with subjective ratings by judges, juries, coaches, etc., or with rankings resulting from round-robin or ladder tournaments. Whenever possible, rankings obtained from actual competition are to be preferred over subjective ratings. If the individuals who score highest on the skill test also are the better performers under game conditions, then the test is said to be valid.

*Internal criterion.* The test scores are correlated with an expanded battery of test items composed of fundamental components (skill elements) of a more complex skill. For example, a battery of 10 badminton skills is purported to measure badminton ability. By multiple correlation techniques, it is determined that 3 of the items correlate highly with all 10. It is then assumed that the 3-item battery is a valid test of badminton ability. This is a highly questionable practice and should be avoided unless the original 10-item test is first validated against an external criterion.

### Reliability

A good test has reliability, i.e., the *same* tester can obtain the *same* results from the *same* group under the *same* testing conditions. This reliability is most often determined by calculation of a split-halves or test-retest reliability coefficient discussed in Chapter 2. Since reliability is influenced by such factors as fatigue, physical (fitness) condition, general health, and emotional state, it is imperative that the testing procedure be standardized carefully.

### Objectivity

A good test has objectivity, i.e., *different* testers can obtain the *same* results from the *same* group under the *same* testing conditions.

Validity, reliability, and objectivity are expressed mathematically as coefficients of correlation, the calculation of which is discussed in Chapter 2.

Some arbitrary standards for their interpretation have been developed by various writers and are shown in Table 8-1.[1]

The above standards should be thought of as guidelines rather than hard-and-fast rules. In some situations, because of the difficulty in controlling certain variables, the above standards might be too high, and slightly lower coefficients might be acceptable.

In addition to the technical qualities of validity and reliability, other major practical considerations must be addressed in constructing and/or selecting an available test:

**1.** Has the researcher examined the sport critically so that the skills finally chosen for study are recognized as important by both students and teachers and/or coaches? This is usually accomplished via the questionnaire technique with which the investigator attempts to gain consensus on the *essential* components (skill elements) of a given sport.

**2.** Will the skills to be tested be measured as closely as possible to a gamelike situation? Students tend to lose interest if the skill tested does not appear to be related to the game.

**3.** Is the test economical in terms of time and equipment? Special and expensive equipment must be minimized for obvious reasons. Time must be viewed in two different ways: (a) time needed in preparation for the test, e.g., for placing of lines and markings on floors or walls; and (b) time needed for actual administration of the test. If there is one universal complaint about the use of testing in physical

**TABLE 8-1    Standards for Coefficients of Correlation**

| COEFFICIENT | VALIDITY | RELIABILITY AND OBJECTIVITY |
|---|---|---|
| .95–.99 | | excellent |
| .90–.94 | | very good |
| .85–.89 | excellent | acceptable |
| .80–.84 | very good | acceptable |
| .75–.79 | acceptable | poor |
| .70–.74 | acceptable | poor |
| .65–.69 | questionable except for very complex tests | questionable except for groups |
| .60–.64 | questionable | questionable except for groups |

Source: Barrow and McGee, p. 42, 1964.

education, it is that testing is too time-consuming, thus detracting from the instructional program. Too often, however, the time factor is used as an excuse for lack of interest, commitment, or expertise.

In any event, a skills test must allow for a sufficient number of trials so that chance fluctuations in performance will be minimized. The number of trials should increase as the element of chance increases, just as trials should increase when a high degree of accuracy is necessary for a good performance[2] (as in archery, for example).

**4.** Is the scoring done easily and objectively? Some controversy exists on the question of whether a second or third person should be involved in the performance of the individual being tested. For example, in a volleyball smash test, should a second individual set up the individual to be tested? Some authors[3] state flatly that only the person being tested should be involved, and game simulation can be obtained by using a wall-rebound situation. Others[4] contend that tests involving a second individual are not necessarily inferior, provided the performance of the second individual is skillful and reliable. It is tempting to generalize here that, as a skills test becomes more objective, it tends to become less gamelike; thus, the test constructor is plagued constantly with the necessity of trading one off with the other.

**5.** Is the test specific as to age group, sex, grade level in school or skill level, i.e., is the test one of beginning, intermediate, or advanced skill? Too often, these distinctions are not clear or are ignored completely in the literature, and potential users are left baffled as to whether certain tests are applicable to their particular sex, age group, etc.

**6.** Does the test include norms? Ordinarily, tests that have an accompanying set of norms are more useful than those that have not. It is often desirable to compare a student's obtained score on a test with standards derived from the testing of a large number of individuals of like age, weight, height, sex, etc. But, unless the norms are quite specific as to the latter criteria, and some attempt has been made at random selection of subjects, it is probably best for potential users to ignore those norms and devise their own. Unfortunately, few sports skills tests in the professional literature have included norms that can be used with a great deal of confidence.

The foregoing list of criteria for constructing or selecting sports skills tests is by no means exclusive. For instance, no mention has been made of factors that might affect a student's motivation in taking the test, such as whether the test is too easy, difficult, strenuous, or unfair.

Chapters 8 through 10 will be devoted to the identification and discussion of sports skills tests available in the professional literature. Some of the better tests, i.e., those that satisfy most of the foregoing criteria, are summarized in table form, whereas one or two tests are singled out for in-depth description.

### Table Format

The table format includes author, source, sex of the sample, number of cases in the sample, age group of the sample, available norms, and reliability and validity coefficients. Some of the above factors are coded to give additional information as follows:

**Symbols for Reading Tables Summarizing**
**Skills Tests in Chapters 8 through 10***

SH = split-halves reliability method
T-R = test-retest reliability method
AV = analysis of variance reliability method
IVC = internal validity criterion used
EVC = external validity criterion used
lit. = the author did not compute reliability coefficients but rather, accepted coefficients published by other authors.
log. = logic or content validity. The author felt no need to obtain statistical validity since the test or test item was to be used as an end in itself rather than as a predictor of a more complex performance.

A summary of the procedures used in writing Chapters 8 through 10 and general observations on all three chapters are discussed at the end of Chapter 10.

## ARCHERY SKILLS TESTS

Few tests of archery skill are available in the professional literature (Table 8–2). The most extensive work in this area was done by Edith I. Hyde in three separate articles.[5,6,7] More recently, the AAHPERD produced an archery test manual[8] for boys and girls ages 10–18. Both tests will be discussed here.

### The Hyde Archery Achievement Test[9]

*Equipment.* Standard 48-inch (1.22 m) target; bows and arrows; measuring tape; line markers; stakes; score cards; pencils.

*Description and administration.* The Columbia Round is a standard event used in archery competition for women. The shooting takes place in the following order:

First range, 24 arrows shot at 50 yards (45.72 m)
Second range, 24 arrows shot at 40 yards (36.58 m)
Third range, 24 arrows shot at 30 yards (27.43 m)

The distances on the archery range are measured and marked so that they are the same for every student at all times. All scores are made on standard 48-inch (1.22 m) target faces placed so that the center of the gold is 4 feet (1.22 m) from the ground. Arrows are shot in ends of 6 arrows each. Not more than one practice end may be shot before beginning to record the score at each distance. The practice

*For the readers' convenience, these symbols are repeated in Appendix D.

**TABLE 8-2  Summary of Archery Skill Tests***

| AUTHOR | SOURCE | SEX | NO. CASES | AGE GROUP | NORMS | RELIABILITY COEFFICIENT | VALIDITY COEFFICIENT |
|---|---|---|---|---|---|---|---|
| Hyde, E.I. | *R.Q., 8*:109–116, May, 1937. | F | 1400 | 10–18 | Yes | — | — |
| AAHPER | *Skills Test Manual: Archery for Boys and Girls*, 1967. | M & F | 600–900 | 12–18 | Yes | lit. | log. |
| Zabik, R.M. and Jackson, A.S. | *R.Q., 40*:254–255, March, 1969. | M | 60 | college freshmen | No | AV .86–.87 | — |

*See Appendix D for explanation of symbols.

163

TABLE 8-3  Achievement Scales in Archery for College Women*

| SCALE | FIRST COLUMBIA TOTAL SCORE (TARGET SCORE) | FINAL COLUMBIA RECORD (TARGET SCORE) | | | |
| | | TOTAL SCORE | (45.72 m.) 50 YARDS | (36.58 m.) 40 YARDS | (27.43 m.) 30 YARDS |
| --- | --- | --- | --- | --- | --- |
| 100 | 436 | 466 | 150 | 176 | 194 |
| 99 | 430 | 460 | 148 | 174 | 192 |
| 98 | 424 | 455 | 146 | 171 | 190 |
| 97 | 418 | 449 | 143 | 169 | 187 |
| 96 | 412 | 443 | 141 | 167 | 185 |
| 95 | 406 | 438 | 139 | 164 | 183 |
| 94 | 400 | 432 | 137 | 162 | 181 |
| 93 | 394 | 426 | 135 | 160 | 179 |
| 92 | 388 | 420 | 132 | 157 | 176 |
| 91 | 382 | 415 | 130 | 155 | 174 |
| 90 | 376 | 409 | 128 | 153 | 172 |
| 89 | 370 | 403 | 126 | 150 | 170 |
| 88 | 364 | 398 | 124 | 148 | 168 |
| 87 | 358 | 392 | 121 | 146 | 165 |
| 86 | 352 | 386 | 119 | 143 | 163 |
| 85 | 346 | 381 | 117 | 141 | 161 |
| 84 | 340 | 375 | 115 | 139 | 159 |
| 83 | 334 | 369 | 113 | 136 | 157 |
| 82 | 328 | 363 | 110 | 134 | 154 |
| 81 | 322 | 358 | 108 | 132 | 152 |
| 80 | 316 | 352 | 106 | 129 | 150 |
| 79 | 310 | 346 | 104 | 127 | 148 |
| 78 | 304 | 341 | 102 | 125 | 146 |
| 77 | 298 | 335 | 99 | 122 | 143 |
| 76 | 292 | 329 | 97 | 120 | 141 |
| 75 | 286 | 324 | 95 | 118 | 139 |
| 74 | 280 | 318 | 93 | 115 | 137 |
| 73 | 274 | 312 | 91 | 113 | 135 |
| 72 | 268 | 306 | 88 | 111 | 132 |
| 71 | 262 | 301 | 86 | 108 | 130 |
| 70 | 256 | 295 | 84 | 106 | 128 |
| 69 | 250 | 289 | 82 | 104 | 126 |
| 68 | 224 | 284 | 80 | 101 | 124 |
| 67 | 238 | 278 | 77 | 99 | 121 |
| 66 | 232 | 272 | 75 | 97 | 119 |
| 65 | 226 | 267 | 73 | 94 | 117 |
| 64 | 220 | 261 | 71 | 92 | 115 |
| 63 | 214 | 255 | 69 | 90 | 113 |
| 62 | 208 | 249 | 66 | 87 | 110 |
| 61 | 202 | 244 | 64 | 85 | 108 |
| 60 | 196 | 238 | 62 | 83 | 106 |
| 59 | 190 | 232 | 60 | 80 | 104 |

TABLE 8-3 (continued)

| SCALE | FIRST COLUMBIA TOTAL SCORE (TARGET SCORE) | FINAL COLUMBIA RECORD (TARGET SCORE) | | | |
|---|---|---|---|---|---|
| | | TOTAL SCORE | (45.72 m.) 50 YARDS | (36.58 m.) 40 YARDS | (27.43 m.) 30 YARDS |
| 58 | 184 | 227 | 58 | 78 | 102 |
| 57 | 178 | 221 | 55 | 76 | 99 |
| 56 | 172 | 215 | 53 | 73 | 97 |
| 55 | 166 | 210 | 51 | 71 | 95 |
| 54 | 160 | 204 | 49 | 69 | 93 |
| 53 | 154 | 198 | 47 | 66 | 91 |
| 52 | 148 | 192 | 44 | 64 | 88 |
| 51 | 142 | 187 | 42 | 62 | 86 |
| 50 | 136 | 181 | 40 | 59 | 84 |
| 49 | 133 | 178 | 39 | 58 | 82 |
| 48 | 131 | 174 | — | 57 | 80 |
| 47 | 128 | 171 | 38 | 56 | 79 |
| 46 | 125 | 167 | 37 | 55 | 77 |
| 45 | 122 | 164 | 36 | 53 | 75 |
| 44 | 120 | 160 | 35 | 52 | 74 |
| 43 | 117 | 157 | — | 51 | 72 |
| 42 | 114 | 153 | 34 | 50 | 70 |
| 41 | 111 | 150 | 33 | 49 | 69 |
| 40 | 109 | 146 | 32 | 47 | 67 |
| 39 | 106 | 143 | 31 | 46 | 65 |
| 38 | 103 | 139 | — | 45 | 64 |
| 37 | 100 | 136 | 30 | 44 | 62 |
| 36 | 98 | 132 | 29 | 43 | 60 |
| 35 | 95 | 129 | 28 | 42 | 59 |
| 34 | 92 | 125 | 27 | 40 | 57 |
| 33 | 89 | 122 | — | 39 | 55 |
| 32 | 87 | 118 | 26 | 38 | 54 |
| 31 | 84 | 115 | 25 | 37 | 52 |
| 30 | 81 | 111 | 24 | 36 | 50 |
| 29 | 78 | 108 | 23 | 34 | 49 |
| 28 | 76 | 104 | — | 33 | 47 |
| 27 | 73 | 101 | 22 | 32 | 45 |
| 26 | 70 | 97 | 21 | 31 | 44 |
| 25 | 67 | 94 | 20 | 30 | 42 |
| 24 | 65 | 90 | 19 | 28 | 40 |
| 23 | 62 | 87 | — | 27 | 39 |
| 22 | 59 | 83 | 18 | 26 | 37 |
| 21 | 56 | 80 | 17 | 25 | 35 |
| 20 | 54 | 76 | 16 | 24 | 34 |
| 19 | 51 | 73 | 15 | 23 | 32 |
| 18 | 48 | 69 | — | 21 | 30 |
| 17 | 45 | 66 | 14 | 20 | 29 |

**TABLE 8-3 (continued)**

| SCALE | FIRST COLUMBIA TOTAL SCORE (TARGET SCORE) | FINAL COLUMBIA RECORD (TARGET SCORE) | | | |
|---|---|---|---|---|---|
| | | TOTAL SCORE | (45.72 m.) 50 YARDS | (36.58 m.) 40 YARDS | (27.43 m.) 30 YARDS |
| 16 | 43 | 62 | 13 | 19 | 27 |
| 15 | 40 | 59 | 12 | 18 | 25 |
| 14 | 37 | 55 | 11 | 17 | 24 |
| 13 | 34 | 52 | − | 15 | 22 |
| 12 | 32 | 48 | 10 | 14 | 20 |
| 11 | 29 | 45 | 9 | 13 | 19 |
| 10 | 26 | 41 | 8 | 12 | 17 |
| 9 | 23 | 38 | 7 | 11 | 15 |
| 8 | 21 | 34 | − | 9 | 14 |
| 7 | 18 | 31 | 6 | 8 | 12 |
| 6 | 15 | 27 | 5 | 7 | 10 |
| 5 | 12 | 24 | 4 | 6 | 9 |
| 4 | 10 | 20 | 3 | 5 | 7 |
| 3 | 7 | 17 | − | 4 | 5 |
| 2 | 4 | 13 | 2 | 2 | 4 |
| 1 | 1 | 10 | 1 | 1 | 2 |

*Scale constructed by F.W. Cozens, University of California at Los Angeles.
Source: Hyde, 1937, pp. 109-16.

end is not scored and may not be used as part of the round. It is not necessary for the entire round to be completed on the same day. However, at least one distance is to be completed at each session.

*Scoring.* There is one official scorekeeper and one assistant for each target. The official scorekeeper records all scores made on that target. The scores are checked by the assistant.

The target values are: gold, 9; red, 7; blue, 5; black, 3; and white, 1. An arrow cutting two colors counts as having hit the inner one. An arrow rebounding from, or passing through, the scoring face of the target does not count as a hit and is recorded as zero on the scorecard. The score for each hit is recorded on the scorecard, beginning with those having the highest value. The hits and score are added for each end and for each distance separately. The Round score is the total score for all three distances.

*Reliability and validity.* No apparent attempt was made to determine the reliability or validity of the test.

A correlation was made, however, between scores in the first versus the final Columbia Round (N = 708), resulting in a correlation of .76, indicating a moderate relationship between initial scores and final accomplishment.[10] However, this cannot be construed as a test of reliability, since instruction had taken place in the interim.

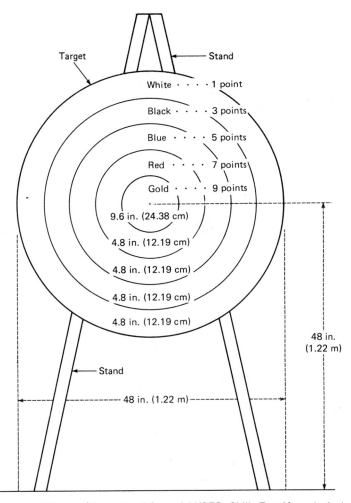

**FIGURE 8.1 Standard Target. (Reproduced from** *AAHPER, Skills Test Manual—Archery for Boys and Girls,* **1967, p. 22.)**

*Normative information.* The final norms were constructed using approximately 1,400 scores collected from 27 colleges in 16 states. A three-part standard score table is presented in Table 8–3. This is a sigma-scale with 50 the average; 100 is 3 standard deviations higher than the mean, and 0 is 3 standard deviations lower than the mean. Thus, separate scale scores may be added or averaged if one wishes to obtain a total achievement score.

*Comments.* The Hyde Archery Test is a test of achievement in archery *per se* rather than a predictor of archery skill from component parts of archery. This test should be of value in classification of college female students into beginning, intermediate, and advanced classes at the beginning of instruction and as a posttest for

*AAHPERD Publications Sales, P.O. Box 704, Waldorf, MD 20601.

grading at the end of instruction. More norms for the Hyde Archery Test need to be constructed for both sexes and various age groups.

### AAHPER Archery Skills Test

*Equipment.* No attempt was made to standardize archery equipment. It was assumed that bows of suitable strength and arrows of appropriate lengths would be available for the appropriate age and ability of the archers to be tested. Other equipment needed: standard 48-inch (1.22 m) target; a measuring tape; line markers; stakes; chalk; whistles; score cards; record sheets; pencils.

*Description and administration.* The tests are designed to measure skill in shooting at the standard 48-inch (1.22 m) target at various distances—10 yards (9.14 m), 20 yards (18.29 m), and 30 yards (27.43 m)—by boys and girls ages 12–18. (See Figures 8.1 and 8.2.)

Archers are allowed 4 practice shots at each distance. They may use any method of aiming. They should be organized into squads of 4 with 1 squad shooting at 1 target.

*Scoring.* Each archer shoots 2 ends of 6 arrows each (a total of 12 arrows) at each distance. An arrow cutting two colors is scored as the higher color. The final score is the sum of the two ends.

Additional hints on administration and safety are found in the manual. Scorecards, class composite record cards, personal record forms, and profile sheets are available for purchase.*

*Reliability and validity.* Selected personnel from 28 colleges and universities assisted in selection and administration of test items to approximately 100 college-age students. No reliability coefficients were presented, the rationale being that reliability and objectivity had been established in previous studies. These studies were not cited, however.

No validity coefficients were presented, the rationale being that the items are identical to the skills tested, i.e., face validity is obvious.

*Normative information.* An effort was made to collect data from as wide a geographical area as possible, i.e., test forms were distributed to schools throughout the United States. For the final percentile tables, between 600 and 900 scores were used for each sex and age (12–18 years). In the AAHPER manual, percentile tables are included for: 1) boys firing 12 arrows at 10, 20, and 30 yards (9.14, 18.29, and 27.43 m), respectively, plus a total score for the three distances, and 2) girls firing 12 arrows at 10 and 20 yards (9.14 and 18.29 m), respectively, plus a total score for the two distances. Only the tables for boys and girls firing 12 arrows at 10 yards (9.14 m) are shown here (Tables 8-4 and 8-5).

*AAHPERD Publications Sales, P.O. Box 704, Waldorf, MD 20601.

**TABLE 8-4   10 Yards (9.14 m), Twelve Arrows—Girls**

| PERCENTILE | AGE | | | | | PERCENTILE |
|---|---|---|---|---|---|---|
| | 12–13 | 14 | 15 | 16 | 17–18 | |
| 100th | 85 | 89 | 96 | 100 | 100 | 100th |
| 95th | 69 | 74 | 82 | 87 | 87 | 95th |
| 90th | 60 | 68 | 75 | 80 | 80 | 90th |
| 85th | 50 | 63 | 70 | 73 | 73 | 85th |
| 80th | 46 | 58 | 66 | 67 | 69 | 80th |
| 75th | 41 | 54 | 63 | 64 | 66 | 75th |
| 70th | 38 | 50 | 60 | 60 | 62 | 70th |
| 65th | 35 | 48 | 56 | 56 | 58 | 65th |
| 60th | 34 | 46 | 53 | 53 | 55 | 60th |
| 55th | 32 | 43 | 51 | 49 | 52 | 55th |
| 50th | 30 | 41 | 49 | 46 | 48 | 50th |
| 45th | 27 | 38 | 46 | 43 | 46 | 45th |
| 40th | 24 | 35 | 43 | 41 | 42 | 40th |
| 35th | 22 | 33 | 40 | 38 | 40 | 35th |
| 30th | 19 | 30 | 37 | 33 | 38 | 30th |
| 25th | 16 | 28 | 34 | 31 | 35 | 25th |
| 20th | 14 | 25 | 31 | 29 | 31 | 20th |
| 15th | 12 | 22 | 27 | 25 | 28 | 15th |
| 10th | 10 | 19 | 21 | 21 | 24 | 10th |
| 5th | 6 | 12 | 13 | 16 | 19 | 5th |
| 0 | 0 | 0 | 0 | 0 | 0 | 0 |

Source: AAHPER, 1967, p. 33.

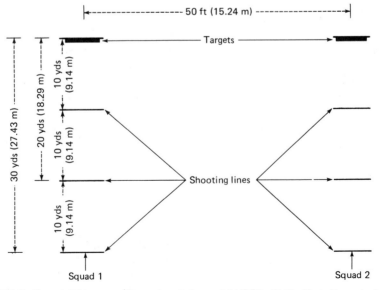

**FIGURE 8.2   Squad Distances. (Reproduced from *AAHPER, Skills Test Manual—Archery for Boys and Girls,* 1967, p. 21.)**

**TABLE 8-5  10 Yards (9.14 m), 12 Arrows—Boys**

| PERCENTILE | AGE | | | | | PERCENTILE |
|---|---|---|---|---|---|---|
| | 12–13 | 14 | 15 | 16 | 17–18 | |
| 100th | 91 | 96 | 100 | 100 | 100 | 100th |
| 95th | 83 | 88 | 97 | 99 | 98 | 95th |
| 90th | 78 | 80 | 94 | 97 | 96 | 90th |
| 85th | 73 | 78 | 90 | 96 | 93 | 85th |
| 80th | 70 | 75 | 88 | 92 | 90 | 80th |
| 75th | 67 | 72 | 84 | 90 | 88 | 75th |
| 70th | 64 | 70 | 80 | 88 | 86 | 70th |
| 65th | 61 | 68 | 78 | 86 | 84 | 65th |
| 60th | 59 | 67 | 76 | 84 | 82 | 60th |
| 55th | 57 | 65 | 73 | 80 | 79 | 55th |
| 50th | 54 | 63 | 69 | 79 | 77 | 50th |
| 45th | 50 | 60 | 65 | 77 | 74 | 45th |
| 40th | 48 | 57 | 62 | 75 | 71 | 40th |
| 35th | 45 | 55 | 59 | 72 | 68 | 35th |
| 30th | 42 | 52 | 55 | 70 | 63 | 30th |
| 25th | 38 | 45 | 51 | 67 | 59 | 25th |
| 20th | 34 | 40 | 48 | 61 | 55 | 20th |
| 15th | 31 | 36 | 43 | 51 | 48 | 15th |
| 10th | 26 | 31 | 36 | 50 | 40 | 10th |
| 5th | 16 | 25 | 25 | 40 | 27 | 5th |
| 0 | 0 | 0 | 0 | 0 | 0 | 0 |

Source: AAHPER, 1967, p. 39.

*Comments.*  This is a very practical test that could be used for classification of students into ability groups as well as to show improvement resulting from instruction. Caution should be used in application of the norms, since no mention is made of the level of ability of the individuals on whom the norms are based.

In general, there is a lack of validiated archery skills tests in the professional literature, and more work needs to be done using the Flint Round and the Chicago Round, as in the work of Zabik.[11]

## BOWLING SKILLS TESTS

Few tests of bowling skills are available in the professional literature (Table 8-6). This is probably due to the fact that the act of bowling itself is an objective measure. Apparently, little need has been felt for predicting bowling ability from components of the bowling act. Consequently, much of the work done in this area involves construction of norms.[12,13,14] The work by Liba and Olsen[15] is a notable exception.

### Liba and Olsen Spot-Bowling Test

*Equipment.* Bowling balls; observation sheets; bowling alley marked with a 3-foot (91.44 cm) sheet of paper taped 17-20 feet (5.18-6.10 m) from the foul line.

*Description and administration.* The ability to spot bowl is judged by the ability of the student to release the ball consistently over the desired release point and to roll the ball so that it passes over the desired point of aim.

*Procedure for making the observation record.* The check-list used to record the observations is illustrated in Figure 8.3. The desired release point and point of aim are indicated by the two vertical lines. As the bowler rolls the ball (the first throw in each frame), an observer notes the actual position of the center of the ball with respect to the dots, i.e., over the desired release point, over the second dot, one board to the left, etc. This is recorded on the observation sheet by placing a heavy vertical line in the first row of dots (Figure 8.3). The next throw is recorded in the second row, etc. The observation and recording procedures for the arrows (point of aim) are identical.

*Procedures for determining the exact path of the ball.* A 3-foot (91.44 cm) wide strip of paper is taped to the alley, just beyond the alley darts (arrows), so that it is 17-20 feet (5.18 m-6.10 m) from the foul line. As the ball is rolled over the paper, it leaves a black line showing its actual path within the 3-foot (91.44 cm) area. Since this portion of the actual straight line path is known, other points can be determined trigonometrically by projecting that line back to the foul line. The original study included a table that provides the exact position of the ball at the foul line and at the arrows (darts), once the actual path of the ball, between the 17-20-foot (5.18 m-6.10 m) area is known.

*Reliability and validity.* Five trials recorded on each of two days, using 33 straight-line bowlers, produced reliability coefficients of .85 for observed point of release and .86 for the actual ball path. When trials were increased to ten, reliabilities increased slightly for both observed point of release (.86 to .88) and for actual ball path (.88).

To determine validity, the records of ball position at release and in relation to point of aim were correlated with the actual ball path as determined mathematically. The validity coefficients for the average of ten trials as recorded on two days were .81 and .83 for point of release, and .94 and .93 for point of aim. The authors attributed the lower coefficients for release point to the fact that, since the ball is still in the hand of the bowler as it passes over the dots, it is more difficult to observe its actual position in relation to the dots.

**TABLE 8-6 Summary of Bowling Skills Tests***

| AUTHOR | SOURCE | SEX | NO. CASES | AGE GROUP | NORMS | RELIABILITY COEFFICIENT | VALIDITY COEFFICIENT |
|---|---|---|---|---|---|---|---|
| Phillips, M. and Summers, D. | *R.Q., 21*:377-385 Dec., 1950. | F | 3634 | college women | Yes | — | — |
| Martin, J. | *R.Q., 31*:113-116, March, 1960. | M & F | 704 | college men & women | Yes | — | — |
| Martin, J. and Keogh, J. | *R.Q., 35*:325-327, Oct., 1964. | M & F | 320 | college men & women | Yes | — | — |
| Liba, M. and Olsen, J.K. | *R.Q., 38*:193-201, May, 1967 | F | 33 | college women | No | T-R .74-.88 | EVC .81-.94 |

*See Appendix D for explanation of symbols.

Trials

| 1 | 1234 • 1234 • 1234 • 1234 • 1234 • 1234 ▌1234 • 1234 |
|---|---|
| 2 | 1234 • 1234 • 1234 • 1234 • 1234 • 1234 • 123▌ • 1234 |
| 3 | 1234 • 1234 • 1234 • 1234 • 1234 • 1234 • 1234 • 1234 |
| 4 | 1234 • 1234 • 1234 • 1234 • 1234 • 1234 • 1234 • 1234 |
| 5 | 1234 • 1234 • 1234 • 1234 • 1234 • 1234 • 1234 • 1234 |
| 6 | 1234 • 1234 • 1234 • 1234 • 1234 • 1234 • 1234 • 1234 |
| 7 | 1234 • 1234 • 1234 • 1234 • 1234 • 1234 • 1234 • 1234 |
| 8 | 1234 • 1234 • 1234 • 1234 • 1234 • 1234 • 1234 • 1234 |
| 9 | 1234 • 1234 • 1234 • 1234 • 1234 • 1234 • 1234 • 1234 |
| 10 | 1234 • 1234 • 1234 • 1234 • 1234 • 1234 • 1234 • 1234 |

POINT OF RELEASE

Trials

| 1 | 1234 ▲ 1234 ▲ 1234 ▲ 1234 ▲ 1234 ▲ 1234 ▌1234 ▲ 1234 |
|---|---|
| 2 | 1234 ▲ 1234 ▲ 1234 ▲ 1234 ▲ 1234 ▲ 123▌▲ 1234 ▲ 1234 |
| 3 | 1234 ▲ 1234 ▲ 1234 ▲ 1234 ▲ 1234 ▲ 1234 ▲ 1234 ▲ 1234 |
| 4 | 1234 ▲ 1234 ▲ 1234 ▲ 1234 ▲ 1234 ▲ 1234 ▲ 1234 ▲ 1234 |
| 5 | 1234 ▲ 1234 ▲ 1234 ▲ 1234 ▲ 1234 ▲ 1234 ▲ 1234 ▲ 1234 |
| 6 | 1234 ▲ 1234 ▲ 1234 ▲ 1234 ▲ 1234 ▲ 1234 ▲ 1234 ▲ 1234 |
| 7 | 1234 ▲ 1234 ▲ 1234 ▲ 1234 ▲ 1234 ▲ 1234 ▲ 1234 ▲ 1234 |
| 8 | 1234 ▲ 1234 ▲ 1234 ▲ 1234 ▲ 1234 ▲ 1234 ▲ 1234 ▲ 1234 |
| 9 | 1234 ▲ 1234 ▲ 1234 ▲ 1234 ▲ 1234 ▲ 1234 ▲ 1234 ▲ 1234 |
| 10 | 1234 ▲ 1234 ▲ 1234 ▲ 1234 ▲ 1234 ▲ 1234 ▲ 1234 ▲ 1234 |

POINT OF AIM

**FIGURE 8.3** Observation sheet for recording point of release and point of aim. (Reproduced from Liba and Olsen, "A Device for Evaluating Spot Bowling Ability," *Res. Quart.*, 38 (May 1967), 196.)

*Normative information.* Although norm tables were not published, normative data were obtained on 98 college women (using a single observer) at the end of a semester of instruction in beginning bowling. For point of release, the mean was 1.45 and the standard deviation, .84; for point of aim, the mean was 2.11 and the standard deviation, .92.

*Comments.* Although ten trials do not increase the reliability of the test greatly, they are feasible for use in a single instructional period (4 or 5 students bowling on one alley in a 45- or 50-minute class period).

The necessity of constructing a table using trigonometric methods should not preclude use of this test. Assistance is readily available in most schools.

It is not known why the authors used actual path of the ball as the validating criterion rather than actual bowling score. The latter could have been included without changing the design of the study or contaminating the results.

## DANCING/RHYTHMS SKILLS TESTS

The controversy as to whether dance should be subjected to analytical measurement has been debated for some time.[16] Possibly as a result of this controversy, the professional literature offers little help to those who would wish to involve themselves in the objective measurement of dance. Understandably, little has been done to measure the creative aspects of dance such as artistic temperament, emotional response, idea projection, etc. Most studies have dealt largely with measurement of rhythm per se, i.e., a person's motor response to a rhythmic pattern. A few of these are summarized in Table 8-7.

### The Ashton Gross Motor Rhythm Test[17]

*Equipment.*   Records.

*Description and administration.*   The purpose of the test is to measure response to beat, correct rhythm pattern, ability to maintain and vary movement, ability to change direction, and style of movement (from forced and mechanical to live and spirited).

Before beginning the test, a standardized instruction sheet is read by the student. It reads as follows:

> In a few moments, you will hear a recording. The first part of this recording has music for walking, running and skipping. Each will be played twice. The first time, listen; the second time after the signal, start. Keep moving until the music stops.
>   The second part of the record consists of musical excerpts. During the musical excerpts you may show any movement that you think fits the music. If you wish to restrict your movement to walking, running and skipping, you may do so. Any movement that you show will be accepted and judged for its value. Please show your best movement.
>   The third part of the recording has music for the schottische, waltz, and polka. For some movements, more than one piece of music will be played. The voice will tell you what to do.

Students are tested in groups of three, using three judges. They are tested on the musical excerpts shown in Table 8-8. The test as recorded takes 8 minutes. Two groups of three students can be scheduled every 15 minutes.

*Scoring.*   Thirteen items comprise the test, judged on a 0-4 scale by the three judges. The range of scores possible is 0-156 for each student, i.e., the sum of the three judges' scores taken from the rating scale shown in Table 8-9.

*Reliability and validity.*   A pilot group of 14 students was tested with a random mixture of forms 1 and 2 on consecutive days under similar circumstances. The reliability coefficient was .86.

No mention of statistical or logical validity was made in this study.

*Normative information.*   No norm tables accompanied this study. However, the author did publish lowest cutoff points, for grading purposes, and ranges, means, and standard deviations from which norm tables could be constructed easily.

**TABLE 8-7  Summary of Dance and Rhythm Skills Tests***

| AUTHOR | SOURCE | SEX | NO. CASES | AGE GROUP | NORMS | RELIABILITY COEFFICIENT | VALIDITY COEFFICIENT |
|---|---|---|---|---|---|---|---|
| Annett, T. | R.Q., 3:183-191, May, 1932. | M & F | 122 | college women | No | .50 | EVC .47 |
| Benton, R.J. | R.Q., 15:137-144, May, 1944. | F | 42 | college women | No | lit. .62-.97 | EVC .83 |
| Ashton, D. | R.Q., 24:253-260, Oct., 1953. | | | fresh. & soph. | No | T-R | — |
| | | F | 79-705 | college women | | .86 | |
| Waglow, I.F. | R.Q., 24:97-101, March, 1953. | M & F | 54 | college men and women | No | T-R .47 | EVC .37 |
| Simpson, S. | R.Q., 29:342-348, Oct., 1958. | F | 42-89 | college women | No | SH & AV .87-.89 | — |

*See Appendix D for explanation of symbols.

175

**TABLE 8–8A   Musical Excerpts (Form #1)**

|  | MEAS. | MM. | TIME (SEC.) |
|---|---|---|---|
| *Section 1* | | | |
| Walk—Wisconsin Blueprint | 12 | 112 | 21.9 |
| Skip—Davies | 16 | 192 | 19.7 |
| Run—Heurter—Fire Dance | 24 | 192 | 29.3 |
| *Section 2* | | | |
| Skip—Kerry Dance | 20 | 208 | 21.6 |
| Run—Concone-Study | 16 | 208 | 24.8 |
| Fast Walk—Prokofieff | 32 | 132 | 29.0 |
| Slow Walk—Beethoven—Waterman ABC | 16 | 104 | 33.1 |
| Skip—New Mown Hay | 24 | 192 | 37.2 |
| Run—Reinhold—Gnomes | 32 | 208 | 27.6 |
| *Section 3* | | | |
| Schottische—Jubilee | 16 | 192 | 24.7 |
| Slow Waltz—Tschaikowsky—Waltz from | | | |
|   Sleeping Beauty | 32 | 138 | 36.1 |
| Moderate Waltz—Schubert, No. 7 | 32 | 168 | 29.0 |
| Polka—Lichner | 32 | 208 | 24.3 |

**TABLE 8–8B   Musical Excerpts (Form #2)**

|  | MEAS. | MM. | TIME (SEC.) |
|---|---|---|---|
| *Section 1* | | | |
| Walk—Davies | 12 | 128 | 20.3 |
| Skip—Queen of Sheba | 16 | 208 | 32.5 |
| Run—Wisconsin Blueprint | 12 | 184 | 14.4 |
| *Section 2* | | | |
| Skip—Schumann—Sicilianish | 24 | 132 | 21.8 |
| Run—Moszkowski—Scherzino | 12 | 208 | 22.3 |
| Fast Walk—Handel—Joshua | 16 | 196 | 21.0 |
| Slow Walk—Hollaender March | 17 | 116 | 31.6 |
| Skip—Marche Lorraine | 32 | 132 | 28.8 |
| Run—Delibes—Passapied | 24 | 208 | 25.5 |
| *Section 3* | | | |
| Schottische—Faust-Up-To-Date | 24 | 168 | 35.1 |
| Slow Waltz—Gurlitt—First Dance | 32 | 138 | 35.7 |
| Waltz—Tschaikowsky—Waltz of the | | | |
|   Flowers | 32 | 168 | 27.2 |
| Polka—Plantation Dance | 24 | 208 | 25.3 |

Source: Ashton, 1953, p. 260.

**TABLE 8-9   Rhythm Rating Scale**

To be used for entire test:

0—No response or incorrect response.

   Correct beat and accent only through chance.

   Step and rhythm incorrect.

   Attempts to start self in motion; undecided as to correct step.

   Starts a preliminary faltering movement; then stops.

1—Correct step but not correct beat (unable to pick up new beat or tempo). Correct movement only by imitation of another student.

   Awkward, uncoordinated movement.

   Ability to start self in movement—maintained only for a measure or two.

   Difficulty in changing direction.

2—Step and rhythm pattern correct. Reaction time slow. Movement uncertain—lapses occasionally into incorrect beat.

   Movements are consistently heavy; shows tension.

   Maintenance of movement is short; phrase.

   Movement is forced; mechanical. Lacking in style.

   It is prosaic—no variety.

3—Uses correct step, beat, and accent. If student loses the accent and gets off the beat, student is aware of it and able to get back on the beat.

   Ability to maintain movement throughout excerpt.

   Varies direction with effort but is able to maintain movement.

   Student shows ability in simple movement. Movement has direction but is not alive and spirited.

4—Immediate response with correct step, beat, and accent.

   Ability to maintain movement throughout excerpt.

   Ability to vary movement (turns, etc.).

   Confidence shown in movement. Movements are definite, spirited, and easily accomplished. Student is relaxed.

Source: Ashton, 1953, p. 259.

*Comments.* It is obvious that the credibility of the test depends upon the consistency (objectivity) of the three judges. It is recommended that, in any new application of this test, objectivity coefficients among the three judges be obtained.

## GOLF SKILLS TESTS

The components of golf for which tests have been devised include driving (distance and target), putting, and approaching. Most of the studies in this area are found in theses and dissertations. Some of these are summarized in Table 8-10.

The following test is selected for further description.

**TABLE 8-10  Summary of Golf Skills Tests***

| AUTHOR | SOURCE | SEX | NO. CASES | AGE GROUP | NORMS | RELIABILITY COEFFICIENT | VALIDITY COEFFICIENT |
|---|---|---|---|---|---|---|---|
| McKee, M.E. | *R.Q., 21*:40-46 March, 1950. | F | 30 | college students & faculty | No | SH .60-.95 | — |
| McKee, M.E. | *R.Q., 21*:40-46, March, 1950. | F | 30-44 | college students & faculty | No | SH .68-.93 | EVC .14-.80 |
| Vanderhoof, E.R. | Master's thesis, U. of Iowa, 1956. | F | 110 | college women | Yes | SH .79-.90 | EVC .66-.82 |
| Rowlands, D.J. | Doctoral dissertation U. of Utah, 1974. | M | 92 | adult men | No | — | EVC .82 |

*See Appendix D for explanation of symbols.

### The Vanderhoof Golf Test[18]

The author experimented with different scoring methods for a drive test, a 5-iron approach test, and a 7-iron approach test. Only the drive test and the 5-iron approach test will be discussed here.

*Equipment.* Gymnasium with high ceiling; 5-iron club; 2-wood club; cocoa mat with a permanent tee inserted; plastic golf balls; 2 standards for supported rope; one rope; a ten pin (as a target distant from the restraining line).

*Description and administration.* The testing station consists of an area 13 feet × 74 feet (3.96 m × 22.56 m) and a rope is suspended eight feet (2.44 m) above the floor, at a distance of 14 feet (4.27 m) from and parallel to the restraining line. Target values and other dimensions are shown in Figure 8.4.

*The approach test.* Prior to the test, the player takes as many swings as desired and then hits two or three balls for warm-up. When ready, the player hits the ball (no tee) with a full swing toward the target, for a total of 15 trials. The ball must go over the rope to score or the ball is considered topped. A second trial is allowed for a topped ball and two successive topped balls count as only one trial.

Directional errors may be measured by using a scorecard that duplicates the scoring area. The direction of each shot is marked on the scorecard.

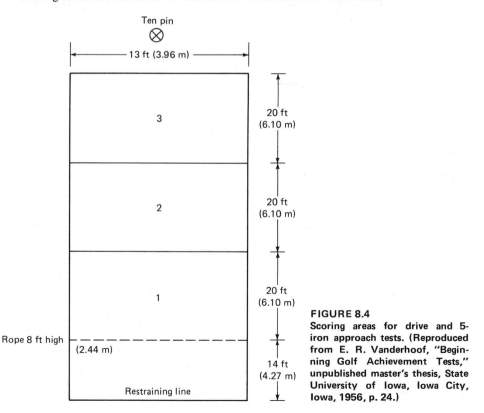

**FIGURE 8.4**
Scoring areas for drive and 5-iron approach tests. (Reproduced from E. R. Vanderhoof, "Beginning Golf Achievement Tests," unpublished master's thesis, State University of Iowa, Iowa City, Iowa, 1956, p. 24.)

*The drive test.* The drive test is conducted exactly as the approach test, except that a 2-wood is used and the ball is teed up.

*Scoring.* For both tests, each trial is scored from 0 to 3 points, according to the area in which the ball lands. (Figure 8.4.) Two "topped" balls in succession are recorded as a trial with 0 score. Trial scores are summed for the final test scores.

*Reliability and validity.* The split-halves method was used to obtain reliability coefficients for 110 college women who had received 15 lessons of group instruction in golf. The coefficients for the various experiments ranged from .79 to .90 but were .84 and .90 for the 5-iron and drive tests, respectively.

Statistical validation was attempted by correlating test scores with subjective ratings of the students' golf form and swing. Coefficients for the various experiments ranged from .66 to .82 but were .66 and .71 for the 5-iron and drive tests, respectively.

*Normative information.* A T-scale was constructed for the drive test and is shown in Table 8–11.

*Comments.* Because plastic balls would be affected by wind, these tests should be used indoors.

It would appear that a better distinction between abilities would be obtained

**TABLE 8-11   T-Scale for Drive Test**

| RAW SCORE | T-SCORE | RAW SCORE | T-SCORE |
|-----------|---------|-----------|---------|
| 45 | 76 | 23 | 50 |
| 44 | 74 | 22 | 49 |
| 43 | 72 | 21 | 48 |
| 42 | 71 | 20 | 47 |
| 41 | 71 | 19 | 46 |
| 40 | 69 | 18 | 44 |
| 39 | 67 | 17 | 43 |
| 38 | 65 | 16 | 43 |
| 37 | 64 | 15 | 42 |
| 36 | 63 | 14 | 41 |
| 35 | 63 | 13 | 40 |
| 34 | 62 | 12 | 38 |
| 33 | 60 | 11 | 37 |
| 32 | 59 | 10 | 36 |
| 31 | 58 | 9 | 35 |
| 30 | 57 | 8 | 34 |
| 29 | 56 | 7 | 31 |
| 28 | 55 | 6 | 26 |
| 27 | 54 | 5 | 26 |
| 26 | 52 | 4 | 26 |
| 25 | 51 | 3 | 24 |
| 24 | 50 | | |

Source: Vanderhoof, 1956, p. 43.

if the number of scoring areas was increased, say from 3 areas 20 feet (6.10 m) apart to 12 areas 5 feet (1.52 m) apart. Statistically, this would also make for a more normal distribution of scores.

Since both tests were validated against a subjective rating of form and swing, it would have been helpful if criteria for rating these items were included in the study.

## GYMNASTICS/TUMBLING SKILLS TESTS

Validated tests in this area are practically nonexistent in professional literature. This is not surprising when one considers the complexity of gymnastics. Generally, the studies attempt to predict *potential* gymnastics ability from selected elements, usually structural and/or physical fitness components. Some of these are summarized in Table 8-12.

The following study is selected for further description mainly because of its availability in the *Research Quarterly,* and because the process followed included the development of prediction equations, a step taken rarely in the development of sports skills tests.

### The Wettstone Gymnastics Potential Test[19]

*Equipment.* Medical tape; stadiometer or meter stick; stall (wall) bars or horizontal bar; parallel bars.

*Description and administration.* The purpose of the test is to measure the complexity called potential "gymnastic ability" from simple structural and physical fitness components, a formidable task at best. The author made it clear that the test was to be used for locating "raw material" for developing good gymnastics teams and for motivating purposes.

In the original study, 34 qualities possessed by a "good gymnast" were identified by questioning authorities in the field. The 15 highest ranked qualities were selected for measurement.

Series of partial and multiple correlations were done to determine which combination of variables correlated highest with the test criterion (gymnastics ability).

Gymnastics ability was rated by the coaches after observing the 22 gymnasts in the sample for seven months. A simple numerical system was used to measure whether the gymnast was champion caliber, good varsity, fair varsity, poor varsity, or nonvarsity material.

The final prediction equation was:

$$\text{Potential Gymnastics Ability} = .355X_1 + .260X_2 + .035X_3 + 13.990$$

**TABLE 8-12  Summary of Gymnastics/Tumbling Skills Tests***

| AUTHOR | SOURCE | SEX | NO. CASES | AGE GROUP | NORMS | RELIABILITY COEFFICIENT | VALIDITY COEFFICIENT |
|---|---|---|---|---|---|---|---|
| Wettstone, E. | *R.Q.*, *9*:115-125, Dec., 1938. | M | 22 | college men | No | — | EVC .75-.79 |
| Gates, J.L. | Doctoral dissertation U. of Arkansas, 1974. | M | 58 | college men | No | — | EVC .72-.75 |
| Michalek, F.H. | Doctoral dissertation, U. of Utah, 1974. | M | 100 | 18-28 | No | — | EVC .61 |

*See Appendix D for explanation of symbols.

Where $X_1$ was thigh circumference divided by height.

$X_2$ was a "strength" test consisting of chinning, dipping, and thigh flexion (leg lift). Thigh flexion was measured by having the subject hang from stall (wall) bars and flex the legs at the hip joint to the horizontal position, as often as possible.

$X_3$ was an agility item called the Burpee (squat thrust).

*Scoring.* 1) Thigh circumference in inches divided by height in inches. Centimeters may be used. 2) Strength: The sum of the number of chins, dips, and leg lifts. 3) Agility: The number of completed 4-count burpees (squat thrusts) in 10 seconds.

Computation tables for converting raw scores on the above variables to scores to be used with the prediction equation were supplied in the original article.

*Reliability and validity.*   Although reliability is mentioned at one point, there is no evidence that any steps were taken to measure the reliability of any of the variables studied.

Validity coefficients were obtained on 22 gymnasts using the coaches' rating system described earlier as the test criterion. A coefficient of .79 was obtained between the test criterion and the 3-item prediction equation described above.

*Normative information.*   No norm tables were included in this study.

*Comments.*   Some researchers continue to study the relationship of structural and functional measures to success in gymnastics,[20] whereas others see the importance of including personality factors.[21] Future gymnastics skills test batteries should probably include combinations of these factors.

The validity of the Wettstone test could probably be improved if the test criterion were a more objective variable—perhaps average of judges' scores for a gymnast for a season.

## SWIMMING AND DIVING SKILLS TESTS

Typically, swimming tests have been of the achievement type rather than the predictive type. This is understandable, since swimming skills are, for the most part, considered ends in themselves, i.e., they are often practiced for their own intrinsic value rather than as simulations of more complex (game) activities. A few of these are summarized in Table 8–13. The study by Fox is selected for further description.

### The Fox Swimming Power Test[22]

This test was developed on the premise that power is fundamental to good swimming, and that the power factor correlates highly with form ratings that are often used as the primary method of evaluation in swimming classes.

**TABLE 8-13  Summary of Swimming/Diving Skills Tests***

| AUTHOR | SOURCE | SEX | NO. CASES | AGE GROUP | NORMS | RELIABILITY COEFFICIENT | VALIDITY COEFFICIENT |
|---|---|---|---|---|---|---|---|
| Bennett, L.M.** | *R.Q., 13*:109–115, March, 1942 | F | 26 | 18–23 | No | SH .95 | EVC .94 |
| Hewitt, J.E. | *R.Q., 14*:391–396, Dec., 1943. | M | 3000 | military men | Yes | — | — |
| Hewitt, J.E. | *R.Q., 19*:282–289, Dec., 1948. | M | 4000 | college men | Yes | SH .89–.95 | IVC .54–.93 |
| Hewitt, J.E. | *R.Q., 20*:170–179, May, 1949. | F<br>M | 647<br>446 | college<br>college | Yes<br>Yes | SH .89–.96 | IVC .59–.94 |
| Fox, M.G. | *R.Q., 28*:233–238, Oct., 1957. | F | 97 | college women | Yes | SH .95–.97 | .69–.83 |
| Rosentswieg, J. | *R.Q., 39*:818–819, October, 1968. | F | 184 | college freshmen & sophomores | No | .89–.96 | EVC .72–.83 |

*See Appendix D for explanation of symbols.

**Diving test

*Equipment.* A rope 20 feet (6.10 m) longer than the width of the pool is tied at one end to some firm object. The other end is free. A weight is suspended from the center of the rope so the rope will drop. The rope is suspended 1 foot (30.48 cm) below the water and 2 feet (60.96 cm) from, and parallel to, the end of the pool.

Starting at rope level, the deck of the pool is marked in 5-foot (1.52 m) intervals up to 55 feet (16.76 m). The markers are numbered.

*Description and administration.* To become oriented with the starting position, the swimmer should practice starting from the rope two or three times. The swimmer then assumes the proper starting position for the stroke to be tested. The feet rest on the rope with the malleoli (ankle bones) at rope level.

At the signal "Go," the rope is dropped and the swimmer starts stroking. In swimming the side, breast, or elementary back stroke, the swimmer does 5 strokes complete with glide.

The distance covered is measured by noting where the ankles are in reference to the deck markers at the beginning of the recovery of the legs for the sixth stroke. Distance is measured to the nearest foot (meter).

For the front and back crawl, distance is measured by noting the position of the ankles at the moment the fingers enter the water to begin the sixth complete arm cycle. This can be simplified by counting the point of entry of each arm as one unit. The measurement is taken at the eleventh entry.

*Scoring.* The distance to the nearest foot (meter) traveled by the malleoli.

*Reliability and validity.* The test-retest method (trial 2 vs. trial 3) was used to obtain reliability coefficients of .95 and .97 for the front crawl and side strokes, respectively.

Although the author claimed face (content) validity, coefficients of .69 and .83 for the crawl and side strokes, respectively, were obtained by correlating test scores with subjective ratings of form. A judge scored form on the basis of 1–10.

*Normative information.* T-score tables were constructed for the crawl and side strokes, using data from 97 female college-age subjects. (Table 8–14.)

*Comments.* Some of the premises on which this test is based are questionable. This is due to the fact that the author did not define power. Since the mechanical formula for power is

$$\frac{\text{work}}{\text{time}}$$

it can be argued by the purist that power was *not* measured.

**TABLE 8-14 T-Scores for Crawl and Side Strokes (N = 97)**

| T-SCORE | CRAWL FEET | CRAWL METERS | SIDESTROKE FEET | SIDESTROKE METERS | T-SCORE | CRAWL FEET | CRAWL METERS | SIDESTROKE FEET | SIDESTROKE METERS |
|---|---|---|---|---|---|---|---|---|---|
| 76 | 50 | 15.24 | 52 | 15.85 | 51 | 27 | 8.23 | 28 | 8.53 |
| 73 | 47-49 | 14.33-14.94 | 51 | 15.55 | 49 | 26 | 7.92 | 26-27 | 7.92-8.23 |
| 72 | 46 | 14.02 | 50 | 15.24 | 48 | 25 | 7.62 | 25 | 7.62 |
| 70 | | | 48-49 | 14.63-14.94 | 47 | | | 24 | 7.32 |
| 69 | 45 | 13.72 | 46-47 | 14.02-14.33 | 46 | 24 | 7.32 | | |
| 68 | 44 | 13.41 | 45 | 13.72 | 45 | | | 23 | 7.01 |
| 67 | 43 | 13.11 | 44 | 13.41 | 44 | 23 | 7.01 | 22 | 6.71 |
| 66 | 40-42 | 12.19-12.80 | 43 | 13.11 | 43 | | | 21 | 6.40 |
| 65 | | | 42 | 12.80 | 42 | 22 | 6.71 | | |
| 64 | 39 | 11.89 | | | 41 | 21 | 6.40 | 19-20 | 5.79-6.10 |
| 63 | | | 40-41 | 12.19-12.50 | 40 | 20 | 6.10 | 18 | 5.49 |
| 62 | 38 | 11.58 | 37-39 | 11.28-11.89 | 39 | | | 17 | 5.18 |
| 61 | 36-37 | 10.97-11.28 | 36 | 10.97 | 38 | 19 | 5.79 | 16 | 4.88 |
| 60 | 35 | 10.67 | 35 | 10.67 | 37 | | | 15 | 4.57 |
| 59 | 34 | 10.36 | 34 | 10.36 | 36 | 18 | 5.49 | | |
| 57 | 33 | 10.06 | 33 | 10.06 | 35 | 17 | 5.18 | 14 | 4.27 |
| 56 | 32 | 9.75 | | | 34 | | | 9-13 | 2.74-3.96 |
| 55 | 31 | 9.45 | 32 | 9.75 | 33 | 16 | 4.88 | 8 | 2.44 |
| 54 | 30 | 9.14 | 31 | 9.45 | 32 | | | 7 | 2.13 |
| 53 | 28-29 | 8.53-8.84 | 30 | 9.14 | 30 | 15 | 4.57 | 6 | 1.83 |
| 52 | | | 29 | 8.84 | 27 | 9-14 | 2.74-4.27 | | |
| | | | | | 24 | 8 | 2.44 | 5 | 1.52 |

Source: Fox, 1957, pp. 233-38.

From the point of view of validation, the reader is cautioned that the test criterion for this study is form, not "swimming ability." The author did not discuss the relationship between form and "swimming ability."

## TRACK AND FIELD SKILLS TESTS

Track and field tests are not normally included in the sports skills area of most measurement and evaluation books in physical education. They are usually discussed in separate chapters, included under tests of general motor ability, or ignored altogether. As in swimming, track events are usually considered ends in themselves. Thus, tests of skill in track and field are usually achievement (performance) tests culminating in norms with which individuals or groups can be compared; they are not tests attempting to predict general ability in track and field from skill elements in track.

Since the skills tests in track are usually the skills themselves, statistical validation is not an important consideration. Reliability must be studied, however, or considerable time, money, or energy may be wasted. In general, track and field skills would tend to be reliable, since they are measured in time or distance, and the literature shows that these types of variables tend to be reliable if sufficient trials are allowed.

Finally, it is quite understandable that track and field events are found in many tests of general motor ability and so-called "fitness" tests. Track and field skills include running, jumping, and throwing. These fundamental skills play a large part in almost all athletic events. Thus, track and field events offer an interesting and convenient approach to the testing of more general athletic abilities.

Probably the most extensive work on development of achievement tests in track and field was done in the 1930s. Some of the studies are summarized in Table 8-15.

The Nielson and Cozens study is selected for further description. Although developed in the 1930s, it deserves mention due to the methods used in developing the achievement scales and on its sheer comprehensiveness.

### Nielson and Cozens Track Skills Achievement Tests[23]

The original test battery consisted of 33 skills tests for boys and 31 for girls, about half of which would be considered track and field skills today. Only the "pure" sprint events—40, 50, 60 and 75 yards (36.58 m, 45.72 m, 54.86 m, and 68.58 m)—will be mentioned here.

*Equipment.* Wool yarn; stopwatch.

*Description and administration.* A starting line and, parallel to it, 4 finish lines are established exactly 40, 50, 60 or 75 yards (36.58 m, 45.72 m, 54.86 m,

**TABLE 8-15 Summary of Track and Field Skills Tests***

| AUTHOR | SOURCE | SEX | NO. CASES | AGE GROUP | NORMS | RELIABILITY COEFFICIENT | VALIDITY COEFFICIENT |
|---|---|---|---|---|---|---|---|
| Neilson, N.P. and Cozens, F.W. | *Achievement Scales,* Cal. Dept. of Ed., 1934. | M & F | 1060 2400 | elem. & jr. high | Yes | — | .98** |
| Mitchell, A.F. | *R.Q., 5*:86-91, (supplement), March, 1934. | F | 600 | college women | Yes | — | log. |
| Coleman, J.W. | *R.Q., 11*:47-53, May, 1940. | M | 75 | 18-24 | No | T-R .82-92 | log. |

*See Appendix D for explanation of symbols.

**Validation coefficient for the authors' classification system rather than track skills.

**TABLE 8-16  Classification Chart for Boys and Girls**

| EXPONENT | HEIGHT — INCHES | HEIGHT — METERS | AGE IN YEARS AND MONTHS | WEIGHT — POUNDS | WEIGHT — KILOGRAMS | SUM OF EXPONENTS | CLASS |
|---|---|---|---|---|---|---|---|
| 1 | 50 to 51 | 1.27 to 1.30 | 10 to 10-5 | 60 to 65 | 27.22 to 29.48 | 9 and below | A |
| 2 | 52 to 53 | 1.32 to 1.35 | 10-6 to 10-11 | 66 to 70 | 29.94 to 31.75 | 10 to 14 | B |
| 3 | | | 11 to 11-5 | 71 to 75 | 32.21 to 34.01 | 15 to 19 | C |
| 4 | 54 to 55 | 1.37 to 1.40 | 11-6 to 11-11 | 76 to 80 | 34.47 to 35.29 | 20 to 24 | D |
| 5 | | | 12 to 12-5 | 81 to 85 | 36.74 to 38.56 | 25 to 29 | E |
| 6 | 56 to 57 | 1.42 to 1.45 | 12-6 to 12-11 | 86 to 90 | 39.01 to 40.82 | 30 to 34 | F |
| 7 | | | 13 to 13-5 | 91 to 95 | 41.28 to 43.09 | 35 to 38 | G |
| 8 | 58 to 59 | 1.47 to 1.50 | 13-6 to 13-11 | 96 to 100 | 43.55 to 45.36 | 39 and above | H |
| 9 | | | 14 to 14-5 | 101 to 105 | 45.81 to 47.63 | | |
| 10 | 60 to 61 | 1.52 to 1.55 | 14-6 to 14-11 | 106 to 110 | 48.08 to 49.90 | | |
| 11 | | | 15 to 15-5 | 111 to 115 | 50.35 to 52.16 | | |
| 12 | 62 to 63 | 1.57 to 1.60 | 15-6 to 15-11 | 116 to 120 | 52.62 to 54.43 | | |
| 13 | | | 16 to 16-5 | 121 to 125 | 54.89 to 56.70 | | |
| 14 | 64 to 65 | 1.63 to 1.65 | 16-6 to 16-11 | 126 to 130 | 57.15 to 58.97 | | |
| 15 | 66 to 67 | 1.68 to 1.70 | 17 to 17-5 | 131 to 133 | 59.42 to 60.33 | | |
| 16 | 68 | 1.73 | 17-6 to 17-11 | 134 to 136 | 60.78 to 61.69 | | |
| 17 | 69 and over | 1.75 and over | 18 and over | 137 and over | 62.14 and over | | |

EXAMPLE FOR USE OF CLASSIFICATION CHART:

| | EXPONENT |
|---|---|
| Height | |
|   inches—57 | |
|   meters—1.45 | 6 |
| Age | |
|   13 yrs., 2 mos. | 7 |
| Weight | |
|   pounds—102 | |
|   kilograms—46.27 | 9 |
| Sum | 22 |
| Pupil is in Class D | |

Source:  Neilson and Cozens, 1934, pp. 5–6.

TABLE 8-17   60-Yard (54.86 m) Run—Boys (Time in Seconds and Tenths of Seconds)

| SCORE | A | B | C | D | E | F | G | H | SCORE |
|---|---|---|---|---|---|---|---|---|---|
| | | | | CLASSES | | | | | |
| 100 | 8.1 | 7.9 | 7.7 | — | 7.4 | — | — | — | 100 |
| 99 | — | — | — | 7.6 | — | 7.2 | 6.9 | — | 99 |
| 98 | — | — | — | — | — | — | — | 6.6 | 98 |
| 97 | 8.2 | 8.0 | 7.8 | — | 7.5 | — | — | — | 97 |
| 96 | — | — | — | 7.7 | — | 7.3 | 7.0 | — | 96 |
| 95 | — | — | — | — | — | — | — | 6.7 | 95 |
| 94 | 8.3 | 8.1 | 7.9 | — | 7.6 | — | — | — | 94 |
| 93 | — | — | — | 7.8 | — | 7.4 | 7.1 | — | 93 |
| 92 | 8.4 | 8.2 | 8.0 | — | — | — | — | 6.8 | 92 |
| 91 | — | — | — | — | 7.7 | — | — | — | 91 |
| 90 | — | — | — | 7.9 | — | 7.5 | 7.2 | — | 90 |
| 89 | 8.5 | 8.3 | 8.1 | — | — | — | — | 6.9 | 89 |
| 88 | — | — | — | — | 7.8 | — | — | — | 88 |
| 87 | — | — | — | 8.0 | — | 7.6 | 7.3 | — | 87 |
| 86 | 8.6 | 8.4 | 8.2 | — | — | — | — | 7.0 | 86 |
| 85 | — | — | — | — | 7.9 | — | — | — | 85 |
| 84 | — | — | — | 8.1 | — | 7.7 | 7.4 | — | 84 |
| 83 | 8.7 | 8.5 | 8.3 | — | — | — | — | 7.1 | 83 |
| 82 | — | — | — | 8.2 | 8.0 | — | — | — | 82 |
| 81 | 8.8 | 8.6 | 8.4 | — | — | 7.8 | 7.5 | — | 81 |
| 80 | — | — | — | — | — | — | — | 7.2 | 80 |
| 79 | — | — | — | 8.3 | 8.1 | — | — | — | 79 |
| 78 | 8.9 | 8.7 | 8.5 | — | — | 7.9 | 7.6 | — | 78 |
| 77 | — | — | — | — | — | — | — | 7.3 | 77 |
| 76 | — | — | — | 8.4 | 8.2 | — | — | — | 76 |
| 75 | 9.0 | 8.8 | 8.6 | — | — | 8.0 | 7.7 | — | 75 |
| 74 | — | — | — | — | — | — | — | 7.4 | 74 |
| 73 | — | — | — | 8.5 | 8.3 | — | — | — | 73 |
| 72 | 9.1 | 8.9 | 8.7 | — | — | 8.1 | 7.8 | — | 72 |
| 71 | — | — | — | — | — | — | — | 7.5 | 71 |
| 70 | — | — | — | 8.6 | 8.4 | — | — | — | 70 |
| 69 | 9.2 | 9.0 | 8.8 | — | — | 8.2 | 7.9 | — | 69 |
| 68 | — | — | — | — | — | — | — | 7.6 | 68 |
| 67 | 9.3 | 9.1 | 8.9 | 8.7 | 8.5 | — | — | — | 67 |
| 66 | — | — | — | — | — | 8.3 | 8.0 | — | 66 |
| 65 | — | — | — | 8.8 | — | — | — | 7.7 | 65 |
| 64 | 9.4 | 9.2 | 9.0 | — | 8.6 | — | — | — | 64 |
| 63 | — | — | — | — | — | 8.4 | 8.1 | — | 63 |
| 62 | — | — | — | 8.9 | — | — | — | 7.8 | 62 |
| 61 | 9.5 | 9.3 | 9.1 | — | 8.7 | — | — | — | 61 |
| 60 | — | — | — | — | — | 8.5 | 8.2 | — | 60 |
| 59 | — | — | — | 9.0 | — | — | — | 7.9 | 59 |
| 58 | 9.6 | 9.4 | 9.2 | — | 8.8 | — | — | — | 58 |
| 57 | — | — | — | — | — | 8.6 | 8.3 | — | 57 |
| 56 | 9.7 | 9.5 | 9.3 | 9.1 | — | — | — | 8.0 | 56 |

190

TABLE 8–17 (continued)

| SCORE | | | | CLASSES | | | | | SCORE |
|---|---|---|---|---|---|---|---|---|---|
| | A | B | C | D | E | F | G | H | |
| 55 | — | — | — | — | 8.9 | — | — | — | 55 |
| 54 | — | — | — | — | — | 8.7 | 8.4 | — | 54 |
| 53 | 9.8 | 9.6 | 9.4 | 9.2 | — | — | — | 8.1 | 53 |
| 52 | — | — | — | — | 9.0 | — | — | — | 52 |
| 51 | — | — | — | — | — | 8.8 | 8.5 | — | 51 |
| 50 | 9.9 | 9.7 | 9.5 | 9.3 | — | — | — | 8.2 | 50 |
| 49 | — | — | — | — | 9.1 | — | — | — | 49 |
| 48 | — | — | — | — | — | 8.9 | 8.6 | — | 48 |
| 47 | 10.0 | 9.8 | 9.6 | 9.4 | — | — | — | 8.3 | 47 |
| 46 | — | — | — | — | 9.2 | — | — | — | 46 |
| 45 | — | — | — | — | — | 9.0 | 8.7 | — | 45 |
| 44 | 10.1 | 9.9 | 9.7 | 9.5 | — | — | — | 8.4 | 44 |
| 43 | — | — | — | — | 9.3 | — | — | — | 43 |
| 42 | 10.2 | 10.0 | 9.8 | — | — | 9.1 | 8.8 | — | 42 |
| 41 | — | — | — | 9.6 | — | — | — | 8.5 | 41 |
| 40 | — | — | — | — | 9.4 | — | — | — | 40 |
| 39 | 10.3 | 10.1 | 9.9 | 9.7 | — | 9.2 | 8.9 | — | 39 |
| 38 | — | — | — | — | — | — | — | 8.6 | 38 |
| 37 | — | — | — | — | 9.5 | — | — | — | 37 |
| 36 | 10.4 | 10.2 | 10.0 | 9.8 | — | 9.3 | 9.0 | — | 36 |
| 35 | — | — | — | — | — | — | — | 8.7 | 35 |
| 34 | — | — | — | — | 9.6 | — | — | — | 34 |
| 33 | 10.5 | 10.3 | 10.1 | 9.9 | — | 9.4 | 9.1 | — | 33 |
| 32 | — | — | — | — | — | — | — | 8.8 | 32 |
| 31 | 10.6 | 10.4 | 10.2 | — | 9.7 | — | — | — | 31 |
| 30 | — | — | — | 10.0 | — | 9.5 | 9.2 | — | 30 |
| 29 | — | — | — | — | — | — | — | 8.9 | 29 |
| 28 | 10.7 | 10.5 | 10.3 | — | 9.8 | — | — | — | 28 |
| 27 | — | — | — | 10.1 | — | 9.6 | 9.3 | — | 27 |
| 26 | — | — | — | — | — | — | — | 9.0 | 26 |
| 25 | 10.8 | 10.6 | 10.4 | — | 9.9 | — | — | — | 25 |
| 24 | — | — | — | 10.2 | — | 9.7 | 9.4 | — | 24 |
| 23 | — | — | — | — | — | — | — | 9.1 | 23 |
| 22 | 10.9 | 10.7 | 10.5 | — | 10.0 | — | — | — | 22 |
| 21 | — | — | — | 10.3 | — | 9.8 | 9.5 | — | 21 |
| 20 | — | — | — | — | — | — | — | 9.2 | 20 |
| 19 | 11.0 | 10.8 | 10.6 | 10.4 | 10.1 | — | — | — | 19 |
| 18 | — | — | — | — | — | 9.9 | 9.6 | — | 18 |
| 17 | 11.1 | 10.9 | 10.7 | — | — | — | — | 9.3 | 17 |
| 16 | — | — | — | 10.5 | 10.2 | — | — | — | 16 |
| 15 | — | — | — | — | — | 10.0 | 9.7 | — | 15 |
| 14 | 11.2 | 11.0 | 10.8 | — | — | — | — | 9.4 | 14 |
| 13 | — | — | — | 10.6 | 10.3 | — | — | — | 13 |
| 12 | — | — | — | — | — | 10.1 | 9.8 | — | 12 |
| 11 | 11.3 | 11.1 | 10.9 | — | — | — | — | 9.5 | 11 |

**TABLE 8-17 (continued)**

| SCORE | A | B | C | CLASSES D | E | F | G | H | SCORE |
|---|---|---|---|---|---|---|---|---|---|
| 10 | — | — | — | 10.7 | 10.4 | — | — | — | 10 |
| 9 | — | — | — | — | — | 10.2 | 9.9 | — | 9 |
| 8 | 11.4 | 11.2 | 11.0 | — | — | — | — | 9.6 | 8 |
| 7 | — | — | — | 10.8 | 10.5 | — | — | — | 7 |
| 6 | 11.5 | 11.3 | 11.1 | — | — | 10.3 | 10.0 | — | 6 |
| 5 | — | — | — | — | — | — | — | 9.7 | 5 |
| 4 | — | — | — | 10.9 | 10.6 | — | — | — | 4 |
| 3 | 11.6 | 11.4 | 11.2 | — | — | 10.4 | 10.1 | — | 3 |
| 2 | — | — | — | — | — | — | — | 9.8 | 2 |
| 1 | — | — | — | 11.0 | 10.7 | — | — | — | 1 |

Source: Neilson and Cozens, 1934, pp. 72–73.

**TABLE 8-18  60-Yard (54.86 m) Run—Girls (Time in Seconds and Tenths of Seconds)**

| SCORE | A | B | C | CLASSES D | E | F | G | H | SCORE |
|---|---|---|---|---|---|---|---|---|---|
| 100 | — | — | — | 7.6 | — | — | — | — | 100 |
| 99 | — | 8.0 | 7.8 | — | 7.5 | — | 7.3 | 7.5 | 99 |
| 98 | 8.2 | — | — | 7.7 | — | 7.4 | — | — | 98 |
| 97 | — | — | 7.9 | — | — | — | 7.4 | 7.6 | 97 |
| 96 | 8.3 | 8.1 | — | — | 7.6 | 7.5 | — | — | 96 |
| 95 | — | — | — | 7.8 | — | — | — | — | 95 |
| 94 | — | 8.2 | 8.0 | — | 7.7 | — | 7.5 | 7.7 | 94 |
| 93 | 8.4 | — | — | 7.9 | — | 7.6 | — | — | 93 |
| 92 | — | — | 8.1 | — | — | — | 7.6 | 7.8 | 92 |
| 91 | 8.5 | 8.3 | — | — | 7.8 | 7.7 | — | — | 91 |
| 90 | — | — | — | 8.0 | — | — | — | — | 90 |
| 89 | — | 8.4 | 8.2 | — | 7.9 | — | 7.7 | 7.9 | 89 |
| 88 | 8.6 | — | — | 8.1 | — | 7.8 | — | — | 88 |
| 87 | — | — | 8.3 | — | — | — | 7.8 | 8.0 | 87 |
| 86 | 8.7 | 8.5 | — | — | 8.0 | 7.9 | — | — | 86 |
| 85 | — | — | — | 8.2 | — | — | — | — | 85 |
| 84 | — | 8.6 | 8.4 | — | 8.1 | — | 7.9 | 8.1 | 84 |
| 83 | 8.8 | — | — | 8.3 | — | 8.0 | — | — | 83 |
| 82 | — | — | 8.5 | — | — | — | 8.0 | 8.2 | 82 |
| 81 | 8.9 | 8.7 | — | — | 8.2 | 8.1 | — | — | 81 |
| 80 | — | — | — | 8.4 | — | — | — | — | 80 |
| 79 | — | 8.8 | 8.6 | — | 8.3 | — | 8.1 | 8.3 | 79 |
| 78 | 9.0 | — | — | 8.5 | — | 8.2 | — | — | 78 |
| 77 | — | — | 8.7 | — | — | — | 8.2 | 8.4 | 77 |
| 76 | 9.1 | 8.9 | — | — | 8.4 | 8.3 | — | — | 76 |
| 75 | — | — | — | 8.6 | — | — | — | — | 75 |
| 74 | — | 9.0 | 8.8 | — | 8.5 | — | 8.3 | 8.5 | 74 |
| 73 | 9.2 | — | — | 8.7 | — | 8.4 | — | — | 73 |
| 72 | — | — | 8.9 | — | — | — | 8.4 | 8.6 | 72 |

TABLE 8-18 (continued)

| SCORE | | | | CLASSES | | | | | SCORE |
|---|---|---|---|---|---|---|---|---|---|
| | A | B | C | D | E | F | G | H | |
| 71 | 9.3 | 9.1 | — | — | 8.6 | 8.5 | — | — | 71 |
| 70 | — | — | — | 8.8 | — | — | — | — | 70 |
| 69 | — | 9.2 | 9.0 | — | 8.7 | — | 8.5 | 8.7 | 69 |
| 68 | 9.4 | — | — | 8.9 | — | 8.6 | — | — | 68 |
| 67 | — | — | 9.1 | — | — | — | 8.6 | 8.8 | 67 |
| 66 | 9.5 | 9.3 | — | — | 8.8 | 8.7 | — | — | 66 |
| 65 | — | — | — | 9.0 | — | — | — | — | 65 |
| 64 | — | 9.4 | 9.2 | — | 8.9 | — | 8.7 | 8.9 | 64 |
| 63 | 9.6 | — | — | 9.1 | — | 8.8 | — | — | 63 |
| 62 | — | — | 9.3 | — | — | — | 8.8 | 9.0 | 62 |
| 61 | 9.7 | 9.5 | — | — | 9.0 | 8.9 | — | — | 61 |
| 60 | — | — | — | 9.2 | — | — | — | — | 60 |
| 59 | — | 9.6 | 9.4 | — | 9.1 | — | 8.9 | 9.1 | 59 |
| 58 | 9.8 | — | — | 9.3 | — | 9.0 | — | — | 58 |
| 57 | — | — | 9.5 | — | — | — | 9.0 | 9.2 | 57 |
| 56 | 9.9 | 9.7 | — | — | 9.2 | 9.1 | — | — | 56 |
| 55 | — | — | — | 9.4 | — | — | — | — | 55 |
| 54 | — | 9.8 | 9.6 | — | 9.3 | — | 9.1 | 9.3 | 54 |
| 53 | 10.0 | — | — | 9.5 | — | 9.2 | — | — | 53 |
| 52 | — | — | 9.7 | — | — | — | 9.2 | 9.4 | 52 |
| 51 | 10.1 | 9.9 | — | — | 9.4 | 9.3 | — | — | 51 |
| 50 | — | — | 9.8 | 9.6 | — | — | — | — | 50 |
| 49 | — | 10.0 | — | — | 9.5 | — | 9.3 | 9.5 | 49 |
| 48 | 10.2 | — | — | 9.7 | — | 9.4 | — | — | 48 |
| 47 | — | — | 9.9 | — | — | — | 9.4 | 9.6 | 47 |
| 46 | 10.3 | 10.1 | — | — | 9.6 | 9.5 | — | — | 46 |
| 45 | — | — | 10.0 | 9.8 | — | — | — | — | 45 |
| 44 | — | 10.2 | — | — | 9.7 | — | 9.5 | 9.7 | 44 |
| 43 | 10.4 | — | — | 9.9 | — | 9.6 | — | — | 43 |
| 42 | — | — | 10.1 | — | — | — | 9.6 | 9.8 | 42 |
| 41 | 10.5 | 10.3 | — | — | 9.8 | 9.7 | — | — | 41 |
| 40 | — | — | 10.2 | 10.0 | — | — | — | — | 40 |
| 39 | — | 10.4 | — | — | 9.9 | — | 9.7 | 9.9 | 39 |
| 38 | 10.6 | — | — | 10.1 | — | 9.8 | — | — | 38 |
| 37 | — | — | 10.3 | — | — | — | 9.8 | 10.0 | 37 |
| 36 | 10.7 | 10.5 | — | — | 10.0 | 9.9 | — | — | 36 |
| 35 | — | — | 10.4 | 10.2 | — | — | — | — | 35 |
| 34 | — | 10.6 | — | — | 10.1 | — | 9.9 | 10.1 | 34 |
| 33 | 10.8 | — | — | 10.3 | — | 10.0 | — | — | 33 |
| 32 | — | — | 10.5 | — | — | — | 10.0 | 10.2 | 32 |
| 31 | 10.9 | 10.7 | — | — | 10.2 | 10.1 | — | — | 31 |
| 30 | — | — | 10.6 | 10.4 | — | — | — | — | 30 |
| 29 | — | 10.8 | — | — | 10.3 | — | 10.1 | 10.3 | 29 |
| 28 | 11.0 | — | — | 10.5 | — | 10.2 | — | — | 28 |

TABLE 8–18 (continued)

| SCORE | A | B | C | D | E | F | G | H | SCORE |
|---|---|---|---|---|---|---|---|---|---|
| | | | | CLASSES | | | | | |
| 27 | — | — | 10.7 | — | — | — | 10.2 | 10.4 | 27 |
| 26 | 11.1 | 10.9 | — | — | 10.4 | 10.3 | — | — | 26 |
| 25 | — | — | 10.8 | 10.6 | — | — | — | — | 25 |
| 24 | — | 11.0 | — | — | 10.5 | — | 10.3 | 10.5 | 24 |
| 23 | 11.2 | — | — | 10.7 | — | 10.4 | — | — | 23 |
| 22 | — | — | 10.9 | — | — | — | 10.4 | 10.6 | 22 |
| 21 | 11.3 | 11.1 | — | — | 10.6 | 10.5 | — | — | 21 |
| 20 | — | — | 11.0 | 10.8 | — | — | — | — | 20 |
| 19 | — | 11.2 | — | — | 10.7 | — | 10.5 | 10.7 | 19 |
| 18 | 11.4 | — | — | 10.9 | — | 10.6 | — | — | 18 |
| 17 | — | — | 11.1 | — | — | — | 10.6 | 10.8 | 17 |
| 16 | 11.5 | 11.3 | — | — | 10.8 | 10.9 | — | — | 16 |
| 15 | — | — | 11.2 | 11.0 | — | — | — | — | 15 |
| 14 | — | 11.4 | — | — | 10.9 | — | 10.7 | 10.9 | 14 |
| 13 | 11.6 | — | — | 11.1 | — | 10.8 | — | — | 13 |
| 12 | — | — | 11.3 | — | — | — | 10.8 | 11.0 | 12 |
| 11 | 11.7 | 11.5 | — | — | 11.0 | 10.9 | — | — | 11 |
| 10 | — | — | 11.4 | 11.2 | — | — | — | — | 10 |
| 9 | — | 11.6 | — | — | 11.1 | — | 10.9 | 11.1 | 9 |
| 8 | 11.8 | — | — | 11.3 | — | 11.0 | — | — | 8 |
| 7 | — | — | 11.5 | — | — | — | 11.0 | 11.2 | 7 |
| 6 | 11.9 | 11.7 | — | — | 11.2 | 11.1 | — | — | 6 |
| 5 | — | — | 11.6 | 11.4 | — | — | — | — | 5 |
| 4 | — | 11.8 | — | — | 11.3 | — | 11.1 | 11.3 | 4 |
| 3 | 12.0 | — | — | 11.5 | — | 11.2 | — | — | 3 |
| 2 | — | — | 11.7 | — | — | — | 11.2 | 11.4 | 2 |
| 1 | 12.1 | 11.9 | — | — | 11.4 | 11.3 | — | — | 1 |

Source: Neilson and Cozens, 1934, pp. 132–133.

or 68.58 m) from the starting line. One student is assigned as official starter, two students are assigned to hold the wool yarn breast high over the finish line, and another student is assigned as recorder. The student to be tested takes a position behind the starting line. The teacher stands at the finish line with stopwatch in hand. The timer (teacher) raises an arm as a signal to the starter when ready; the starter raises an arm and says, "On your mark, get set, go!" With the word "go" the starter brings the arm down quickly, the student starts the run, and the timer starts the watch. When the student breasts the yarn over the finish line, the timer stops the watch. The time is given aloud to the recorder.

*Scoring.* Time is taken to the nearest tenth of a second.

*Reliability and validity.* No reliability coefficients were obtained in this study. Content validity was assumed. No attempt was made to establish statistical validity, since prediction of general track ability was not a consideration.

*Normative information.* T-scale norm tables were developed for all 33 items for samples ranging from 1,060 to 2,400 boys and girls for each of eight classifications. The classification system was based on age, height, and weight and is shown in Table 8-16. Examples of the T-scales are shown in Tables 8-17 and 8-18.

*Comments.* Too often, studies involving a large number of subjects do not report reliability coefficients. It is understandable that the test-retest method might be prohibitive in these instances. However, the split-halves, odd-even method can be utilized, precluding the necessity for testing the same large group twice.

## BIBLIOGRAPHY

AAHPER. *Skills Test Manual-Archery for Boys and Girls.* Washington: AAHPERD Publications, 1967.

ANNETT, THOMAS. "A Study of Rhythmical Capacity and Performance in Motor Rhythm in Physical Education Majors." *Research Quarterly,* 3 (May 1932), 183–91.

ASHTON, DUDLEY. "A Gross Motor Rhythm Test." *Research Quarterly,* 24 (October 1953), 253–60.

BARROW, HAROLD M. and ROSEMARY McGEE. *A Practical Approach to Measurement in Physical Education.* Philadelphia: Lea and Febiger, 1964.

BENNETT, La VERNE M. "A Test of Diving for Use in Beginning Classes." *Research Quarterly,* 18 (March 1942), 109–15.

BENTON, RACHEL J. "The Measurement of Capacities for Learning Dance Movement Techniques." *Research Quarterly,* 15 (May 1944), 137–44.

BOSCO, JAMES S. "The Physical and Personality Characteristics of Champion Male Gymnasts." Unpublished doctoral dissertation, University of Illinois, 1962.

COLEMAN, JAMES W. "Pure Speed as a Positive Factor in Some Track and Field Events." *Research Quarterly,* 11 (May 1940), 47–53.

DiGIOVANNA, VINCENT. "The Relation of Structural and Functional Measures to Success in College Athletics." *Research Quarterly,* 14 (May 1943), 199–216.

FOX, MARGARET G. "Swimming Power Test." *Research Quarterly,* 28 (October 1957), 233–38.

GATES, JOHN L. "The Validity of Selected Structural and Functional Measures in Predicting Potential Gymnastics Ability for the Purpose of Homogeneous Grouping." Unpublished doctoral dissertation, University of Arkansas, 1974.

HEWITT, JACK E. "Achievement Scale Scores for High School Swimming." *Research Quarterly,* 20 (May 1949), 170–79.

_____. "Achievement Scale Scores for Wartime Swimming." *Research Quarterly,* 14 (December 1943), 391–96.

_____. "Swimming Achievement Scale Scores for College Men." *Research Quarterly,* 19 (December 1948), 282–89.

HYDE, EDITH I. "An Achievement Scale in Archery." *Research Quarterly,* 8 (May 1937), 109–16.

_____. "The Measurement of Achievement in Archery." *Journal of Educational Research,* 27 (May 1934), 673–86.

____. "National Research Study in Archery." *Research Quarterly*, 7 (December 1936), 64–73.

JOHNSON, BARRY L. and JACK K. NELSON. *Practical Measurements for Evaluation in Physical Education*. Minneapolis: Burgess Publishing Co., 1969.

LIBA, MARIE and JANICE K. OLSEN. "A Device for Evaluating Spot Bowling Ability." *Research Quarterly*, 38 (May 1967), 193–201.

MARTIN, JOAN. "Bowling Norms for College Men and Women." *Research Quarterly*, 31 (March, 1960), 113–16.

____ and JACK KEOGH. "Bowling Norms for College Students in Elective Physical Education Classes." *Research Quarterly*, 35 (October 1964), 325–27.

McKEE, MARY ELLEN. "A Test for the Full Swinging Shot in Golf." *Research Quarterly*, 21 (March 1950), 40–46.

MICHALEK, FRANK H. "Selected Measures as Predictors of Success in Gymnastics." Unpublished doctoral dissertation, University of Utah, 1974.

MITCHELL, A. VIOLA. "A Scoring Table for College Women in the Fifty-Yard (45.72 m.) Dash, the Running Broad Jump and the Basketball Throw for Distance." *Research Quarterly*, Supplement, 5 (March 1934), 86–91.

NEILSON, N.P. and FREDERICK COZENS. *Achievement Scales in Physical Education Activities for Boys and Girls in Elementary and Junior High School*. Sacramento: California State Department of Education, 1934.

PHILLIPS, MARJORIE and DEAN SUMMERS. "Bowling Norms and Learning Curves for College Women." *Research Quarterly*, 21 (December 1950), 377–85.

ROSENTSWIEG, JOEL. "A Revision of the Power Swimming Test." *Research Quarterly*, 39 (October 1968), 818–19.

ROWLANDS, DAVID J. "A Golf Skills Test Battery." Unpublished doctoral dissertation, University of Utah, 1974.

SCOTT, M. GLADYS and ESTHER FRENCH. *Measurement and Evaluation in Physical Education*. Dubuque, Iowa: Wm. C. Brown, Co., 1959.

SHELLY, MARY JO. "Some Aspects of the Case For and Against Objective Testing of Dance in Education." *Research Quarterly*, 1 (October 1930), 119–24.

SIMPSON, SHIRLEY. "Development and Validation of an Objective Measure of Locomotor Response to Auditory Rhythmic Stimuli." *Research Quarterly*, 29 (October 1958), 342–48.

VANDERHOOF, ELLEN R. "Beginning Golf Achievement Tests." Unpublished master's thesis, State University of Iowa, 1956.

WAGLOW, I.F. "An Experiment in Social Dance Testing." *Research Quarterly*, 24 (March 1953), 97–101.

WETTSTONE, EUGENE. "Tests for Predicting Potential Ability in Gymnastics and Tumbling." *Research Quarterly*, 9 (December 1938), 115–25.

ZABIK, ROBERT M. and ANDREW S. JACKSON. "Reliability of Archery Achievement." *Research Quarterly*, 40 (March 1969), 254–55.

## SUGGESTED READINGS

AUTREY, ELIZABETH B. "A Study of a Battery of Tests for Measuring Playing Ability in Golf." Unpublished master's thesis, University of Wisconsin, Madison, Wisconsin, 1937.

BRODERICK, KATHLEEN E. "A Normative Study of Track and Field Events for the Alberta Special Games." Unpublished master's thesis, University of Alberta, Edmonton, Canada, 1974.

BUCK, NADINE. "A Comparison of Two Methods of Testing Response to Auditory Rhythms." *Research Quarterly,* 7 (October 1936), 36–45.

CLEVETT, MELVIN A. "An Experiment in Teaching Methods of Golf." *Research Quarterly,* 2 (December 1931), 104–12.

COFFEY, MARGARET. "Achievement Tests in Golf." Unpublished master's thesis, State University of Iowa, Iowa City, Iowa, 1946.

COZENS, FREDERICK W. *Achievement Scales in Physical Education Activities for College Men.* Philadelphia: Lea and Febiger, 1936.

COZENS, FREDERICK W., HAZEL J. CUBBERLEY, and N.P. NEILSON. *Achievement Scales in Physical Education Activities for Secondary School Girls and College Women.* New York: A.S. Barnes and Company, 1937.

COZENS, FREDERICK W., MARTIN H. TRIEB, and N.P. NEILSON. "The Classification of Secondary School Boys for Purposes of Competition." *Research Quarterly,* 7 (March 1936), 36–43.

CURETON, THOMAS K. *Beginning and Intermediate National YMCA Progressive Aquatic Tests.* New York: Association Press, 1938.

_____. "Standards for Testing Beginning Swimming." *Research Quarterly,* 10 (December 1939), 54–59.

EDGREN, HARRY D. and G.G. ROBINSON. *Individual Skill Tests in Physical Activities.* Chicago: published by the authors, 1937.

FREY, HAROLD J. "Analysis of Beginning Tumbling." Unpublished master's thesis, University of Illinois, 1951.

GAUTHEIR, ROGER B. "The Reliability of Gymnastic Ratings and Gymnastic Judges." Unpublished doctoral dissertation, University of Alberta, 1974.

GIRARDIN, YVAN and DALE HANSON. "Relationship between Ability to Perform Tumbling Skills and Ability to Diagnose Performance Errors." *Research Quarterly,* 38 (December 1967), 556–61.

HEINLEIN, CHRISTIAN P. "A New Method of Studying Rhythmic Responses of Children Together with an Evaluation of the Method of Simple Observation." *Journal of Genetic Psychology,* 36 (June 1929), 205–28.

JEFFERSON, HILARY W. "Coefficient Performance Chart." *Research Quarterly,* 11 (October, 1940), 148–54.

KELLY, NANCY. "A Study of a Battery of Tests for Measuring Golf Playing Ability of Beginners." Unpublished master's thesis, University of Texas, 1944.

KORANDO, CATHERINE A. "The Determination of Valid Measures of Balance Beam Performance." Unpublished master's thesis, Southern Illinois University, 1970.

KRAKOWER, HYMAN. "Testing in Physical Education." *Research Quarterly,* 8 (March 1937), 45–67.

LEMON, ELOISE and ELIZABETH SHERBON. "A Study of the Relationship of Certain Measures of Rhythmic Ability and Motor Ability in Girls and Women." *Research Quarterly Supplement,* 5 (March 1934), 82–85.

McCRISTAL, KING J. "Experimental Study of Rhythm in Gymnastic and Tap Dancing." *Research Quarterly,* 4 (May 1933), 63–75.

NATIONS, TEENA. "Relationship between Brown's Golf Skills Battery and Scores on 18 Holes of Golf at the University of Oklahoma." Unpublished master's thesis, University of Oklahoma, 1973.

NOYES, ELIZABETH. "A Survey of Methods of Grading Women in Individual Gymnastics in Colleges and Universities." *Research Quarterly,* 4 (October 1933), 71–75.

PARKHURST, MARY G. "Achievement Tests in Swimming." *Journal of Health and Physical Education,* 5 (May 1934), 58–59.

PATTERSON, D.G., R.M. ELLIOT, L.D. ANDERSON, H.A. TOOPS, and E. HEIDBREDER. *Minnesota Mechanical Ability Tests.* University of Minnesota, 1930.

RUCKNICK, C.A. "The Role of Kinaesthesis in the Perception of Rhythm." *American Journal of Psychology,* 24 (July 1913), 305–59.

SCOTT, M. GLADYS. "Learning Rate of Beginning Swimmers." *Research Quarterly,* 25 (March 1954), 91–99.

SEASHORE, C.E. "New Rhythm Apparatus." *Science, New Series,* 19 (February 1924), 146–47.

SHAMBAUGH, MARY E. "The Objective Measurement of Success in the Teaching of Folk Dancing to University Women." *Research Quarterly,* 6 (March 1935), 33–58.

WATTS, HARRIET. "Construction and Evaluation of a Target for Testing the Approach Shot in Golf." Unpublished master's thesis, University of Wisconsin, 1942.

WHYMAN, DEANNA. "Two Methods of Evaluating the Front Crawl in Swimming." Unpublished master's thesis, Southern Illinois University, 1970.

WILLIAMS, H.M. "A Study in the Prediction of Motor Rhythmic Performance of School Children." *Journal of Genetic Psychology,* (December 1932).

WILSON, COLIN T. "Coordination Tests in Swimming." *Research Quarterly,* 5 (December 1934), 81–88.

WOOD, JANET I. "A Study for the Purpose of Setting up the Specifications of a Golf Driving Cage Target and Test for the Mid-iron and the Brassie Clubs." Unpublished master's thesis, University of Wisconsin, 1933.

# CHAPTER NINE
# SPORTS SKILLS TESTS: DUAL-PARTICIPANT SPORTS

## BADMINTON SKILLS TESTS

A number of badminton skill tests are available in the professional literature. A few are summarized in Table 9-1. Two tests will be discussed in more detail.

### The French Short Serve and Clear Tests[1]

*Equipment for the Short Serve Test.*   Badminton court; rope; plastic shuttle-cocks; racket; floor markings. Floor markings are circular lines, 1½ inches (3.81 cm) wide. Widths are included in diameters of the various circles. Diameters of the circles are 22 inches (55.88 cm), 30 inches (76.20 cm), 38 inches (96.52 cm), and 48 inches (1.22 m), respectively (Figure 9.1).

*Description and administration of the Short Serve Test.*   The purpose of the test is to measure ability to serve accurately and low.

The players must stand in the regulation court for serving and serve 20 times into the opposite right service court for the doubles game. The shuttlecock must go under the rope, which is placed 20 inches (50.80 cm) above and parallel to the net. The serve must be a legal one. Additional hints on the administration of this test may be obtained in Eckert.[2]

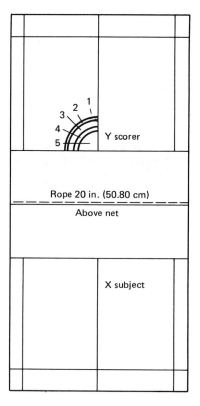

**FIGURE 9.1**
**Floor markings and scoring values for French's Short-Serve Test. (Reproduced from E. French and E. Stalter, "Study of Skill Tests in Badminton for College Women,"** *Res. Quart.,* **20 (October, 1949), 257–72.)**

**TABLE 9-1  Summary of Badminton Skills Tests***

| AUTHOR | SOURCE | SEX | NO. CASES | AGE GROUP | NORMS | RELIABILITY COEFFICIENT | VALIDITY COEFFICIENT |
|---|---|---|---|---|---|---|---|
| Scott, M.G. | *R.Q., 12*:242–253, May, 1941. | F | 149 | college women | Yes | SH .77–.98 | EVC .85 |
| French, E. and Stalter, E. | *R.Q., 20*:257–272, Oct., 1949. | F | 59 | college women | No | SH .51–.93 | EVC .69 |
| Lockhart, A and McPherson, F.A. | *R.Q., 20*:402–405 Dec., 1949 | F | 50 | college women | Yes | T-R .90 | EVC .60–.72 |
| Miller, F.A. | *R.Q., 22*:208–213, May, 1951. | M & F | 100<br>115 | college women<br>college men | No<br>No | T-R .94 | EVC .83 |
| Kowert, E.A. | Master's thesis, U. of Iowa, 1968. | M | 46 | college men | No | .50–.99 | EVC .84 |

*See Appendix D for explanation of symbols.

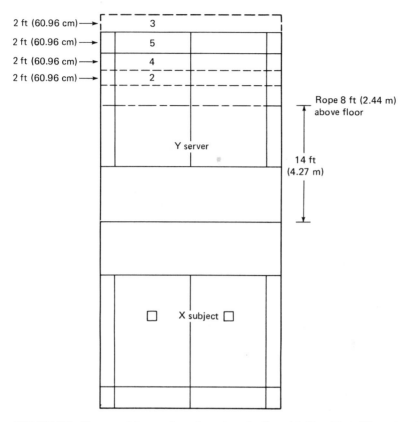

2 ft (60.96 cm) ⟶ 3

2 ft (60.96 cm) ⟶ 5

2 ft (60.96 cm) ⟶ 4

2 ft (60.96 cm) ⟶ 2

Rope 8 ft (2.44 m) above floor

Y server

14 ft (4.27 m)

X subject

**FIGURE 9.2 Floor markings and scoring values for French's Clear Test. (Reproduced from E. French and E. Stalter, "Study of Skill Tests in Badminton for College Women," *Res. Quart.*, 20 (October, 1949), 257-72.)**

*Scoring.* Each serve is given the numerical value of the area in which it first lands. Shuttlecocks that land on a line are given the higher value. Those serves that fail to go between the rope and the net, fall out of bounds, or are not served legally are scored zero. The final score is the sum of the values scored on the 20 serves.

*Equipment for the Clear Test.* Same as the Short Serve Test, except for the floor markings (Figure 9.2).

*Description and administration of the Clear Test.* The purpose of the test is to return a serve with an accurate clear shot. The player stands between the two square marks that are 2 inches (5.08 cm) square, 11 feet (3.35 m) from the net, and 3 feet (91.44 cm) from the center line on the target side of the net. The bird must cross the net with enough force to carry it to the line between the two squares before it touches the floor. As soon as the bird is served, the player may move about as desired. The player attempts to clear the bird over a rope stretched 8 feet (2.44 m) from the floor and 14 feet (4.27 m) from (and parallel to) the net, into the marked target area. The target area consists of: 1) a line across the court 2 feet

**TABLE 9-2  Norms (T-Scores) for the French Short Serve and Clear Tests**

| BEGINNERS | | ADVANCED | |
|---|---|---|---|
| SCORE | T-SCORE | SCORE | T-SCORE |
| 140 | 76 | 175 | 74 |
| 135 | 72 | 170 | 69 |
| 130 | 71 | 165 | 67 |
| 125 | 70 | 160 | 66 |
| 110 | 69 | 155 | 65 |
| 115 | 66 | 150 | 64 |
| 110 | 65 | 145 | 64 |
| 105 | 62 | 140 | 63 |
| 100 | 60 | 135 | 63 |
| 95 | 59 | 130 | 61 |
| 90 | 57 | 125 | 60 |
| 85 | 55 | 120 | 59 |
| 80 | 54 | 115 | 58 |
| 75 | 53 | 110 | 56 |
| 70 | 52 | 105 | 55 |
| 65 | 50 | 100 | 55 |
| 60 | 49 | 95 | 54 |
| 55 | 47 | 90 | 53 |
| 50 | 46 | 85 | 52 |
| 45 | 45 | 80 | 51 |
| 40 | 45 | 75 | 50 |
| 35 | 44 | 70 | 49 |
| 30 | 42 | 65 | 47 |
| 25 | 40 | 60 | 46 |
| 20 | 38 | 55 | 45 |
| 15 | 35 | 50 | 43 |
| 10 | 32 | 45 | 41 |
| 5 | 27 | 40 | 40 |
| 0 | 23 | 35 | 38 |
| | | 30 | 37 |
| | | 25 | 34 |
| | | 20 | 33 |
| | | 15 | 32 |
| | | 10 | 31 |
| | | 5 | 25 |

Source: Scott, 1941, p. 253.

(60.96 cm) nearer the net than the rear service line in the doubles game; and 2) a line across the court 2 feet (60.96 cm) farther from the net than the rear service line in the singles game. Additional hints on the administration of this test may be found in Clarke.[3]

*Scoring.*  Scoring is done according to the values in Figure 9.2. Trials that fail to clear the rope or fail to land in the target area are scored zero. A bird landing on a line dividing two scoring areas receives the higher score. The score on the entire test is the sum of 20 trials.

*Reliability and validity.*    The Service and Clear tests were selected from a battery of 6 items used in a preliminary study. The players were separated into two groups, beginning and advanced. They were given 20 trials on each test. The reliability coefficients on the 20 trials ranged from .63 to .77. Study of the reliability on alternate halves (odd vs. even) indicated that 10 trials would be sufficient for the advanced but not the beginning group.

A validity coefficient of .66 was obtained by correlating the tests with a combination of instructors' subjective ratings on a seven-point scale and standings in tournament play. This is an example of validation by use of an external criterion.

*Normative information.*    Norms were based on only 59 college women and should, therefore, be used with caution (Table 9-2).

The following grading plan was suggested:

| BEGINNERS | | ADVANCED | |
|---|---|---|---|
| A | 115–145 | A | 170–180 |
| B | 85–114 | B | 110–169 |
| C | 40–84 | C | 55–109 |
| D | 15–39 | D | 25–54 |
| Fd | 0–14 | Fd | 0–24 |

*Comments.*    The Service and Clear tests are easy to administer, consume little time, and would have some value in quick classification of students into ability groups prior to the start of instruction. The small number of cases used to construct the norms precludes their use as a credible standard of performance. The practice of combining the sum of the scores of two test items to arrive at a single score is a questionable practice in that the assumption is being made that the two items are of equal value in measuring the criterion.

### Lockhart and McPherson
### Badminton Wall-Volley Test[4]

*Equipment.*    Badminton racket in good condition; new indoor shuttlecock; unobstructed wall space at least 10 feet (3.05 m) in height and 10 feet (3.05 m) in length; stopwatch; score sheets. Floor markings should be made as follows: a 1-inch (2.54 cm) net line marked on the wall 5 feet (1.52 m) above and parallel to the floor; a starting line drawn on the floor 6 feet 6 inches (1.98 m) from the base of the wall; a restraining line marked on the floor three feet (91.44 cm) from the base of the wall and parallel to the starting line (Figure 9.3).

*Description and administration.*    The player to be tested stands behind the starting line 6 feet 6 inches (1.98 m) from the wall (Figure 9.3). On the signal "Ready, go," the bird is served legally against the wall on or above the net line.

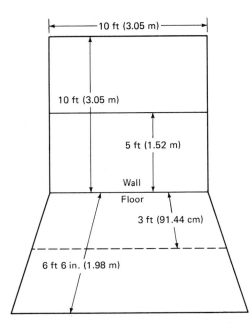

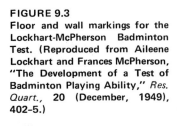

**FIGURE 9.3**
Floor and wall markings for the Lockhart-McPherson Badminton Test. (Reproduced from Aileene Lockhart and Frances McPherson, "The Development of a Test of Badminton Playing Ability," *Res. Quart.*, **20** (December, 1949), 402–5.)

The bird is volleyed continuously for 30 seconds. Only those shots hit from behind the 3-foot (91.44 cm) restraining line and above the 5-foot (1.52 m) net line are counted for the score. Once the volley is stopped, it may be restarted anytime during the 30-second test period with another legal serve from behind the starting line. Additional hints on the administration of this test may be obtained in Eckert[5] and Mathews.[6]

*Scoring.* With the exception of the serve(s), each legal hit merits one point. The final score is the total number of points in three 30-second trials. Rest periods are allowed between trials.

*Reliability and validity.* A reliability coefficient of .90 was obtained by using the test-retest (3 days apart) method on 50 sophomore college women.

Two different validity schemes were attempted by correlating scores on this test with the following external criteria: 1) judges' ratings; and 2) a round-robin tournament.

A third validity scheme correlated the judges' ratings with percentages of games won in the round-robin tournament. The resulting validity coefficients were .71, .60, and .90, respectively.

*Normative information.* T-scale values were calculated from data on 178 female college students on a total of three trials on a wooden blackboard surface. (Table 9-3).

*Comments.* This test is easy to administer, requires little time, and has some practical value as a quick means of classification into ability groups. However, since

**TABLE 9-3  T-Scales for Badminton Volleying Test**

| RAW SCORE | T SCORE | RAW SCORE | T SCORE | RAW SCORE | T SCORE |
|---|---|---|---|---|---|
| 148 | 78 | 108 | | 68 | 46.5 |
| 147 | | 107 | 62 | 67 | 46 |
| 146 | | 106 | | 66 | |
| 145 | | 105 | 61.5 | 65 | 45.5 |
| 144 | | 104 | 61 | 64 | 45 |
| 143 | 74 | 103 | 60.5 | 63 | 44.5 |
| 142 | | 102 | | 62 | 44 |
| 141 | | 101 | 60 | 61 | 43 |
| 140 | | 100 | 59.5 | 60 | 42.5 |
| 139 | | 99 | | 59 | 42.5 |
| 138 | 72 | 98 | | 58 | 42 |
| 137 | | 97 | 59 | 57 | 42 |
| 136 | 71 | 96 | 58.5 | 56 | 41.5 |
| 135 | | 95 | 58 | 55 | 41.5 |
| 134 | | 94 | 57.5 | 54 | 41 |
| 133 | | 93 | | 53 | 40.5 |
| 132 | | 92 | 57 | 52 | 40 |
| 131 | | 91 | 57 | 51 | 39.5 |
| 130 | | 90 | 56.5 | 50 | 38.5 |
| 129 | | 89 | 56 | 49 | 38 |
| 128 | 69.5 | 88 | 55.5 | 48 | 37.5 |
| 127 | 68.5 | 87 | 55 | 47 | 37 |
| 126 | | 86 | 54 | 46 | 36.5 |
| 125 | | 85 | 53.5 | 45 | 35.5 |
| 124 | | 84 | 53 | 44 | 34.5 |
| 123 | 67.5 | 83 | 53 | 43 | 34 |
| 122 | 67 | 82 | 52.5 | 42 | 33 |
| 121 | | 81 | 52 | 41 | |
| 120 | 66.5 | 80 | 51.5 | 40 | |
| 119 | | 79 | 51.5 | 39 | 31.5 |
| 118 | | 78 | 51 | 38 | 30.5 |
| 117 | | 77 | 51 | 37 | 29 |
| 116 | | 76 | 51 | 36 | |
| 115 | 66 | 75 | 50.5 | 35 | |
| 114 | 65 | 74 | | 34 | |
| 113 | 64.5 | 73 | 50 | 33 | |
| 112 | 64 | 72 | 48.5 | 32 | 25.5 |
| 111 | 63 | 71 | 48 | 31 | |
| 110 | 63 | 70 | 47.5 | 30 | |
| 109 | 62.5 | 69 | 47 | 29 | 21.0 |

Source: Lockhart and McPherson, 1949, pp. 402-5.

it contains only 1 item, low validity coefficients are to be expected, i.e., it would appear unlikely that a simple wall-volleying test would correlate highly with something as complex as "badminton playing ability." This test, combined with a Clear item and a Service item, would quite likely result in a more valid test.

## FENCING SKILLS TESTS

Interestingly, the majority of the material in this area appears to be unpublished, i.e., it is in the form of theses and dissertations. A few of these are summarized in Table 9–4.

The basic elements studied have been agility in footwork, body control, speed and accuracy of attack, speed of reaction time in defense, and ability to outwit the opponent.

One of the tests is selected for description as an example of a typical thesis in this area.

### Kuhajda Fencing Skill Test[7]

*Equipment.* Two fencing foils (one right-handed and one left-handed, with white tape placed on each foil 11 inches (27.94 cm) from the bell guard; two bamboo poles six feet (1.83 m) in height, tied together at the top in order to maintain a distance of 14 inches (35.56 cm) between the poles; two one-hundredth-of-a-second stopwatches; a flat wall surface 4 feet (1.22 m) wide and 6 feet (1.83 m) high.

*Description and administration.* The purpose of the test is to measure the speed and accuracy of the riposte-lunge from the parry four position.

The subject assumes an on-guard position with respect to the colored restraining lines assigned prior to the test. The back foot is placed behind and parallel to the restraining line farthest from the wall. The heel of the forward foot is on the restraining line nearest the wall. The fencing arm is in guard position six, with that portion of the blade between the bell guard and the tape resting against the pole to the right for a right-handed fencer and to the left for a left-handed fencer.

When the signal "Go" is given, the subject executes a parry four, ripostes, and lunges toward the wall target. The parry four is executed by touching the pole opposite the one from which the subject started with that section of the blade between the bell guard and the tape. The subject recovers to an on-guard position and repeats each trial when the signal is given. A total of five trials is allowed.

The wall target consists of 10 concentric circles. The center circle and each successive circle have a diameter of 2 inches (5.08 cm). The center of the center circle is placed at a perpendicular distance of 45 inches (1.14 m) from the floor (Figure 9.4).

A reference line is drawn on the floor perpendicular to the wall and directly under the center of the target. The reference line extends to the restraining line farthest from the wall. This reference line serves as a guideline for the remaining markings of the test.

**TABLE 9-4 Summary of Fencing Skills Tests\***

| AUTHOR | SOURCE | SEX | NO. CASES | AGE GROUP | NORMS | RELIABILITY COEFFICIENT | VALIDITY COEFFICIENT |
|---|---|---|---|---|---|---|---|
| Schutz, H.J. | Master's thesis, Univ. of Washington, 1940 | F | 150 | college women | No | T-R .69-.96 | — |
| Safrit, M.J. | Master's thesis, Univ. of Wisconsin, 1962. | F | — | college women | No | AV .85-.94 | — |
| Cooper, C.K. | Master's thesis, Western Illinois Univ., 1968 | F | 76 | college women | No | AV .62-.75 | log. |
| Kuhajda, P.F. | Master's thesis, Southern Illinois Univ., 1970 | F | 38 | college women | No | AV .65-.96 | log. |

*See Appendix D for explanation of symbols.

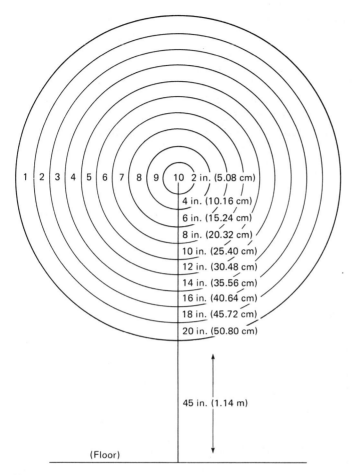

| 1 | 2 | 3 | 4 | 5 | 6 | 7 | 8 | 9 | 10 | 2 in. (5.08 cm) |

4 in. (10.16 cm)
6 in. (15.24 cm)
8 in. (20.32 cm)
10 in. (25.40 cm)
12 in. (30.48 cm)
14 in. (35.56 cm)
16 in. (40.64 cm)
18 in. (45.72 cm)
20 in. (50.80 cm)

45 in. (1.14 m)

(Floor)

Note: Vertical numbers indicate the circle diameters.
Horizontal numbers indicate the value of each circle.

**FIGURE 9.4  Wall Target for Fencing Skill Test. (Reproduced from P. F. Kuhajda, master's thesis, Carbondale, Illinois: Southern Illinois University, 1970.)**

On the floor directly in front of the target and parallel to the wall are three pairs of colored restraining lines. The horizontal distances of these lines from the wall are as follows:

green     7 feet 8 inches (2.34 m) and 6 feet 9 inches (2.06 m)
red        8 feet 1 inch (2.46 m) and 7 feet 2 inches (2.19 m)
blue      8 feet 6 inches (2.59 m) and 7 feet 7 inches (2.31 m)

Each line is one foot (30.48 cm) in length with 6 inches (15.24 cm) on each side of the reference line.

Three pairs of colored X's are placed on the floor. These X's are used in determining the placement of the parrying target. If a subject uses the red restraining lines, the poles are placed perpendicular to the floor on the red X's. If a subject uses the blue lines, the poles are placed on the blue X's. The same procedure is followed if the green restraining lines are used. The horizontal distances of the X's from the reference line and the vertical distances of the X's from the restraining lines are as follows: The X's are placed at points 7 inches (17.78 cm) to the right and left of the reference line and 17 inches (48.13 cm) toward the wall from the restraining lines nearest the wall (Figure 9.5).

Time penalties are imposed if the student starts the trial before the signal is given, neglects to parry before lunging toward the wall, or fails to keep the back

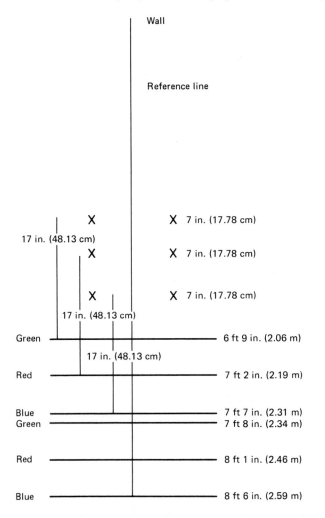

X = placement of the parrying targets (poles).

FIGURE 9.5   Dimensions of restraining lines for Fencing Skill Test. (Reproduced from P. F. Kuhajda, master's thesis, Carbondale, Illinois: Southern Illinois University, 1970.)

foot behind the restraining line farthest from the wall. One-tenth of a second is added to the time score for each trial in which the error is made.

*Scoring.*    An accuracy score and a time score are obtained for each subject. Each trial is timed from the moment the subject touches the parrying target until the foil tip contacts the wall target. Time is recorded to the nearest one hundredth of a second. An accuracy score is obtained by recording the number that corresponds to the circle contacted with the foil tip. Line contacts are awarded the higher of the two values.

*Reliability and validity.*    College women (N = 38) were given a total of five trials each. The analysis of variance method was used to obtain reliability coefficients ranging from .65 to .96.

No attempt was made to obtain statistical validity. Since the purpose of the test was simply to measure specific elements of fencing (speed and accuracy of the riposte-lunge) and not "fencing ability," content validity was considered sufficient.

*Normative information.*    No norms were established for this test.

*Comments.*    The reader is reminded that a master's thesis is often the first research experience of its writer, and acceptance of results should be viewed with caution. This should in no way be construed as a negative reflection on the writer of this thesis.

In view of the work of Singer,[8] who found little relationship between movement and accuracy elements when compared with foil fencing ability, future studies should probably include additional variables in the test battery.

## HANDBALL SKILLS TESTS

Few validated studies have been published since 1935, when the first empirically determined tests began to appear in the professional literature. A considerable number of unpublished studies are available in the form of masters' theses, however. Examples of each of the above are summarized in Table 9-5.

### The Pennington/Drowatzky/ Day/Hansan Test[9]

The study was conducted to develop a handball skills test that would discriminate between good and poor performances.

In the original study, 17 strength, motor ability, and handball skill items were used as experimental variables. No specific practice or warm-up was prescribed before administration of the test items. Subjects were involved in regular handball participation before and after testing.

After a series of zero-order correlations (correlating each variable with each

**TABLE 9-5 Summary of Handball Skills Tests***

| AUTHOR | SOURCE | SEX | NO. CASES | AGE GROUP | NORMS | RELIABILITY COEFFICIENT | VALIDITY COEFFICIENT |
|---|---|---|---|---|---|---|---|
| Cornish, C. | *R.Q., 20:*215–222, May, 1949. | M | 134 | college men | No | — | EVC .69 |
| Pennington, G.G. et al. | *R.Q., 38:*247–253, May, 1967. | M | 37 | college men | No | — | EVC .80 |
| Tyson, K.W. | Master's thesis, U. of Tex., 1970 | M | 64 | college men | No | T–R .64–.82 | EVC .87–.92 |
| Hemmer, J.C. | Master's thesis, E. Ky. Univ., 1972 | M | 125 | college men | No | T–R .20–.78 | EVC .60–.83 |

*See Appendix D for explanation of symbols.

other variable), a series of multiple correlations was made between various *combinations* of the variables and the test criterion. The test criterion was the subject's average score per game multiplied by 10 to eliminate the decimal. An average of 10 games was played by each participant in the tournament.

The final test consisted of three variables and was expressed in the following regression (prediction) equations in both raw score and standard score forms:

1. Standard score form:

Criterion = .425 service placement score + .430 total wall volley score
+ .175 back-wall placement score.

2. Raw score form:

Criterion = 1.37 service placement score + 2.27 total wall volley score
+ 1.59 back-wall placement score + .29.

*Equipment.*    Properly marked 4-wall handball court; handballs.

*Description and administration.*    The tests are described as follows:

1. Service placement test:    The court is divided into areas that are assigned numerical values (Figure 9.6). Serving in a regulation manner, the student attempts

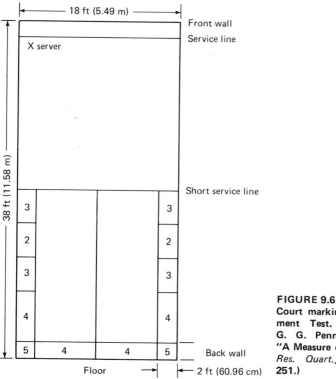

**FIGURE 9.6**
**Court markings for Service Place-
ment Test. (Reproduced from
G. G. Pennington and others,
"A Measure of Handball Ability,"**
*Res. Quart.,* **38 (May, 1967),
251.)**

to place the service into the area having the highest numerical value. Each subject is given 10 trials.

2. Wall-volley test: a) 30-second wall volley with the dominant hand. The subject stands at the center of the court behind the short service line, drops the ball to the floor and strokes it against the front wall repeatedly for 30 seconds. The subject is permitted to step ahead of the line for one return, but the next must be played behind the line. If subjects violate this rule or lose control, they must recover the ball and begin a new series in the same way.

b) 30-second wall volley with the nondominant hand. This test is administered in the same manner as the previous test, but the subject may not strike the ball with the dominant hand.

3. Back-wall placement test: The front wall is divided into different areas with assigned numerical values (Figure 9.7). The subject throws the ball high and hard against the front wall and, after it hits the floor and rebounds off the back wall, attempts to stroke it into the high scoring areas of the front wall. The subject is allowed 5 trials with the right hand off the right back wall and 5 trials with the left hand off the left back wall.

*Scoring.*
1. Service placement test: the sum of 10 trials.
2. 30-second wall-volley test: the sum of the number of times the ball is stroked against the front wall in 30 seconds with the dominant hand and the nondominant hand.

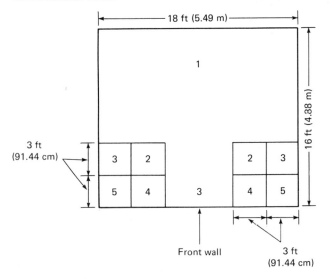

FIGURE 9.7    Court markings for Wall Placement Tests. (Reproduced from G. G. Pennington and others, "A Measure of Handball Ability," *Res. Quart.*, 38 (May, 1967), 251.)

3. Back-wall placement test: the sum of 5 trials with the right hand off the right back wall and 5 trials with the left hand off the left back wall.

*Reliability and validity.*   No mention of reliability was made in the study.

A validity coefficient of .80 was obtained by correlating the three test items with the test criterion.

*Normative information.*   No norms were published with the study, possibly because of the small number of cases used (N = 37). Norms based on so few cases would probably have little value for comparison with other groups or individuals. However, means and standard deviations were published for those who wish to construct their own norm tables.

*Comments.*   With the exception of failure to check the reliability of the experimental variables, this study "touched most of the bases" required for good research in test construction. It should also have reported the method of arriving at the experimental variables selected finally.

Unfortunately, the study was done on a nonregulation court, and one can only speculate if the same results would be obtained on a regulation court 20 feet (6.10 m) high by 40 feet (12.19 m) long. The reader is referred to the Tyson study[10] done on a regulation court.

## TENNIS SKILLS TESTS

In comparison with many other sports, tennis has been studied rather extensively from the point of view of construction of validated skills tests. The tests have dealt predominantly with three skill elements—forehand drive, backhand drive, and serve. Some of them are summarized in Table 9-6. One of the tests is selected for further description.

### The Hewitt Tennis Achievement Test[11]

The test consists of forehand, backhand, and service elements and is categorized according to beginning, advanced, and varsity levels.

*Equipment for all tests.*   A 7-foot × 2-inch × 2-inch (2.13 m × 5.08 cm × 5.08 cm) wood pole is installed at each net post and a one-quarter-inch (6.35 mm) rope is strung between the poles at a height of 7 feet (2.13 m) above the net; 36 new, heavy-duty tennis balls; tennis rackets; court markings.

*Description and administration for Forehand and Backhand tests.*   The court is marked as in Figure 9.8. All students are given a demonstration of the tests to be taken. A 10-minute warm-up period is provided for each student on another court prior to testing. The student stands at the intersection of baseline at X

**TABLE 9-6** Summary of Tennis Skills Tests*

| AUTHOR | SOURCE | SEX | NO. CASES | AGE GROUP | NORMS | RELIABILITY COEFFICIENT | VALIDITY COEFFICIENT |
|---|---|---|---|---|---|---|---|
| Dyer, J.T. | R.Q., 6:63-74, March, 1935. | F | 13-534 | college women | No | T-R .87-.90 | EVC .38-.96 |
| Dyer, J.T. | R.Q., 9:25-31, March, 1938. | F | 15-37 | college women | Yes | T-R .86-.92 | EVC .92 |
| Scott, M.G. | R.Q., 12:40-49, March, 1941 | F | 167-358 | college women | No | — | EVC .41-.92 |
| Broer, M.R. and Miller, D.M. | R.Q., 21:303-321, Oct., 1950. | F | 59 | college women | No | SH .80 | EVC .35-.87 |
| Fox, K. | R.Q., 24:1-7, March, 1953. | F | 41 | college women | No | — | EVC .81 |
| Miller, W.K. | R.Q., 24:81-90, March, 1953. | F | 672 | college women | Yes | — | — |
| Hewitt, J.E. | R.Q., 36:153-157, May, 1965 | M | 31-91 | college men | No | T-R .82-.93 | EVC .68-.89 |
| Hewitt, J.E. | R.Q., 37:231-240, May, 1966. | M & F | 16-91 | college men & women | Yes | T-R .75-.94 | EVC .52-.93 |
| Hewitt, J.E. | R.Q., 39:552-555, Oct., 1968. | M | 9-15 | college men | Yes | T-R .83-.88 | EVC .23-.88 |
| DiGennaro, J. | R.Q., 40:496-501, Oct., 1969. | M | 64 | college men | Yes | T-R .66-.80 | EVC .40-.78 |

*See Appendix D for explanation of symbols.

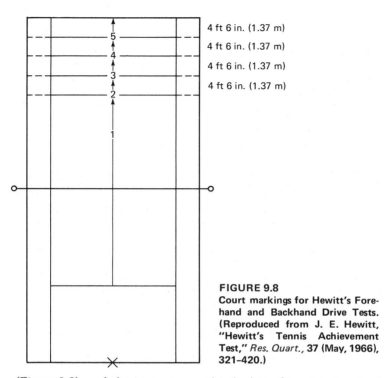

4 ft 6 in. (1.37 m)

4 ft 6 in. (1.37 m)

4 ft 6 in. (1.37 m)

4 ft 6 in. (1.37 m)

**FIGURE 9.8**
Court markings for Hewitt's Forehand and Backhand Drive Tests. (Reproduced from J. E. Hewitt, "Hewitt's Tennis Achievement Test," *Res. Quart.*, **37** (May, 1966), **321–420.**)

(Figure 9.8), and the instructor, with a basket of tennis balls, stands across the net at the intersection of the center service line and service line. The instructor hits 5 practice balls to the student just beyond the service court. The student moves into proper position for the forehand and drives the ball over the net into the zoned areas. The student tries to drive the ball as near the baseline as possible. Ten trials each are given, and the student chooses any ten balls to return with the forehand and the backhand. It is important that the same instructor hit all balls to the students in order to standardize the procedure. If a school possesses an automatic ball-throwing machine, this can be used most effectively.

*Scoring (Forehand and Backhand tests).* All scores are recorded on the score sheet for each of the 10 forehand and 10 backhand drives going over the net and under the restraining rope. Scores are awarded according to the values marked on the lines for the respective spaces—5, 4, 3, 2, and 1. The sum of the 10 trials is the final score. Balls hit over the 7-foot (2.13 m) restraining rope and into the scoring zones score one-half the regular value. Balls that are hit into the net, go over the baseline, or go wide of the sidelines are given a zero score. All net balls (balls hitting the top of the net and dropping into the opposite court) are replayed.

*Description and administration (Service tests).*

Service test (placement). The court is marked according to Figure 9.9. The instructor demonstrates the test. The student is allowed a 10-minute warm-up on another court. The student starts the test at the right of the center line and behind the baseline at X (Figure 9.9). The student serves 10 balls into the right service court target area.

Service test (speed). The court is marked according to Figure 9.10. Actually, the word speed is a misnomer, since what is measured is the distance the ball travels on the second bounce after it has been served in the proper service court.

*Scoring.*

Service test (placement). Every ball hit over the net and under the 7-foot (2.13 m) restraining line is scored on the basis of the value of the target area in which it lands. Balls hitting out of the service court or over the restraining line are scored zero. Net balls are re-served. The sum of the ten trials is the final score.

Service test (speed). For each of 10 good serve placements (described above), the score is the distance the ball bounces into the respective zones shown in Figure 9.10. Balls landing in zones 1, 2, 3, and 4 are scored 1, 2, 3, and 4 points, respectively.

*Reliability and validity.* The test-retest method, over two successive class periods, was used to obtain reliability coefficients of .75, .78, .94, and .84 for the

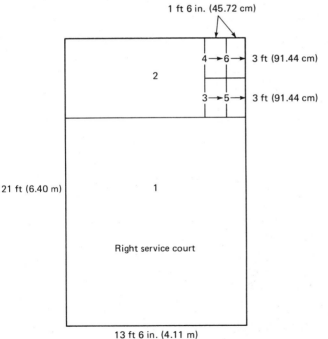

FIGURE 9.9  Court markings for Hewitt's Service Placement Test. (Reproduced from Hewitt, "Hewitt's Tennis Achievement Test," p. 235.)

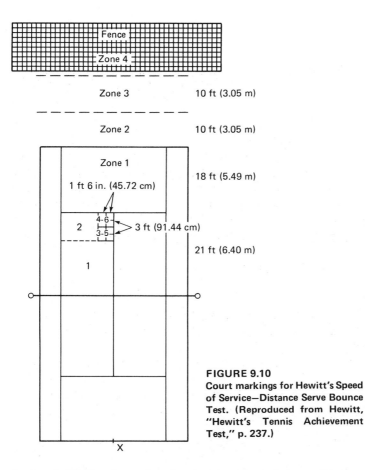

FIGURE 9.10
Court markings for Hewitt's Speed of Service—Distance Serve Bounce Test. (Reproduced from Hewitt, "Hewitt's Tennis Achievement Test," p. 237.)

Fence
Zone 4
Zone 3       10 ft (3.05 m)
Zone 2       10 ft (3.05 m)
Zone 1
1 ft 6 in. (45.72 cm)       18 ft (5.49 m)
4-6
2   3-5   3 ft (91.44 cm)
      21 ft (6.40 m)
1
X

forehand, backhand, service placement, and service speed tests, respectively. Apparently, all subjects, regardless of ability level, were combined for these calculations.

Validity coefficients were obtained by correlating test scores with the test criterion, namely, a ranking of all players from the results of a round-robin tournament. For beginners, the coefficients were .67, .62, .72, and .89; for advanced players, they were .61, .61, .62, and .72; for varsity-level players, they were .57, .52, .92, and .86 for forehand, backhand, service placement, and service speed tests, respectively.

*Normative information.* Graded achievement T-scale norms for different ability groups were constructed and are presented in Table 9-7.

*Comments.* Future research with this test should include correlations of combinations of the skill elements tested with the test criterion, culminating in a regression (predictive) equation. Also included with the above skill elements should be the Dyer[12] (wall-volley) test, which Hewitt has also studied.

**TABLE 9-7   Hewitt Tennis Achievement Scales Norms**

| GRADE | SERVICE PLACEMENTS | SERVICE SPEED | FOREHAND PLACEMENTS | BACKHAND PLACEMENTS |
|---|---|---|---|---|
| | | Junior Varsity and Varsity Tennis (16 cases—5 S.D.) | | |
| F | 20–24 | 20–22 | 25–28 | 20–23 |
| D | 25–29 | 23–25 | 29–32 | 24–27 |
| C | 30–39 | 26–32 | 33–39 | 28–34 |
| B | 40–45 | 33–36 | 40–45 | 35–40 |
| A | 46–50 | 37–40 | 46–50 | 41–47 |
| | | Advanced Tennis (36 cases—5 S.D.) | | |
| F | 11–14 | 8–9 | 24–25 | 22–26 |
| D | 15–19 | 11–13 | 26–29 | 27–30 |
| C | 20–30 | 14–21 | 30–39 | 31–37 |
| B | 31–37 | 22–25 | 40–44 | 38–42 |
| A | 38–44 | 26–30 | 45–48 | 43–46 |
| | | Beginning Tennis (91 cases—5 S.D.) | | |
| F | 1–2 | 1–3 | 1–3 | 1–2 |
| D | 3–6 | 4–7 | 4–8 | 3–7 |
| C | 7–16 | 8–13 | 9–21 | 8–19 |
| B | 17–21 | 14–17 | 22–28 | 20–26 |
| A | 22–26 | 18–21 | 29–26 | 27–34 |

Source: Hewitt, 1966, p. 239.

## WRESTLING SKILLS TESTS

As is the case with many other sports, very little systematic research has been done on the construction of skills tests for wrestling. However, a few master's theses have attempted to deal with the problem. These studies have sought to predict wrestling ability from general motor ability tests, agility, balance, specific wrestling skills, strategy, and aggressiveness. The results of these studies have been disappointing, generally, which probably explains the lack of interest in the area in professional literature.

The study by Seavers (Table 9-8) is singled out for brief mention, since it at least attempted to follow some of the proper procedures of skills test construction.

### The Seavers Test
### for Wrestling Potential[13]

*Equipment.*   Parallel bars; horizontal bar; hand grip dynamometer; stopwatch.

*Description and administration.*   The purpose of the original study was to develop a battery of tests that would predict potential wrestling ability and, there-

**TABLE 9-8 Summary of Wrestling Skills Tests***

| AUTHOR | SOURCE | SEX | NO. CASES | AGE GROUP | NORMS | RELIABILITY COEFFICIENT | VALIDITY COEFFICIENT |
|--------|--------|-----|-----------|-----------|-------|------------------------|----------------------|
| Seavers, H.L. | Master's thesis, Univ. of Iowa, 1934. | M | 30 | college men | Yes | — | EVC .57-.92 |

*See Appendix D for explanation of symbols.

fore, be of value to coaches in the selection of the most desirable candidates for interscholastic wrestling activities. After communicating with wrestling coaches and wrestlers, the author concluded that the attributes most associated with success in wrestling were: 1) strength in the shoulders and arms; 2) competitive spirit, desire to excel, and determination to succeed; 3) the desire to be a wrestler and interest in the sport; 4) the ability to react quickly to an applied force; and 5) speed and agility in moving about on the mat.

The following tests were used to measure the above qualities: 1) Athletic Fitness Index (short form) including right and left grip strength, number of chins, and number of dips; 2) the Sargent Jump; 3) the sustained grip on the hand dynamometer ($\frac{2}{3}$ maximum); 4) 40 mm U-tube test for time; 5) the switch; and 6) the front-to-back leaning rest test.*

Intercorrelations between each test item and the test criterion (wrestling ability) were made; these were followed by multiple correlations combining groups of the test items and correlating them with the test criterion. Finally, a regression (prediction) equation was developed including only three of the six original test items: 1) The Athletic Fitness Index; 2) hand grip dynamometer test ($\frac{2}{3}$ maximum); and 3) the front-to-back leaning rest test.

*Scoring.** The final regression equation was:

Wrestling potential = .4954 (Athletic Fitness Index) + .3105 (grip dynamometer test) + .2404 (front-to-back leaning rest).

*Reliability and validity.*   No reliability coefficients were reported for any of the six original test items.

Validity coefficients for the three test items in the above regression equations were .92, .88, and .90, respectively. The multiple correlation of the final three items with the test criterion was .97.

*Normative information.*   Norms were included in the original study.

*Comments.*   The author should have determined reliability coefficients for the test items, or, at least, cited them from other studies.

The high validity coefficients reported in this study have been questioned by others. Bremner[14] reported only a "fair" degree of success in predicting wrestling ability with Seavers' regression equation. Several other studies (see suggested readings) have reported conflicting and negative results as to the value of strength and agility items in predicting wrestling ability.

---

*Complete descriptions and scoring of the individual test items are included in the original study.

BREMNER, BARRON J. "Measurement of Potential Wrestling Ability." Unpublished master's thesis, University of Iowa, 1964.

BROER, MARION R. and DONNA M. MILLER. "Achievement Tests for Beginning and Intermediate Tennis." *Research Quarterly,* 21 (October 1950), 303–21.

CLARKE, H. HARRISON. *Application of Measurement to Health and Physical Education,* 2nd ed. Englewood Cliffs N.J.: Prentice-Hall, Inc., 1950.

COOPER, CYNTHIA. "The Development of a Fencing Skill Test for Measuring Achievement of Beginning Collegiate Women Fencers in Using the Advance, Beat, and Lunge." Unpublished master's thesis, Western Illinois University, 1968.

CORNISH, CLAYTON. "A Study of Measurement of Ability in Handball." *Research Quarterly,* 20 (May 1949), 215–22.

Di GENNARO, JOSEPH. "Construction of Forehand Drive, Backhand Drive, and Service Tennis Tests." *Research Quarterly,* 40 (October 1969), 496–501.

DYER, JOANNA T. "Revision of the Backboard Test of Tennis Ability." *Research Quarterly,* 9 (March 1938), 25–31.

____. "The Backboard Test of Tennis Ability." *Research Quarterly, Supplement,* 6 (March 1935), 63–74.

ECKERT, HELEN M. *Practical Measurement of Physical Performance.* Philadelphia: Lea and Febiger, 1974.

FOX, KATHARINE. "A Study of the Validity of the Dyer Backboard Test and the Miller Forehand-Backhand Test for Beginning Tennis Players." *Research Quarterly,* 24 (March 1953), 1–7.

FRENCH, ESTHER and EVELYN STALTER. "Study of Skill Tests in Badminton for College Women." *Research Quarterly,* 20 (October 1949), 257–72.

HEMMER, JOHN C. "A Determination of the Reliability and Validity of the Cornish Handball Skill Tests." Unpublished master's thesis, Eastern Kentucky University, 1972.

HEWITT, JACK E. "Classification Tests in Tennis." *Research Quarterly,* 39 (October 1968), 552–55.

____. Hewitt's Tennis Achievement Test." *Research Quarterly,* 37 (May 1966), 231–40.

____. "Revision of the Dyer Backboard Tennis Test." *Research Quarterly,* 36 (May 1965), 153–57.

KOWERT, EUGENE A. "Construction of a Badminton Ability Test Battery for Men." Unpublished master's thesis, University of Iowa, 1968.

KUHAJDA, PATRICIA F. "The Construction and Validation of a Skill Test for the Riposte Lunge in Fencing." Unpublished master's thesis, Southern Illinois University, 1970.

LOCKHART, AILEENE and FRANCES A. McPHERSON. "The Development of a Test of Badminton Playing Ability." *Research Quarterly,* 20 (December 1949), 402–405.

MATHEWS, DONALD K. *Measurement in Physical Education,* 3rd ed. Philadelphia: W.B. Saunders, Co., 1968.

MILLER, FRANCES A. "A Badminton Wall Volley Test." *Research Quarterly,* 22 (May 1951), 208–13.

MILLER, WILMA K. "Achievement Levels in Tennis Knowledge and Skill for Women Physical Education Major Students." *Research Quarterly,* 24 (March 1953), 81–90.

PENNINGTON, G. GARY, JOHN K. DROWATZKY, JAMES A.P. DAY, and

JOHN F. HANSAN. "A Measure of Handball Ability." *Research Quarterly,* 38 (May 1967), 247–53.

SAFRIT, MARGARET J. "Construction of Skill Tests for Beginning Fencers." Unpublished master's thesis, University of Wisconsin, 1962 (Microcard).

SCHUTZ, HELEN JOAN. "Construction of an Achievement Scale in Fencing for Women." Unpublished master's thesis, University of Washington, 1940.

SCOTT, M. GLADYS. "Achievement Examinations for Elementary and Intermediate Tennis Classes." *Research Quarterly,* 12 (March 1941), 40–49.

——. "Achievement Examinations in Badminton." *Research Quarterly,* 12 (May 1941), 242–53.

SEAVERS, HARRY L. "The Measurement of Potential Wrestling Ability." Unpublished master's thesis, State University of Iowa, 1934.

SINGER, ROBERT N. "Speed and Accuracy of Movement as Related to Fencing Success." *Research Quarterly,* 29 (December 1968), 1080–1083.

TYSON, KENNETH W. "A Handball Skill Test for College Men." Unpublished master's thesis, University of Texas, 1970.

## SUGGESTED READINGS

BOLDRICK, EVELYN L. "The Measurement of Fundamental Skills in Badminton." Unpublished master's thesis, Wellesley College, 1945.

BOWER, MURIEL. "Bower Test of General Fencing Ability." *1964–66 Bowling-Fencing-Golf Guide.* Washington: AAHPERD Publications, 1964.

CAMPBELL, VIRGINIA M. "Development of Achievement Tests in Badminton." Unpublished master's thesis, The University of Texas, 1938.

CLEVETT, MELVIN A. "All Around Athletic Championship." *Journal of Health and Physical Education,* 6 (March 1935), 48.

COZENS, FREDERICK W., HAZEL J. CUBBERLEY, and N.P. NEILSON. *Achievement Scales in Physical Education Activities for Secondary School Girls and Women.* New York: A.S. Barnes, 1937.

DAVIS, BARBARA. "The Relationship of Certain Skill Tests to Playing Ability in Badminton." Unpublished master's thesis, Wellesley College, 1946.

DAVIS, PHYLLIS, R. "The Development of a Combined Short and Long Badminton Service Skill Test." Unpublished master's thesis, University of Tennessee, 1968.

EDGREN, HARRY D. and G.G. ROBINSON. *Individual Skill Tests in Physical Activities.* Chicago: Edgren and Robinson, 1937.

EMERY, LYNN. "Criteria for Rating Selected Skills of Foil Fencing." *1960–62 Bowling-Fencing-Golf Guide.* Washington: AAHPERD Publications, 1960.

FAGAN, CLIFFORD B. "A Further Study of the Use of Psycho-Motor Tests for the Measurement of Potential Wrestling Ability." Unpublished master's thesis, State University of Iowa, 1940.

FEIN, J.T. "Construction of Skill Tests for Beginning Collegiate Women Fencers." Unpublished master's thesis, State University of Iowa, 1964.

FRIERMOOD, H.T. "A Handball Classification Plan." *Journal of Health and Physical Education,* 8 (February 1937), 106–7; 127.

GREINER, M. "Construction of a Short-Serve Test for Beginning Badminton Players," Unpublished master's thesis, University of Wisconsin, 1964.

GRIFFITH, M.A. "An Objective Method for Evaluating Ability in Handball Singles." Unpublished master's thesis, The Ohio State University, 1960.

GROSS, E.A., D.C. GRIESEL, and A. STULL. "Relationship Between Two Motor

Educability Tests, a Strength Test, and Wrestling Ability after Eight Weeks' Instruction." *Research Quarterly* 27 (December 1956), 395.

HALE, P.A., "Construction of a Badminton Long Serve Test for Beginning Players (Singles)." Unpublished master's thesis, University of Wisconsin, 1970.

HICKS, V. "The Construction and Evaluation of a Battery of Five Badminton Skill Tests." Unpublished doctoral dissertation, Texas Women's University, 1967.

HULAC, G.M. "The Construction of an Objective Indoor Test for Measuring Effective Tennis Serve." Unpublished master's thesis, Women's College of the University of North Carolina, 1958.

KROLL, W. "Selected Factors Associated with Wrestling Success." *Research Quarterly* 29 (December 1958), 389.

LEINBACK, C.H. "The Development of Achievement Standards in Handball and Touch Football for Use in the Department of Physical Training for Men at the University of Texas." Unpublished master's thesis, University of Texas, 1952.

MALINAK, NINA. "The Construction of an Objective Measure of Accuracy in the Performance of the Serve." Unpublished master's thesis, University of Illinois, 1961.

MASTROPAOLO, JOSEPH ANTHONY. "An Analysis of the Fundamentals of Fencing." Unpublished doctoral dissertation, State University of Iowa, 1958.

McCACHREN, JAMES R., "A Study of the University of Florida Handball Skill Test." Unpublished master's thesis, University of North Carolina, 1949.

McDONALD, E.D. "The Development of a Skill Test for the Badminton High Clear." Unpublished master's thesis, Southern Illinois University, 1968.

MONTOYE, HENRY J. and JOHN BROTZMAN. "An Investigation of the Validity of Using the Results of a Doubles Tournament as a Measure of Handball Ability." *Research Quarterly,* 22 (May 1951), 214-18.

MUMBY, H. HUGH. "Kinesthetic Acuity and Balance Related to Wrestling Ability." *Research Quarterly,* 24 (October 1953), 327.

ROYER, MIRIAM. "Achievement Tests in Badminton for College Women." Unpublished master's thesis, State University of Iowa, 1950.

SCHIFF, F.S. "A Test of Skills Performed in the Game Situation of Handball." Unpublished master's thesis, The Ohio State University, 1938.

SCHMITTER, CHARLES. "Evaluating Fencing Classes." *1958-60 Bowling-Fencing Golf Guide.* Washington: AAHPERD Publications, 1958.

SCOTT, JAMES H. "A Study in the Evaluation of Playing Ability in the Game of Badminton." Unpublished master's thesis, The Ohio State University, 1941.

SHAY, CLAYTON T. "An Application of the Dyer Tennis Test." *Journal of Health, Physical Education and Recreation,* 20 (April 1949), 273-74.

SICKELS, WILLIAM L. "A Rating Test of Amateur Wrestling Ability." Unpublished master's thesis, San Jose State College, 1967.

SIMOS, THOMAS. "A Handball Classification Test." Unpublished master's thesis, Springfield, Mass.: Springfield College, 1952.

SWANSON, ALLYS HAINS. "Measuring Achievement in Selected Skills for Beginning Women Fencers." Unpublished master's thesis. Iowa City, State University of Iowa, 1967.

THORPE, JO ANNE. "Intelligence and Skill in Relation to Success in Singles Competition in Badminton and Tennis." *Research Quarterly,* 38 (March 1967), 119-25.

_____, and CHARLOTTE WEST. "A Test of Game Sense in Badminton." *Perceptual Motor Skills,* 28 (February 1969), 159-69.

WAGNER, MIRIAM M. "An Objective Method of Grading Beginners in Tennis." *Journal of Health and Physical Education,* 6 (March 1935), 24–25; 79.

WASHINGTON, JEAN. "Construction of a Wall Test for the Badminton Short Serve, and the Effect of Wall Practice on Court Performance." Unpublished master's thesis, North Texas State University, 1968.

WILLIAMS, GLENNA R. "A Study of Badminton Skills Tests." Unpublished master's thesis, Texas State College for Women, 1945.

YEO, DAVID G. "The Relationship of Reaction Time, Performance Time and Handball Velocity to Success in Handball." Unpublished master's thesis, Springfield College, 1968.

YETTER, HENRY. "A Test of Wrestling Aptitude: Preliminary Exploration." Unpublished master's thesis, University of Wisconsin, 1963.

# CHAPTER TEN
# SPORTS SKILLS TESTS: MULTIPLE-PARTICIPANT SPORTS

## BASEBALL/SOFTBALL
## SKILLS TESTS

Some problem in semantics was encountered in this area because authors use such terms as baseball, softball, playground baseball, hardball, etc., without defining them. Unless the researcher used the term "baseball" specifically, it was assumed that softball was the game under discussion, since none of the studies described the size of the ball. For the purpose of this section, baseball is that game played with a ball approximately 9 inches (22.86 cm) in circumference, which is pitched overhand; softball uses a ball approximately 12 inches (30.48 cm) in circumference, which is pitched underhand. There are variations of softball where a 16-inch (40.64-cm) ball is used.

Since baseball and softball skills are so similar, they will be combined in this section. Summaries of some of the better known skills tests are found in Tables 10-1 and 10-2.

The AAHPER softball skills tests for boys[1] and girls[2] have been selected for discussion. Together, these two booklets include the following tests: throw for distance; overhand throw for accuracy, underhand pitching; speed-throw; fungo hitting; base running; fielding ground balls; and catching fly balls. The tests for girls are the same as those for boys, with two exceptions. The throw for accuracy and underhand pitching tests involve shorter distances than those for boys. Separate percentile scales have been developed for boys and girls. Two of the above tests will be described.

### AAHPER Softball Skills Test—
### Underhand Pitching (Boys)[3]

*Equipment.* Gymnasium or outdoor space adjacent to a smooth wall; a target as shown in Figure 10.1; softballs; measuring tape; chalk.

*Description and administration.* The purpose of the test is to measure the accuracy with which a softball can be pitched. The target is rectangular; it contains an inner rectangle 17 inches (43.13 cm) wide and 30 inches (76.20 cm) high and an outer rectangle 6 inches (15.24 cm) larger on all sides. Lines 1 inch (2.54 cm) wide are painted on canvas or marked on a wall. The target is placed so that the bottom of the outer rectangle is exactly 18 inches (45.72 cm) above the floor. A pitching line 24 inches (60.96 cm) long is marked on the floor opposite the center of the target and parallel to its face. This line is 46 feet (14.02 m) from the target. The player is allowed 1 practice pitch and then takes 15 underhand pitches at the target. The player must keep one foot on the pitching line while delivering the ball but can take a forward step in making the pitch. In addition, a legal underhand softball pitch must be used and one foot must be in contact with the pitching line until the ball has been delivered. A total of 15 pitches is taken.

**TABLE 10-1 Summary of Baseball Skills Tests***

| AUTHOR | SOURCE | SEX | NO. CASES | AGE GROUP | NORMS | RELIABILITY COEFFICIENT | VALIDITY COEFFICIENT |
|---|---|---|---|---|---|---|---|
| Everett, P.W. | *R.Q., 23*:15-19, March, 1952. | M | 30 | college men | No | — | EVC .20-.52 |
| Kelson, R.E. | *R.Q., 24*:304-307, Oct., 1953. | M | 64 | 8-12 | Yes | — | EVC .85 |
| Hooks, G.E. | *R.Q., 30*:38-43, March, 1959. | M | 56 | college freshmen | No | T-R .82-.96 | EVC .42-.79 |

*See Appendix D for explanation of symbols.

**TABLE 10-2  Summary of Softball Skills Tests***

| AUTHOR | SOURCE | SEX | NO. CASES | AGE GROUP | NORMS | RELIABILITY COEFFICIENT | VALIDITY COEFFICIENT |
|---|---|---|---|---|---|---|---|
| Rodgers, E.G. | *R.Q., 2*:113–131, Dec., 1931. | M | 450–755 | grades 5 & 6 | Yes | T-R .83 | EVC .62–.65 |
| Fox, M.G. and Young, O.G. | *R.Q., 25*:26–27, March, 1954. | F | 62–64 | college women | No | SH .81–.96 | EVC .64 |
| Latchaw, M. | *R.Q., 25*:439–449, Dec., 1954 | F | 50 | grades 4, 5, 6 | No | T-R .80–.85 | — |
| Latchaw, M. | *R.Q., 25*:439–449, Dec., 1954. | M | 50 | grades 4, 5, 6 | No | T-R .77–.85 | — |
| Broer, M.R. | *R.Q., 29*:139–145, May, 1958. | F | 52–239 | grades 7 & 8 | No | T-R & SH .42–.97 | — |
| AAHPER | *Skills Test Manual: Softball for Boys,* 1966. | M | 600–900 | 12–18 | Yes | lit. | log. |
| AAHPER | *Skills Test Manual: Softball for Girls,* 1966. | F | 600–900 | 12–18 | Yes | lit. | log. |
| Schick, J. | *R.Q., 41*:82–87, March 1970. | F | 59 | college women | No | T-R .88 | EVC .75 |

*See Appendix D for explanation of symbols.

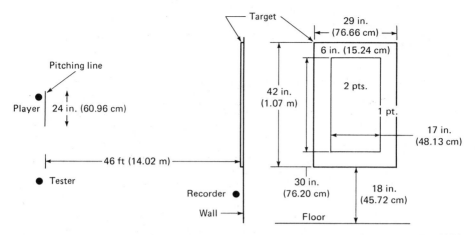

FIGURE 10.1 Target for the Underhand Pitching Test. (Reproduced from *AAHPER, Skills Test Manual—Softball for Boys,* 1966, p. 22.)

*Scoring.* Pitched balls hitting in the center area or on its boundary line count 2 points, and balls hitting in the outer area or on its outside boundary line count 1 point. The score is the sum of all points made on 15 pitches. Each score is recorded as made. The maximum score is 30 points.

*Reliability and validity.* No reliability or validity coefficients were given for this test. Instead, a statement was made that reliability and objectivity had been established in previous studies.[4] No attempt was made to establish validity, since the purpose of the test was to measure *current* level of performance in the particular skill rather than to measure a complexity called "softball ability."

*Normative information.* An effort was made to collect data from as wide a geographical area as possible. Percentile tables were constructed from approximately 700 scores for boys, ages 10-18. Thus, the abilities of boys of the same age can be compared, as can the improvement made by a boy between tests (Table 10-3).

*Comments.* This is a practical, easily administered test that can be used for measuring present ability in underhand pitching. This skill test should be regarded as a "practice test," since it was intended to be used by players as a way of improving skill in fundamentals of the game.

The test could be used with more confidence had actual reliability coefficients been published. However, a quick reliability check could be made prior to its use in a local setting.

Finally, some consideration should be given to the combination of a speed element with this test in order to make it more representative of the game situation.

## AAHPER Softball Skills Test—
## Catching Fly Balls (Girls)

*Equipment.* A standard softball diamond, with boundaries marking a catching

**TABLE 10-3  Softball Underhand Pitch (Boys)**

| PERCENTILE | | | | AGE | | | | PERCENTILE |
|---|---|---|---|---|---|---|---|---|
| | 10–11 | 12 | 13 | 14 | 15 | 16 | 17–18 | |
| 100th | 18 | 23 | 21 | 22 | 24 | 25 | 25 | 100th |
| 95th | 12 | 14 | 15 | 16 | 18 | 19 | 19 | 95th |
| 90th | 10 | 12 | 13 | 15 | 16 | 17 | 17 | 90th |
| 85th | 9 | 11 | 11 | 14 | 15 | 15 | 16 | 85th |
| 80th | 8 | 9 | 10 | 12 | 14 | 14 | 15 | 80th |
| 75th | 7 | 9 | 10 | 12 | 13 | 13 | 14 | 75th |
| 70th | 7 | 8 | 9 | 11 | 12 | 12 | 13 | 70th |
| 65th | 6 | 7 | 8 | 10 | 11 | 12 | 12 | 65th |
| 60th | 6 | 7 | 8 | 9 | 10 | 11 | 12 | 60th |
| 55th | 5 | 6 | 7 | 9 | 10 | 10 | 11 | 55th |
| 50th | 4 | 6 | 7 | 8 | 9 | 9 | 10 | 50th |
| 45th | 4 | 5 | 6 | 7 | 8 | 9 | 10 | 45th |
| 40th | 3 | 4 | 5 | 7 | 7 | 8 | 9 | 40th |
| 35th | 3 | 4 | 5 | 6 | 7 | 8 | 8 | 35th |
| 30th | 2 | 3 | 4 | 6 | 6 | 7 | 8 | 30th |
| 25th | 2 | 3 | 4 | 5 | 5 | 6 | 7 | 25th |
| 20th | 1 | 2 | 3 | 4 | 4 | 5 | 6 | 20th |
| 15th | 1 | 2 | 3 | 4 | 4 | 4 | 5 | 15th |
| 10th | 1 | 1 | 2 | 3 | 3 | 3 | 4 | 10th |
| 5th | 0 | 0 | 1 | 2 | 2 | 2 | 3 | 5th |
| 0 | 0 | 0 | 0 | 0 | 0 | 0 | 0 | 0 |

Source: AAHPER, 1966, p. 39.

zone, as shown in Figure 10.2; softballs; rope and 2 standards or posts 8 feet (2.44 m) high.

*Description and administration.* The player stands at second base in the center of a 60-foot (18.29 m) square. The thrower stands in a restraining zone 5 feet (1.52 m) behind home plate and throws fly balls to the player as directed. The thrower must throw the ball over the rope, which is fastened between 2 standards that are located 5 feet (1.52 m) in front of home plate. The thrower must throw with regular speed. Spare balls should be available. The player must catch the ball, toss it aside, and be immediately ready to catch the next ball. The tester stands behind the player being tested and indicates to the thrower whether to throw left, right, or straight into the catching zone. Approximately one-third of the balls should be thrown to the right, one-third to the left, and one-third to the middle of the catching zone. Each player is given 2 trials of 10 balls each. A practice trial is allowed. Balls not properly thrown into the catching zone are not counted. The ball must be thrown so that it describes an arc in flight. A total of 20 good fly balls must be thrown, and the player must make a good catch of each ball before tossing it aside.

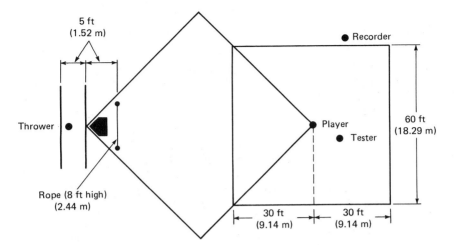

**FIGURE 10.2** **Layout for testing the catching of fly balls. (Reproduced from AAHPER,** *Skills Test Manual—Softball for Girls,* **1966, p. 32.)**

*Scoring.* The score is the number of balls caught successfully during 2 trials of 10 balls each, for a total of 20 balls. One point is recorded for each ball that is caught and a zero for each one that is missed. (If desired, an X may be recorded for each ball contacted by the player but not held.) The maximum score is 20 points.

*Reliability and validity.* The same rationale is used for this test as was used for reliability and validity for the underhand pitching test for boys.

*Normative information.* The norms for this test were based on between 600 and 900 scores collected from as wide a geographical area as possible. Thus, it should be possible to measure improvement in this skill and to compare performance with that of other girls of the same age (Table 10-4).

*Comments.* This test is designed to measure performance level and is not intended to predict potential ability in softball. It is a teaching aid and may be practiced as a way of improving performance in that particular skill.

## BASKETBALL SKILLS TESTS

In comparison to many other sports, basketball has enjoyed rather extensive study in the development of specific skills tests. A number of tests are available for shooting, passing, dribbling, and jumping.

The field goal shooting tests are categorized as those that include a series of single shots, those that sum the number of repeated goals in a certain length of time, and those in which goal shooting is combined with other skills.

The passing tests predominantly have dealt with speed passing, accuracy passing, and a combination of speed and accuracy passing.

**TABLE 10-4  Catching Fly Balls (Girls)**

| PERCENTILE | | | | AGE | | | | PERCENTILE |
|---|---|---|---|---|---|---|---|---|
| | 10–11 | 12 | 13 | 14 | 15 | 16 | 17–18 | |
| 100th | 15 | 17 | 19 | 19 | 20 | 20 | 20 | 100th |
| 95th | 13 | 15 | 17 | 17 | 19 | 19 | 19 | 95th |
| 90th | 10 | 13 | 15 | 16 | 18 | 19 | 19 | 90th |
| 85th | 9 | 11 | 13 | 15 | 18 | 18 | 18 | 85th |
| 80th | 9 | 10 | 12 | 14 | 17 | 17 | 17 | 80th |
| 75th | 8 | 9 | 11 | 13 | 16 | 16 | 16 | 75th |
| 70th | 7 | 8 | 10 | 12 | 15 | 15 | 16 | 70th |
| 65th | 7 | 7 | 9 | 11 | 14 | 14 | 15 | 65th |
| 60th | 6 | 7 | 8 | 10 | 13 | 13 | 15 | 60th |
| 55th | 6 | 6 | 7 | 9 | 12 | 13 | 14 | 55th |
| 50th | 5 | 6 | 6 | 9 | 11 | 12 | 13 | 50th |
| 45th | 4 | 5 | 5 | 8 | 10 | 11 | 12 | 45th |
| 40th | 4 | 5 | 5 | 8 | 9 | 10 | 11 | 40th |
| 35th | 3 | 4 | 4 | 7 | 8 | 9 | 10 | 35th |
| 30th | 3 | 3 | 3 | 6 | 7 | 8 | 9 | 30th |
| 25th | 2 | 3 | 3 | 5 | 6 | 7 | 8 | 25th |
| 20th | 2 | 2 | 2 | 4 | 5 | 6 | 7 | 20th |
| 15th | 1 | 2 | 2 | 3 | 4 | 5 | 6 | 15th |
| 10th | 1 | 1 | 1 | 2 | 3 | 4 | 5 | 10th |
| 5th | 0 | 0 | 0 | 1 | 2 | 3 | 4 | 5th |
| 0 | 0 | 0 | 0 | 0 | 0 | 0 | 0 | 0 |

Source: AAHPER, 1966, p. 44.

The dribbling tests are characterized by the use of benches, chairs, or hurdles as obstacles to test the ability to complete the test in the shortest possible time.

The jumping tests consist of a straight jump or a jump and reach. Apparently, the importance of timing a vertical jump with coordination of catching a basketball has been neglected in the construction of jumping tests.

Fourteen tests are summarized in Table 10-5. Many of the above tests are described in a doctoral dissertation by A.R. Leilich.[5]

The AAHPER basketball skills tests for boys[6] and girls[7] have been selected for discussion below. Together, these two booklets include such specific items as the front shot, side shot, foul shot, under-basket shot, speed pass, jump and reach, overarm pass for accuracy, push pass for accuracy, and dribble. Although the same tests are used for boys and girls, separate percentile scales have been constructed. Two of the above tests will be described here.

### AAHPER Basketball Skills Test—
### Overarm Pass for Accuracy (Boys)

*Equipment.* Standard inflated basketballs; target painted or marked on a wall, a mat, or a piece of canvas hung on a smooth wall; chalk; measuring tape. The floor should be measured and marked properly, as shown in Figure 10.3.

**TABLE 10-5  Summary of Basketball Skills Tests***

| AUTHOR | SOURCE | SEX | NO. CASES | AGE GROUP | NORMS | RELIABILITY COEFFICIENT | VALIDITY COEFFICIENT |
|---|---|---|---|---|---|---|---|
| Young, G. and Moser, H. | R.Q., 5:3-23, May, 1934. | F | 19-65 | college seniors | Yes | T-R .47-.98 | EVC .85 |
| Schwartz, H. | R.Q., 8:143-156, March, 1937. | F | 1000 | senior high | Yes | — | — |
| Glassow, R.G., et al. | R.Q., 9:60-68, Dec. 1938. | F | 51 | college women | No | T-R .74-.82 | .66 |
| Dyer, J.T., et al. | R.Q., 10:128-147, Oct., 1939. | F | 25-39 | college women | Yes | T-R .70-.92 | EVC .80-.90 |
| Dyer, J.T., et al. | R.Q., 10:128-147, Oct., 1939. | F | — | high school girls | Yes | T-R — | EVC .76-.80 |
| Dyer, J.T., et al. | R.Q., 10:128-147, Oct., 1939. | F | 35 | junior high girls | Yes | T-R .57-.96 | EVC .87-.98 |
| Leilich, A.R. | Doctoral dissertation, Indiana Univ., 1952. | F | 110 | college women | No | — | — |
| Latchaw, M. | R.Q., 25:439-449, Dec., 1954. | M | 50 | grades 4, 5, 6 | No | T-R .78-.91 | — |
| Latchaw, M. | R.Q., 25:439-449, Dec., 1954. | F | 50 | grades 4, 5, 6 | No | T-R .83-.94 | — |
| Broer, M.R. | R.Q., 29:139-145, May, 1958. | F | 50-237 | junior high girls | No | T-R SH .69-.86 | — |
| AAHPER | Skills Test Manual: Basketball for Boys, 1966 | M | 600-900 | 12-18 | Yes | lit. | log. |

**TABLE 10-5 (continued)**

| AUTHOR | SOURCE | SEX | NO. CASES | AGE GROUP | NORMS | RELIABILITY COEFFICIENT | VALIDITY COEFFICIENT |
|---|---|---|---|---|---|---|---|
| AAHPER | *Skills Test Manual: Basketball for Girls*, 1966. | F | 600-900 | 12-18 | Yes | lit. | log. |
| Harrison, E.R. | Master's thesis, Univ. of Florida, 1969. | M | 116 | grades 7-12 | Yes | T-R .72-.97 | EVC .77-.89 |
| Clark, W.J. | Doctoral dissertation Ohio State Univ., 1973. | M | 38-44 | college men | Yes | T-R .89 | EVC .62-.87 |

*See Appendix D for explanation of symbols.

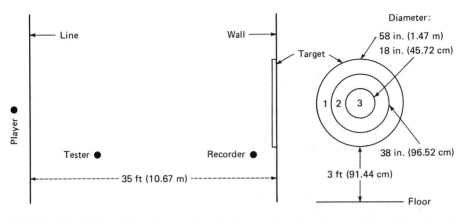

**FIGURE 10.3 Wall and floor layout for the Overarm Pass for Accuracy Test. (Reproduced from AAHPER,** *Skills Test Manual—Basketball for Boys,* **1966, p. 30.)**

*Description and administration.* The purpose of the test is to measure the accuracy with which a player can make a single overarm pass at a target. The player stands behind a line parallel to and 35 feet (10.67 m) from the target marked or hung on a wall. The player throws the ball single overarm at the target. The target is circular, with 3 concentric circles separated by 1-inch (2.54 cm) wide white or black lines. The inner circle is 18 inches (45.72 cm) in diameter, the next circle is 38 inches (96.52 cm) in diameter, and the outer circle is 58 inches (1.47 m) in diameter. The bottom of the outer circle is 3 feet (91.44 cm) above the floor. A practice pass is allowed. In addition, the ball can be held in both hands prior to the throw. The throw must be made from behind the line. The player may take a step in throwing, but both feet must be behind the throwing line. Ten passes are taken.

*Scoring.* 3 points are scored for balls hitting in the center circle, 2 points for balls hitting in the next circle, and 1 point for balls hitting in the outer circle. Balls hitting on a line count as hitting in the area of the higher score. Points should be recorded as made on each throw, and the total is the score. The maximum possible score is 30 points made on 10 passes at the target.

*Reliability and validity.* Neither was attempted.

*Normative information.* The norms for this test were based on approximately 800 scores collected from 82 cities in 40 states. This should make it possible to compare the abilities of boys of the same ages and to measure improvements made by a boy from one testing to the next. The norms also show the teacher the range of ability in a specific skill to be expected of boys of different ages (Table 10-6).

*Comments.* In view of the fact that no reliability coefficients were published for this test, it is recommended that potential users perform their own simple reliability checks.

The test can then be used by the physical education teacher as a device to

TABLE 10-6  Overarm Pass for Accuracy (Boys)

| PERCENTILE | AGE | | | | | | | | PERCENTILE |
|---|---|---|---|---|---|---|---|---|---|
| | 10 | 11 | 12 | 13 | 14 | 15 | 16 | 17–18 | |
| 100th | 18 | 27 | 27 | 27 | 29 | 31 | 31 | 31 | 100th |
| 95th | 14 | 18 | 20 | 20 | 22 | 24 | 24 | 25 | 95th |
| 90th | 13 | 15 | 18 | 19 | 21 | 22 | 22 | 23 | 90th |
| 85th | 11 | 14 | 17 | 18 | 20 | 21 | 21 | 22 | 85th |
| 80th | 10 | 12 | 16 | 17 | 19 | 20 | 20 | 21 | 80th |
| 75th | 8 | 11 | 15 | 16 | 18 | 19 | 19 | 20 | 75th |
| 70th | 7 | 11 | 14 | 16 | 18 | 19 | 19 | 19 | 70th |
| 65th | 6 | 10 | 13 | 15 | 17 | 17 | 18 | 18 | 65th |
| 60th | 6 | 9 | 12 | 15 | 17 | 17 | 17 | 17 | 60th |
| 55th | 5 | 9 | 12 | 14 | 16 | 17 | 17 | 17 | 55th |
| 50th | 4 | 7 | 11 | 13 | 16 | 16 | 16 | 16 | 50th |
| 45th | 3 | 6 | 10 | 12 | 15 | 15 | 15 | 15 | 45th |
| 40th | 2 | 5 | 10 | 12 | 14 | 15 | 15 | 15 | 40th |
| 35th | 2 | 4 | 9 | 11 | 14 | 14 | 14 | 14 | 35th |
| 30th | 1 | 3 | 8 | 10 | 13 | 13 | 13 | 13 | 30th |
| 25th | 0 | 2 | 7 | 9 | 12 | 12 | 12 | 12 | 25th |
| 20th | 0 | 2 | 6 | 9 | 10 | 11 | 11 | 11 | 20th |
| 15th | 0 | 1 | 5 | 8 | 10 | 10 | 11 | 11 | 15th |
| 10th | 0 | 1 | 3 | 6 | 9 | 9 | 9 | 9 | 10th |
| 5th | 0 | 0 | 2 | 4 | 7 | 7 | 8 | 9 | 5th |
| 0 | 0 | 0 | 0 | 0 | 0 | 0 | 0 | 2 | 0 |

Source: AAHPER, 1966, p. 45.

make instruction more effective. Test scores can provide students with an objective measure of their own levels of performance before and after instruction. Whereas the test is intended primarily as an instructional aid, it can be used effectively by the coach as an aid in discovering the better players, finding those with special talents in a particular skill, and diagnosing faults that need correction.

### AAHPER Basketball Skills Test— Dribbling (Girls)

*Equipment.*  Standard inflated basketballs; stopwatch; 6 chairs arranged as shown in Figure 10.4.

*Description and administration.*  The purpose of the test is to measure the speed with which a player can dribble a ball around obstacles. The player stands behind the starting line with a ball in hand and, on the signal "Go," starts with a dribble to the right of the first chair, continues to dribble in and out alternately around the remaining 5 chairs, and returns to cross the starting line. The chairs are arranged single file so that the front of the first chair is 5 feet (1.52 m) from the

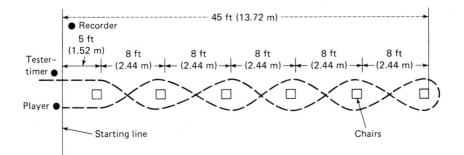

**FIGURE 10.4  Court layout for the Dribble Test. (Reproduced from AAHPER,** *Skills Test Manual—Basketball for Girls,* **1966, p. 34.)**

starting line and the chairs behind it are 8 feet (2.44 m) apart, measured from the front of each chair. All chairs have their backs toward the starting line. The overall distance from the starting line to the far edge of the sixth chair is 45 feet (13.72 m). A practice trial is allowed. Additionally, the ball may be dribbled with either hand, legal dribbles must be used, and the ball must be dribbled at least once as each chair is passed (but need not be dribbled opposite a chair). Each player is allowed 2 trials.

*Scoring.* The score is the time (recorded in seconds and tenths of seconds) that it takes to dribble around and between the chairs and back. Time is started on the signal "Go" and stopped the instant the player crosses the starting line at the end of the trip. Two trials are timed and recorded. The better time of the 2 trials is the player's score on the test.

*Reliability and validity.* Neither was attempted.

*Normative information.* The norms for this test were constructed from 900 scores collected from 82 cities in 40 states (Table 10-7). The table shows the range of ability in a specific skill to be expected of girls of different ages.

*Comments.* The test and percentile-rank table can be used to help establish class and grade-level norms for a school or a school system. It is intended primarily as a teaching aid to help measure students' performances and evaluate teaching procedures and programs. However, it can be used as a competitive event in intraclass and intramural programs.

## FIELD HOCKEY SKILLS TESTS

The first tests of field hockey to appear in the professional literature were tests such as Hartley's,[8] developed empirically by the author. The first statistically validated test apparently did not appear until 1940. Since that time, a number of tests have appeared in master's theses. A few of these are summarized in Table 10-8.

TABLE 10-7 Basketball Dribbling (Girls)

| PERCENTILE | | | | AGE | | | | PERCENTILE |
|---|---|---|---|---|---|---|---|---|
| | 10–11 | 12 | 13 | 14 | 15 | 16 | 17–18 | |
| 100th | 9.5 | 9.5 | 9.5 | 9.5 | 9.5 | 8.5 | 7.5 | 100th |
| 95th | 13.7 | 12.0 | 11.7 | 11.7 | 11.7 | 10.9 | 10.8 | 95th |
| 90th | 14.5 | 12.9 | 12.8 | 12.6 | 12.3 | 11.7 | 11.7 | 90th |
| 85th | 14.9 | 13.5 | 13.3 | 13.0 | 12.8 | 12.1 | 12.0 | 85th |
| 80th | 15.2 | 14.0 | 13.7 | 13.4 | 13.1 | 12.5 | 12.4 | 80th |
| 75th | 15.6 | 14.3 | 14.0 | 13.7 | 13.4 | 12.7 | 12.7 | 75th |
| 70th | 15.9 | 14.6 | 14.4 | 14.0 | 13.6 | 13.0 | 13.0 | 70th |
| 65th | 16.2 | 14.9 | 14.7 | 14.3 | 13.8 | 13.2 | 13.2 | 65th |
| 60th | 16.5 | 15.2 | 14.9 | 14.5 | 14.0 | 13.5 | 13.4 | 60th |
| 55th | 16.8 | 15.5 | 15.1 | 14.8 | 14.2 | 13.7 | 13.6 | 55th |
| 50th | 17.1 | 15.8 | 15.4 | 15.0 | 14.5 | 14.0 | 14.0 | 50th |
| 45th | 17.5 | 16.2 | 15.7 | 15.2 | 14.7 | 14.3 | 14.3 | 45th |
| 40th | 17.8 | 16.5 | 16.1 | 15.5 | 15.0 | 14.6 | 14.5 | 40th |
| 35th | 18.2 | 16.9 | 16.4 | 15.8 | 15.3 | 14.9 | 14.7 | 35th |
| 30th | 18.5 | 17.3 | 16.7 | 16.2 | 15.6 | 15.2 | 15.0 | 30th |
| 25th | 19.0 | 17.7 | 17.1 | 16.5 | 16.0 | 15.5 | 15.2 | 25th |
| 20th | 19.5 | 18.2 | 17.5 | 17.0 | 16.3 | 16.0 | 15.5 | 20th |
| 15th | 20.4 | 18.7 | 18.0 | 17.5 | 16.9 | 16.5 | 16.3 | 15th |
| 10th | 21.1 | 20.5 | 18.2 | 17.8 | 17.2 | 17.1 | 17.0 | 10th |
| 5th | 22.4 | 21.2 | 20.6 | 19.8 | 18.9 | 18.4 | 18.0 | 5th |
| 0 | 29.0 | 24.5 | 24.5 | 24.5 | 24.5 | 24.5 | 24.5 | 0 |

Source: AAHPER, 1966, p. 45.

One of the studies from Table 10-8 is selected for further description. Although developed in 1940, it still provides a good demonstration of the process of test construction from selection of test items to development of regression (prediction) equations.

### The Schmithals-French Field Hockey Skills Test[9]

In the original research, the skill elements selected for study were obtained from the subjective opinions of three nationally rated umpires as to the frequency with which the skills were used by college women in the game itself.

Tests were constructed in the following skills and combination of skills: 1) dribble, dodge, circular tackle, and drive; 2) drive for goal (straight, to right, to left); 3) fielding and drive; 4) push pass; 5) drive for distance; and 6) receiving of ball from teammate (left and right).

A series of intercorrelations was completed among all six variables. The rationale for this step was:

1. If two items correlate highly with each other, they are probably measuring the *same* skill; thus, one could be eliminated.

**TABLE 10-8  Summary of Field Hockey Skills Tests***

| AUTHOR | SOURCE | SEX | NO. CASES | AGE GROUP | NORMS | RELIABILITY COEFFICIENT | VALIDITY COEFFICIENT |
|---|---|---|---|---|---|---|---|
| Schmithals, M. and French, E. | *R.Q., 11*:84-92, Oct., 1940. | F | 51 | college women | No | .67-.92 | EVC .62 |
| Strait, C.J. | Master's thesis Smith College, 1960. | F | 51-62 | college & sports-club women | No | T-R .86 | EVC .60-.76 |
| Perry, F.L. | Master's thesis Penn. State Univ., 1969 | F | 52-63 | college women | No | T-R .34-.81 | EVC .34-.71 |
| Henry, M.E. | Master's thesis Temple Univ., 1970 | F | 31 | high school & college | No | T-R & AV .71-.81 | EVC .79-.83 |

*See Appendix D for explanation of symbols.

2. If two items do not correlate, they are probably measuring two *different* skills and both might need to be retained.

A series of multiple correlations were computed to determine which *combination* of skills correlated highest with the test criterion, i.e., field hockey playing ability. The test criterion consisted of subjective rating by three nationally rated umpires, all of whom were players and teachers of considerable experience. The judges were asked to rate the players on general hockey playing ability during two successive periods and to classify them into five groups: 1) superior; 2) above average; 3) average; 4) below average; and 5) inferior. The rating of the instructor of each particular group involved was weighted so that the criterion consisted of twice the instructor's score plus the sum of the other two raters. The final regression (prediction) equation was:

$$x_0 = .38\,x_1 + .17\,x_2 + .48\,x_3 - 1.62$$

in which

$x_0$ = the test criterion, i.e., playing ability

$x_1$ = goal shooting left test

$x_2$ = dribble, dodge, circular tackle, and drive test

$x_3$ = fielding and drive test

Only the dribble, dodge, circular tackle, and drive test will be described here. This test was considered by the authors as the most economically administered. The other tests in the final battery are described in the original article.

*Equipment.* Hockey stick for each participant; stopwatch; 1 ball necessary; 2 balls convenient; high jump standards; field markings 2 inches (5.08 cm) wide (see Figure 10.5) as follows:

1.  A line 20 feet (6.10 m) long to be used for a starting line.
2.  A line perpendicular to the midpoint of the starting line and extending 35 feet (10.67 m) from it. This is the foul line.
3.  A line 10 feet (3.05 m) long, perpendicular to and bisected by the foul line at a point 30 feet (9.14 m) from the starting line. This is the restraining line.
4.  A line 1 foot (30.48 cm) long, perpendicular to and bisected by the foul line at a point 35 feet (10.67 m) from the starting line.
5.  Two lines, each one foot (30.48 cm) long, bisecting each other at a point 45 feet (13.72 m) from the starting line and in a straight line with the foul line.

Positions of standards are as follows:

1.  One standard is placed so that the middle of the base of the standard is directly over the point where the foul line and the line described in 4 above bisect each other.

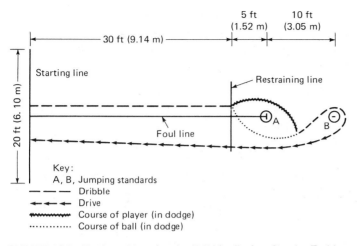

**FIGURE 10.5** Field markings for the Dribble, Dodge, Circular Tackle and Drive Test. (Reproduced from Schmithals and French, "Achievement Tests in Field Hockey for College Women," *Res. Quart.,* **11 (October, 1940), 84–92.)**

2. The other standard is placed in similar fashion over the point formed by the two lines described in 3 above.

*Description and administration.* The player being tested stands behind the starting line with the hockey ball placed on the starting line at any point to the left of the foul line. At the signal "Ready? Go!," the player dribbles the ball forward to the left and parallel to the foul line. As soon as the restraining line is reached, the ball is hit from the left side of the foul line to the right of the first obstacle (from the player's point of view), and the player runs around the left side of the obstacle to recover the ball. (This is analogous to a dodge.) Next, the player executes a turn toward the right around the second obstacle, still keeping control of the ball. (This is analogous to a circular tackle.) As soon as possible after that, the ball is driven toward the starting line. If the drive is not hard enough to reach the starting line, the player may follow it up and hit the ball again.

This procedure is repeated until six trials have been given, care being taken that no player is fatigued.

*Scoring.* One practice trial is given. The score for one trial is the time it takes from the signal "Go" until the player's ball again crosses the starting line. The score for the entire test is the average of the six trials. It is considered a foul and the trial does not count if: 1) the ball or player crosses the foul line before reaching the restraining line; 2) in executing the dodge, the ball is not hit from the left side of the foul line; or 3) the player makes "sticks."

*Reliability and validity.* Reliability coefficients were obtained for 51 college women on all six original test items. These ranged from .67 to .92. Coefficients for the three test items composing the final test battery ranged from .87 to .92. The method of obtaining reliability was not stated.

Validity coefficients were obtained for each of the original test items correlated with the external test criterion (field hockey playing ability). These ranged from .41 to .48. The validity coefficient for the final test battery correlated with the test criterion was .62.

*Normative information.*  No norm tables were included in the original study, but means and standard deviations for each test item were published, making it a simple matter for readers to develop their own standard score tables by use of the formulas given in Chapter 2.

*Comments.*  The relatively high reliability of most of the test items coupled with the relatively low validity of the test battery indicate that some important skill elements may have been omitted inadvertently from the original study. The authors themselves recommended possible inclusion of a change-of-direction test in future studies.

## FOOTBALL—TACKLE/TOUCH SKILLS TESTS

There is a scarcity of tests purported to measure football ability in the professional literature. The few available are tests of achievement, i.e., they attempt to measure present status in specific football skills rather than *predict* performance in football playing ability. Some of these are summarized in Table 10-9.

The AAHPER football skills tests[10] are probably the first tests to be put into general use. These consist of forward pass for distance; 50-yard (45.72 m) dash with football; blocking; forward pass for accuracy; football punt for distance; ball-changing zigzag run; catching the forward pass; pull out; kick off; dodging run.

Two of the above are selected for further description.

### AAHPER Football Blocking Skill Test

*Equipment.*  A football field or other smooth grass field; three blocking bags; measuring tape; stopwatch. For the blocking bags, canvas bags 18 inches (45.72 cm) in diameter and 4 feet (1.22 m) high can be used. They should be filled with sand and closed at the top.

*Description and administration.*  The purpose of this test is to measure the player's speed and agility in executing three cross-body blocks. The course is set up so that the three blocking bags are arranged as shown in Figure 10.6. Bags 1 and 2 are placed on end 15 feet (4.57 m) apart and 15 feet (4.57 m) from the starting line. Bag 3 is placed on end 15 feet (4.57 m) from bag 2 in the direction of the starting line and at a 45° angle to the line between bag 1 and bag 2. This will put bag 3 about 5 feet (1.52 m) from the starting line. A player stands behind the start-

**TABLE 10-9 Summary of Football—Tackle/Touch Tests***

| AUTHOR | SOURCE | SEX | NO. CASES | AGE GROUP | NORMS | RELIABILITY COEFFICIENT | VALIDITY COEFFICIENT |
|---|---|---|---|---|---|---|---|
| Cozens, F.W. | *R.Q., 8:72–78,* May, 1937. | M | Five Classes | college men | No | — | EVC–.85 IVC–.88–.92 |
| McElroy, H.N. | *R.Q., 9:82–88* Oct., 1938. | M | — | grades 7–12 | No | T–R .74–.79 | — |
| Brace, D.K. | *R.Q., 14:372–377,* Dec., 1943 | M | 65 | college athletes | No | — | EVC .33–.48 |
| Manolis, G.G. | *R.Q., 26:170–178,* May, 1955. | M | 31 | college athletes | No | T–R .97 | EVC .28–.34 |
| AAHPER | *Skills Test Manual: Football,* 1966. | M | 600–900 | 10–18 | Yes | lit. | log. |

*See Appendix D for explanation of symbols.

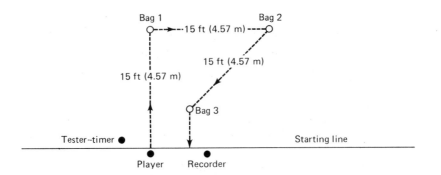

**FIGURE 10.6  Blocking. (Reproduced from AAHPER,** *Skills Test Manual—Football,* **Washington, D.C.: AAHPER, 1966, p. 20.)**

ing line opposite bag 1 and, on the signal "Go," charges forward and cross-body blocks bag 1 to the ground. The player then recovers immediately, charges across to bag 2, and blocks it to the ground. The player recovers again, charges back to bag 3, blocks it to the ground, recovers again, and charges across the starting line. The players are timed from the signal "Go" to the instant they cross the starting line after blocking down bag 3. In addition, the player must warm up before being tested and is allowed one practice run-through. Each bag must be cross-body blocked to the ground with the player on top. The bag cannot just be bumped down. The player is given two trials and each time is recorded.

*Scoring.* The score is the time (recorded in seconds and tenths of seconds) required for the player to finish the test; time is started on signal "Go" and stopped as the player crosses back over the line. The best time is the player's score.

*Reliability and validity.* Neither was attempted.

*Normative information.* The norms (Table 10-10) were based on scores received from approximately 700 boys. Data were collected from a wide geographical range including 74 cities in 36 states.

*Comments.* This test can be used to identify performance levels of boys of different ages before and after units of instruction or before and after seasons of competition. Although not devised statistically to test general football playing ability, practice in this skill should serve to improve overall performance.

### AAHPER Football Skills Test—
### Catching the Forward Pass

*Equipment.* Football field or other smooth grass field marked for the test as shown in Figure 10.7; standard footballs; measuring tape; baseball bases or white cloths to mark points.

**TABLE 10-10  Blocking**

| PERCENTILE | AGE | | | | | | | | PERCENTILE |
|---|---|---|---|---|---|---|---|---|---|
| | 10 | 11 | 12 | 13 | 14 | 15 | 16 | 17–18 | |
| 100th | 6.9 | 5.0 | 5.0 | 5.0 | 5.0 | 5.0 | 5.0 | 5.0 | 100th |
| 95th | 7.5 | 6.6 | 6.6 | 5.9 | 5.8 | 5.8 | 5.8 | 5.5 | 95th |
| 90th | 7.7 | 7.1 | 7.1 | 6.5 | 6.2 | 6.2 | 6.1 | 5.7 | 90th |
| 85th | 7.9 | 7.5 | 7.5 | 6.7 | 6.6 | 6.3 | 6.3 | 5.8 | 85th |
| 80th | 8.1 | 8.0 | 7.7 | 6.9 | 6.8 | 6.5 | 6.5 | 6.0 | 80th |
| 75th | 8.3 | 8.3 | 7.9 | 7.2 | 6.0 | 6.7 | 6.7 | 6.2 | 75th |
| 70th | 8.5 | 8.6 | 8.1 | 7.4 | 7.1 | 6.9 | 7.0 | 6.3 | 70th |
| 65th | 8.9 | 9.1 | 8.4 | 7.6 | 7.3 | 7.0 | 7.2 | 6.5 | 65th |
| 60th | 9.3 | 9.5 | 8.5 | 7.7 | 7.5 | 7.2 | 7.4 | 6.7 | 60th |
| 55th | 9.6 | 9.7 | 8.8 | 7.9 | 7.7 | 7.4 | 7.6 | 7.0 | 55th |
| 50th | 9.8 | 9.9 | 9.0 | 8.1 | 7.8 | 7.5 | 7.8 | 7.2 | 50th |
| 45th | 10.1 | 10.2 | 9.2 | 8.3 | 8.0 | 7.8 | 8.0 | 7.4 | 45th |
| 40th | 10.5 | 10.4 | 9.4 | 8.4 | 8.1 | 7.9 | 8.3 | 7.6 | 40th |
| 35th | 10.7 | 10.6 | 9.6 | 8.6 | 8.3 | 8.2 | 8.6 | 7.8 | 35th |
| 30th | 11.0 | 10.9 | 9.7 | 8.9 | 8.5 | 8.3 | 8.8 | 8.0 | 30th |
| 25th | 11.3 | 11.1 | 9.9 | 9.1 | 8.7 | 8.5 | 9.1 | 8.2 | 25th |
| 20th | 11.6 | 11.3 | 10.2 | 9.4 | 9.0 | 8.8 | 9.5 | 8.5 | 20th |
| 15th | 12.0 | 11.6 | 10.5 | 9.8 | 9.2 | 9.0 | 9.0 | 8.9 | 15th |
| 10th | 12.8 | 12.0 | 10.9 | 10.2 | 9.5 | 9.4 | 10.6 | 9.4 | 10th |
| 5th | 14.4 | 13.1 | 11.6 | 11.2 | 10.3 | 10.4 | 10.7 | 10.8 | 5th |
| 0 | 17.5 | 18.0 | 15.0 | 15.0 | 15.0 | 13.0 | 15.0 | 14.0 | 0 |

Source: AAHPER, 1966, p. 41.

*Description and administration.*  The success of this test depends upon having one or more expert passers who can pass the ball mechanically over the passing point without paying attention to the player trying to catch the pass.

A scrimmage line is laid out. An assistant serves as center over the ball on the scrimmage line. The player being tested takes a position as an end, 9 feet (2.74 m) from the center on the right. A "turning point" is marked 30 feet (9.14 m) directly ahead of the player on the scrimmage line. A "passing point" is marked 30 feet (9.14 m) from the turning point to the right and 30 feet (9.14 m) from the scrimmage line. A similar turning point and passing point are laid out to the left of the center. The passer stands 15 feet (4.57 m) directly behind the center. On the signal "Go" the center snaps the ball to the passer, who takes a step and passes the ball directly over the passing point above head height. On the signal "Go" the player runs straight ahead around the turning point and out beyond the passing point, where he or she tries to catch the ball. Additionally, the player must warm up before being tested and is allowed one practice run-through on each side. The player must go around the turning point. To be good, the pass must go over the passing point. The player is thrown 10 passes on each side and need not try for bad balls.

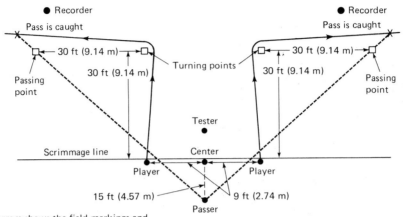

This diagram shows the field markings and action for catching passes from both sides

**FIGURE 10.7  Catching the forward pass. (Reproduced from AAHPER,** *Skills Test Manual—Football,* **1966, p. 28.)**

*Scoring.*  One point is scored for each pass caught after the pass has crossed over the passing point. The score is the sum of passes caught from both sides.

*Reliability and validity.*  Neither was attempted.

*Normative information.*  The norms (Table 10-11) were based on scores received from approximately 700 boys. Data were collected from a wide geographical range including 74 cities in 36 states.

*Comments.*  Care must be taken that the individual(s) selected to pass the ball over the passing point be able to concentrate on the passing point rather than the receiver.

In addition to measuring present status, this skill should prove to be an interesting and challenging practice item.

## ICE HOCKEY SKILLS TESTS

Statistically analyzed ice hockey skills tests are practically nonexistent in the professional literature. Two of these are summarized in Table 10-12. The more comprehensive of the two is selected for further description.

### The Merrifield-Walford Ice Hockey Skills Test[11]

In the original test, six skill elements were selected for study, based upon the subjective judgment of the investigators. These included: 1) forward skating speed; 2) backward skating speed; 3) skating agility; 4) puck-carry; 5) shooting; and 6)

**TABLE 10-11** Catching the Forward Pass

| PERCENTILE | AGE | | | | | | | | PERCENTILE |
|---|---|---|---|---|---|---|---|---|---|
| | 10 | 11 | 12 | 13 | 14 | 15 | 16 | 17-18 | |
| 100th | 20 | 20 | 20 | 20 | 20 | 20 | 20 | 20 | 100th |
| 95th | 19 | 19 | 19 | 20 | 20 | 20 | 20 | 20 | 95th |
| 90th | 17 | 18 | 19 | 19 | 19 | 19 | 19 | 19 | 90th |
| 85th | 16 | 16 | 18 | 18 | 18 | 19 | 19 | 19 | 85th |
| 80th | 14 | 15 | 18 | 17 | 18 | 18 | 18 | 18 | 80th |
| 75th | 13 | 14 | 16 | 17 | 17 | 18 | 18 | 18 | 75th |
| 70th | 12 | 13 | 16 | 16 | 16 | 17 | 17 | 17 | 70th |
| 65th | 11 | 12 | 15 | 15 | 15 | 16 | 16 | 16 | 65th |
| 60th | 10 | 12 | 14 | 15 | 15 | 16 | 16 | 16 | 60th |
| 55th | 8 | 11 | 14 | 14 | 14 | 15 | 15 | 15 | 55th |
| 50th | 7 | 10 | 13 | 13 | 14 | 15 | 15 | 15 | 50th |
| 45th | 7 | 9 | 12 | 13 | 13 | 14 | 14 | 14 | 45th |
| 40th | 6 | 8 | 12 | 12 | 12 | 13 | 13 | 13 | 40th |
| 35th | 5 | 7 | 11 | 11 | 11 | 12 | 12 | 13 | 35th |
| 30th | 5 | 7 | 10 | 10 | 10 | 11 | 11 | 12 | 30th |
| 25th | 4 | 6 | 10 | 9 | 9 | 10 | 10 | 11 | 25th |
| 20th | 3 | 5 | 8 | 8 | 8 | 9 | 9 | 10 | 20th |
| 15th | 2 | 4 | 7 | 7 | 8 | 8 | 8 | 9 | 15th |
| 10th | 1 | 3 | 6 | 6 | 6 | 7 | 6 | 8 | 10th |
| 5th | 1 | 1 | 5 | 4 | 4 | 6 | 4 | 6 | 5th |
| 0 | 0 | 0 | 0 | 0 | 0 | 0 | 0 | 0 | 0 |

Source: AAHPER, 1966, p. 45.

passing. Because of low reliability, the passing and shooting tests were dropped from further analysis. The remaining four test items were intercorrelated and then correlated with the test criterion. The test criterion consisted of the coach's ranking of each individual in overall playing ability. No attempt was made to make use of partial and multiple correlation techniques to arrive at regression equations that could be used to predict overall performance from a validated battery of skills tests.

Of the four remaining test items, only one, the puck-carry test, will be described here. The others are discussed in the original article.

*Equipment.* Seven wooden obstacles; whistle; stopwatch; hockey sticks; hockey pucks; markings as shown in Figure 10.8.

*Description and administration.* Seven wooden obstacles are placed on the ice in a straight line 30 feet (9.14 m) apart. The first obstacle is situated at the 4-foot (1.22 m) start-finish line (Figure 10.8).

The test includes maneuvers of skating to the left, to the right, and performing a loop around obstacles while stickhandling a puck. The skater stands behind the start-finish line with the puck resting on the line to the left of the obstacle.

**TABLE 10-12  Summary of Ice Hockey Skills Tests***

| AUTHOR | SOURCE | SEX | NO. CASES | AGE GROUP | NORMS | RELIABILITY COEFFICIENT | VALIDITY COEFFICIENT |
|---|---|---|---|---|---|---|---|
| Doroschuk, E. and Marcotte, G. | Canadian AAHPER, June, 1965. | M | 27 | college men | No | T–R .93 | EVC .83 |
| Merrifield, H. and Walford, G. | R.Q., 40:146–152, March, 1969. | M | 15 | college men | No | T–R .37–.94 | EVC .75–.96 |

*See Appendix D for explanation of symbols.

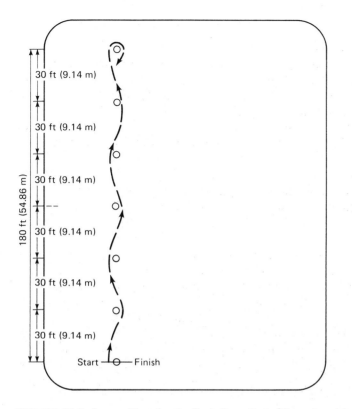

**FIGURE 10.8 Ice markings for the Puck-Carry Test. (Reproduced from H. H. Merrifield and G. A. A. Walford, "Battery of Ice Hockey Skill Tests,"** *Res. Quart.,* **40 (March, 1969), 146–152.)**

When the signal is given, the skater moves through the zig-zag course, passing to the left of the first obstacle, to the right of the second obstacle, etc., then skates around the farthest obstacle and zig-zags back to the starting line. If 2 or more obstacles are knocked over, the skater must repeat the test. The performer is required to maintain control over the puck throughout the test. If the subject fails during a test performance, the trial is repeated. The test is described to the subject prior to the test. Each subject is allowed to first go through the test at approximately half speed to ensure familiarization.

*Scoring.* A stopwatch is used to record the time to the nearest one tenth of a second. Time is recorded from the whistle signal until the skater's first skate reaches the finish line.

*Reliability and validity.* The test-retest method was used to obtain reliability coefficients for 15 subjects on all of the original six skill elements. These ranged from .37 to .94. The reliability of the puck-carry test described here was .93.

Validity coefficients were obtained for each of the four skill items deemed reliable by correlating them with the subjective test criterion (coach's ranking). These ranged from .75 for skating agility to .96 for the puck-carry test.

*Normative information.*   No norms were included in the study. This is understandable, since, with only 15 cases, the likelihood of a resultant normal distribution is remote.

*Comments.*   The unusually high validity coefficient of .96 between the puck-carry test and the subjective ranking of overall playing ability is, indeed, surprising. Until this study can be duplicated with a larger sample (between, say, 100–200 cases) and employing perhaps two or more judges and a more sophisticated rating scale, it would be "chancy" to conclude that the puck-carry test can account for over 92% of the variance included in something as complex as ice hockey playing ability.

## SOCCER SKILLS TESTS

Few validated soccer skills tests are available in the professional literature. A relatively large number of studies involving a variety of soccer skill elements can be found in the form of masters' theses. A few of these are summarized in Table 10-13. One of the more commonly used tests is selected for further description.

### The McDonald Soccer Skill Test[12]

The author selected controlled kicking as a most fundamental skill element of soccer. A test of this skill could be administered easily, promised to be an objective measure of general soccer ability, and could be used at the high school or college level. Actually, the test combined the requirements of accurate kicking, ball control, and judgment of a moving ball.

In the original study, experiments were conducted at distances of 9 feet (2.74 m), 15 feet (4.57 m), 21 feet (6.40 m) and 30 feet (9.14 m) from the kickboard. The scores at the various distances were correlated with the test criterion, consisting of a subjective rating by three coaches, of overall soccer playing ability. The kickboard test, with a 9-foot (2.74 m) restraining distance, provided the highest validity coefficients and is described here.

*Equipment.*   Soccer field; 3 regulation soccer balls; stopwatch; kickboard; markings as shown in Figure 10.9.

*Description and administration.*   One ball is placed on the 9-foot (2.74 m) restraining line for the subject to commence kicking at the starting signal. The two other balls are placed the same distance (9 feet—2.74 m) behind the restraining line and 18 feet (5.49 m) from the kickboard. The subject commences kicking the stationary ball from or behind the restraining line and continues kicking the rebound-

**TABLE 10-13  Summary of Soccer Skills Tests***

| AUTHOR | SOURCE | SEX | NO. CASES | AGE GROUP | NORMS | RELIABILITY COEFFICIENT | VALIDITY COEFFICIENT |
|---|---|---|---|---|---|---|---|
| Heath, M.L. and Rodgers, E.G. | *R.Q.*, 3:33-53, Dec., 1932. | M | 210-318 | grades 5-6 | Yes | T-R .60-.74 | EVC .60-.62 |
| Schauffle, E.F. | Master's thesis, State U. of Iowa, 1940. | F | 84 | grades 9-10 | Yes | SH .73-.97 | EVC .52-.78 |
| McDonald, L.G. | Master's thesis, Springfield College, 1951. | M | 17-53 | college men | No | — | EVC .63-.94 |
| Crew, V.N. | Master's thesis, U. of Ore., 1968. | M | 51 | college men | Yes | .97-.99** | EVC .73-.99 |

*See Appendix D for explanation of symbols.

**Objectivity coefficients.

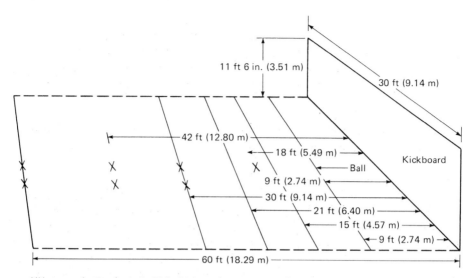

11 ft 6 in. (3.51 m)

30 ft (9.14 m)

42 ft (12.80 m)

18 ft (5.49 m)

Kickboard

Ball

9 ft (2.74 m)

30 ft (9.14 m)

21 ft (6.40 m)

15 ft (4.57 m)

9 ft (2.74 m)

60 ft (18.29 m)

XX = spots for 2 extra balls 18 ft, 30 ft, 42 ft, and 60 ft from
kickboard (5.49 m, 9.14 m, 12.80 m, and 18.29 m)

**FIGURE 10.9** Diagram of markings for soccer kickboard test. (Reproduced from L.G. Mc-
Donald, "The Construction of a Kicking Skill Test as an Index of General Soccer
Ability," unpublished master's thesis, Springfield, Mass.: Springfield College,
1951, p. 25.)

ing ball as rapidly as control permits until the 30-second time limit expires. Any
type of kick and any ball control methods may be used, but the kicking, to be
scored, has to be done with the supporting leg on or behind the restraining line. If
the ball fails to rebound sufficiently, the subject may retrieve it with either hands
or feet and, after placing it on or behind the restraining line, continue kicking; or,
as an alternative, one of the spare balls may be put into play, again using hands or
feet to get the ball into the desired kicking position on or behind the restraining
line. A subject losing control of the ball as a result of kicking it out of the boundaries of the testing area also has the option of either retrieving it or putting a spare
ball into play.

*Scoring.* The timing is begun with the command "Go." The subject kicks
the controlled ball into the backboard as often as possible in 30 seconds. Four trials
are given, and the final test score is the sum of the three best trials.

*Reliability and validity.* Apparently, no reliability coefficients were obtained
for this test. However, in a later study, Johnson[13] obtained reliabilities of .74 to .80
on consecutive trials for a similar wall-volley test.

Validity coefficients were obtained for the McDonald test by correlating the
scores of three skill-level groups with the test criterion (coach's rating). The coefficients were .94, .63, .76, and .85 for varsity, junior varsity, freshman varsity, and
combined groups, respectively.

*Comments.*    A number of steps might have been taken to improve the quality of this study.

1. First to be questioned is the arbitrary selection of just one skill element to measure soccer ability. A better approach would have been to: a) identify important skill elements from opinions of a panel of "experts"; b) reduce the number of items by the process of intercorrelation and remove some items that correlate highly with each other; and c) identify, by multiple correlation, a small battery of skills that correlate highly with the test criterion.

2. Reliability coefficients should have been obtained routinely.

3. A kickboard the size of a regulation goal (8 feet × 24 feet—2.44 m × 7.32 m) might have been used rather than one 11½ feet × 30 feet (3.51 m × 9.14 m).

4. It would probably have been better not to have allowed the use of the hands to recover a stray ball. Incidentally, the Johnson test mentioned previously corrects the criticisms in numbers 3 and 4 above.

5. Finally, the researcher allowed unlimited warm-up and rest periods. These should probably be controlled.


## SPEEDBALL SKILLS TESTS

Apparently there are no statistically validated tests of speedball skill in the published professional literature. In an unpublished doctoral dissertation, Crawford[14] studied both soccer and speedball skills. References for a few empirically determined tests were included in her study and may be used for future scientific research.


## VOLLEYBALL SKILLS TESTS

Volleyball, like tennis, has enjoyed a considerable amount of test-construction study in comparison to most other sports. Most of the studies have employed some type of repeated wall-volley test with the use of restraining lines. Variations in these wall-volley tests have included; 1) distance of restraining lines from the wall; 2) length and number of trials; and 3) trials used to determine a player's score. A few passing tests have also been published. Some of the better known tests are summarized in Table 10–14. Two of these have been selected for further description.

### The Cunningham and Garrison High
### Wall-Volley Test[15]

*Equipment.*    Official leather volleyball, properly inflated; unobstructed wall space 9 feet (2.74 m) wide and 15 feet (4.57 m) high; stopwatch.

*Description and administration.*    A target area is formed by three lines: one horizontal line 3 feet (91.44 cm) long and 10 feet (3.05 m) from the floor, and two

**TABLE 10-14 Summary of Volleyball Skills Tests***

| AUTHOR | SOURCE | SEX | NO. CASES | AGE GROUP | NORMS | RELIABILITY COEFFICIENT | VALIDITY COEFFICIENT |
|---|---|---|---|---|---|---|---|
| Bassett, G., et al. | R.Q., 8:60-72, Dec., 1937. | F | 119 | college women | No | T-R .62-.89 | EVC .51-.78 |
| French, E.L. and Cooper, B.I. | R.Q., 8:150-157, May, 1937 | F | 227 | grades 9-12 | No | – | EVC .61-.81 |
| Russell, N. and Lange, E. | R.Q., 11:33-41, Dec., 1940. | F | 52-70 | grades 7-9 | Yes | T-R .87-.91 | EVC .67-.77 |
| Crogan, C. | Phys. Educ., 4:34-37, Oct., 1943. | F | 113-129 | grades 9-12 | No | T-R .45-.83 | – |
| Brady, G.F. | R.Q., 16:14-17, March, 1945. | M | 537 | college men | No | T-R .92 | EVC .86 |
| Lamp, N.A. | R.Q., 25:189-200, May, 1954. | M & F | 90 | jr. high 11-16 | No | T-R .56-.64 | IVC .71-.98 |
| Mohr, D.R. and Haverstick, M.J. | R.Q., 26:179-184, May, 1955. | F | 69 | college women | No | T-R .93-.94 | EVC .68-.79 |
| Broer, M.R. | R.Q., 29:139-145, May, 1958. | F | 136-199 | grades 7-8 | No | SH & T-R .66-.94 | – |
| Butler, W.M. | R.Q., 32:261-262, May, 1961. | F | 32 | grade 10 | No | SH .84-.98 | EVC .60** |
| Clifton, M.A. | R.Q., 33:208-211, May, 1962. | F | 45 | college women | No. | T-R .63-.86 | EVC .58-.74 |
| Liba, M.R. and Stauff, M.R. | R.Q., 34:56-63, March, 1963. | F | 2 classes | college | No | AV .70-.95 | – |
|  |  | F | 1 class | grades 7 & 8 | No | .55-.93 |  |

**TABLE 10-14 (continued)**

| AUTHOR | SOURCE | SEX | NO. CASES | AGE GROUP | NORMS | RELIABILITY COEFFICIENT | VALIDITY COEFFICIENT |
|---|---|---|---|---|---|---|---|
| Cunningham, P. and Garrison, J. | *R.Q., 39*:486–490, Oct., 1968. | F | 111 | college women | No | T-R .87 | EVC .62–.72 |
| Kronqvist, P., and Brumbach, W. | *R.Q., 39*:116–120, March, 1968. | M | 33–71 | grades 10–11 | No | T-R .71–.83 | EVC .68–.82 |
| AAHPER | *Skills Test Manual—Volleyball*, 1969 | M & F | 600–900 | 10–18 | Yes | lit. | log. |

*See Appendix D for explanation of symbols.

**The original study did not attempt statistical validity. This validity coefficient was obtained in the study by Cunningham and Garrison.

vertical lines 3 feet (91.44 cm) long (at each end of the horizontal line) extending upward at right angles to the horizontal line.

The test consists of two 30-second trials. The player stands anywhere in front of the target (no restraining line). With the signal "Ready, go," the player uses any type of toss or hit to send the ball into the target area on or above the 10-foot (3.05 m) line and on or between the two vertical lines or their extensions. When the ball returns, the player volleys it repeatedly into the target area. Only one contact with the ball is allowed on each volley.

If control of the ball is lost, the player recovers the ball and starts again as before. The player may not use the sequence "toss, volley, catch; toss, volley, catch" but must make an attempt to perform a repeated volley. Following the first trial, the player rests while the other members of the group (6 to 8 players) take their first trials. A second trial is given.

*Scoring.* One point is scored each time the ball hits in the target area or on the lines bounding it (including imaginary extensions of the vertical lines) following a legal volley of a ball rebounding from the wall. The toss or hit to start the ball does not count. If the player loses control of the ball, scoring continues with the next legal hit. Two 30-second trials are given, and the final score is the better of the two trials.

*Reliability and validity.* The test-retest method was used on 111 college-age female subjects to obtain a reliability coefficient of .87.

Validity coefficients were obtained by correlating various scoring schemes of the test with the test criterion, namely, volleyball playing ability as obtained by subjective ratings by three experienced judges. Coefficients were .62, .65, .67, and .72 for trial one, trial two, sum of trials one and two, and the better of trials one and two, respectively.

*Normative information.* No norms were published for this study, nor were means and standard deviations made available.

*Comments.* The test has some advantages over other wall-volley tests in that it has: 1) eliminated the restraining line; 2) raised the height factor; and 3) decreased the size of the target area, thus making the skill requirements more gamelike.

### The AAHPER Volleyball Skills Test (Boys and Girls)[16]

The original publication includes tests of the following skill elements: 1) volleying; 2) serving; 3) passing; and 4) setting. Only the passing test will be described here.

*Equipment.* Volleyballs; volleyball net and standards; 4-foot (1.22m) X 6-foot (1.83 m) mats or marked areas on floor (Figure 10.10); 30-foot (9.14 m) rope; two standards 8 feet (2.44 m) high.

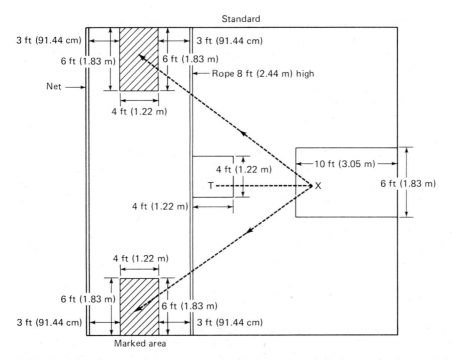

**FIGURE 10.10 Floor markings for Volleyball Passing Test. (Reproduced from AAHPER,** *Skills Test Manual—Volleyball,* **1969, p. 22.)**

*Description and administration.* Passer X (person being tested) stands in the center-back position of the court, receives a high throw (similar to a two-hand basketball shot) from the thrower T, and executes a pass so that it goes over the rope and onto the mat or marked area. The passer is given 20 trials performed alternately to the right and to the left. The trial counts, but no points are recorded if the ball touches the rope or net or does not fall on the target area.

*Scoring.* One point is scored for each pass going over the rope and landing on or hitting any part of the target area (including lines), with 20 being the maximum.

*Reliability and validity.* Neither was attempted.

*Normative information.* Percentile-rank norm tables have been constructed for the passing test for both boys and girls. These are presented in Tables 10-15 and 10-16.

*Comments.* Before this test is used, it seems critical that the reliability of the test for the particular age group in question be determined. It is highly unlikely that the reliability would be the same for ten-year olds as for eighteen-year olds.

TABLE 10-15  Passing Test (Boys)

| PERCENTILE | | | | AGE | | | | PERCENTILE |
|---|---|---|---|---|---|---|---|---|
| | 10-11 | 12 | 13 | 14 | 15 | 16 | 17-18 | |
| 100 | 19 | 19 | 20 | 20 | 20 | 20 | 20 | 100 |
| 95 | 12 | 14 | 16 | 17 | 17 | 17 | 17 | 95 |
| 90 | 10 | 13 | 14 | 16 | 16 | 16 | 16 | 90 |
| 85 | 9 | 12 | 13 | 15 | 15 | 15 | 15 | 85 |
| 80 | 8 | 11 | 12 | 14 | 14 | 14 | 14 | 80 |
| 75 | 7 | 10 | 12 | 13 | 13 | 13 | 13 | 75 |
| 70 | 6 | 9 | 11 | 12 | 12 | 12 | 13 | 70 |
| 65 | 5 | 8 | 10 | 12 | 12 | 12 | 13 | 65 |
| 60 | 4 | 8 | 9 | 11 | 11 | 12 | 12 | 60 |
| 55 | 4 | 7 | 9 | 10 | 10 | 12 | 12 | 55 |
| 50 | 3 | 6 | 8 | 10 | 10 | 11 | 11 | 50 |
| 45 | 3 | 5 | 7 | 9 | 9 | 10 | 10 | 45 |
| 40 | 2 | 4 | 7 | 8 | 8 | 9 | 9 | 40 |
| 35 | 2 | 4 | 6 | 8 | 8 | 9 | 9 | 35 |
| 30 | 1 | 3 | 5 | 7 | 7 | 8 | 8 | 30 |
| 25 | 1 | 2 | 4 | 6 | 6 | 7 | 8 | 25 |
| 20 | 0 | 2 | 4 | 5 | 5 | 6 | 7 | 20 |
| 15 | 0 | 1 | 3 | 4 | 4 | 5 | 6 | 15 |
| 10 | 0 | 0 | 2 | 3 | 3 | 4 | 4 | 10 |
| 5 | 0 | 0 | 1 | 2 | 2 | 2 | 2 | 5 |
| 0 | 0 | 0 | 0 | 0 | 0 | 0 | 0 | 0 |

Source: AAHPER, 1966, p. 31.

## WATER POLO SKILLS TEST

No statistically validated tests were found in the professional literature. Books on the subject maintain that all players on a team, with the exception of the goalie, are expected to do all things. They must shoot, pass, swim, and play defense.[17] Skill elements have been identified by Anttila[18] as including conditioning, ball handling, passing and receiving, dribbling, spinning, breaking, and shooting.

Walton[19] proposed a 10-item skill test to be used for drill purposes. A graduate student attempted to validate this test while fulfilling a requirement for a research methods class. His findings are presented here in hopes of stimulating more research on this and other tests.[20]

### The Walton Water Polo Decathlon

1. Reversals

*Equipment.*  Two poles extended 5 feet (1.52 m) from the sides of the pool, 4 yards (3.66 m) apart; a 2-inch × 4-inch (5.08 cm × 10.16 cm) float hung 2 inches (5.08 cm) above the surface of the water from each pole.

260

**TABLE 10-16  Passing Test (Girls)**

| PERCENTILE | AGE | | | | | | | PERCENTILE |
|---|---|---|---|---|---|---|---|---|
| | 10–11 | 12 | 13 | 14 | 15 | 16 | 17–18 | |
| 100 | 19 | 19 | 20 | 20 | 20 | 20 | 20 | 100 |
| 95 | 10 | 12 | 12 | 13 | 13 | 14 | 15 | 95 |
| 90 | 8 | 10 | 10 | 11 | 11 | 12 | 13 | 90 |
| 85 | 7 | 8 | 9 | 10 | 10 | 11 | 12 | 85 |
| 80 | 6 | 7 | 8 | 9 | 9 | 10 | 11 | 80 |
| 75 | 5 | 6 | 7 | 8 | 8 | 8 | 9 | 75 |
| 70 | 4 | 6 | 6 | 7 | 7 | 8 | 9 | 70 |
| 65 | 3 | 5 | 5 | 6 | 6 | 8 | 8 | 65 |
| 60 | 3 | 4 | 4 | 6 | 6 | 7 | 8 | 60 |
| 55 | 2 | 4 | 4 | 5 | 5 | 6 | 7 | 55 |
| 50 | 2 | 3 | 4 | 5 | 5 | 6 | 6 | 50 |
| 45 | 1 | 3 | 3 | 4 | 4 | 5 | 6 | 45 |
| 40 | 1 | 2 | 3 | 4 | 4 | 4 | 5 | 40 |
| 35 | 0 | 2 | 2 | 3 | 3 | 4 | 4 | 35 |
| 30 | 0 | 1 | 2 | 3 | 3 | 3 | 4 | 30 |
| 25 | 0 | 1 | 1 | 2 | 2 | 3 | 3 | 25 |
| 20 | 0 | 0 | 1 | 1 | 2 | 2 | 3 | 20 |
| 15 | 0 | 0 | 0 | 1 | 1 | 2 | 2 | 15 |
| 10 | 0 | 0 | 0 | 0 | 1 | 1 | 1 | 10 |
| 5 | 0 | 0 | 0 | 0 | 0 | 0 | 0 | 5 |
| 0 | 0 | 0 | 0 | 0 | 0 | 0 | 0 | 0 |

Source: AAHPER, 1966, p. 35.

*Description and administration.* The purpose is to measure change in direction and quick start ability. The participant starts with the head next to and outside a float. On the whistle, the participant swims back and forth between the floats, executing a reversal. The use of the bottom or the side of the pool is not permitted.

*Scoring.* The clock starts on the whistle. A count is made of each float touched during a 1-minute period.

2. Five shot accuracy

*Equipment.* Markers placed 8 yards (7.32 m) from the front of the goal; 5 balls; a target suspended 1 foot (30.48 cm) inside goal area; scoring areas marked clearly, with point values indicated.

*Description and administration.* The purpose of this test is to measure throwing accuracy. The participant's head is on a line 8 yards (7.32 m) from the front of the center of the goal. The ball is thrown at a target area suspended 1 foot (30.48 cm) inside the goal area.

*Scoring.* Points, corresponding with the target, are awarded for hitting scoring areas on the fly. Five points are awarded each time a ball hits a 1-foot-square (30.48 cm) area and 2 points are awarded for each ball striking anywhere else on the 16-inch-wide (40.64 cm) target area. The ball must strike entirely inside the scoring area on the fly to receive the highest point value.

### 3. Dribble sprint

*Equipment.* A course 25 yards (22.86 m) in length; stopwatch.

*Description and administration.* The purpose of this test is to measure the ability to dribble a ball quickly from one point to another while maintaining control of the ball. The ball is held on the fingertips above the surface of the water, with the opposite hand gripping the gutter and the feet against the wall. On the push-off, the ball is set directly in front of the participant's head and dribbled.

*Scoring.* The participant is timed from the whistle start to the hand-touch finish. The ball must be between the participant's arms. If control is lost, the participant must retrieve the ball without using the palm of the hand or fingers and continue swimming without touching the ball with    fingers or hands. Control of the ball may be lost only twice during the trial.

### 4. Ball handling

*Equipment.* A pole 2 inches, (5.08 cm) in diameter, extended 5 feet (1.52 m) from the side of the pool and 5 feet (1.52 m) from the surface of the water.

*Description and administration.* The purpose of this test is to measure throwing, catching, and control of the ball with either hand, and to measure eye-hand coordination. The participant starts under a pole and treads water. The ball is held in the left hand, passed over the pole to the right hand, and caught. Immediately, the ball is passed back over the pole and caught with the left hand.

*Scoring.* A score is given for each time the ball is passed over the pole to the opposite hand and caught during a 1-minute timed period.

### 5. Kick-reach

*Equipment.* A kick-reach board calibrated in inches (or centimeters) suspended over the surface of the water 4 feet (1.22 m) from the edge of the pool.

*Description and administration.* The purpose of this test is to measure power of legs, sculling action, and ability to raise one's body out of the water. The participant is in a vertical position in the water; the chin is on the surface of the water; one arm is stretched vertically upward. With the fingers, a mark is placed on the board. The participant, facing the marking board, sculls and kicks, touching the highest point possible on the board.

*Scoring.* The distance the participant can kick and scull above the original mark is measured in inches (centimeters).

6. 200-yard (182.88 m) head-high sprint

*Equipment.* A 25-yard (22.86 m) course; stopwatch.

*Description and administration.* The purpose of this test is to measure speed, form, and endurance using the water polo swimming stroke. The participants start in the water, with one hand holding the gutter. On the whistle, they swim 200 yards (182.88 m) with the chin on the surface of the water. One stroke may be taken with head down on the start and on each turn. Open turns are used.

*Scoring.* The clock starts on the whistle and runs until the course is completed. Time is measured to the nearest one tenth of a second.

7. Push pass for distance

*Equipment.* A restraining line; pool edge marked in feet (meters).

*Description and administration.* The purpose of this test is to measure an important water polo throwing and scoring method. A push pass is thrown from behind a restraining line. The participant must be in motion a minimum of 2 strokes. The body is parallel to the surface of the water. The elbow is behind and parallel to the wrist.

*Scoring.* The distance is measured to the nearest foot (meter) from the restraining line to the point where the ball strikes the water. Two passes are allowed and the better of the two is the score.

8. Rebounding

*Equipment.* Restraining bar; target 3 feet $\times$ 4 feet (0.91 m $\times$ 1.22 m), placed with its bottom edge at the water's surface. The face of the reinforced target is sloped back 3 inches (7.62 cm) from the bottom edge.

*Description and administration.* The purpose of this test is to measure finger dexterity and hand-eye coordination. The target area is placed on the pool edge. From behind a restraining bar 4 feet 6 inches (1.37 m) from the edge of the pool, the ball is tapped or thrown against the target area and controlled.

*Scoring.* A stopwatch starts on the whistle. A count is made of each strike against the target and return during a 1-minute period.

9. Distance throw

*Equipment.*    A marked pool area; an unobstructed course of at least 125 feet (38.10 m).

*Description and administration.*    The purpose of this test is to measure the power the individual has when throwing from a set position in the water. From behind a restraining line, the participant, using an overarm throw, throws the ball as hard and as far as possible.

*Scoring.*    The distance is measured in feet (meters). The best of three throws is the participant's score.

10. Three-shot accuracy

*Equipment.*    Markers placed 8 yards (7.32 m) from the front of the goal; five balls; target suspended 1 foot (30.48 cm) inside the goal area; marked scoring areas, lines marked at 2 yards (1.83 m) and 4 yards (3.66 m); anchored ball holders.

*Description and administration.*    The purpose of this test is to measure a variety of shooting techniques and scoring accuracy. The participant starts 8 yards (7.32 m) from the front of the goal. Within a 10-second time limit, the participant dribbles toward the goal outside of the 2-yard (1.83 m) line, shoots a push shot, swims to station number 2 (4 yards or 3.66 m in front of the right corner of the cage), pops the ball out of the holder from beneath with the left hand, and shoots a right-handed shot. The participant then swims to station 3 (2 yards or 1.83 m from the goal), pops the ball out of the holder with the right hand, and shoots a left-handed shot.

*Scoring.*    Points are awarded for hitting scoring areas. Five points are awarded each time a ball hits an area 1-foot-square (.093 sq. m), and two points are awarded for each ball striking anywhere else on the 16-inch-wide (40.64 cm) target area.

*Reliability and validity.*    No usual reliability coefficients of the test-retest or split-halves variety were obtained, but objectivity coefficients (simultaneous testing by the author and the coach) were calculated from data on 13 highly skilled, college-age, male water polo players (Table 10-17).
Internal validity coefficients were obtained by correlating each item with a composite score for all items. External validity coefficients were obtained by correlating each item with the coach's ranking of the players in overall ability (test criterion). All of the above coefficients are shown in Table 10-17.

*Normative information.*    No norms were included in this study.

*Comments.*    Intercorrelations showed that some items correlated highly with others. The test could probably be trimmed to 5 items. Multiple correlations could

TABLE 10-17  Objectivity and Validity of the Walton Water Polo Decathlon

| TEST ITEMS | INTERNAL VALIDITY | EXTERNAL VALIDITY | OBJECTIVITY |
|---|---|---|---|
| Kick-Reach | .711 | .039 | .988 |
| Reversals | .573 | .409 | 1.000 |
| 5-Shot Accuracy | .018 | -.036 | .876 |
| Dribble Sprint | .702 | .443 | .992 |
| Push Pass | .368 | .438 | 1.000 |
| Ball Handling | .780 | .552 | 1.000 |
| 3-Shot Accuracy | .555 | .073 | .859 |
| 200 yd. Crawl (182.88 m) | .862 | .622 | 1.000 |
| Rebounding | .393 | .548 | .976 |
| Distance Throw | .003 | .122 | 1.000 |
| Total (all ten events) | — | .595 | .987 |

Source: Tully, 1970, p. 15.

be used to determine which combinations of items should be retained. Regression (prediction) equations should be used to determine the relative contribution (weight) of each item in predicting overall water polo playing ability. Finally, the reliability of each item should be determined.

## GENERAL COMMENTS ON CHAPTERS ON SPORTS SKILLS (CHAPTERS 8 THROUGH 10)

The following procedure was used in writing these three chapters:

1. A search of the published professional literature.
2. A search of the unpublished literature (theses and dissertations).
3. Tables were constructed summarizing studies that tended to approach validation of tests scientifically.
4. One or two tests in each sport were selected for broader description and discussion. Whenever possible, diagrams and norms were included.

Some general observations are:

1. The main purpose of a predictive-type test is to "measure something complex with something simple" with a high degree of validity. If the predictive-type test proves to be complex or its validity questionable, it probably should not be used.

2. There seems to be considerable confusion as to whether a test is a predictive one or whether an author has simply developed achievement (performance) scales on specific sports skills. The reader is reminded that, in the former case, statistical reliability and validity are absolutely necessary, because the attempt is

to predict something complex (e.g., basketball playing ability) from something simple (e.g., vertical jump).

In the latter case, statistical reliability is also necessary but statistical validation is not, because the vertical jump is considered a *component* of basketball playing ability and is measured as an *end* in itself.

3. Very few sports skills tests have been taken to the point of development of regression (prediction) equations. Most have a) determined the correlation of each test item with the test criterion and b) selected a test battery from those items that correlated more highly with the test criterion. The problem with stopping the analysis at this point is the underlying false assumption that each item in the test battery contributes equally to the prediction of the test criterion.

4. There is a great disparity in the amount and quality of research done on specific sports skills tests. An arbitrary, rough categorization might be:

   a. Reasonably adequate:
      badminton, basketball, field hockey, handball, softball, soccer, tennis, and volleyball.

   b. Moderate but inadequate:
      archery, bowling, dancing, fencing, golf, gymnastics, swimming, and track and field.

   c. Little or none:
      baseball, boxing, canoeing, diving, horseback riding, ice hockey, lacrosse, martial arts, racquetball, rugby, skiing, speedball, squash, water polo, wrestling, and weight lifting.

Admittedly, some of the sports in the last category have become popular in America only in recent years. They are listed in hopes of motivating the reader to contribute research in this important area.

## BIBLIOGRAPHY

*AAHPER Skills Test Manual—Basketball for Boys.* Washington: AAHPERD Publications, 1966.

*AAHPER Skills Test Manual—Basketball for Girls.* Washington: AAHPERD Publications, 1966.

*AAHPER Skills Test Manual—Football.* Washington: AAHPERD Publications, 1966.

*AAHPER Skills Test Manual—Softball for Boys.* Washington: AAHPERD Publications, 1966.

*AAHPER Skills Test Manual—Softball for Girls.* Washington: AAHPERD Publications, 1966.

*AAHPER Skills Test Manual—Volleyball for Boys and Girls.* Washington: AAHPERD Publications, 1969.

ANTTILA, W.K. *Water Polo Drills and Playing Hints.* Stockton: San Joaquin Delta College, 1963.

BASSETT, GLADYS, RUTH GLASSOW and MABEL LOCKE. "Studies in Testing Volleyball Skills." *Research Quarterly,* 8 (December 1937), 60–72.

BRACE, DAVID K. "Validity of Football Achievement Tests as Measures of Motor Learning and as a Partial Basis for the Selection of Players." *Research Quarterly,* 14 (December 1943), 372–77.

BRADY, GEORGE F. "Preliminary Investigations of Volleyball Playing Ability." *Research Quarterly,* 16 (March 1945), 14–17.

BROER, MARION R. "Reliability of Certain Skill Tests for Junior High School Girls." *Research Quarterly,* 29 (May 1958), 139–45.

BUTLER, WILLIE M. "Comparison of Two Methods of Measuring the Degree of Skill in the Underarm Volleyball Serve." *Research Quarterly,* 32 (May 1961), 261–62.

CLARK, WILLIAM J. "Development and Validation of a Basketball Potential Skill Test." Unpublished doctoral dissertation, The Ohio State University, 1973.

CLIFTON, MARGUERITE A. "Single Hit Volley Test for Women's Volleyball." *Research Quarterly,* 33 (May 1962), 208–11.

COZENS, FREDERICK W. "Ninth Annual Report of the Committee on Curriculum Research of the College Physical Education Association." *Research Quarterly,* 8 (May 1937), 73–78.

CRAWFORD, ELINOR A. "The Development of Skill Test Batteries for Evaluating The Ability of Women Physical Education Major Students in Soccer and Speedball." Unpublished doctoral dissertation, University of Oregon, 1958.

CREW, VERNON N. "A Skill Test Battery for Use in Service Program Soccer Classes at the University Level." Unpublished master's thesis, University of Oregon, 1968.

CROGAN, CORRINEE. "A Simple Volleyball Classification Test for High School Girls." *Physical Educator,* 4 (October 1943), 34–37.

CUNNINGHAM, PHYLLIS and JOAN GARRISON. "High Wall Volley Test for Women's Volleyball." *Research Quarterly,* 39 (October 1968), 486–90.

DOROSCHUK, EUGENE V. and GASTON MARCOTTE. "An Agility Test for Screening Ice Hockey Players." Paper presented at the national convention of the Canadian Association of Health, Physical Education and Recreation, St. John, N.B., Canada (June 1965).

DYER, JOANNA T., JENNIE C. SCHURIG, and SARA L. APGAR. "A Basketball Motor Ability Test for College Women and Secondary School Girls." *Research Quarterly,* 10 (October 1939), 128–47.

EVERETT, PETER W. "The Prediction of Baseball Ability." *Research Quarterly,* 23 (March 1952), 15–19.

FOX, MARGARET G. and OLIVE G. YOUNG. "A Test of Softball Batting Ability." *Research Quarterly,* 25 (March 1954), 26–27.

FRENCH, ESTHER L. and BERNICE I. COOPER. "Achievement Tests in Volleyball for High School Girls." *Research Quarterly,* 8 (May 1937), 150–57.

GLASSOW, RUTH B. "Studies in Measuring Basketball Playing Ability of College Women." *Research Quarterly,* 9 (December 1938), 60–68.

HARRISON, EDWARD R. "A Test to Measure Basketball Ability for Boys." Unpublished master's thesis, University of Florida, 1969.

HARTLEY, GRACE. "Motivating the Physical Education Program for High School Girls." *American Physical Education Review,* 34 (May, June, September, 1929), 284, 344, 405.

HEATH, MARJORIE L. and ELIZABETH G. RODGERS. "A Study in the Use of Knowledge and Skill Tests in Soccer." *Research Quarterly,* 3 (December 1932), 33–53.

HENRY, MALVARY E. "The Validation of a Test on Field Hockey Skill." Unpublished master's thesis, Temple University, 1970.

HOOKS, G. EUGENE. "Prediction of Baseball Ability Through an Analysis of Measures of Strength and Structure." *Research Quarterly,* 30 (March 1959), 38–43.

JOHNSON, JOSEPH R. "The Development of a Single-Item Test as a Measure of Soccer Skill." Unpublished master's thesis, University of British Columbia, 1962.

KELSON, ROBERT E. "Baseball Classification Plan for Boys." *Research Quarterly,* 24 (October 1953), 304–7.

KRONQVIST, ROGER A. and WAYNE B. BRUMBACH. "A Modification of the Brady Volleyball Skill Test for High School Boys." *Research Quarterly,* 39 (March 1968), 116–20.

LAMBERT, ARTHUR F. and ROBERT GAUGHRAN. *The Technique of Water Polo.* Hollywood: Swimming World, 1969.

LAMP, NANCY A. "Volleyball Skills of Junior High School Students as a Function of Physical Size and Maturity." *Research Quarterly,* 25 (May 1954), 189–200.

LATCHAW, MARJORIE. "Measuring Selected Motor Skills in Fourth, Fifth and Sixth Grades." *Research Quarterly,* 25 (December 1954), 439–49.

LEILICH, AVIS. "The Primary Components of Selected Basketball Tests for College Women." Unpublished doctoral dissertation, Indiana University, 1952.

LIBA, MARIE R., and MARILYN R. STAUFF. "Test for the Volleyball Pass." *Research Quarterly,* 34 (March 1963), 56–63.

MANOLIS, GUS G. "Relation of Charging Time to Blocking Performance in Football." *Research Quarterly,* 26 (May 1955), 170–78.

McDONALD, LLOYD G. "The Construction of a Kicking Skill Test as an Index of General Soccer Ability." Unpublished master's thesis. Springfield, Mass.: Springfield College, 1951.

McELROY, H.N. "A Report on Some Experimentation with a Skill Test." *Research Quarterly,* 9 (October 1938), 82–88.

MERRIFIELD, H.H. and GERALD A. WALFORD. "Battery of Ice Hockey Skill Tests." *Research Quarterly,* 40 (March 1969), 146–52.

MOHR, DOROTHY R. and MARTHA J. HAVERSTICK. "Repeated Volleys Tests for Women's Volleyball." *Research Quarterly,* 26 (May 1955), 179–84.

PERRY, ELLEN L. "An Investigation of Field Hockey Skills Tests for College Women." Unpublished master's thesis, Pennsylvania State University, 1969.

RODGERS, ELIZABETH G. and MARJORIE L. HEATH. "An Experiment in the Use of Knowledge and Skill Tests in Playground Baseball." *Research Quarterly,* 2 (December 1931), 113–31.

RUSSELL, NAOMI and ELIZABETH LANGE. "Achievement Tests in Volleyball for Junior High School Girls." *Research Quarterly,* 11 (December 1940), 33–41.

SCHAUFFLE, EVELYN F. "The Establishment of Objective Tests for Girls of the Ninth and Tenth Grades to Determine Soccer Ability." Unpublished master's thesis, State University of Iowa, 1940.

SCHMITHALS, MARGARET and ESTHER FRENCH. "Achievement Tests in Field Hockey for College Women." *Research Quarterly,* 11 (October 1940), 84–92.

SCHWARTZ, HELEN. "Knowledge and Achievement Tests in Girls' Basketball on the Senior High School Level." *Research Quarterly,* 8 (March 1937), 143–56.

SHICK, JACQUELINE. "Battery of Defensive Softball Skills Tests for College Women." *Research Quarterly,* 41 (March 1970), 88–94.

STRAIT, CLARA J. "The Construction and Evaluation of a Field Hockey Skills Test." Unpublished master's thesis, Smith College, 1960.

TULLY, LOUIS J. "A Statistical Analysis of the Walton Water Polo Decathlon." Unpublished project, San Jose State College, 1970.

WALTON, LEE A. "Water Polo Decathlon." *Water Polo Illustrated,* 1 (May 1966), 10–12.

YOUNG, GENEVIEVE and HELEN MOSER. "A Short Battery of Tests to Measure Playing Ability in Women's Basketball." *Research Quarterly,* 5 (May 1934), 3–23.

## SUGGESTED READINGS

BARROW, HAROLD M. "Basketball Skill Test." *Physical Educator,* 16 (March 1959), 26–27.

BETTENCOURT, RICHARD M. "The Relationship Between Selected Fundamental Skills and Team Success in Intramural Junior College Basketball." Unpublished master's thesis, Springfield College, 1970.

BLACKMAN, CLAUDIA J. "The Development of a Volleyball Test for the Spike." Unpublished master's thesis, Southern Illinois University, 1968.

BLISS, J.G., *Basketball.* Philadelphia: Lea & Febiger, 1929.

BORLESKE, STANLEY, E. "A Study of the Achievement of College Men in Touch Football." Unpublished master's thesis, University of California at Berkeley, 1936.

BOYD, CLIFFORD A., JAMES R. McCACHREN and I.F. WAGLOW. "Predictive Ability of a Selected Basketball Test." *Research Quarterly,* 26 (October 1955), 364–65.

BRACE, DAVID K. *Measuring Motor Ability, A Scale of Motor Ability Tests.* New York: A.S. Barnes and Co., 1927.

_____. "Testing Basketball Techniques." *American Physical Education Review,* 29 (April 1924), 159–65.

BRONTZ, JEAN. "An Experiment in the Construction of a Test for Measuring Ability in Some of the Fundamental Skills used by Fifth and Sixth Grade Children in Soccer." Unpublished master's thesis, State University of Iowa, 1942.

BROWN, HARRIET, M. "The Game of Ice Hockey." *Journal of Health and Physical Education,* 6 (January 1935), 28–30; 54–55.

BUCHANAN, RUTH E. "A Study of Achievement Tests in Speedball for High School Girls," Unpublished master's thesis, State University of Iowa, 1942.

BUICE, MARY. "Selected Achievement Standards as a Practice Test for Beginners." *Official Soccer-Speedball Guide.* Washington: AAHPERD Publications, 1956–58.

COLEMAN, JIM, BILL NEVILLE and BEA GORTON. "A Statistical System for Volleyball and its Use in Chicago Women's Association." *International Volleyball Review,* 27 (Post-season World Championship issue, 1970), 72–73, 110.

COLEMAN, JIM, BILL NEVILLE and GREG MILLER. "The Four-point Statistical S stem used for Back Court Defense." *International Volleyball Review,* 28 (April 1971), 38–39; 112.

COMEAUX, BARBARA A. "Development of a Volleyball Selection Test Battery for Girls." Unpublished master's thesis, Lamar University, 1974.

COX, RICHARD A. "Relationship Between Selected Volleyball Skill Components and Team Performance of Men's Northwest 'AA' Volleyball Teams." *Research Quarterly,* 45 (December 1974), 441–46.

COZENS, FREDERICK W. and HAZEL J. CUBBERLEY. "Achievement Tests in Soccer and Speedball." In *Spaldings Official Soccer and Speedball Guide, No. 116R.* New York: American Sports Publishing Company, 1936.

CRAWFORD, ELINOR A. "The Development of Skill Test Batteries for Evaluating the Ability of Women Physical Education Major Students in Soccer and Speedball." Unpublished doctoral dissertation, University of Oregon, 1958.

CUBBERLEY, HAZEL J. and FREDERICK W. COZENS. *The Measurement of Achievement in Basketball, Spaldings 17R.* New York: American Sports Publishing Company, 1935–36.

EDGREN, H.D. "An Experiment in the Testing of Ability and Progress in Basketball." *Research Quarterly,* 3 (March 1932), 159–71.

ELBEL, E.R. "Evaluating Team and Individual Performance in Basketball." *Research Quarterly,* 12 (October 1941), 538–55.

ELROD, JOE M. "Construction of a Softball Skill Test Battery for High School Boys." Unpublished master's thesis, Louisiana State University, 1969.

FARROW, BERNICE E. "Development of a Volleyball Selection Test Battery." Unpublished master's thesis, Lamar State College of Technology, 1970.

FRIEDEL, JEAN E. "The Development of a Field Hockey Skill Test for High School Girls." Unpublished master's thesis, Illinois State Normal University, 1956.

FRIERMOOD, H.T. "Basketball Progress Tests Adaptable to Class Use." *Journal of Health, Physical Education and Recreation,* 5 (January 1934), 45–47.

FRINGER, MARGARET N. "A Battery of Softball Skills Tests for High School Girls." Unpublished master's thesis, University of Michigan, 1961.

GILBERT, RAYMOND R. "A Study of Selected Variables in Predicting Basketball Players." Unpublished master's thesis, Springfield College, 1968.

GLASSOW, RUTH B. and MARION R. BROER, *Measuring Achievement in Physical Education,* p. 103. Philadelphia: W.B. Saunders Co., 1938.

GORTON, BEATRICE A. "An Evaluation of the Serve and Pass in Women's Volleyball Competition." Unpublished master's thesis, George Williams College, 1970.

HALVERSON, DONALD E. "Validation of the AAHPER Basketball Skills Test for Male Physical Education Majors at the University of North Dakota." Unpublished master's thesis, University of North Dakota, 1968.

HARRISON, JO ANN. "Selected Speedball Skills Tests." In *Official Soccer-Speedball-Flag Football Guide.* Washington: AAHPERD Publications, 1972. 1972.

HOWARD, G.W. *Motor Skills in the Game of Basketball.* New York: Teachers College, 1937.

HOWLAND, AMY R. *National Physical Achievement Standards for Girls.* New York: National Recreation Association, 1936.

ILLNER, JULEE A. "The Construction and Validation of a Skill Test for the Drive in Field Hockey." Unpublished master's thesis, Southern Illinois University, 1968.

JESSELINE, THOMAS. "Skill Tests." In *Official Softball-Volleyball Guide.* New York: A.S. Barnes and Company, 1943.

JOHNSON, L. WILLIAM. "Objective Test in Basketball for High School Boys." Unpublished master's thesis, State University of Iowa. 1934.

KESSLER, ADRIAN. "The Validity and Reliability of the Sandefur Volleyball Spiking Test." Unpublished master's thesis, California State College, Long Beach, 1968.

KNIGHT, LINDA. "The Relationship of the Repeated Wall Volleys, the Volleyball Pass, and the Volleyball Playing Ability of Eleventh Grade Girls." Unpublished master's thesis, North Texas State University, 1969.

KNOX, ROBERT D. "An Experiment to Determine the Relationship Between Performance in Skill Tests and Success in Playing Basketball." Unpublished master's thesis, University of Oregon, 1937.

LAMBERT, ANN T. "A Basketball Test for College Women." Unpublished master's thesis, University of North Carolina, 1969.

LATCHAW, MARJORIE. "Measuring Selected Motor Skills in Fourth, Fifth, and Sixth Grades." *Research Quarterly,* 25 (December 1954), 439–49.

LEE, HARRY C. "An Evaluation of Brock's Soccer Skill Test and a Rating Scale of Physical Endurance, Tackling and Personality Traits in Soccer on the Secondary School Level." Unpublished master's thesis, Springfield College, 1941.

LEHSTEN, NELSON. "A Measure of Basketball Skills in High School Boys." *Physical Educator,* 5 (December 1948), 103–9.

_____. "Basketball Aptitude Tests." *Scholastic Coach,* 19 (October 1949), 62–65.

LEINBACK, C.H. "The Development of Achievement Standards in Handball and Touch Football for Use in the Department of Physical Training for Men at the University of Texas." Unpublished master's thesis, University of Texas, 1952.

LUCEY, MILDRED. "Study of Reliability in Relation to the Construction of Field Hockey Tests." Unpublished master's thesis, University of Wisconsin, 1934.

MacGILLIVARY, WILLIAM W. "The Relationship of Certain Underlying Capacities to Ability Level in a Complex Gross Motor Skill." Unpublished master's thesis, University of Alberta, 1965.

MacKENZIE, JOHN. "The Evaluation of a Battery of Soccer Skill Tests as an Aid to Classification of General Soccer Ability." Unpublished master's thesis, University of Massachusetts, 1968.

McELROY, H.N. "A Report of Some Experimentation with a Skill Test." *Research Quarterly,* 9 (October, 1938), 82–88.

MILLER, SHIRLEY B. "Speedball Skill Tests." In *Soccer-Speedball.* Washington: AAHPERD Publications, 1962–64.

MILLER, WILMA K. "Achievement Levels in Basketball Skills for Women Physical Education Majors." *Research Quarterly,* 25 (December 1954), 450–55.

MITCHELL, REID. "The Modification of the McDonald Soccer Skill Test for Upper Elementary School Boys." Unpublished master's thesis, University of Oregon, 1963.

MOHR, DOROTHY R., and MARTHA J. HAVERSTICK. "Relationship Between Height, Jumping Ability, and Agility to Volleyball Skill." *Research Quarterly,* 27 (March 1956), 74–78.

MONEY, C.V. "Tests for Evaluating the Abilities of Basketball Players." *Athletic Journal,* 14 (November 1933), 32; 34, and (December 1933), 18–19.

MOSBEK, ELLEN. "Baseball Skills Tests." In *Spalding's 121R.* New York: American Sports Publishing Company, 1937.

MOSER, HELEN A. "The Use of Basketball Skills Tests for Girls and Women." *Journal of Health, Physical Education and Recreation,* 6 (March 1935), 53–55.

PRITCHETT, RITA J. "Reliability and Validity of a Passing Skill Test in Women's Basketball." Unpublished master's thesis, Eastern Kentucky University, 1971.

REYNOLDS, H.J. "Volleyball Tests." *Journal of Health and Physical Education,* 1 (March 1930), 42.

RUSSELL, NAOMI and ELIZABETH LANGE. "Studies Relating to Achievement Scales in Physical Education Activities." *Research Quarterly*, 9 (December 1938), 43–56.

RYAN, MARY F. "A Study of Tests for the Volleyball Serve." Unpublished master's thesis, University of Wisconsin, 1969.

SCOTT, M. GLADYS and ESTHER FRENCH. *Measurement and Evaluation in Physical Education*, pp. 373–74. Dubuque: Wm. C. Brown, Co., 1959.

SCOTT, RICHARD J. "The Relationship of Statistical Charting to Team Success in Volleyball." Unpublished master's thesis, University of California, Los Angeles, 1971.

STEIN, JULIAN U. "Better Basketball Through Skill Classification." *Journal of Health, Physical Education and Recreation*, 28 (November 1957), 10–11; 37.

STEWART, HARRIET E. "A Test for Measuring Field Hockey Skill of College Women." Unpublished doctoral dissertation, Indiana University, 1965.

____. "A Test for Measuring Field Hockey Skill of College Women." in *Field Hockey-La Crosse Guide*, 1966–68. Washington: AAHPERD Publications, 1966–68.

STROUP, FRANCIS. "Game Results as a Criterion for Validating a Basketball Skill Test." *Research Quarterly*, 26 (October 1955), 353–57.

VANDERHOOF, MILDRED. "Soccer Skills Tests." *Journal of Health and Physical Education*, 3 (October 1932), 54–56.

VOLTMER, E.F. and TED WATTS. "A Rating Scale of Player Performance in Basketball." *Journal of Health, Physical Education and Recreation*, 11 (February 1940), 94–95.

WARNER, GLENN F.H. "Testing in Soccer." *Scholastic Coach*, 20 (December 1950), 18–20, 46.

WHITNEY, ALTHIA H. and GRACE CHAPIN. "Soccer Skill Testing for Girls." In *Official Soccer-Speedball Guide*. New York: A.S. Barnes and Co., 1946–48.

WILEY, ROGER C., *Soccer Syllabus for Teachers*. Ann Arbor: Edward Brothers, Inc., 1962.

WRIGHT, LOGAN and PATSY K. WRIGHT. "An Instrument for Evaluation of Skill in Women's Physical Education Classes." *Research Quarterly*, 35 (March 1964), 69–74.

# CHAPTER ELEVEN
# KNOWLEDGE APPRAISAL

Knowledge tests are designed to provide instructors with information from which they can evaluate, to a considerable extent, student acquisition of pertinent knowledge and understanding. Such information often helps to identify those areas of study in which the learning has been deficient. Such deficiencies may be due to failure to present material clearly and interestingly; to inadequate application by the student; or to a variety of other causes, some of which may never be fully ascertained. It is also quite possible that the test may be inadequate to provide sufficient discrimination between those who have learned and those who have not. An understanding of the principles and corresponding problems of test construction and of the of the several varieties of test items will assist the teacher in the preparation of tests that satisfy the purposes for which they are designed.

## PROBLEMS IN TEST CONSTRUCTION

Students who are in the process of preparing for a written examination often conjecture about the kinds of questions that are likely to appear on a test. If they were able to predict the test form and content accurately, they would be in a more favorable position to prepare for the test. Seldom are they aware that the teacher, too, may be in a similar quandary, although, admittedly, of a slightly different kind.

### Conceiving Testable Ideas

First of all, the teacher is faced with the basic and difficult problem of conceiving testable ideas. Typical sources for these ideas include tests that have been given in the past, textbooks, other printed matter that has been distributed to the class, and notes used in the presentation of lectures and demonstrations. Hopefully, the teacher has also compiled a list of student misconceptions that have been observed in written assignments, past tests, and class discussions and activities. A final ingredient is a good deal of old-fashioned cogitation.

### Constructing the Test: Considerations

Once a testable idea is identified, the teacher must then construct the test item, a process that involves considerable decision making. Should the item be in the form of a free-response (often called subjective or essay) in which a question or statement is presented and to which students are to frame answers or reactions in their own words? If this decision is in the affirmative, is there a particular form of the item that will best tend to elicit the desired response?

Or, possibly, one of the objective forms should be used. If so, which is most adaptable to the idea at hand? How should the item be phrased so that the intent is unmistakable?

Consideration must also be given to the length of the total test. Will all students have sufficient time to complete the test, or is it desirable that not everyone (or even anyone) finish all of the items?

Yes, the task of constructing the test is every bit as difficult as that of taking the test and demands as much skill and greater knowledge. The greater requisite knowledge stems from the need of the teacher to be not only a master of the test subject matter but to be a highly skilled test constructor as well.

### Ability to Convey Meaning

Among the general skills that must be perfected, the ability to write clearly and concisely is undoubtedly the most important. Most of us fully understand the intent of questions or statements that we have written. Seldom, on the other hand, are we aware of the difficulties that readers encounter in attempting to understand our meaning. To avoid this pitfall, it is most advisable that the test items be submitted to at least one and preferably to two or more colleagues so that they may pass on the clarity. Even with this safeguard, some items may still be unclear to students, and they will likely ask about the meaning during the test. Whether the teacher attempts to clarify the meaning at this time is a matter of individual judgment. Certainly, the confusion encountered should be noted and the item revised before it is included again as part of the test.

## KINDS OF TEST ITEMS AND THEIR GENERAL ADVANTAGES AND DISADVANTAGES

There are two basic kinds of test items; objective and free-response. Typically, the objective item demands a form of *recognition* from the student of the correct response to a statement or question. The free-response, on the other hand, requires that students be able either to *recall* from their reservoirs of knowledge the appropriate response or to apply this knowledge to the solution of a problem. In the hands of a skilled test constructor, each of the basic forms of test item can be designed to require wide degrees of intellectual powers on the part of respondents.

In the selection of the best form for a particular item, teachers must first decide whether they wish to test a limited area of knowledge in depth (the free-response item is usually most effective for this purpose) or to test a broad sampling of knowledge with a corresponding reduction in depth (in which case they will select one or more from among the several forms of objective items; such a choice permits many more items to be included on the test than if free-response items were used). If the free-response form is selected, a relatively small proportion of time will be spent in constructing the test with considerably more time necessarily devoted to reading and evaluating the responses. Conversely, if an objective form is chosen, virtually all effort will be directed to test construction and very little to scoring the test (once a key is developed, any responsible person can score the test or, as is happening more and more, a machine may be used for scoring).

Although there may be differences of opinion as to whether free-response or objective forms are more economical of the teacher's time, it is fairly clear that the former may save more time if the number of respondents is rather small, whereas the latter may save time when the number of respondents grows larger. If the same test may be used repeatedly without sacrifice of integrity, it is obvious that the objective form's economic advantage increases greatly. Economy of time, however, should not be the major criterion in the resolution of the form to be used. Many teachers combine free-response and objective forms in their comprehensive examinations.

### Free-Response Items

The free-response form of test item usually consists of either a question or statement to which the student is to react in accord with its specific demands. The item's demands upon the respondent may span the spectrum from very simple to highly complex, not only in terms of its difficulty but also with respect to the degree and kind of direction that is provided. It is generally more difficult for students to frame responses if they are asked only to react than if a particular kind of reaction desired is identified. The former structure may also complicate the instructor's evaluation, since the responses may include several kinds of reaction that had not been anticipated. Now it must be decided whether these unanticipated reactions are appropriate to the demands of the question and, if so, to compare their relative values with those responses that had been anticipated. The obvious conclusion is that the less structured question will elicit more varied kinds of responses and will give the student greater freedom to demonstrate his or her intellectual and creative talents.

Critics of free-response items claim that they are less reliable indicators of student abilities than objective items, and there is considerable substance to this claim. By its very nature, the free-response form is not objective, i.e., competent scorers may often disagree as to the value of a response, and a single scorer may, at two widely separated times, provide evaluations that are in considerable disagreement. Difficulties is obtaining satisfactory reliability are due to a number of causes, each of which may require a different remedy.

*Common causes of low reliability in scoring.*     The subsequent discussion applies to the reliability of a single evaluator as well as to the reliability between or among two or more evaluators, unless otherwise indicated.

The most common cause of low reliability is the failure to agree upon the key elements that a complete response should contain. Often these elements are only hazily defined, and their relative importance to the response is given little concern. Too frequently an inexperienced (or perhaps lazy or indifferent) teacher will begin to read responses before giving serious and thorough consideration to what is to be expected in a satisfactory response. The score assigned to a response is then often based upon a general, and usually unclear, impression of its quality.

Let us examine several of the pitfalls that face practitioners of this technique. They may consider one of the first responses they read to be extremely good and, somewhat arbitrarily, assign a mark of A. Later, a response that is clearly better than the one previously marked appears, and certainly this response deserves a higher mark; since no higher mark is available, however, the mark on the earlier response must be reduced. To do this, at least a quick review of the earlier paper is required to provide a fresh comparison to use as a guide in the reduction of the earlier mark. Once this is accomplished, the reader is now faced with the prospect of rereading all papers previously marked. With each new paper read, the teacher may again be faced with the need of repeating the entire process. We are all aware that a teacher who is unwilling to take the time (or, even worse, is unable) to identify the key elements expected in the response is not likely to reread the responses, either. If any adjustments are to be made in the responses read previously, they are likely to be across-the-board adjustments, i.e., the same deduction for each paper, a procedure that is not without criticism.

A second cause of low reliability, one not totally unrelated to the first, is what is often termed the "halo effect." The halo effect occurs if the score awarded to a paper (or response) is influenced unduly by the quality of the previous paper (or response) that the teacher has read. Thus, if the tenth paper is of the same quality as the third paper, the mark awarded the tenth may be higher or lower than the third, depending upon the degree to which the ninth paper is inferior to or superior to the tenth, respectively. Hence, the order in which the papers are read can affect the scores. The halo effect can be minimized somewhat by shuffling the papers after a given question has been scored on all of the papers. Trained evaluators who know what they expect in a response are considerably less subject to the halo effect.

As implied earlier, reliability tends to be lowered if the question is structured so that the range of appropriate and acceptable responses is quite wide. This is truer still if the length of the response is not controlled, particularly if the respondents are provided too generously with time in which to complete their replies. Again, precision and clarity in the construction of the statement or question will limit the variety of acceptable responses. Further, an appropriate limit to the number of words that may be used in the reply, or to the total time limit for the test, will tend to standardize the length of responses and will increase reliability. It is true that students often complain that the time was insufficient to complete the test. It is equally true, however, that such "power" tests discriminate among student abilities as well as, if not better than, longer tests (or easier tests) in which most or all students have time to finish.

*General guides for the development, administration, and scoring of free-response items.*   Free-response items are especially suited for the testing of certain kinds of knowledge, understanding, and talent. They are most useful in such tasks as problem-solving; development of logical arguments in support of a stand or point of view; and analyses of events, actions, rulings, causes and effects, beliefs, and similar concerns. The first step, then, is to ascertain the type of quality that is to be tested. If the type falls into a category for which free-response items are well suited, the broad and important concepts to be tested must be identified so as to serve as guides to the framing of appropriate problem statements or questions. The number of different problem statements to be used and the time allotted for the test will be controlling factors in the selection of topics for each. The fewer to be included, the greater the care that must be exercised to ensure that the statements will adequately cover the important concepts.

Upon completion of these preliminary steps, the statements may then be composed. Before the test is considered ready for administration, it should be read by several colleagues who may be able to suggest valuable revisions for increasing the clarity and completeness of the separate statements or of the entire test. They may also be able to assist in estimating the time that will be needed to complete the test.

It is desirable for each student to have a copy of the complete test. If this is not feasible, it is next best for the instructor to print the statements on one or more blackboards in such a way that each student will be able to read them without difficulty. The instructor might also read the statements as a supplement to the blackboard. Least desirable is for the instructor to simply read the statements, since the necessity for transcription onto their papers by the students takes time away from responding and introduces the distinct possibility of misinterpretation due to faulty transcription.

Once the test has begun, it is wise to discourage student queries. Such interruptions disturb the concentration of other students. If the instructor wishes to permit such inquiries, his answers should be directed to the entire class so that no student gains an undeserved advantage. No questions relating to the test content can be permitted if any other students have turned in their papers.

Many methods are available to provide the respondent with a measure of anonymity. The purpose of anonymity is to ensure that the instructor, as a response is being evaluated, is not influenced by knowledge of the respondent's past performance. The simplest method is to limit responses to one side of the sheet with the respondent's name on the reverse side. Increased security may be obtained, although it is seldom necessary, if the instructor consecutively numbers a series of 3 inch × 5 inch cards equal to the number of class members. Each card is put into a separate envelope and distributed at random to the class. Each student signs a card, places the card in the envelope, seals the envelope, and returns it to the instructor. The number contained on the card is written on each sheet of the response. The envelopes remain sealed until a final mark has been assigned to each test paper. It is unlikely that competent instructors will be influenced by knowledge of the respondent. Providing anonymity largely eliminates such influence and also helps assure students that all papers will be evaluated on merit.

In addition to the suggestion provided in the section describing the causes of low reliability, other aids in the objectification of the evaluative process are practiced by diligent teachers. The first is that it is decidedly preferable to read all responses to a single item in turn than to read each paper in its entirety before turning to the next. This procedure allows the teacher to focus attention on a narrower train of thought and thereby increase objectivity. Likewise, all responses to a given item should be read in a single session that is free from extensive distractions.

As a rule, questions should be marked on a numerical basis rather than on a letter basis. Numerical scores generally provide for a greater range of discrimination and, hence, for increased precision and reliability. Furthermore, it is often necessary to convert separate letter marks to numerical scores before a final mark for the whole test can be computed; a step can be saved by using numerical scores at the outset.

Finally, objectivity and reliability are improved if points are assigned to as many discrete elements of the response as is feasible rather than if a single score is awarded on the basis of the entire response. The former guards against overevaluating the total response because of one particularly well-developed section, especially if this section is near the end of the response and thus leaves a fresher impression upon the evaluator. It also tends to ensure that no critical element of a satisfactory response is ignored by the reader.

### Objective Items

Although there often appear to be many varieties of objective items, all of these are only forms of four basic types: 1) multiple-choice; 2) true-false; 3) short-answer (fill-in); and 4) matching. Each has its special features, with the multiple-choice possessing the greatest versatility and potential for discrimination among student abilities. Under certain conditions, objective-item tests are economical of the teacher's time. This is not to infer that it is an easy task to construct items that are of an appropriate difficulty and that are also discriminating. To the contrary, item writing requires infinite skill and, possibly more so, patience. After a few brilliant strokes, test constructors often find themselves devoid of further ideas for items. This predicament is often compounded if preparation of the test has been delayed until shortly before it is scheduled to be administered. Not uncommonly, this leads to the inclusion of items that are inadequate, simply to provide a test that is long enough to fill the testing period.

Although most teachers are aware of the difficulties just described, few have developed an organized plan for constructing objective items. An organized plan involves the employment of several general principles as well as of some specific guidelines that are singular to each of the basic forms. The general principles will be considered first.

*General principles for constructing objective tests.*   The major topics included in the course (or unit) that are to be covered by the test must be identified. Estimates must be made of the relative emphasis that has been placed upon each of these topics. Normally, but not in every instance, the proportion of class time devoted to a topic is a direct function of its importance. Each topic is next subdivided into its major elements and their relative importance is estimated, as was done with the major topics. The purpose of the procedure is to develop a guide for item content for the test. Thus, the greater the importance of a topic or concept, the greater the proportion of the test that should be devoted to this topic or concept. Many poorly constructed tests are invalid measures of student abilities because of their preoccupation with trivia. Unfortunately, it is often easier to develop items around trivia than around important concepts.

If time permits, each item should be read by one or more fellow teachers.

Items that lack clarity or that are superficial or obvious are more likely to be discovered by someone other than the original writer. Colleagues should be forewarned not to sacrifice their objectivity in an effort to spare the feelings of the item writer.

The aforementioned guidelines apply to all forms of objective items. Also, each item form has its own special guidelines, and these will be treated in order, for each item, in the basic discussion of objective forms.

*Forms of objective test items.*   Each of the four basic types of objective items, multiple-choice, true-false, short-answer, and matching, is designed for a particular use. Multiple-choice items are the most versatile and probably test the student's powers of discrimination to a greater degree than do the others. True-false items are designed to offer the respondent only two choices, and yet a skillful test constructor can design items of this type that will probe students' depth of knowledge to a considerable extent. Short-answer items bear some resemblance to the free-response items discussed earlier but are confined mainly to single-word or short-phrase responses that tend to limit the freedom of the respondent to very few choices. Matching items are confined to the identification of relatedness between items in one listing with those in another or among items in three or more listings.

Although each basic form has its own special use, it is still possible to use any of the four in the treatment of a particular concept or set of facts. Which form the test constructor should employ depends primarily upon the depth of understanding that needs to be evaluated.

*Multiple-choice.*   This item is composed of a *stem*, in the form of a statement (or question), that is to be completed (or answered) by selecting one from among three or more choices that are presented below the stem as single words, phrases, or sentences. Respondents are instructed to select the only correct choice or, if so directed, the best choice. In either case, a major problem in the construction of the item is the development of appealing distractors, i.e., incorrect choices that are likely to be selected by the less knowledgeable. Sources for appealing distractors include incorrect replies made by students to questions posed in class; incorrect answers to other item forms such as short-answer and free-response; and observations by the teacher of misconceptions of pupils with respect to playing rules, procedures, strategies, and techniques.

Many authorities recommend that the responses (choices) be of approximately the same length. The fear is that if one response is significantly longer than others, it is, more often than not, the correct answer. Perhaps this fear is overemphasized. It is not the length of the response that should be the main concern but whether the correct response is indicated inadvertently. A good response, whether the correct one or a distractor, should never be discarded simply because its length is inconsistent with those of the associated responses.

Another recommendation, one that possesses considerably more merit, is that the responses contain what is called parallelism, i.e., that all responses be of a parallel quality or state. For example:

Where did volleyball originate?

1. Asia
2. England
3. Massachusetts
4. Mexico City

This item lacks the quality of parallelism since the possible responses include a continent, a country, a state, and a city. If it is desired to retain the correct response, Massachusetts, in its present form, then the other responses should also be states. If Massachusetts is to be replaced by Holyoke, the city of volleyball's origin, then the distractors should also be cities. The rationale for demanding parallelism among responses is that it eliminates unnecessary confusion on the part of the respondent and also prevents unintentional overlapping of ostensibly correct responses with those of incorrect responses.

Caution must be exerted to avoid the use of words in the stem that would preclude the selection of one or more of the responses, either in terms of grammatical construction or of logic. Stems ending in "a" or "an" may provide unintentional clues if some or all of the distractors are written so that the constructions of the completed statements are incorrect grammatically. Stems that demand a response in a singular form (e.g., procedure, cause, effect, etc.) must not be followed by responses that include plural forms.

The critical matter of the order in which the four or five responses are to be listed merits careful concern. Foremost, of course, is that the order should not reveal a pattern of correct responses such that the examinee will have more than the normal probability of guessing successfully. Among the patterns that often develop is the one in which a particular numbered response is the correct one an inordinate number of times. In preparing responses to a multiple-choice stem, it is easiest to list the correct response first and to then begin the search for distractors. If this practice is followed, it is evident that the position of the correct reply must be alternated before the final draft is completed. Failure to alternate will provide a most obvious pattern even for the less informed respondents. The foregoing is not to imply that there must be an equal number of correct responses in each of the positions, as this practice might produce a pattern of its own.

Probably the wisest means of determining the position of the correct response is to employ a random method of selection. An example of this method is to number slips of paper from 1 through $n$ ($n$ = number of responses following the stem). For each item, one slip is drawn from a container, with the number on the slip corresponding to the position of the correct response for that item. The slip is returned to the container, the slips are shaken thoroughly within the container, and the process is repeated for each subsequent item.

At times, it may be desirable to arrange the positions of the four or five responses in certain logical orders. Among the kinds of responses that may be so ordered are: 1) dates and other numerical data that are listed in order of chronology or of increasing magnitude; and 2) names, statements, and similar verbal replies that are alphabetized according to the first principal word. These orders tend to distribute the positions of the correct responses in a reasonably random fashion and have the added advantage of being less time-consuming than the slip-drawing process.

*True-false.* The most widely used objective test item in teacher-made tests is the true-false variety (or its variations—yes-no, right-wrong, etc.). It is employed more frequently than the multiple-choice item because it does not require that distractors be devised. As a result, this form of objective item does not possess the versatility of the multiple-choice item, but it does permit the testing of certain types of material for which it would be difficult to develop the necessary three or four distractors.

True-false items, because of their dichotomous nature, must be stated with unmistakable clarity and precision so that the intent of the writer is not lost in a profusion or confusion of words. In most instances, a statement must be true in its entirety and without exception if it is to be marked as "true." Thus, great care must be exercised so that imprecision does not permit exceptions that would demand a "false" response if a "true" response were the original intent of the writer. Again, submission of items to colleagues will help to eliminate imprecise or ambiguous statements.

Normally, a true-false item is limited to a single sentence in the interest of focusing the respondent's concentration upon a single concept. If more than one sentence is necessary to convey intent, the writer must be certain not to introduce contradictions or excessive qualifications that will tend to blur this focus. A good item-writer never wastes a word.

Writers of true-false items are often cautioned against the use of words such as *never* and *always* on the grounds that, inevitably, items containing these words are false. There seems to be no logical basis for an inflexible rule on the use of these words, and it is often the case that statements are clearer with the inclusion of such qualifying words. The concern, as always, is that inadvertent clues to the correct response are avoided. The same defense can be made for the negative words *no* and *never.* To avoid confusion, the use of two or more negatives in a single statement should occur only in rare instances.

Textbooks, rulebooks, and other printed matter are among the sources from which true-false statements may be taken. Skilled item-writers will eschew, with occasional exceptions, direct transcriptions of statements from these sources. Instead, they will use these printed sources for suggestions of ideas, facts, and concepts from which to develop their own statements. Those statements that are transcribed verbatim will serve at best to test the students' powers of recall but will seldom challenge their reasoning capacities. It is not enough to simply reword the statements; they must be revised so that they test the students' understanding of the concepts with which they are concerned.

*Matching items.* The matching type of item is not so highly recommended as the prior two forms. The basic form consists of two parallel columns of words, statements, names, numbers, or symbols. For each entry in the left-hand column, there is one entry (or occasionally two or more entries) in the right-hand column that is in some way related to it. The left-hand column might, for example, contain a listing of sports. The right-hand column could then contain a listing of dates (e.g., relating to the origin of the sports), numbers (e.g., official scores of forfeited games), or names (e.g., persons closely associated with the sports). The possibilities are almost unlimited, but the form is restricted largely to the recall of facts and offers few opportunities for testing in depth.

This form of item is generally employed to test simple recognition of the "who," "what," "when," and "where" of a fact or circumstance; but it is not particularly effective for investigating a student's understanding of the "why" of a concept. Guessing tends to play a larger role in matching items than for multiple-choice or true-false items. This is especially true if the number of entries in each of the columns is the same, a circumstance that often permits correct identification to be accomplished solely by a process of elimination. This defect may be overcome one of two ways. First, the number of entries in the right-hand column is made greater than in its parallel column, in which case some of the entries will not be used. An alternative, if column length is to be identical, is to permit the matching of entries in the right-hand column with more than one entry in the left-hand column. In either case, guessing as a built-in factor would be reduced somewhat.

It is desirable (as with multiple-choice responses) that each entry in a given column possess a reasonable degree of parallelism. Entries in an adjoining column need not agree with the first column but would contain entries that were agreeable with others in its column.

More complex varieties of matching items exist, such as those that employ three columns (e.g., one containing events, a second of dates corresponding to the events' occurrences, and a third of names of individuals associated with the events).

*Short-answer (fill-in).* The final distinct type of objective question is the short-answer variety, in which a statement contains one or more blanks that must be filled in with a single word for each blank. A variation finds the blank listed after the statement, to be filled in with the response demanded by the statement. The latter type resembles the free-response form, except that the response is limited invariably to one word, or, at most, several words.

Well-written short-answer items are those that restrict each blank to a single correct response. Thus, if the response is to be considered correct, only one word (or a suitable synonym) can fill a given blank correctly. This restriction requires that considerable care be given by the writer to the phrasing of the statement and to the placement of the blanks to ensure that multiple correct responses are unlikely to be elicited. Although there is no precise mathematical formula, it is fairly safe to say that the degree of precision of a short-answer item is inversely proportional to the frequency of the blanks.

The short-answer item is inferior to other items in terms of reliability; but it does possess the advantage of demanding recall, even if often of a somewhat limited nature, instead of recognition. Whether this advantage is sufficient to offset the generally lower reliability can only by judged by each teacher. The view from here is that its use should be discouraged, except in rare instances, and then only if the item-writer is proficient with this form.

## ITEM ANALYSIS

Item analysis is a topic that alone could fill, at the very least, a small textbook. Its purpose is to provide the teacher with a mathematical description of the effectiveness of each test item. An item's effectiveness is measured by its ability to distinguish, in terms of correct responses, between the better and poorer students. An effective item is one that would produce a larger number of correct responses from those who score well on the entire test than from those who score poorly on the total test. This quality in a test item, of distinguishing between those in the high and low groups for the total test, is termed the *validity index* or *discriminative power* of the item.

### Discriminative Power of an Item

The range of an item's discriminative power is from 1.00 (all members of the high group responded correctly and all members of the low group responded incorrectly) to 0.00 (an equal number of members from each of the groups responded correctly) to –1.00 (all members of the low group responded correctly and all members of the high group responded incorrectly). Several methods for computing the discriminative power of an item are available to the teacher. Some methods, such as the biserial $r$ and the Flanagan, are particularly useful for machine-scored tests but are too time-consuming for the teacher's use. A modified method, based upon the biserial $r$, which will provide fairly reliable estimates of an item's discriminative power, utilizes the formula

$$\text{Discriminative power} = \frac{R_h - R_1}{N}$$

in which

$R_h$ is the number responding correctly in the high group
$R_1$ is the number responding correctly in the low group
$N$ is the number in the high group

Thus, if there are 20 pupils each in the high and low groups (these groups are equal in size and should represent 25–27% each of the total number taking the test) and 12 in the high group and 8 in the low group respond correctly to the item, the discriminative power is

$$\frac{12 - 8}{20} = .20$$

If the group taking the test is fairly large and an item is found to have a discrimination index that is close to zero or negative, it becomes obvious that the item is not serving its intended purpose. Before it is next used, it must be revised in order to eliminate ambiguous or misleading portions. For small groups, chance might on occasion produce zero or negative discrimination indices, and, unless some obvious flaws in the item appear upon perusal, a teacher might wish to subject the item to additional testing before undertaking a revision.

### A Basic Assumption in Computing the Discrimination Index

All of the foregoing discussion concerned with the index of discrimination is based upon a most critical assumption. Furthermore, it is an assumption that may, upon rare occasions, be false, and one which could go unnoticed by the teacher. This assumption is that the members of the high group are, in fact, the best students of the subject matter that is supposedly covered by the test, and that the members of the low group are the poorest students. This assumption is usually valid, but it is possible to imagine a test so poorly prepared that those who are the most competent students would tend to earn the lowest scores, whereas those who are the poorest students would tend to earn the highest scores. Under such a condition, most of the items would appear to be discriminating positively, whereas, in reality, they would be discriminating negatively. Fortunately, it is exceedingly unlikely that a test of any length would produce this effect. The probability of such an occurrence in a short test is considerably higher and should not be ignored.

### Index of Difficulty

A second concern in item analysis is the computation of the index of difficulty of an item. Simply put, the index of difficulty is the percentage of students taking the test who respond correctly to the item:

$$\text{Index of Difficulty} = \frac{\text{Number responding correctly}}{\text{Number responding to the item}}$$

Thus, if 40 students responded to the item, and 30 of these responded correctly, the index of difficulty would be 30/40 or .75. As can be seen, the higher the index of difficulty, the less difficult the item is.

A wise teacher will select items with a mean index of difficulty of approximately .50 and with a distribution of difficulty indices approximating a normal distribution. The majority of items should have difficulty indices ranging between .10 and .90, and all those with indices of .00 or 1.00 must be discarded or revised, since they have no effect upon the relative positions or ranks of the students taking the test, i.e., they do not discriminate between members of the high and low groups.

### Effectiveness of Multiple-Choice Distractors

An additional means of analyzing multiple-choice items is available and permits an estimate to be made of the effectiveness of distractors. As an example, if response 3 is correct and the distribution of choices among the responses is

| Choice | 1 | 2 | 3 | 4 | N |
|---|---|---|---|---|---|
| Number Selecting | 0 | 3 | 16 | 6 | 25 |

it becomes clear that distractor 1 appeals to none of the students in the test group and probably should be revised or replaced. (It is possible that the teacher might wish to administer the test to another group before making a decision to revise or replace.) If revision or replacement is undertaken and proves successful in that some students select the new distractor, the teacher may find one of two effects produced: 1) distractor 1 now appeals to some of the 16 who originally selected the correct response or 2) distractor 1 appeals only to those who had previously selected either distractor 2 of distractor 4.

The first effect is desirable, as the item now contains three distractors, each of which possesses some degree of attraction. The second effect has, at best, only revealed the relative weakness of either distractor 2 or distractor 4 or, possibly, of both. It may now be necessary to revise or replace one or both of these distractors.

## SCORING OF TESTS

The most direct method of scoring objective tests is to count the number of correct responses and to multiply this count by the value of each of the items (assuming that the items are weighted equally). This product, if divided by the total points possible, is the percentage of correct responses. Other systems of scoring are designed to increase the test's ability to discriminate among students' knowledge.

Of the other systems, the two basic ones are those that weight certain items, e.g., multiple-choice, more heavily than they do others, and those that employ scoring formulas that are intended to counteract the effects of guessing.

If items are weighted, it is usually on the precept that some items or forms of items require comprehension of more complex knowledge or understanding than do others. Theoretically, true-false items are the easiest to respond to, since the respondents have an even chance of guessing correctly, even if they don't bother to read the item. The odds against guessing a multiple-choice item correctly are 3 or 4 to 1, depending upon the number of choices and assuming that the item is not read by the teacher.

### Scoring Formulas for Correction Against Guessing

Those systems that involve the use of scoring formulas penalize incorrect responses and ignore omitted responses. Thus, for true-false items, the formula is normally $R - W$ (number of correct responses minus number of incorrect responses). A modification of this formula adds one-half the number of omitted items to the $R - W$ score, since it is assumed that the student would have gotten half of the omitted items correct simply by guessing. This modification is not recommended, for several reasons that are beyond the scope of this presentation.

Multiple-choice formulas are also modified to account for the increased difficulty faced by the respondent who attempts to guess the correct response. The modified formula is:

$$\frac{R - W}{N - 1}$$

in which $N$ is the number of choices available for response in each of the items. If some items contain four choices and others contain five, then those items with four choices will have to be scored separately from those with five choices.

For matching items, the multiple-choice formula is utilized, with $N$ representing the number of entries in the left-hand column. If used in this manner the formula is less precise than for the multiple-choice items but is a reasonable approximation.

Correction formulas are difficult to establish for short-answer items; since the potential number of blanks usually varies from item to item, it would almost be necessary to have a separate formula for each item. If a correction formula is desired, and if there is only one blank per item, then it is probably best to employ the same one as for true-false items, i.e., $R - W$.

### Should Correction Formulas be Used?

The teacher is faced, at this point, with the decision of whether to use a correction formula for objective tests. Several studies have produced findings that indicate that scoring formulas for the correction of guessing seldom alter the rank order of a group of tests scored originally on the basis of the number of correct answers. Studies also show that the weighting of items does not significantly disturb the rank order of test scores. In the interest of economy of time, and unless contradictory evidence is disclosed, it is not recommended that teachers employ scoring formulas that correct for guessing or that weight objective items.

## CONSTRUCTING THE TEACHER-MADE TEST

Some standardized knowledge tests in physical education are available (see *Suggested Readings* at the end of the chapter), but too often they are inappropriate in terms of content or level for use in a particular class. One exception to this generalization is the *AAHPER Cooperative Physical Education Tests.*[1] Separate tests (each with two forms) are available for grades 4-6, 7-9, 10-12, respectively. Each test consists of 60 multiple-choice items, each of which offers four choices. Content validity is determined on the basis of the procedures used in preparing final forms. Two types of reliability coefficient—internal consistency measures and alternate form—were calculated. The former yielded coefficients ranging from .72 to .82, whereas the latter coefficients were found to be between .69 and .76.[2]

Hence, teachers must be prepared to construct their own tests. Although means have been provided earlier in this chapter for analyzing a test once it has been administered, attention must also be given to considerations for constructing a test that will provide scores that are *valid* representations of student abilities in the particular course of study.

### Test Validity

It is possible to determine experimentally the validity of a test after it has been administered, but steps can be taken at the outset to develop a fairly valid test. If the test is to be valid, its content and emphases must parallel closely those of the instruction. Thus, if 10 percent of a unit of instruction is devoted to a certain concept, then 10 percent of the test covering that unit should also be devoted to this concept. Teachers who follow this procedure in constructing their classroom tests can be quite confident that their tests will possess *content validity*.

*BIBLIOGRAPHY*

*AAHPER Cooperative Physical Education Tests.* Princeton: Educational Testing Service, 1970.
*Handbook (for) The AAHPER Cooperative Physical Education Tests.* Princeton: Educational Testing Service, 1971.


*SUGGESTED READINGS*

DIETZ, D. and B. FRENCH. "Hockey Knowledge Tests for Girls." *Journal of Health, Physical Education and Recreation,* 11 (June 1940), 366.
EBEL, ROBERT. "Writing the Test Item." In *Educational Measurement,* E.F. Lindquist, ed. Washington: American Council on Education, 1951.
FOX, KATHARINE. "Beginning Badminton Written Examination." *Research Quarterly,* 24 (May 1953), 135–46.
FRENCH, ESTHER L. "The Construction of Knowledge Tests in Selected Professional Courses in Physical Education." *Research Quarterly,* 14 (December 1943), 406–24.
GERSHON, ERNEST. "Apparatus Gymnastics Knowledge Test for College Men in Professional Physical Education." *Research Quarterly,* 28 (December 1957), 332–41.
GRISIER, GERTRUDE J. "The Construction of an Objective Test of Knowledge and Interpretation of the Rules of Field Hockey for Women." *Research Quarterly,* Supplement, 5 (March 1934), 79–81.
HEATH, M.L. and E.G. RODGERS. "A Study in the Use of Knowledge and Skill Tests in Soccer." *Research Quarterly,* 3 (December 1932), 33–53.
HEMPHILL, FAY. "Information Tests in Health and Physical Education for High School Boys." *Research Quarterly,* 3 (December 1932), 83–96.

HENNIS, GAIL M. "Construction of Knowledge Tests in Selected Physical Education Activities for College Women." *Research Quarterly*, 27 (October 1956), 301–9.

HEWITT, JACK E. "Comprehensive Tennis Knowledge Test." *Research Quarterly*, 8 (October 1937), 74–84.

____. "Improving the Construction of the Essay and Objective and New Type Examination." *Research Quarterly*, 10 (October 1939), 148–54.

HOOKS, EDGAR W. "Hooks' Comprehensive Knowledge Test in Selected Physical Education Activities for College Men." *Research Quarterly*, 37 (December 1966), 506–14.

KELLY, ELLEN D. and JANE E. BROWN. "The Construction of a Field Hockey Test for Women Physical Education Majors." *Research Quarterly*, 23 (October 1952), 322–29.

KNIGHTON, MARIAN. "Soccer Questions." *Journal of Health and Physical Education*, 1 (October 1930), 29.

LANGSTON, DEWEY F. "Standardization of a Volleyball Knowledge Test for College Men Physical Education Majors." *Research Quarterly*, 26 (March 1955), 60–68.

*Making the Classroom Test*, 2nd ed. Princeton, N.J.: Educational Testing Service, 1961.

MOHR, DOROTHY R. "Knowledge Tests in Physical Education." *California Association for Health, Physical Education, and Recreation Journal*, 31 (November–December 1968), 24.

MURPHY, MARY AGNES. "Criteria for Judging a Golf Knowledge Test." *Research Quarterly*, 4 (December 1933), 81–88.

PHILLIPS, MARJORIE. "Standardization of a Badminton Knowledge Test for College Women." *Research Quarterly*, 17 (March 1946), 48–63.

PHILLIPS, M.F. "Two Practical Questions Involving Grading of Papers." *Clearing House*, 36 (December 1961), 237–39.

RODGERS, ELIZABETH G. "The Standardization and Use of Objective Type Information Tests in Team Game Activities." *Research Quarterly*, 10 (March 1939), 102–12.

RODGERS, ELIZABETH G. and MARJORIE L. HEATH. "An Experiment in the Use of Knowledge and Skill Tests in Playground Baseball." *Research Quarterly*, 2 (December 1931), 113–31.

SCHWARTZ, HELEN. "Knowledge and Achievement Tests in Girls' Basketball on the Senior High School Level." *Research Quarterly*, 8 (March 1937), 143–51.

SCOTT, M. GLADYS. "Achievement Examinations for Elementary and Intermediate Swimming Classes." *Research Quarterly*, 11 (May 1940), 100–111.

____. "Achievement Examinations for Elementary and Intermediate Tennis Classes." *Research Quarterly*, 12 (March 1941), 40–49.

____. "Achievement Examinations in Badminton," *Research Quarterly*, 12 (May 1941), 242–53.

SNELL, CATHERINE. "Physical Education Knowledge Tests." *Research Quarterly*, 6 (October 1935), 78–94; 7 (March, 1936), 73–82; 7 (May, 1936), 77–91.

STRADTMAN, H.D. and T.K. CURETON. "A Physical Fitness Knowledge Test for Secondary School Boys and Girls." *Research Quarterly*, 21 (March 1950), 53–57.

WAGLOW, I.F. and C.H. REHLING. "A Golf Knowledge Test." *Research Quarterly*, 24 (December 1953), 463–70.

WAGLOW, I.F. and FOY STEPHENS. "A Softball Knowledge Test." *Research Quarterly*, 26 (May 1955), 234–43.

# CHAPTER TWELVE
# SOCIAL APPRAISAL

Many physical educators have long held to the article of faith that social adjustment (often identified by terms such as attitudes, leadership, sportsmanship, appreciation, citizenship, etc.) is an expected and desirable outcome of participation in programs of physical education including interscholastic and other forms of athletics competition. Cowell has summarized the findings of numerous investigations that are purported to describe "the effects of physical activity upon the personal and social adjustment of people."[1] What these studies have demonstrated is the *associative* relationship between certain social traits and a variety of other factors including participation in physical activity.

Kenyon has identified and described two types of social roles: 1) *specific*, including ascribed roles such as teenager and sister and achieved roles such as teacher, doctor, and athlete, and 2) *diffuse* roles, exemplified by being a democratic citizen, having good moral character, etc.[2] The dearth of longitudinal studies examining the effects of participation in physical education activity, per se, upon social adjustment leads to the conclusion that "at present there is little evidence to support the proposition that instructional programs in physical education are particularly effective for socialization into diffuse roles."[3] This is not to say that socialization into diffuse roles does not occur during physical activity. What is suggested is that it has not been established that whatever diffuse socialization happens to take place is a direct result of participation (i.e., similar socialization may occur in many other forms of human activity), and that some forms of socialization may even be undesirable!

Certainly there is substantial evidence that instructional programs in physical education do provide effectively for the socialization of students into specific, achieved roles such as baseball player, advanced swimmer, or social dancer. But seldom are these achieved roles among the subheadings found under the various designations that are commonly used to describe the general objective of social adjustment or social development. Instead, one finds listed under this objective such diffuse social characteristics as "cooperative," "has desirable attitude," and "observes department rules."

Thus, it would seem that physical educators too often seek to measure and evaluate that which is most elusive—diffuse social qualities—and correspondingly ignore as objectives those specific, achieved roles that most students are capable of attaining to one degree or another. Why is this so? Is it that some physical educators believe the long-standing professional claim that participation in their programs will produce in their pupils positively altered diffuse social traits? Or has their frequently regimented training (for example as members of teams directed by authoritarian coaches) inclined them to institute a series of "behavior" rules in the interest of uniformity and the maintenance of discipline? Or could it be that some physical educators don't believe that the substantive content of their programs is of enough importance to deserve major emphasis? Or is it conceivable that they have little interest in or time for the instructional program, because they are so tied up with coaching concerns that the use of vague criteria provides a convenient and uncomplicated method of assigning marks?

Whatever the reason, it is time that the profession took a realistic look at what it is capable of accomplishing and focused its energies upon those ends. There is evidence that the profession is beginning to come to grips with the problem, and that improved programs may be realizable if school administrators will hire physical educators as much for their competency in and dedication to the instructional program as for their excellence in coaching competitive teams. Much of the blame must also be placed upon college and university professors who continue to espouse the social objective in unrealistic terms and thereby perpetuate the "Pollyannaish" claims.

What are some of the major deterrents to the attainment of positively altered diffuse roles? Kenyon suggests three: 1) lack of class time; 2) failure of the teacher to adequately delineate the socialization outcomes desired or to establish effective means for attaining those that have been delineated; and 3) competition from an endless variety of other social stimuli.[4] But even if those deterrents were not present, the crucial question remains: what motivates physical educators more than other teachers to be preoccupied with the development of their pupils into diffuse social roles? A corollary to this question is whether this preoccupation deleteriously affects the teacher's capability of fulfilling what would logically seem to be the primary responsibility—that of providing stimulating and well-conceived instruction in the substantive content of physical education.

If, in fact, they would be candid, many physical educators would have to admit that their primary purposes for including a diffuse social objective are to provide: 1) an external control (through the medium of the course mark) over the behavior of their pupils; and 2) a justification whereby those pupils who fail to meet even minimal standards in the substantive content may still be assured of a moderately high mark by the simple expedients of not causing trouble and by giving the appearance of "trying." The latter criterion is often based upon vague, subjective evaluations by the teacher and may represent little more than "good behavior."

But what is "good behavior?" Cowell implies that, among other factors, it involves learning the way of the group, acting according to its standards, and being accepted by the group.[5] This kind of conformity, it would seem, would leave little hope for the "rugged individualist," the one whose inner resources and security free him from the burden of group dependence. This is not to suggest, of course, that instruction in team sports and other group activities should give free rein to the individual at the expense of the group, but it is a declaration that it is not the special responsibility of the physical educator to attempt to socialize pupils into diffuse roles in which standards of behavior are often arbitrary.

Etzioni has concluded from his analyses of studies conducted by fellow social scientists that "human beings are not very easily changed after all."[6] He indicates that, in spite of changes in environment, process, or other similar factors, seldom is much produced in the way of permanent social change. He summarized his findings in this way:

> The contention that personal growth and societal changes are much harder to come by than we had assumed, especially via one version or another of the

educationist-enlightenment approach, is not a joyful message, but one whose full implications we must learn to accept before we can devise more effective social programs.[7]

Thus, one might conclude that the best hope for effecting social change is not to attack the social behavior directly but rather to develop those qualities and competencies in individuals that give promise of producing socially adjusted humans. But even in this realm, some caution must be exercised against the temptation to become too optimistic about the prospects of consistent success. First of all, research findings are not in agreement as to the relationship between the acquisition of highly developed skills on the one hand and the display of desirable social traits on the other. Stevenson, for example, concluded, from his analysis of 54 research investigations involving the socializing effects of participation in sport that, "the results were divided between support and nonsupport . . . of socialization effects, and, in addition, some results suggested unexpected and undesirable relationships between personal characteristics and participation in sports."[8]

A related investigation by Cratty concludes: "Athletic competition produces environments which are at times highly charged with emotional content and in which social forces interact violently with personal aspirations and sometimes evoke marked changes in individuals' personalities and in group performance."[9] This would seem to suggest that the environment as well as one's personal aspiration has a determining influence upon the kind of social change, if any, that occurs from participation in a vigorous competitive setting. Cratty argues that additional research is required to learn whether participation in vigorous activity has a greater effect upon social adjustment and group cohesiveness than does association in more passive endeavors.[10]

Further, American society is not of a singular mind as to whether certain social qualities, characteristics, and beliefs are desirable. Most humans are confronted with circumstances from time to time that place conflicting calls upon their consciences and ensuing social behavior. Controversy abounds over what represents appropriate social behavior of citizens faced with decisions ordered by legally constituted authorities. If a decision is unpopular with a citizen, should he or she react by acquiescing loyally to the will of the majority (sometimes called the "tyranny of the majority") or by engaging in protest, and, if the latter, what form should it take? Even more difficult, perhaps, is the determination of appropriate social behavior if the legal decision appears not to be in concert with the will of the majority, e.g., unpopular executive actions. In what way does the extent to which an unpopular decision directly affects the individual influence the resulting social behavior? Will the reaction be of one kind to some decisions and of another kind to other decisions? Should one always be consistent in his or her reactions?

The questions go on and on with the realization that conclusive answers may be beyond reach. What should be clear is that the unilateral and authoritarian imposition of expected social behaviors for all citizens in all circumstances is inappropriate. In fact, it is not too difficult to defend the proposition that one of the great strengths of Americans (no inference is intended that this strength is unique to Americans) lies in their diversity.

## INSTRUMENTS FOR THE ASSESSMENT
## OF SOCIAL FACTORS

Many instruments have been developed over the years for the measurement of a variety of social characteristics or qualities, including attitudes, character, personality, anxiety, and cohesiveness. Some of these instruments have been validated; others have not. For those that have been validated, issue might be taken with the methods used in several instances.

The focus of this section will be to analyze representative instruments for two processes: 1) subject response to inventories; and 2) sociometry, designed by means of sociograms to illustrate group cohesiveness. To the extent that they are available, estimates of validity and reliability will be cited.

### Assessment of Attitudes

Numerous instruments have been developed for the assessment of attitudes of selected groups toward various matters. Instruments described in this section are restricted to those designed to assess attitudes toward physical education, activity, exercise, competition, and physical education as a career.

*Physical education attitude inventory (PEAI).*[11]   Carlos Wear developed this initial 120-item inventory, which would make reliable and valid assessments of individual and group attitudes toward physical education as an activity course. Likert's recommendation was followed with respect to the form of response to the items.[12]

Validity was computed by correlating scores earned on PEAI with the respondents' self-ratings of their general attitudes toward physical education. Further, a one-page questionnaire was administered with the expectation that it would tend to support validity or at least serve as a check on validity. The coefficient of correlation between the inventory scores and the self-ratings was .80, indicating a substantial relationship between the respondents' "general" and "specific" attitudes toward physical education as an activity course. Reliability of the PEAI was determined by the split-halves method to be .96, which, when corrected by the Spearman-Brown prophecy formula, was adjusted to .98.

Wear reduced the inventory from 120 to 40 items, in terms of their indices of discrimination and their tendency to avoid duplication in the coverage of aspects of attitude toward physical education. Convenience was gained in administering the shorter form, and there was no serious loss of precision. Validity, determined against the self-rating criterion, was .80, and reliability, again using the split-halves method, was .94 and, after correction, .97.

In a later study, Wear developed alternate forms of what he called Physical Education Attitude Scales, each of which contained 30 items.[13] He reasoned that the construction of equivalent scales would facilitate the measurement and evaluation of differences in attitude before and after involvement in an experience in physical education. The 60 items contained in the two forms were taken from the original list of 120 items used in the development of the first inventory.

Correlation of Form A with the self-rating was .80 and of Form B, .78. Reliability of Form A using split-halves with correction was .94 and for Form B, .96. The correlation of scores on the two forms yielded a coefficient of .96. Thus, the forms would seem to merit the designation of equivalent.

Broer used Wear's inventory in assessing the attitudes of college women.[14] Reliability was found to be .96 (method is not identified, but, since no indication is given of a second administration, it is presumed that the corrected split-halves method was used), and validity, as determined by correlating inventory scores with the self-rating scale, was reported as .71, slightly less than that which Wear obtained for college men.

Wessel and Nelson also used Wear's inventory in their study of college women.[15] Correlation of inventory scores with self-rating scales yielded a validity coefficient of .81. Test-retest resulted in an objectivity coefficient of .84 for the attitude inventory and .81 for the self-rating scale.

*Kappes attitude inventory.*[16]   This inventory is in two parts: Part I requires Likert-type responses to three aspects of 31 activities (enjoyment of, desire for instruction in, and estimation of ability in); and Part II contains 55 items, 20 of which are specifically related to attitude toward physical education. Validity was estimated in several ways. Correlating total score on the 20 attitude items with teachers' ratings of student attitudes yielded a coefficient of .26. Use of the Dickey G method revealed that scores for 739 subjects ranged from −3.88 to 2.58 standard deviations; this is greater than normal expectations and should thus contribute to higher validity. Reliability of the 20 items was estimated by corrected split-halves and test-retest methods and generated coefficients of .94 and .90, respectively.

*Adams attitude scales.*[17]   Adams designed two 20-item scales for measuring attitude toward physical education. Responses could be made with either a Likert-type or a Thurstone-type arrangement. If the former approach is used, four items must be discarded from each of the scales for failing to fulfill the requirements of a Likert scale. Validity was estimated by correlating Thurstone scores with those yielded by the Likert scale, and by each of the scores with a cumulative self-rating scale. Coefficients thus produced ranged from .61 to .80. The split-halves coefficient corrected for the 32-item Likert scale was .89. For one of the scales in which Thurstone scores were computed, reliability was .71; for the combined scales, it was .84.

*Plummer attitude inventory.*[18]   Mista used this inventory in her inquiry into the attitudes of college women toward their high school physical education programs.[19] Validity was estimated by the criterion of internal consistency. In other words, the 30 items from the original inventory (consisting of 48 from the Plummer Attitude Inventory and 10 of the investigator's creation) that best discriminated between the top and bottom 40 scores on the 58 items were retained. Validity was not estimated against an external criterion.

Reliability was calculated for both the 58-item and the 30-item inventories, using the test-retest method. The coefficient for the longer inventory was .93 and for the shorter, .90. Mista argues that the difference in coefficients is due to the respective inventories' lengths, a conclusion that seems justified.

*Edgington attitude scale.*[20]    This scale was designed to assess the attitudes toward physical education of high school freshman boys. The scale contains 66 items of the type used by Likert, 34 of which are deemed to be negative statements and 32 positive.

Construct validity was estimated in two ways: 1) through Likert's technique of internal consistency; and 2) through correlation between scores of 30 respondents and ratings of their attitudes by their teachers. In the first instance, items were eliminated that did not elicit a difference of at least 1.5 between those in the highest and lowest 10 percent in terms of overall score; i.e., only the "valid" items were retained. This method assumes the validity of the entire inventory in establishing the validity of each item which, collectively, serve as a valid scale—a kind of circular method. This is not to say that the method is not defensible, but rather that it is not without potential error.

In the second instance, the respondents' teachers were asked to identify subjectively the 15 with the "most favorable" attitudes and the 15 with the "most unfavorable" attitudes. The observed scores of the respondents were compared with the expected frequencies by means of chi-square, with a resultant level of significance of .01.

*Thurstone scale of attitudes toward physical fitness and exercise.*[21]    Richardson constructed two equivalent forms of an equal-appearing-intervals scale, each with 19 items. Thus, based upon the judgment of experts, the items are ordered from least to most favorable, with the intervals between successive statements being of equal degree. The respondent circles the scale value for each of the statements with which there is agreement; the median of these scale values is designated as the respondent's score.

Based upon evidence of other studies, it was assumed that the expert judges were capable of making valid judgments of the favorability of the statements, independent of their own attitudes toward physical fitness and exercise. Test-retest yielded a reliability coefficient of .83. Reliability as estimated by correlating scores made by 300 respondents on each of the two forms was .87.

*McPherson-Yuhasz attitude inventory.*[22]    This 50-item inventory was designed by the investigators to detect intensity of attitudes of men toward exercise and physical activity. Validity was estimated by administering the inventory to two groups. One of the groups, physical education teachers, was presumed to have favorable attitudes toward physical activity and exercise, whereas the other group, composed of teachers of other subjects, was believed to have unfavorable attitudes. Two tests detected significant differences between the mean scores of the two groups.

Reliability was estimated by administering the inventory twice to the group of physical education teachers. Coefficients yielded by test-retest and by corrected split-halves for the two administrations were .95 and .81, respectively.

*ATPA scales.*[23]   The scales are designed to measure attitude toward physical activity and are subdivided into six domains: social experience; health and fitness; pursuit of vertigo; aesthetic experience; catharsis; and ascetic experience. Seven-point, Likert-type options appropriate for each domain were provided for responses. Two forms, CM for college men and CW for college women, were combined into a single form, C.

Validity was estimated using the respondents' preferences, weak or strong, for generalized physical activity as the criterion. Except for catharsis, scale scores discriminated significantly between those with strong and those with weak preferences. It was assumed that those with stronger preferences had more favorable attitudes. Hoyt reliabilities were calculated for college men and for college women for each of the scales. Maximum reliabilities in both instances were identified for the "pursuit of vertigo" scale (.89 and .86, respectively), whereas minimum reliabilities were calculated for the "social experience" scale (.72 for both sexes). Kenyon had previously reported on the construct validity of his conceptual model.[24]

Simon and Smoll[25] and Zaichkowsky[26] utilized modified inventories based upon Kenyon's scales. Smoll, et al.,[27] further modified the scales for use with children (CATPA) and reported Hoyt reliabilities ranging from .80, for the social and the health-and-fitness dimensions, to .89, for the aesthetic subdomain.

Apgar modified ATPA to include a pursuit-of-victory-dimension.[28] To investigate the effects of the modifications upon the integrity of ATPA, reliability coefficients were computed for the eight dimensions and were found to range from .64 to .88, the latter for the pursuit-of-victory dimension. Validity was estimated on the basis of dimensional independence (low intercorrelations ranging from -.02 to .57) and factor analysis (addition of the pursuit-of-victory dimension had little or no effect on factor loadings, as orthogonal rotation yielded two factors).

*Physical activity attitude inventories.*[29]   This 76-item inventory was developed by Sonstroem and was designed to reflect an estimation of one's ability to perform in vigorous physical activity as well as attraction to various kinds of vigorous physical activity. No validity coefficient is given, but a factor analysis is reported to have identified one prominent psychological factor from the estimation subscale. A Kuder-Richardson reliability coefficient of .90 was computed. A low relationship (.21) was observed between estimation and self-esteem.

*Physical estimation and attraction scales (PEAS).*[30]   Sonstroem revised and renamed the Physical Activity Attitude Inventories. The new inventory, PEAS, contained 89 short, first-person, true-false items designed to assess one's attraction to vigorous physical activity and an estimation of one's ability to perform in vigorous physical activity. Validity coefficients between inventory scores (seven factors plus estimation and attraction scores) and outside criteria ranged from -.46 to .00 to .53. Kuder-Richardson reliability coefficients ranged from .70 to .90.

*Drinkwater attitude inventory.*[31]   Two 36-item forms of this inventory were constructed, in which a Likert scale was used for responses. Validity was determined by calculating the critical ratio between the means of the 27 percent who scored highest on the inventory and the 27 percent who scored lowest. The difference between means was found to be significant well beyond the .01 level. The assumption here is that those 27 percent who scored highest had a more positive attitude toward physical education as a career for women. If one item is used as an illustration, "Girls look forward to their physical education classes with enthusiasm," a respondent is faced with a dilemma. Should she respond in terms of her personal feelings or in terms of her perception of how girls feel in general? If the latter, and her perception is that girls, in fact, do not look forward to physical education classes with enthusiasm, will the interpretation be that it is the respondent's attitude that is negative or the attitudes of girls?

Reliability was determined by means of split-halves ($r$ = .93; .96 corrected) and by test-retest ($r$ = .87).

*Attitudes toward intensive competition.*[32]   A survey of attitudes toward athletic competition generated 145 statements that were reduced to 77 by the elimination of ambiguous or duplicate items. Responses were of the type required by Likert, ranging on a 5-point scale from "strongly agree" to "strongly disagree." Test-retest with a 10- to 13-week interval yielded a reliability coefficient of .70. Reliability estimates for the various subcategories of the scale ranged from 1.00 (public relation) to .28 (safety). Rewording or replacement of several items was undertaken to improve the reliability, but no additional data were reported.

*Scott attitude scale.*[33]   This 79-item scale is a revision of the McCue attitude scale. A 5-point, Likert-type response indicating agreement, neutrality, or disagreement with the items was administered to 1,099 parents, teachers, and school officials. No validity coefficient is reported, although reference is made to the submission of the scale to a group of physical educators for their agreement as to whether a statement reflected a favorable or unfavorable attitude. Presumably, those statements that elicited considerable agreement were retained, but this is not made clear. Two administrations of the test yielded a reliability coefficient of .90.

*McGee attitude scale.*[34]   McGee observed Thurstone and Likert recommendations in constructing a 70-item scale designed to measure attitudes toward high school girls' athletic competition. The scale was subdivided into seven sections of general topics related to competition: personality development; recreation; physical development and conditioning; public relations; human relations; health; and safety.

Test-retest yielded a reliability estimate of .95 when the items were submitted to a panel of graduate students. Although validity is not specified, each item was identified by at least 70 percent of the graduate students as being either favorable or unfavorable toward competition. An attempt was made to word the statements so that about half were favorable and half were unfavorable.

*Lakie competitive attitude scale (CA scale).*[35]   This 22-item scale was designed to reveal the degree to which a respondent embraced the win-at-any-cost conduct of athletics. A Likert-type scale was used for responses that could range from strongly approve to strongly disapprove. Each item describes a sports situation in which ethical conduct is involved. All but three are phrased so that a "strongly disapprove" response is assigned the lowest score. The higher the total score, the more the respondent subscribes to the win-at-any-cost approach to the conduct of athletics.

Validity was assumed, based upon the comprehensiveness and thoroughness of the item analysis (the final 22 items were selected from a pool of 55), recommendations of a four-member "board of experts," and the belief that the respondents were truthful. Reliability was estimated in two ways: test-retest and an application of a modified Kuder-Richardson formula. Test-retest yielded coefficients of .61 for a group of varsity athletes and .64 for a group of graduate students. The modified Kuder-Richardson formula provided an estimate of .81 for scores of 80 subjects selected randomly. Lakie suggests that the reliability of the scale is not high enough to predict individual behavior, but that scales reporting similar reliabilities have been used for differentiating between groups.

*Children's attitudes toward female involvement in sports (CATFIS).*[36]   This Likert-type questionnaire was developed to assess grade and junior high school children's attitudes toward female involvement in sport. Twenty items, selected from an original pool of 60 items, were found to have a test-retest reliability of .81 and to correlate with battery means over a range of .59 to .84. Responses to statements such as "Only boys, not girls, should try to become famous sports players," were measured on a 5-point scale from completely agree to completely disagree.

*The Sportsmanship preference record.*[37]   This inventory describes 20 situations that recur in physical education classes in junior high schools. Following each description of a situation, the subject is asked to select one of four responses to a question concerned with a critical aspect of the situation. Correlation between Preference Record scores and teachers' evaluations of the subjects' sportmanship attitudes resulted in a coefficient of .53. A retest after six months produced a reliability coefficient of .80. Since significant differences are reported among the three grade levels (statistics not cited), it might be hypothesized that larger reliability coefficients might have been found if the retest had occurred sooner.

*Problem-solving test of sportsmanship.*[38]   A 40-item test was developed by Haskins that can be administered as two separate forms of 20 items each. Items are similar in form to those developed by McAfee, except that five possible responses are provided. Further, whereas McAfee's Preference Record was for junior high school use, Haskins' was administered to, and validity and reliability estimates derived from, college students.

Validity was calculated by correlating sportsmanship ratings (students rated each other) with test scores. Coefficients ranged from .39 (Form B) to .43 (Form A) for freshmen, from .08 (Form A) to .14 (Form B) for sophomores, and from .62 (Form B) to .66 (40 items) for juniors. Reliability coefficients derived from correlating scores on Form A with those on Form B were .94 for freshmen, .52 for sophomores, and .86 for juniors. Corrected coefficients for the 40-item test were .97, .68, and .92, respectively.

Johnson[39] criticized Haskins' tests for failing to satisfy eight of the basic informal criteria suggested by Edwards.[40]

*Sportsmanship attitude scales.*[41]    Two 21-item forms were constructed. Empirical validity coefficients of from -.01 to .43 were computed by correlating scores with sportsmanship behavior ratings in which students and teachers participated. Correlation of scores on Form A and Form B yielded a reliability estimate of .86. Coefficients of reproducibility were reported to be .81 for Form A and .86 for Form B.

*Debate over statistics to be used.*    Before concluding this section, brief mention should be made regarding the debate, as exemplified by Petrie[42] and Brumbach,[43] over the appropriate statistics, parametric or nonparametric, for use in the analysis of attitude scale scores.

Petrie argued that it is inappropriate to use parametric statistics under the assumption that there is equality of intervals along the scale. Brumbach, in his rebuttal, claimed that statisticians are not in agreement over the appropriateness of using parametric statistics, particularly if the distribution is relatively normal.

### Assessment of Personality Traits

The expansion of the literature concerned with the assessment of personality has been phenomenal during the 1960s and 1970s. This section will not attempt to review the many studies and will not even attempt to describe all the various instruments that have been used by sports and physical education investigators. But a number of the more prominent instruments and investigations will be described briefly.

*Booth scale.*[44]    Booth administered the 550-item Minnesota Multiphasic Personality Inventory (MMPI) to 141 athletes and 145 nonathletes. Twenty-two of the items were reported to discriminate significantly between good and poor competitors. Competitors were defined as good or poor, based upon independent ratings made by teammates and coaches of two dimensions of competition—competitive spirit and competitive performance. Validity coefficients of correlation between ratings of competitive performance and scores on the 22 items were .67, and between ratings of competitive spirit and scores, .65. Although these coefficients are significant, they represent marginal predictability at best. The 22 items were supplemented by 15 items of the L (Lie) scale of the MMPI and by three other MMPI items chosen at random and then administered to a university varsity track team. Scores were correlated with the coach's rank-order estimates of the athletes' competitive behavior and yielded an *r* of .63.

Keogh[45] challenged the statistical analysis of the Booth Scale, particularly with reference to the omission of data. Booth[46] offered a rebuttal.

Rasch, et al.,[47] administered the 40-item Booth Scale to 33 varsity wrestlers at two universities. For one of the teams, the *r* between the wrestlers' scores on the scale and the coach's ratings of their competitive behavior was .500, and for the other team it was .171. The investigators concluded that the Booth Scale did not predict the competitive behavior of these wrestlers. It must be cautioned, however, that if the coaches' ratings were not accurate estimates of competitive behavior, then the coefficient of correlation between the ratings and the Booth Scale would be adversely affected. It may well be that a single rater is inadequate, and that this inadequacy may be aggravated by the closeness of the relationship between coach and athlete, which may reduce rater objectivity. In fairness, it should be noted that the same kind of criticism may be leveled at Booth in his attempts to validate the scale.

Kroll and Petersen[48] conducted a study somewhat similar to the one by Rasch, et al., with the crucial exception that team success was used as the criterion to represent competitive behavior. They concluded that the Booth Scale did not discriminate between successful and unsuccessful teams or between either of these groups and a group of nonathletes. It is not inconceivable that there are simply too many factors involved in a performer's success in athletics to permit reasonably accurate prediction based upon only a very few of these factors.

Several investigations have produced test-retest reliability estimates for the MMPI.[49] In a study of unselected normals ($N$ = 40–47), Hathaway and McKinley obtained a range of .57 (Hysteria) to .83 (Hypomania) for six of the scales; Cottle, for 100 unselected normals, obtained a range of from .46 (Lie) to .91 (Masculinity-Femininity); and Holzberg and Alessi obtained reliability estimates for 30 psychiatric patients of from .52 (Psychopathic deviate) to .93 (Validity). "As for validity, a high score on a scale has been found to predict positively the corresponding final clinical diagnosis or estimate in more than 60 percent of new psychiatric admissions."[50]

*California psychological inventory.*[51]   This inventory includes 18 scales subdivided into four classes. These are measures of: 1) poise, ascendancy, self-assurance, and interpersonal adequacy; 2) socialization, maturity, responsibility, and intrapersonal structuring of values; 3) achievement, potential, and intellectual efficiency; and 4) intellectual and interest modes. Test-retest (1-year interval) reliability coefficients for high school students ranged from .44 (communality) to .73 (achievement via conformance) for females and from .38 (communality) to .75 (self-control) among the males. For male prisoners (1- to 3-week intervals), coefficients ranged from .49 (flexibility) to .87 (tolerance). Gough cited numerous cross-validation studies of the 18 items, with most of the correlation coefficients falling into the lower ranges.

*Sixteen personality factor questionnaire.*[52]   This questionnaire is designed to assess the broad range of personality by means of 16 paired factors, e.g., reserved vs. outgoing, tough-minded vs. tender-minded, group-dependent vs. self-sufficient, etc., represented by the items within the questionnaire. Validity coefficients ranged from .58 to .87, and reliability estimates ranged from .61 to .83. Cattell later reported multiple correlation validities, when all 16 PF items are used for estimating factors, of from .76 (factor M) to .90 (Factor H).[53]

A companion inventory is the High School Personality Questionnaire (HSPQ) that assesses 14 factors for ages 12 years to 18 years.[54] Reliabilities (immediate retest) ranged from .74 to .96, .72 to .93 (retest after 1 day), .53 to .82 (retest after 6 months), and .38 to .80 (retest after 1 year).

Kroll and Petersen[55] concluded that there was possible merit in the Cattell 16 PF profile for personality work in football investigations.

Tillman[56] found that the Allports' A-S Reaction Study discriminated significantly better on the ascendance-submission trait than did factor E of the Cattell profile, which purports to measure the same trait. He concluded that the former instrument is more extensive with regard to the trait.

Brown and Shaw[57] selected two of Cattell's factors—C, emotional stability, and O, confidence and self-assurance—because of their split-halves reliabilities of .71 and .93 and their validity coefficients of .73 and .96, respectively.

Widdop and Widdop[58] also concluded that more than one inventory should be administered if the full range of personality is to be evaluated. They found, for example, that factor E, humble/assertive on the Cattell and dominance on the California Psychological Inventory, were not significant factors, whereas the corresponding personality factor was found to be significant on the Edwards Personal Preference Schedule.

*Athletic motivation inventory.*[59]   This inventory (AMI) contains 190 items designed to assess 11 personality traits: drive; aggressiveness; determination; guilt-proneness; leadership; self-confidence; emotional control; mental toughness; coachability; conscientiousness; and trust. These traits are believed to be pertinent to success in athletics participation. Four purposes for which the AMI was developed are to 1) permit athlete and coach to improve communication and motivation; 2) enable the athlete to experience positive personal growth through participation; 3) assess causes of changes; and 4) provide an instrument to be used in sports-psychology research. The items are so constructed as to permit the respondent three Likert-type options.

Two types of reliability—internal consistency as measured by the Alpha coefficient and stability as measured by test-retest—have been computed. Alpha coefficients range from .78, for determination, to .93, for mental toughness, when computed from a combination of 100 professional, college, and high school athletes and coaches. Test-retest coefficients were computed for 56 high school soccer players and ranged from .58, for trust, to .80, for guilt-proneness.

Four types of validity assessments are provided. Face validity is presumed from the nature of the items, in that they are sports-specific. No supporting evidence for this assumption is offered in the manual. Four studies are cited to establish content validity by comparing inventory scores for athletes and nonathletes. For several comparison groups, significant differences were obtained for most of the traits.

Construct validity has been estimated by comparing AMI scores with coaches' and athletes' ratings. Among coaches, however, rating reliabilities were often very low. Many studies are reported with mixed results. It must be noted that failure to obtain high correlations between ratings and AMI scores is not necessarily an indictment of the AMI but may reflect rater inability. One study of predictive validity found only one significant difference.

Fosdick[60] found significant correlations between eight of the AMI traits and one or more of the 16 personality factors identified by Cattell. Further, four significant negative correlations were obtained. The largest coefficient (-.717) between the AMI trait of Emotional Control and its corresponding 16 PF factor of Relaxed vs. Tense, is marginal as a predictor. Regrettably, Fosdick did not attempt to validate the AMI by comparing scores with those derived from the 16 PF Questionnaire.

*Implicit values instrument for physical education.*[61]   Bain developed this instrument to identify positions on six value dimensions. The bases for the selection of the six dimensions were emphasis reflected in professional literature, applicability to physical education, and the opportunity to measure by means of observation.

A two-way analysis of variance of partial dimension scores resulted in these estimates of reliability: .28 for achievement; .86 for autonomy; .76 for orderliness; .38 for privacy; .57 for specificity; and .54 for universalism. Content validity was based upon the assumption that it adequately sampled a previously defined universe of behaviors.[62]

*Coaching behavior assessment system (CBAS).*[63]   This system involves the coding and analysis of the behaviors of coaches in naturalistic settings. Twelve kinds of behavior, subdivided into two main categories—reactive and spontaneous—are identified. Reactive behaviors included those in response to: 1) desirable performances; 2) mistakes; and 3) misbehaviors. Spontaneous behaviors included two categories: game-related and game-irrelevant.

Reliability was estimated by comparing accuracy of scoring and consistency of scoring of the observers and by computing interobserver reliability coefficients as well as reliability coefficients between observers and the criterion codings of the investigators. In the first instance, accuracy of agreement averaged 97.8 percent, and the index of consistency mean was 96.4 percent. Inter-observer reliabilities ranged from .77 to .99, with a mean of .88. Reliability coefficients reflecting agreement between observers and investigators ranged from .62 to .98, with a mean of .86.

*Teacher competency questionnaire (TCQ).*[64]   This 89-item inventory uses a Likert-type response ("of very great importance" to "of little importance") to assess professional competence of female teachers of physical education in three realms—knowledge, skill, and behavior. Content validity was determined by submitting the items to a panel of judges deemed knowledgeable as to the role of physical education teachers. Seventy-three of the statements were classified as definitely appropriate to the role, whereas the other 16 were considered less appropriate. None was considered unimportant. Initial steps in the process of establishing construct validity involved a factor analysis that identified 14 subroles, although the investigator failed to suggest what these subroles were. Test-retest reliability was estimated to be .99 when the questionnaire was completed by female major students and their faculty during a 10-day interval.

### Assessment of Anxiety

It is clear that the assessment of anxiety has become an increasingly important concern of students of physical education including sports. Evidence of this increasing concern is seen in the expansion of research studies investigating the phenomenon. Two distinct anxiety factors have been isolated. The first of these, trait anxiety, may be described as a kind of inherent anxiety that is relatively resistant to change. The second, state anxiety, is more transitory and is related to the tension of the moment.

*The state-trait anxiety inventory (STAI).*[65]    STAI was developed to provide relatively brief self-report measures of state (A-State) and trait (A-Trait) anxiety. Validation was assumed if items were demonstrated to be related to other measures of anxiety. It proved difficult, however, to draft statements that measured A-Trait and A-State simultaneously. Therefore, separate scales were constructed. Twenty-statement scales each were developed for the STAI A-State and STAI A-Trait. Items for the latter scale were chosen on the basis of being correlated significantly with other widely accepted anxiety scales.[66] The A-Trait scale attempts to assess how subjects feel generally, whereas the A-State asks subjects to describe how they feel at a particular moment in time. Both scales use 4-item Likert-type responses.

Basler et al. reported an A-Trait reliability coefficient of .83 and A-State reliability coefficients of from .86 to .88, as derived from precompetition measures.[67]

*Sport competition anxiety test.*[68]    According to Scanlan,[69] an extensive review of the reliability and validity studies for SCAT are included in Martens' book. Presumably, Scanlan is satisfied with SCAT, since she uses it to assess competition trait anxiety—a predisposition to respond to competitive sport situations with varying levels of state anxiety—in 306 male youths ages 10–12.

Martens and Simon[70] found that SCAT was a considerably better predictor of precompetitive A-State than was Spielberger's A-Trait inventory. Both were superior to coaches' ratings in women's volleyball and basketball. The investigators concluded that their findings were consistent with previous research in which situation-specific A-Trait instruments have been found to be better behavior predictors than general A-Trait instruments and, hence, supported the construct and predictive validity of SCAT.

Martens and Gill,[71] in a study of 490 fifth- and sixth-grade children, concluded that the results provided clear support for the construct validity of SCAT.

*Taylor manifest anxiety scale (TMAS).*[72]   Some 200 items drawn from the MMPI were submitted to a panel of clinicians, who were asked to identify those that were indicative of manifest anxiety (anxiety that is evident to others). Sixty-five items were agreed upon, and these were reduced to 50 by statistical analysis. The 50 items were contained in a Biographical Inventory that included some 250 statements nonindicative of anxiety. Coefficients of reliability were computed by test-retest. Pearson product-moment coefficients for 59 subjects retested after three weeks, for 113 subjects retested after five months, and for 50 subjects retested after from 9 to 17 months were .89, .82, and .81, respectively.

*Movement satisfaction scale.*[73]   Eight experts in psychology and physical education were asked to judge 129 items, believed to represent motor satisfaction, in terms of three criteria: 1) relevance of content; 2) clarity of meaning; and 3) appropriateness of content and vocabulary for males and females 14 to 21 years of age. The 75 items with the highest agreement among the judges were retained. Responses to the items were on a Likert-type scale ranging from "have strong negative feelings" to "have strong positive feelings." Kuder-Richardson reliability coefficients were .96 for 176 subjects ages 18–21, and .95 for 877 subjects ages 14–21.

Some interesting comparisons between the Movement Satisfaction Scale scores and those made by subjects on the STAI were made by Burton.[74] High A-Trait subjects had higher A-State scores and lower movement satisfaction scores than did the low A-Trait subjects. She concluded that STAI and Movement Satisfaction Scale measure related qualities.

*Other works.*   Martens[75] has provided a useful review of the literature on anxiety as it relates to motor behavior. Critical reactions to this review have been presented by Carron,[76] Marteniuk,[77] Spence,[78] and Spielberger.[79] Issues addressed in these papers include conflicting research findings and conceptual ambiguities.

### Sociometry

Inventories used in sociometry follow the general form of asking subjects to select, on one basis or another, two or more associates, e.g., "Which five persons would you most (least) want on your team (as a friend)?" The purpose is to attempt to assess social status in terms of the frequency with which each member of the group is selected, rejected, or ignored. Based upon these assessments, efforts are made to manipulate class organization, teams, etc., so as to facilitate wider socialization. Although there is some evidence to support the effectiveness of the process in some settings, sociometry is not without hazard. This is particularly so in the instance of younger subjects for whom this may well be the first time that they are introduced to the concept of human rejection. Who is to say what the long-range effect may be when rejection is not only acceptable but also may even be encouraged? Perhaps it would be better if the choices available to the respondent were reduced by eliminating the rejection component.

Breck[80] adopted tests used by Moreno[81] and Jennings. She obtained reliability data for three activities—swimming, dance, and volleyball—based upon skill ($r$ = .64 to .72) and upon friendship ($r$ = .60 to .70). Validity was assumed, based upon the work of those from whom she adopted her tests.

Hale[82] has suggested five criteria—number of isolates, reciprocated choices, number of overchosen, acceptance curve, and structural analysis—to serve as a frame of reference in analyzing sociometric data. Assumptions underlying two or three of the criteria, however, are subject to contention if considered from the individual's and not from the group's perspective. The line of reasoning by which these criteria could be challenged has already been expressed in this chapter and will not be repeated here.

Nelson and Johnson[83] used a sociometric measuring device in an attempt to determine if arrangement of classes in prescribed ways would facilitate social status change. Their two principal findings were that 1) inducing those who are initially incompatible to work together can produce positive social change; and 2) such changes do not result naturally from mere participation in a sports activity. The measuring device used in the investigation consisted of each subject listing the five class members with whom he or she would most like to play and the five with whom he or she would not like to play.

Yukie[84] used a sociometric test involving selection of two class members most wanted as teammates. The test was administered in January, March, and June, to detect class growth. Ten criteria of a "good group," agreed to by five authorities, were used as a standard against which the class could be measured. Also used was Dimock's Best Friends Test,[85] in which class members select their ten best friends. The degree to which members of the class are included among the best friends is claimed to be a measure of group cohesiveness. Yukie concluded that the sociograms do reveal group structure changes, and that they were more efficient, productive, and meaningful than Dimock's test. Implicit in her discussion is that democratic procedures produce positive changes. With no control group, however, it is speculative to suggest the cause or causes that may have led to whatever changes may appear during the course of a semester of instruction.

Skubic utilized an acquaintance test in which each class member is asked to list all those whose names the class member knows.[86] The extent to which acquaintance increases over a period of time is designated as the class member's expansiveness. A reliability coefficient of .93 is indicated and appears to be computed from test-retest data. She also found that acquaintance volume was greatest in volleyball classes, followed by dance and then by swimming classes. Lack of adequate control precludes clear establishment of cause-effect relationships. Skubic provided a fairly extensive bibliography.

Todd[87] has also reviewed some of the early investigations into sociometry.

*Cowell personal-distance scale.*[88]    Cowell developed a Personal-Distance Ballot that was to be completed by each student for all other students in the group. Response options indicated the degree to which each student was accepted by other students (e.g., "into my family as a brother" . . . "into my city"). Mean scores for each student were calculated and compared with norms compiled from 191 cases. Cowell claims that being accepted as a member of one's social group is an important criterion of adjustment to the group. This seems to be the extent of the attempt to validate the Ballot as a measure of social adjustment, in spite of the fact that the Ballot is used subsequently as a criterion for the validation of two forms of the Cowell Social Behavior Trend Index.

Cowell reports no reliability coefficients derived from high school students' data. It appears that the Ballot was used by Trapp in his study of a college football squad. He reported reliability coefficients of .91, .88, and .93 from three separate administrations of the Ballot during the season.[89] Presumably, the coefficients resulted from intercorrelations between each possible pair of Ballot scores. Whether similar reliability estimates would result from administration to younger or less cohesive groups appears not to have been determined.

One aspect of the Personal-Distance Ballot of which Cowell makes no mention is whether it reveals anything about the adjustment of the ones giving the ratings in somewhat the same way that it purports to assess the adjustment of those being rated. For example, what might be concluded about a rater whose evaluations tended to be distant (i.e., unwillingness to accept into close relationship) for most or all of those being rated? Conceivably, a variety of interpretations are possible, and it is probable that no definitive judgment could be made without considerable depth analysis. Similar questions could be asked about raters who accept *everyone* into close relationship. Perhaps such acceptance would be indicative of a lack of appropriate discrimination on the part of these raters.

## BIBLIOGRAPHY

ADAMS, R.S. "Two Scales for Measuring Attitude Toward Physical Education." *Research Quarterly,* 34 (March 1963), 91–94.

APGAR, FRED M. "Emphasis Placed on Winning in Athletics by Male High School Students." *Research Quarterly,* 48 (May 1977), 253–59.

BAIN, LINDA L. "An Instrument for Identifying Implicit Values in Physical Education Programs." *Research Quarterly,* 47 (October 1976), 307–15.

BASLER, MARILYN L., A. CRAIG FISHER, and NANCY L. MUMFORD. "Arousal and Anxiety Correlates of Gymnastic Performance." *Research Quarterly,* 47 (December 1976), 586–89.

BOOTH, E.G., Jr. "Personality Traits of Athletes as Measured by the MMPI." *Research Quarterly,* 29 (May 1958), 127–38.

____. "Personality Traits of Athletes as Measured by the MMPI: a Rebuttal." *Research Quarterly,* 32 (October 1961), 421–23.

BRECK, SABIN JUNE. "A Sociometric Measurement of Status in Physical Education Classes." *Research Quarterly,* 21 (May 1950), 75–82.

BROER, MARION R. "Evaluation of a Basic Skills Curriculum for Women Students of Low Motor Ability at the University of Washington." *Research Quarterly,* 26 (March 1955), 15–27.

BROWN, ELIZABETH YECKEL and CARL N. SHAW. "Effects of a Stressor on a Specific Motor Task on Individuals Displaying Selected Personality Factors." *Research Quarterly,* 46 (March 1975), 71–77.

BRUMBACH, WAYNE B.   "A Response to Petrie's Note on Statistical Analysis of Attitude Scale Scores." *Research Quarterly*, 40 (May 1969), 436–37.

BURTON, ELSIE CARTER.   "Relationship Between Trait and State Anxiety, Movement Satisfaction, and Participation in Physical Education Activities." *Research Quarterly*, 47 (October 1976), 326–31.

CARRON, ALBERT V.   "Reactions to 'Anxiety and Motor Behavior.'" *Journal of Motor Behavior*, 3 (June 1971), 181–88.

CATTELL, RAYMOND B.   *Personality and Mood by Questionnaire*. San Francisco: Jossey-Bass Publishers, 1973.

CATTELL, RAYMOND B. and MARY D.L. CATTELL.   *Handbook for the Jr.-Sr. High School Personality Questionnaire*. Champaign, IL: Institute for Personality and Ability Testing, 1969.

CATTELL, RAYMOND B. and HERBERT W. EBER.   *Handbook for the Sixteen Personality Factor Questionnaire*. Champaign, IL: Institute for Personality and Ability Testing, 1964.

COWELL, CHARLES C.   "Validating an Index of Social Adjustment for High School Use." *Research Quarterly*, 29 (March 1958), 7–18.

"The Contributions of Physical Activity to Social Development." *Research Quarterly*, 31 (May 1960), 286–306.

CRATTY, BRYANT J.   *Social Dimensions of Physical Activity*. Englewood Cliffs: Prentice-Hall, Inc., 1967.

DIMOCK, HEDLEY S.   *Rediscovering the Adolescent*. New York: Association Press, 1937.

DRINKWATER, BARBARA L.   "Development of an Attitude Inventory to Measure the Attitude of High School Girls Toward Physical Education." *Research Quarterly*, 31 (December 1960), 575–80.

EDGINGTON, CHARLES W.   "Development of an Attitide Scale to Measure Attitudes of High School Freshman Boys Toward Physical Education." *Research Quarterly*, 39 (October 1968), 505–12.

EDWARDS, ALLEN L.   *Techniques of Attitude Scale Construction*. New York: Appleton-Century-Crofts, 1957.

ETZIONI, AMATAI.   "Human Beings are not Very Easy to Change After All." *Saturday Review*, June 3, 1972.

FOSDICK, DENNIS HARRY.   "The Relationship of the Athletic Motivation Inventory and the 16 Personality Factor Questionnaire as Measures of the Personality Characteristics of College Varsity Swimmers." Unpublished master's thesis, San Jose State College, 1972.

GOUGH, HARRISON G.   *California Psychological Inventory Manual*. Palo Alto: Consulting Psychologist Press, Inc., 1969.

HALE, PATRICIA WHITAKER.   "Proposed Method for Analyzing Sociometric Data." *Research Quarterly*, 27 (May 1956), 152–61.

HASKINS, MARY JANE.   "Problem-Solving Test of Sportsmanship." *Research Quarterly*, 31 (December 1960), 601–6.

HATHAWAY, S.R. and J.C. McKINLEY.   *Minnesota Multiphasic Personality Inventory Manual*. New York: The Psychological Corporation, 1967.

JOHNSON, MARION LEE.   "Construction of Sportsmanship Attitude Scales." *Research Quarterly*, 40 (May 1969), 312–16.

KAPPES, EVELINE E.   "Inventory to Determine Attitudes of College Women Toward Physical Education and Student Services of the Physical Education Department." *Research Quarterly*, 25 (December 1954), 429–38.

KENYON, GERALD S.   "A Conceptual Model for Characterizing Physical Activity." *Research Quarterly*, 39 (March 1968), 96–105.

_____. "Six Scales for Assessing Attitudes Toward Physical Activity." *Research Quarterly*, 39 (October 1968), 566–74.

_____. "Sociological Considerations." *Journal of Health, Physical Education, and Recreation*, 39 (November-December 1968), 31–33.

KEOGH, JACK.    "Comments on the Selection of Data for Presentation." *Research Quarterly*, 31 (May 1960), 240.

KROLL, WALTER and KAY H. PETERSEN.    "Personality Factor Profiles of Collegiate Football Teams." *Research Quarterly*, 36 (December 1965), 433–40.

_____. "Cross-Validation of the Booth Scale." *Research Quarterly*, 37 (March 1966), 66–70.

LAKIE, WILLIAM L.    "Expressed Attitudes of Various Groups of Athletes Toward Athletic Competition." *Research Quarterly*, 35 (December 1974), 497–503.

LIKERT, RENSIS.    "A Technique for the Measurement of Attitudes." *Archives of Psychology*, 22 (June 1932), 5–43.

MARTENIUK, RONALD G.    "Two Factors to be Considered in the Design of Experiments in Anxiety and Motor Behavior." *Journal of Motor Behavior*, 3 (June 1971), 189–92.

MARTENS, RAINER.    "Anxiety and Motor Behavior: A Review." *Journal of Motor Behavior*, 3 (June 1971), 151–79.

_____. *Sport Competition Anxiety Test*. Champaign, IL: Human Kinetics Publishers, 1977.

MARTENS, RAINER and DIANE L. GILL.    "State Anxiety Among Successful and Unsuccessful Competitors Who Differ in Competitive Trait Anxiety." *Research Quarterly*, 47 (December 1976), 698–708.

MARTENS, RAINER and JULIE A. SIMON.    "Comparisons of Three Predictors of State Anxiety in Competitive Situations." *Research Quarterly*, 47 (October 1976), 381–87.

McAFEE, ROBERT A.    "Sportsmanship Attitudes of Sixth, Seventh, and Eighth Grade Boys." *Research Quarterly*, 26 (March 1955), 120.

McCUE, BETTY FOSTER.    "Constructing an Instrument for Evaluating Attitudes Toward Intensive Competition in Team Games." *Research Quarterly*, 24 (May 1953), 205–9.

McGEE, ROSEMARY.    "Comparison of Attitudes Toward Intensive Competition for High School Girls." *Research Quarterly*, 27 (March 1956), 60–73.

McPHERSON, B.D. and M.S. YUHASZ.    "An Inventory for Assessing Men's Attitudes Toward Exercise and Physical Activity." *Research Quarterly*, 39 (March 1968), 218–20.

MISTA, NANCY J.    "Attitudes of College Women Toward Their High School Physical Education Programs." *Research Quarterly*, 39 (March 1968), 166–74.

MORENO, J.L.    "The Three Branches of Sociometry." *Sociometry Monographs*, No. 21. New York: Beacon House, 1949.

NEALE, DANIEL C., ROBERT J. SONSTROEM, and KENNETH F. METZ.    "Physical Fitness, Self-Esteem, and Attitudes Toward Physical Activity." *Research Quarterly*, 40 (December 1969), 743–49.

NELSON, BARBARA A. and DOROTHY J. ALLEN.    "Scale for the Appraisal of Movement Satisfaction." *Perceptual and Motor Skills*, 31 (1970), 795–800.

NELSON, JACK M. and BARRY L. JOHNSON.    "Effects of Varied Techniques in Organizing Class Competition upon Changes in Sociometric Status." *Research Quarterly*, 39 (October 1968), 634–39.

PETRIE, BRIAN M.    "Statistical Analysis of Attitude Scale Scores." *Research Quarterly*, 40 (May 1969), 434–36.

RASCH, PHILIP J., M. BRIGGS HUNT, and PORT G. ROBERTSON.    "The Booth

Scale as a Predictor of Competitive Behavior of College Wrestlers." *Research Quarterly,* 31 (March 1960), 117–18.

RICHARDSON, CHARLES E. "Thurstone Scale for Measuring Attitudes of College Students Toward Physical Fitness and Exercise." *Research Quarterly,* 31 (December 1960), 638–43.

SAFRIT, MARGARET J., *Evaluation in Physical Education.* Englewood Cliffs, N.J.: Prentice-Hall, Inc., 1973.

SCANLAN, TARA KOST. "The Effects of Success-Failure on the Perception of Threat in a Competitive Situation." *Research Quarterly,* 48 (March 1977), 144–53.

SCOTT, PHEBE MARTHA. "Attitudes Toward Athletic Competition in Elementary Schools." *Research Quarterly,* 24 (October 1953), 352–61.

SELBY, ROSEMARY and JOHN H. LEWKE. "Children's Attitudes Toward Females in Sport: Their Relationship with Sex, Grade, and Sports Participation." *Research Quarterly,* 47 (October 1976), 453–63.

SIMON, JULIE A. and FRANK L. SMOLL. "An Instrument for Assessing Children's Attitudes Toward Physical Activity." *Research Quarterly,* 45 (December 1974), 407–15.

SKUBIC, ELVERA. "A Study in Acquaintanceship and Social Status in Physical Education Classes." *Research Quarterly,* 20 (March 1949), 80–87.

SMITH, RONALD E., FRANK L. SMOLL, and EARL HUNT. "A System for the Behavioral Assessment of Athletic Coaches." *Research Quarterly,* 48 (May 1977), 401–7.

SMOLL, FRANK L., ROBERT W. SCHUTZ, and JOAN K. KEENEY. "Relationships Among Children's Attitudes, Involvement, and Proficiency in Physical Activities." *Research Quarterly,* 47 (December 1976), 797–803.

SONSTROEM, ROBERT J. "Attitude Testing Examining Certain Psychological Correlates of Physical Activity." *Research Quarterly,* 45 (May 1974), 93–103.

SPENCE, JANET TAYLOR. "What Can You Say About a Twenty-Year Old Theory That Won't Die?" *Journal of Motor Behavior,* 3 (June 1971), 193–203.

SPIELBERGER, CHARLES D. "Train-State Anxiety and Motor Behavior." *Journal of Motor Behavior,* 3 (September 1971), 265–79.

____ ed., *Anxiety, Vol. 1.* New York: Academic Press, 1972.

SPIELBERGER, C.D., R.L. GORUSCH, and R.E. LUSHENE. *Manual for the State-Trait Anxiety Inventory.* Palo Alto: Consulting Psychologist Press, 1970.

STEVENSON, CHRISTOPHER L. "Socialization Effects of Participation in Sport: A Critical Review of the Research." *Research Quarterly,* 46 (October 1975), 287–301.

TAYLOR, JANET A. "A Personality Scale of Manifest Anxiety." *Journal of Abnormal and Social Psychology,* 48 (1953), 285–290.

THURSTONE, L.L. and E.J. CHAVE. *The Measurement of Attitude.* Chicago: University of Chicago Press, 1929.

TILLMAN, KENNETH. "Relationship Between Physical Fitness and Selected Personality Traits." *Research Quarterly,* 36 (December 1965), 483–89.

TODD, FRANCES. "Sociometry in Physical Education." *Journal of Health, Physical Education, and Recreation,* 24 (May 1953), 23–24, 36.

TRAPP, WILLIAM G. "A Related Study of Social Integration in a College Football Squad." Unpublished minor research project, Purdue University, 1953.

TUTKO, THOMAS A., LELAND P. LYON, and BRUCE C. OGILVIE. *Athletic Motivation Inventory Manual.* San Jose: The Institute of Athletic Motivation, 1975.

WEAR, CARLOS L. "The Evaluation of Attitude Toward Physical Education as an Activity Course." *Research Quarterly,* 22 (March 1951), 114–26.

____. "Construction of Equivalent Forms of an Attitude Scale." *Research Quarterly,* 26 (March 1955), 113–19.

WEBER, MARIE. "Physical Education Teacher Role Identification Instrument." *Research Quarterly,* 48 (May 1977), 445–51.

WESSEL, JANET A. and RICHARD NELSON. "Relationship Between Strength and Attitudes Toward Physical Education Activity Among College Women." *Research Quarterly,* 35 (December 1964), 562–69.

WIDDOP, JAMES H. and VALERIE A. WIDDOP, "Comparison of the Personality Traits of Female Teacher Education and Physical Education Students." *Research Quarterly,* 46 (October 1975), 274–81.

YUKIE, ELEANOR C. "Group Movement and Growth in a Physical Education Class." *Research Quarterly,* 26 (May 1955), 222–33.

ZAICHKOWSKY, LINDA B. "Attitudinal Differences in Two Types of Physical Education Programs." *Research Quarterly,* 46 (October 1975), 364–70.

# CHAPTER THIRTEEN
# MARKING (GRADING)

The physical education profession has long and consistently been plagued by inefficient evaluative and marking systems and procedures. Prominent among the evidence in support of this contention is the fact that many colleges and universities do not include marks earned in physical education courses in the computation of high school students' overall grade-point averages. Why is this so?

At least two possibilities may account for this current practice. First, it is likely that college policy-makers have concluded (the bases for such conclusion may be ill-founded) that physical education course marks do not predict success in college studies and would serve no useful purpose if included in such computations. In this context, it should be noted that some other high-school-level courses, such as art, music, and industrial arts, are considered in grade-point-average computations, even though the content of these courses reflects remarkably similar elements to those found in properly conceived physical education programs. To illustrate these similarities, it is probably sufficient to cite the respective disciplines' historical and cultural foundations and their emphases upon development of appropriate motor skills and the acquisition of relevant knowledge. Thus, the basic factor of physical education course content should not, and probably does not, underlie the decision of these policy makers.

A second and much more likely reason for this policy decision is that physical education marks have not represented student achievement but, instead, have been a composite of a wide variety of elements, many of which are difficult to justify as legitimate components of physical education programs. Among these are such elements as attendance, costume, comportment, and showering, which are utilized typically as direct factors in the computation of students' marks. The felony is further compounded by instructors who insist upon applying a set of standards so low that one is led to believe, on the basis of marks awarded, that there are no average or below-average students enrolled in physical education courses. For some unknown reason, physical education instructors seem obsessed with the belief that students who try, or who appear to try, should not be penalized simply because they are in our opinion, unable to meet reasonable standards of performance. Many also believe, erroneously in our opinion, that if students are awarded above-average marks, they will be motivated to try even harder in the future. On the contrary, such students are more likely to believe that they are doing quite well and may be content to work no harder or even to diminish their efforts.

Such practices on the part of physical educators ultimately lead to a distribution of marks so skewed to the high side that it is no surprise that college admissions officers are inclined to conclude that physical education marks cannot reliably predict success in college studies. The end result has been the virtual elimination of marks in physical education courses as partial determinants of the eligibility of students for entrance into colleges.

It is not the intent here to argue that the primary reason for the establishment of appropriate standards of performance as criteria in the determination of physical education marks is to convince college policy-makers to review their decision. On the contrary, the crucial reason is that inferior standards almost certainly produce inferior performances. Not only should instructors expect high levels of performance, but students should also expect and demand quality instruction as well as the opportunity to practice so that they can achieve these high levels of performance for their own benefit and personal satisfaction. Under present practices, few are able to interpret accurately just what a mark in physical education really represents, and it is not astonishing that large segments of the lay and professional publics feel that physical education programs are vague in purpose.

## THE PURPOSE OF MARKS

The major purpose of marks is to provide a valid representation of student attainment of legitimate program objectives. As such, marks inform students, their parents, and other interested parties of student achievement in various courses of study. Marks may also identify areas of strength and weakness and may serve to motivate students to exert increased effort.

If marks awarded in physical education are to be taken as seriously as those awarded in other subjects, then the bases upon which physical education marks are determined must be similar in kind to those in other subjects, and, furthermore, they must be equally subject to valid interpretation. Marks in other courses are almost universally interpreted as being representative of student achievement, i.e., students with the highest marks have demonstrated the greatest mastery of the course content. There is no logical reason why the physical education mark should not represent the same kind of mastery. Many writers in physical education agree that the mark should indicate the degree of student attainment of program objectives.[1,2,3,4,5] These statements of agreement, although essentially valid, are fraught with potential pitfalls. The basic validity is sapped of its strength *unless* the program objectives are also valid, i.e., they are legitimate objectives of physical education programs. Further exploration of legitimate program objectives appears later in this chapter.

## MARKING SYSTEMS

Many different marking systems are being utilized by schools and colleges in the 1980s. Undoubtedly, the most common is the 5-point letter system (usually comprised of A, B, C, D, and E or F; or E, S+, S, S-, and U; or some similar combination of five letters or symbols). Other systems include the percentage system, in which the marks reflect the percentage of attainment of some standard, often unidentified; dichotomous systems such as pass-fail or plus-minus, in which the only decision to be determined is whether a minimum standard has been attained,[6] and the percentile-rank system, in which the students' standings are indicated in terms of the percentages of peers that their achievements equal or exceed. Most of the subsequent discussion will revolve around the 5-point scale, since that is the system within which most teachers will have to work.

### Defining Marks

Whatever marking system is employed, one factor is of major concern. This is that each mark in the system must be unmistakably defined in order to readily permit clear and specific interpretation. This demand, regrettably, is seldom met in most marking systems.

The preponderance of report cards and transcripts, issued by schools at all levels, that employ a 5-point scale will commonly define the five points in such vague terms as superior, excellent, above average, average, below average, passing, unsatisfactory but passing, not passing, and failing in some combination of five. It is true that such descriptions do provide students and others with a rough approximation of relative status within peer groups. The question is, however, whether a rough approximation is sufficient for adequate separation of students into categories appropriate to their respective achievements and necessary to their subsequent proper placement. A perusal of marks awarded by teachers in any given school will inevitably reveal that some teachers tend to be "easy marks" whereas others are "harder marks," i.e., the proportion of high marks awarded by some is greater than that awarded by others. The crux of the matter is that it is difficult enough to interpret marks that possess vague descriptions and almost impossible if even the vague descriptions are ignored. In order to illustrate this a bit more, the reader is asked to consider the middle mark in a 5-point system (typically identified as C), the description of which is invariably that of average.

*What is average?*  Among the many dictionary definitions is one that is apt for the discussion: ". . . the usual, typical, or most often encountered thing, happening, or person . . .".[7] Translated into marking language, the C or average mark should represent the point at or around which the achievements of all members of a particular population (e.g., students in a particular course of instruction) should balance. Further, the middle of the C range should represent the usual, typical, or most often encountered achievement. That the C is gradually, if not rapidly, losing its identity is undeniable.*[8] The causes are many and include the "easy mark," who deludes students, and the policy-makers, who delude themselves by mistakenly believing that by raising grade-point-average requirements for entrance into or retention in schools and colleges they are raising standards of achievement. In fact and practice, the reverse is usually true, but this is another topic.

If it could be assumed (a short flight into fantasy) that teachers would agree to and, further, would adhere to the above description of the C mark, the problem of the total process of marking would still be a long distance from solution. Prime among the remaining difficulties—and it is of major importance—is the determining of how many points separate the five marks. If a mark of B, for example, is to represent above-average achievement, how is the above-average achievement at the top of the C range to be distinguished from that at the bottom of the B range?

---

*This was one of the earliest published warnings of the advent of the phenomenon that has come to be known as "grade inflation."

*Chance mark ranges.* The distinction between one mark and its neighboring marks is often made in terms of a so-called "natural break-point," characterized by clear gaps in the distribution of student performances. This method lacks precision, as the break-point position is often subject to wide fluctuations that result in loss of consistency from semester to semester, and some students will be either over-marked or undermarked.

*Arbitrary mark ranges.* Other instructors will establish arbitrary mark ranges and assign marks accordingly. A common scheme of this type involves, for example, the awarding of A to all students whose class averages are equal to or higher than a predetermined point (often 95). The difficulty is that, very likely, the teacher may have no conception of how these arbitrary break-points will affect the ultimate distribution of marks. If standards are exceedingly low, everyone might earn A, whereas if the minimum standards are too high, everyone might fail. It might be argued by some that nothing is wrong with such a procedure, and each student received the mark deserved. The weakness of the argument is that the system fails to distinguish adequately among varying levels of performance and, hence, fails to serve the purpose for which it was intended.

*Percentage mark ranges.* A much more desirable approach to the establishment of the break-points is to predetermine the percentage of students who, over the long run, should receive each of the five marks. When this system is first used, it will be necessary for the teacher to assess the relative achievements of the pupils, usually in terms of points earned for the various parts of the course, and then to determine the break-points in terms of the percentages of the students that are to fall into each letter range. These cumulative scores should be retained by the teacher and combined with scores earned by other students in subsequent semesters or in other sections. As the total number of scores in the compilation increases, so does the reliability of the break-points. At first, it will probably be necessary to make some adjustments in the locations of the break-points as a result of the chance variations typical of relatively small groups. As the total number of scores in the compilation increases, these adjustments will become increasingly small, and the distribution will tend to more closely approximate normal.

At this point, the discussion must regress to the question of the manner in which the predetermination of the various percentages allotted to each mark will be accomplished. No universally followed plan is available as a model. If it is desired that the ranges for each of the marks be equal in size (at least in terms of scores typically achieved instead of scores that might conceivably be achieved), then each range will be of a size equal to 1.2 standard deviations (on the basis that 99.73 percent of the total distribution will be included within ± 3.0 standard deviations from the mean and 6/5 = 1.2). This division will produce a distribution containing approximately 3.5 percent each of As and Fs, approximately 24 percent each of Bs and Ds, and approximately 45 percent of Cs. As can readily be seen, such a division nearly eliminates the A and F marks, a less than desirable effect.

An alternative system would involve an arbitrary reduction of the percentage of Cs to 35, for example, and a corresponding increase of the percentages of As and Fs to about 8.5 each.

Whatever distribution decision is eventually reached, the critical concern is that *all* teachers be fully apprised of this decision and that each teacher conscientiously adhere to the system of distribution. This is not to say that, for a small class, the distributions must conform necessarily to the stated percentages; but over a longer period of time, the marks will tend to be distributed according to the principles of the system. Ideally, of course, there should be uniformity of distribution among all school systems, but this ideal is probably beyond reasonable implementation. Even if such implementation is not forthcoming, it will still be possible to fairly accurately assess the marks awarded by the several systems if each one has quite specifically stated its mark descriptions in terms of percentages.

### Suggestions for Further Improving Marking Systems

Before concluding this section, two brief notes should be appended. First, it is suggested that serious consideration be given by school administrators to the feasibility of eliminating the F mark and its connotation of failure. Failure, per se, is a rather elusive concept. Would it not be better if the lowest mark were designated as E, with the corresponding description of "the lowest *n* per cent in terms of attainment of course objectives?" The principal reason for this suggestion is that so few Fs are given presently that, for practical purposes, the marking system has been compacted into a 4-point scale. With the elimination of the failure connotation from the lowest mark, and with the establishment of a fixed percentage for this mark, there will be a corresponding return to a full 5-point scale.

Now that this suggestion has been given for a return to the 5-point scale, it is next advocated that an even more expanded scale is not only desirable but is also feasible and practiced de facto. This proposal involves expansion of the scale to as many as 15 points and is accomplished by the division of each of the present ranges into equal thirds. The upper third of each range will be identified by a "+" and the lower third by a "-." The rationale for this proposal is that the greater the number of marks, the higher is their reliability as representations of student achievement.[9]

It has often been argued that instructors are not capable of making finer distinctions among levels of achievement than is afforded by a five-point scale. One needs only to observe representative report cards to recognize that teachers almost uniformly follow the practice, at least occasionally, of appending a + or - to the mark, even though they realize that such refinements have no effect upon students' grade-point averages. They do this because they are cognizant of distinct levels of achievement within the range of a single mark, and they wish the students to also be aware of these distinctions. Errors in judgment will be made with a 15-point scale, but they will not be built into the system.

### Gustafson's Law: "The More Standards are Raised, the More They are Lowered"

It should also be noted that efforts of policy makers to raise standards by increasing grade-point-average requirements have consistently produced the reverse effect. A case in point is the typical requirement of graduate schools that candidates for advanced degrees maintain B averages in their course work. The basis for this practice probably had its origin in the fundamentally sound thesis that graduate degrees should be restricted to superior scholars. The unfortunate outcome has been that the 5-point scale has been compacted to a 3-point scale, at most, by the virtual elimination of the two lowest marks. Graduate students have come to expect that average work will be rewarded with a mark of at least B, and they are seldom disappointed. And thus it is that advanced studies and degrees are no longer restricted to superior students. In fact, it is generally easier for a below-average student to get a B in a graduate course than to get a C in an undergraduate course.

Similarly, the large increases in admissions applications that occurred during the 1960s and 1970s required these institutions to be more selective in their acceptance practices. One of the steps employed in this effort was to raise the high school grade-point-average requirements for admission. Little if any consideration has been given to the academic standards of the various high schools. It has become quite obvious that, in some schools, teachers have skewed their marks to the high end of the scale so that more of their students will qualify for admission to colleges. And, again, the net effect has been to compact the 5-point scale and to lower standards of scholarship.

## EVALUATIVE CRITERIA

Earlier reference was made to several criteria often used by physical educators in the evaluation of student achievement. It was suggested that not all of the criteria typically employed in marking systems are legitimate (legitimate is used in this context as meaning logically and does not infer legal status). The question may then be asked, "What are legitimate criteria upon which final course marks in physical education may be based?"

### Legitimate Criteria

Several aspects of the problem must be explored in order to identify these legitimate criteria. As stated earlier, many authorities have claimed that the mark must reflect student attainment of course objectives. If this is so (and the claim is supported here), then the question becomes one of determining course objectives that are legitimate. Course objectives have been developed, in most instances, in one of two ways. Some have been passed from generation to generation as traditions, with little critical examination of their appropriateness. Others have been revised periodically, in emphasis if not in particulars, and too often in reaction to local or national demand rather than as a result of a creative response to logical analysis. Regardless of the approach, and with some variations in terms or classification, program objectives have rather uniformly been and continue to be development of: 1) organic efficiency; 2) neuromuscular facility; 3) social adjustment; and 4) certain knowledge and understanding. So the problem becomes one of establishing a logical basis for determining which of these program objectives are legitimate.

One basis is whether an objective is unique to programs of physical education, i.e., is not among the charges of other school programs.[10] A second basis would demand that objectives not unique to physical education programs at least lie within their proper domain. If the four general objectives that have been listed are submitted to these tests of legitimacy, it is quite clear that objective 1, development of organic efficiency, passes both tests. Objectives 2 and 4 are not unique as stated, since other school programs may be engaged in their development. They are unique, however, in the sense that the development of neuromuscular facility is restricted to the development of motor skills that serve as bases for efficient performances in games, sports, aquatics, exercise, and dance, and that the acquisition of knowledge and understanding is directed primarily toward those associated with the aforementioned activities and with the efficient organic functioning of the body.

In the case of objective 3, development of social adjustment, the evidence in support of its legitimacy is less impressive and occasionally misleading. It is accepted that a vigorous period of exercise will reduce tension, and this is usually desirable. Still, there must be a more education-oriented purpose for an exercise period, or the purpose loses its significance in an educational program. It is also accepted that many participants in physical education programs exhibit improved social adjustment as they continue to participate. To attribute this outcome to a particular cause, however, proves difficult, and it is likely that there is a multitude of factors that play causative roles in the process. There is no evidence, to writers' knowledge, to support the claim that participation in a program of physical education, per se, produces significant social change.[11,12]

Regardless of the point of view held by the writers with respect to social adjustment, instructors, if they are not restricted unduly by a department marking plan to which they are expected to adhere, will ultimately have to resolve the question of what are legitimate evaluative criteria. Many, unfortunately, will continue to employ criteria that are neither program objectives nor even implied in the statements that describe their programs' objectives. These are what the writers choose to call "means to the end," instead of the end product itself. Among these are such factors as attendance, proper uniform, and a vague concept generally termed "attitude." This is not to say that these factors are not important, but rather that they are simply means of attaining the end. If attendance in class is important, then its importance is in its presumed contribution to the attainment of the legitimate program objectives and will be reflected by such attainment. There appears to be no virtue in attendance for attendance's sake; attendance only increases the opportunity for a student to attain the legitimate program objectives. Thus, it is the *quality* of the participation and not the *quantity* that is critical (it is not denied that quantity may affect quality, but not always directly or positively), and only the former is reflected properly in students' marks. In a similar manner, an appropriate uniform serves primarily to facilitate participation.

No person in the profession, it is presumed, would deny the desirability of a student acquiring positive attitudes toward physical education. Too frequently, however, instructors who evaluate what they call attitude are in reality evaluating student comportment. A major portion of the attitude mark is generally composed of negative elements such as gum chewing, improper language, towel snapping, failure to lock lockers, and other behaviors equally irrelevant to the attainment of legitimate program objectives. Again, it is not intended that the foregoing behaviors are to be ignored; they are not, however, aspects of program objectives *except* insofar as they influence the attainment of these objectives, in which case the influence will be measurable as an end product and not as a means to the end:

> Until physical educators become aware of the distinction between course outcomes that are merely incidental to the instruction, that are concomitants of natural processes (e.g., maturation), or are due to influences other than the instruction and those course outcomes that accrue from the intelligent planning of and effective instruction in programs whose components lie within the proper domain of physical education, it is likely that criticisms of the profession's contributions to the educative process will continue and probably increase in intensity.[13]

## METHODS OF EVALUATING STUDENT ACHIEVEMENT

Before a mark that is based upon achievement is assigned to a student, it is necessary that this achievement be assessed. This involves, on the part of the teacher, an effort to ascertain to what extent a student satisfied each of the program objectives. Factors in this evaluation include test scores, subjective judgments, in-class and homework assignments, and tournament results in individual sports.* The total process involves these steps: 1) establishment of the program objectives with the emphasis that each will receive in the instruction and, hence, in the evaluation; 2) the compilation of data related to student achievement of each of the objectives; 3) the application of the emphasis weightings to the achievement data; 4) construction of a distribution curve of these weighted data; and 5) the assignment of marks.

### Weighted Program Objectives

It is advisable for each instructor to develop a course-description sheet to be distributed to a class at the beginning of a course of instruction. On this sheet should be listed the specific course objectives, together with the relative emphasis (as indicated by a weighting factor) that each will receive. Normally, the weighting will

---

*Rational means of comparing and otherwise treating scores of a dissimilar nature are discussed in Chapter 2 in the section dealing with scale scores.

reflect the proportion of time, in class and out, that is to be devoted to a particular objective. It also follows that the amount of time devoted to a particular objective will be in almost direct proportion to its importance.

### The Compilation of Data Related to Student Achievement

It is imperative that every instructor maintain an up-to-date record of each student's accomplishments in all phases of the program. Scores earned on tests, marks for homework and class assignments, subjective evaluations of performance in activities, and results of individual tournament play are typical of the kinds of information that must be compiled for each student before the identification of relative performance can be undertaken. It is noted that some instructors hesitate to use subjective judgments in their evaluations of performance in the mistaken belief that judgments of this kind are unfair to students. To the contrary, subjective judgment is not only proper but also is often necessary, particularly for activities such as team games, gymnastics, and dance, which are not well suited to objective evaluation. After all, skills tests for these activities are inevitably validated directly or indirectly, against the criterion of expert subjective judgment. By identifying the critical elements in each kind of performance and then determining their relative contributions to the total performance, instructors can objectify their subjective ratings to a considerable extent. Of course, they must also be able to recognize and distinguish among the wide variations in performance that they are likely to observe, but this does not seem to be too much to expect from trained physical educators.

Evaluations should be recorded as close to the time of observation as is practical to reduce the retrogressive effects of elapsed time upon recollection. If possible, cumulative student-performance records should be available to permit students to know their relative status at any point during the course.

### The Application of Relative Weights to Compiled Data

Before a cumulative score can be determined for each student, it is necessary to apply weightings to each of the course elements. The procedure is not particularly difficult, and yet certain pitfalls must be recognized and avoided.

If scores earned in various kinds of performances were in the same units and were of approximately the same magnitude, the task of applying the weightings would be fairly simple. For example, both the high jump and long jump are measured in feet and inches or in meters. Performances in the long jump are greater in magnitude than those occurring in the high jump, and, if the two events are to contribute equally to the final mark, it is clear that high jump scores must be weighted more heavily. How is the appropriate weight to be calculated?

Although the method to be used is essentially the same, the basis that is to be used in calculating the weight must be established. Two possibilities are available—mean scores or maximum scores. The latter is not recommended for two reasons: 1)

It is not always possible to estimate a maximum score (how high or far is it possible for a person to leap?); and 2) even if maximum scores may be known, the maximum score may not be most representative of the typical contribution of that particular event to overall performance.

Instead, it is recommended that mean performance scores be used in calculating the relative weightings of the various elements that comprise overall course performance. Thus, if two elements, A and B, are to contribute equally, their weights should be calculated on the basis of class members' mean performance scores in each of the elements. One means for calculating the weights is illustrated here. Four program elements are considered:

| ELEMENT | WEIGHTING | MEAN SCORES (UNWEIGHTED) | SCORES ACHIEVED (UNWEIGHTED) | SCORES ACHIEVED* (WEIGHTED) |
|---------|-----------|--------------------------|------------------------------|-----------------------------|
| W | 40% | 150 | 175 | (1.6 × 175) = 280 |
| X | 30% | 140 | 140 | (1.29 × 140) = 180.6 |
| Y | 20% | 50 | 42 | (2.4 × 42) = 100.8 |
| Z | 10% | 60 | 68 | (1 × 68) = 68 |
| | | | | 629.4 |

### Construction of a Frequency Distribution of Student Scores

After total scores for all class members have been compiled, these scores are next arranged in a frequency distribution containing from 10 to 20 intervals, depending upon the number of scores in the distribution. The greater the number of scores, the greater the number of intervals. Methods are readily available for computing the mean and the standard deviation for the scores in the distribution. If greater precision is desired, these two values may be computed directly from the ungrouped scores.

### Assignment of Marks

The final step is the assignment of a mark to each class member. Errors in this step are every bit as critical as those in any of the prior four steps. As an illustration,

*The method used in calculating the *relative* weightings that are to be multiplied by the unweighted scores achieved involves an arbitrary assignment of a relative weight of 1.0 to element $Z$, the element with the smallest initial weighting. Since element $Y$ is to have twice the initial weighting of element $Z$, a relative weighting must be calculated to take into account the difference in unweighted mean scores as well as the difference in initial weighting. The formula for computing the relative weighting is:

$$\text{relative weighting} = \frac{\text{mean score for Z} \times \text{Y weighting}}{\text{mean score for Y} \times \text{Z weighting}} = \frac{60 \times 20}{50 \times 10} = 2.4$$

let us consider two students in different classes. Student X earned more points, but student Y earned a higher percentage of points possible. Which student deserves the higher mark? To answer the question, two assumptions will be made: 1) The courses are not comparable in all respects (if these were simply two sections of the same course taught by the same instructor employing the same standards, it is virtually assured that the points possible would be the same for each section); and 2) student aptitudes in the courses are not necessarily the same.

In the case of assumption 1, it is impossible to immediately identify the better achievement. First, the means of the distributions of student performances for the two courses must be computed to serve as the middle of the C ranges for the two distributions. If percentage mark ranges are to serve as the basis for assigning marks in which the distribution is to be 8½%, 24%, 35%, 24%, and 8½%, respectively, of A, B, C, D, and E, then all those whose percentile ranks fell at or below 8.5 would receive E, all those above 8.5 and at or below 32.5 would receive D, all those above 32.5 and at or below 67.5 would receive C, all those above 67.5 and at or below 91.5 would receive B, and all those above 91.5 would receive A. At this point, it may be determined which of the two students had the higher achievement, a status reflected by the respective percentile ranks. Comparisons of this kind, however, reflect only relative, and not absolute levels of achievement, and each must be considered within its own context.

Before analyzing the situation under assumption 2, some added discussion of the percentage mark ranges of assigning marks will be helpful. As previously described, percentage mark ranges become increasingly reliable as the number of scores in the distribution also increases. This fact suggests a practice that teachers would be well advised to follow: the collection of scores for all classes of a given course, taught by the same teacher year after year. These scores would be compiled on a master frequency distribution, with the mean computed anew each time that new scores were added to the distribution. At first, when the number of scores is small, the distribution's characteristics may change somewhat abruptly; but as $N$ increases, the mean and standard deviation will fluctuate very little. Once this stability has been accomplished, students will know their status at any point during the course and will also be aware of what they must achieve if they are to earn a particular mark. The major feature of this practice is that no students will receive marks to which they are not entitled, simply because the luck of the draw has placed them in a class composed primarily of high achievers or of low achievers. It should also be noted that as $N$ increases, achievement scores will tend to approach a normal distribution.

An example of assumption 2 is the situation in which two sections of a given course are taught by different instructors. If, by chance or by some selective factor, student aptitudes in the two sections are in marked contrast, this contrast is unlikely to be reflected in the distribution of student marks, since each instructor usually compiles his marks independently of the other. It is quite possible that each of the sections will have approximately the same percentage of each of the letter marks, in spite of the fact that one of the sections may contain superior students. Bender[14]

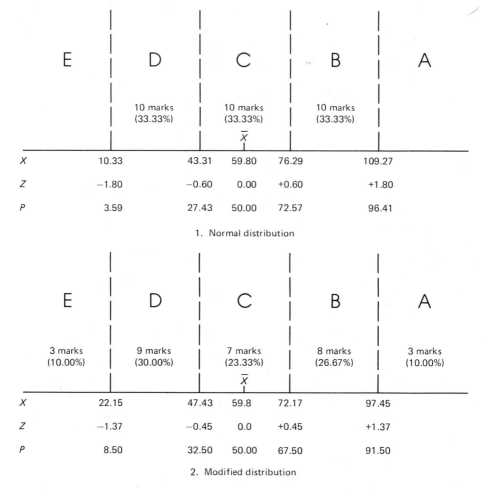

FIGURE 13.1 Two marking plans.

has proposed a solution that offers promise, especially in some situations. He suggests the use of what he calls the "Aptitude Grade Guide" in assisting in the determination of the relative aptitudes of students for particular courses of study. The basic thesis is that if a standardized test, e.g., ACT, which has been determined to predict academic success, is administered to all students, then those who score highest on the test should be expected to earn the bulk of the highest marks in the course, regardless of the section in which they happen to fall. Thus, if one section has more students with higher aptitudes, that section will be assigned more than a normal share of the higher marks. The converse also holds true.

If this guide is to be used, it becomes obvious that the criterion test must be highly related to success in the course to which it is to be applied. Whereas the ACT reasonably predicts success in some college-level courses, it has not been established to the writers' knowledge that the ACT, or any other test for that matter, consistently predicts success in high school physical education courses. In view of the broad nature of physical education course content, it remains necessary to develop a test that measures physical as well as intellectual aptitude. Bender's proposal merits admiration as a step toward the elimination of chance as an important factor in the assignment of student marks, but much work needs to be done before it would be suitable for use in physical education courses.

*Illustrations of two marking plans.*   If we once again return to Table 2-1, with the purpose of assigning marks to the 30 pupils based upon their scores on the knowledge examination, how may we proceed?

Two methods will be discussed. How each would be represented in terms of the distribution of marks is illustrated in Figure 13.1.

In examining Figure 13.1, two factors must be kept in mind: 1) the values defining the limits of each of the mark ranges is computed from the Table of Normal Probability (Table 2-5); and 2) the distribution of scores found in Table 2-1 is *not* representative of normal. Thus, the actual number of marks awarded to the 30 pupils, in terms of A, B, C, D, and E, is often strikingly different from the marks that would be expected if the scores in Table 2-1 were normally distributed. For example, in the top illustration, whereas with a set of scores sufficiently large and distributed normally, one would expect approximately 3.5% of As and Es, 24% of Bs and Ds, and 45% of Es, the 30 scores were so distributed that they yielded no As or Es and 33.33% each of Bs, Cs, and Ds. Similar disparities are found in the other illustration.

These disparities do not invalidate the theoretical principles upon which these plans are devised. If the teacher maintains a cumulative record of achievement scores, it will be found that, as the number of scores grows, the closer the scores will come to approximating a normal distribution.

## Norm-Referencing Versus Criterion-Referencing

This recommended method is based upon the principle of norm-referencing, i.e., the norm of the group determines the standards against which each member of the group will be evaluated. Some mention must, however, be made of an approach to marking, criterion-referencing, which its proponents[15,16,17] claim permits the instructor to evaluate each student independently of the performance of other students within the group. There is no question but that this claim is accurate. What is at issue is whether criterion-referenced marking and its offspring, contract grading, are appropriate methods for evaluating student attainment of program objectives. To do this, it is first necessary to describe the main characteristics of criterion-referenced marks.

One of the onerous tasks of teaching is the necessity for most teachers in most schools to assign marks at the close of various courses of instruction. Not only is the chore difficult and time-consuming, it leaves many teachers with uneasy feelings over at least some of the marks they have assigned. Often, they feel pangs of sorrow, if not regret, if they assign a low mark to a student who has tried very hard but has not achieved well, at least in comparison to his or her peers. How to resolve this dilemma and still have achievement rather than effort serve as the basis for the evaluation? Some believe the answer to be found in criterion-referenced marking. How does it work?

First, the teacher identifies the various forms of achievement that would be elements of the course objectives. For each of these, an estimate (more of this later) is made of what it is possible for students to achieve. Thus, for an A mark, the teacher rather precisely identifies (or so it is hoped) what must be done in order to be assigned that mark. In a badminton course, for example, the kinds of achievement might be identified, in various combinations, as winning $x$ percent of one's singles games in a round-robin tournament, playing $n$ singles and $m$ doubles games, learning to execute $y$ strokes, writing a paper on court etiquette, participating in a local tournament, demonstrating knowledge of rules by attaining a score of $k$ on a rules test, and serving as an official in an intramural tournament. Teachers are to be commended, of course, for making known to their students precisely what is expected of them in a given course. Course objectives that are stated vaguely tend to cause students to be uncertain and instruction to drift somewhat aimlessly.

Using the same system, achievement standards for marks of B, C, and so on would be identified in a similar manner, with the demands becoming less rigorous as the marks become lower. Once these standards are identified, it becomes possible for the student and instructor to enter into a "contract" in which the student affirms her or his intention to work toward those achievements that would merit a given mark. In this connection, Callahan found that "contract grading . . . may significantly lower the mean grade for a class."[18]

It is not inconceivable that a majority of students might enter into contracts for the same mark. It is possible, too, that most, if not all, of the contracts would be fulfilled. To the extent that this might occur, the lack of discrimination among student performances would become apparent. And, as argued earlier in this chapter, discriminating among various levels of achievement is important if marks are to have any real meaning.

In this regard, one problem faced not infrequently by teachers is the means by which failure to fulfill a given contract should be treated. If a student contracts for a mark of B but fails to fulfill the contract, should the mark be F (or whatever the lowest mark happens to be) or should the mark correspond to the specifications of some less demanding contract? In the first option, an F mark might be punitive if the student had achieved satisfactorily to fulfill the requirements of a C or D contract. But if the second option is elected, one might argue that there would be no real need for students to enter into contracts in the first place.

In summary, there are two major benefits inherent in criterion-referenced marking: 1) precise identification of course objectives and those achievements that are elements of the objectives and 2) awareness by students of what is expected of them in order to merit various marks. A third benefit, at least as perceived by teachers, is that they are "off the hook" in assigning marks, i.e., the students are aware of marks they have earned and they cannot blame the teacher for low marks. Several disadvantages to the system must also be cited. One is that many teachers have difficulty precisely identifying just what is expected in the way of student achievement[19] (in fairness, however, this disadvantage affects norm-referenced marking almost as seriously). A second is that, too often, requirements for a given mark or contract are specified in quantitative rather than qualitative terms (i.e., so much of this or so many of those—which obviates the need for the teacher to make those difficult distinctions in the quality of the achievements). A third disadvantage is the difficulty in resolving cases in which students fail to fulfill terms of a given contract to the letter.

In the final analysis, the perceptive reader will observe that since intelligent criterion-referenced marking depends upon instructors having accurate knowledge of the kinds and levels of achievement that might reasonably be expected of students in a given course, and since evidence of student performance results from adequate observation and collection of both quantitative and qualitative data, norm-referencing serves ultimately as the basis for criterion-referenced marking systems. Regardless of the system used, the critical factor is that the marks be fair representations of student achievement. As Hull has explained, ". . . it appears that strictness and conservative grading practices do not strongly influence student attitudes regarding fairness. It is instead perceptions of inconsistency which are most critical."[20]

### Implications of Title IX

Title IX of the Education Amendments Act of 1972 (with which compliance was mandated at varying intervals depending upon the level of the institution) provided that educational institutions, public or private, that receive federal funds may not discriminate on the basis of sex. Although several classes of institutions were exempted from the provision, its interpretation by the Department of Health, Education, and Welfare* was sufficiently expansive to include nearly all educational institutions in the country.

One of the immediate effects, due at times to misinterpretation of the Act, was to open most physical education courses to coeducational enrollment. Concurrently, single-sex sections of courses in most activities, body contact sports and activities excepted, began to disappear from the nation's gymnasiums, pools, playfields, and dance studios.

Although there was considerable hand wringing on the parts of physical education faculties of both sexes, the transition to almost exclusively coeducational sections has proceeded smoothly and with little if any negative effect upon the quality of the educational experience provided to physical education students.

For a period of time immediately after enactment of Title IX, a number of articles analyzing the potential effects, as well as predictions of the means by which the transition would likely proceed, were to be found in professional journals. In-

*Now called Department of Health and Human Services.

terestingly, scant attention was paid to the implications of Title IX for evaluating student achievement of course objectives as represented by course marks. Why this was so is uncertain, but a possible explanation is that initial concerns, at least, focused upon the more apparent problems associated with instruction; class management; purchase and utilization of equipment; class and facilities scheduling; and faculty rights and prerogatives related to salaries, opportunities, workloads, and assignments. Or it simply may have been that potential problems connected with marking were not recognized. What are some of these problems? Although a variety of classifications of problems could perhaps be identified, the central issue centers on the performance capability disparity, actual or perceived, biologically determined or culturally induced, between females and males.

What is known about this disparity? Research findings have not always been in agreement with respect to differences in motor ability between the sexes, particularly prior to adolescence. It appears clear that males at maturation are stronger, but this does not always hold true among children. Regardless of the extent or nature of these differences, it seems clear that separate performance norms for males and females would violate the principle of nondiscrimination mandated in Title IX. On the other hand, if students are evaluated on the basis of a single set of norms, it seems clear that, on that criterion at least and particularly during and after adolescence, males would achieve a greater proportion of the higher marks.

*One possible solution to the dilemma.* As suggested by Cheffers,[21] psychophysiological indices might be used, instead of the male-female dichotomy, in developing norms. Females under this system would be compared to males as well as females whose capabilities generated similar index scores. Similar systems have been utilized in several sports activities for many years for purposes of classifications, e.g., weight divisions in boxing and wrestling and, in some areas, in football; height as a basis for dividing basketball teams; and playing ability as a means of creating different levels of play such as A, B, and C, or open and novice, or varsity and junior varsity.

If such a system of psychophysiological indices is used, it seems critical in assigning marks to also identify the classification within which a particular mark can be judged. The dilemma is not unlike that presented in the evaluation of achievement in tasks requiring intellectual abilities. Just as an A earned by a third grader in mathematics does not represent the same level of achievement represented by an A earned by a sixth grader in mathematics, so should we not expect the third grader to do as well as the sixth grader in those tasks that require physical abilities of one kind or another. But we normally know in each instance that the As represent performances at different levels of complexity and, hence, are not the same A. But within a given class in mathematics, we should not award a mark of A to a student who is simply the best of those students whose academic abilities would limit their performances to the D level. Similarly, the authors believe, only those differences that result from differences in size or maturation level should be taken into account when awarding marks in courses involving physical performances, and, when those factors are considered, this fact should be indicated on the report card.

## SOME ERRORS IN ASSIGNMENT
## OF MARKS

In spite of the care exercised by teachers in devising marking plans that will accurately reflect student achievement of course objectives, it is still possible for errors to occur. Several examples are given here.

Once the relative weightings for each of the course elements have been determined and provisions made to apply these weightings in the computation of the final mark, it is imperative that no extraneous factor be permitted to affect the final mark. This statement seems self-evident, and yet countless examples of violations of this precept are well known to students, to teachers, and even to parents.

### Automatic Reduction of the Final Mark

One common violation is the automatic reduction of a student's mark, for example from a B to a C, if she or he has exceeded a predetermined number of unexcused absences. First, the distinction between excused and unexcused absences in terms of their effect upon the attainment of program objectives is nonexistent. There are other school officers charged with the responsibility for dealing with truancy, and the teacher should not be concerned from the standpoint of the course mark. More to the point, however, is that if the automatic-reduction approach is used, it is apparent that the number of unexcused absences may become the overriding factor in the determination of the final mark. Arguments have previously been made in this chapter against the use of attendance as a factor in course marks, but, if it must be used, its relative contribution to the mark must be resolved (as reflected in its weighting) and applied as for all other weighted elements.

### Inconsistent Conversion Scales

A second common error, which will be discussed briefly, is the use of inconsistent scales in the conversion of letter marks to numerical values and, thence, back to letter marks. If, for example, a C earned in some aspect of the course is assigned a point value of 2.0, then upon later reconversion to the letter system, 2.0 must serve as the midpoint of the C range. In too many conversion scales, the midpoints of the various mark ranges deviate from the numerical values assigned to the respective letter marks, and errors are thus introduced.

### Adjustment of Borderline Marks

A third error is a tendency of many teachers, after total points have been computed, to adjust borderline marks upward and thereby skew the curve to the high side. Seldom, if ever, are borderline students awarded marks below those they earn, but often they are given a "break" by the teacher, who awards them the next higher mark because they were close. Adjustments in either direction are equally erroneous and serve to nullify much of the effort put into devising and executing a rational marking system.

One final important note. No matter how important the evaluative process is, it must always remain subservient to the instructional phase of the program. It is far better to have an excellent program of instruction inadequately evaluated than to have a poorly planned and instructed program perfectly evaluated. There is no reason, of course, why both instruction and evaluation should not be of the finest quality. Normally, if one is of high quality, so is the other.

## *BIBLIOGRAPHY*

BENDER, HARRY. "From Anarchy Toward Order in Grading." *The Tower,* 1 (Spring 1964), 33–53.

BOYD, CLIFFORD A. "A Philosophy of Assigning Grades in Physical Education Classes." *The Physical Educator,* 14 (May 1957), 64–65.

BROER, MARION R. "Are Our Physical Education Grades Fair?" *Journal of Health, Physical Education and Recreation,* 30 (March 1959), 27, 84.

BUCHER, CHARLES A. *Administration of School Health and Physical Education Programs,* 2nd ed. St. Louis: C.V. Mosby, 1958.

CALLAHAN, RICHARD C. "Contract Grading and Student Performance." *Journal of Instructional Psychology,* 6 (Summer 1979), 3–7.

CHEFFERS, JOHN. "Teacher Behavior and Attitudes: Is Change Needed?" *Briefings 1, Title IX: Moving Toward Implementation,* The National Association for the Physical Education of College Women and the National College Physical Education Association for Men, 1975.

CLARK, EDWARD L. "Reliability of Grade-Point Averages." *Journal of Educational Research,* 57 (April 1964), 428–430.

ETZIONI, AMATAI. "Human Beings Are Not Very Easy to Change After All." *Saturday Review,* (June 3, 1972), 45–47.

FRALEIGH, WARREN P. and WILLIAM F. GUSTAFSON. "Can We Defend Required Programs?" *Journal of Health, Physical Education and Recreation,* 35 (February 1964), 32.

GUSTAFSON, WILLIAM F. "Are Grades Losing Their Significance?" *The Physical Educator,* 15 (October 1958), 93–94.

_____. "A Look at Evaluative Criteria in Physical Education." *The Physical Educator,* 20 (December 1963), 172–73.

HULL, RÅY. "Fairness in Grading: Perceptions of Junior High School Students." *The Clearing House,* 58 (March 1980), 340–43.

LADAS, HAROLD. "Grades: Standardizing the Unstandard Standard." *Phi Delta Kappan,* LVI (November 1974), 185–87.

MORIARTY, MARY J. "How Shall We Grade Them?" *Journal of Health, Physical Education, and Recreation,* 25 (January 1954), 27, 55.

PARTIN, RONALD L. "Multiple Option Grade Contracts." *The Clearing House,* 53 (November 1979), 133–35.

POSTMAN, NEIL. "A D+ for Mr. Ladas." *Phi Delta Kappan,* LVI (November 1974), 187–88.

SHEA, JOHN B. "The Pass-Fail Option and Physical Education." *Journal of Health, Physical Education and Recreation,* 42 (May 1971), 19–20.

VOLTMER, EDWARD F. and ARTHUR A. ESSLINGER. *The Organization and Administration of Physical Education,* 3rd ed. New York: Appleton-Century-Crofts, Inc., 1958.

*Webster's Collegiate Dictionary,* 5th ed. Springfield, Mass.: G. & C. Merriam Co., 1945.

## SUGGESTED READINGS

BOOKWALTER, KARL W. "Marking in Physical Education." *Journal of Health and Physical Education.* 7 (January 1936), 16–19.

BOYD, CLIFFORD and I.F. WAGLOW. "The Individual Achievement Profile." *The Physical Educator*, 21 (October 1964), 117–118.

BREIT, NICK. "Grading in Physical Education—A Philosophical Problem." *CAHPER Journal*, 31 (January-February 1969), 6, 12.

CALLON, RUTH. "Marks or Misjudgments?" *The Physical Educator*, 12 (December 1955), 125.

COYKENDALL, R., et al. "Grading Guidelines in Physical Education." *CAHPER Journal*, 26 (November-December 1963), 7.

CUMMINGS, ROBERT H. "Rewards for Work." *Journal of Physical Education and Recreation*, 46 (October 1975), 31.

DRATZ, JOHN. "Grading in Physical Education." *The Physical Educator*, 14 (March 1957), 14.

FLEMING, THOMAS J. "The Mess in Marks." *This Week Magazine,* (September 25, 1966), 4.

GRIGSON, W.H. "The Physical Education Report Card." *The Physical Educator*, 16 (May 1959), 57–61.

HALLADAY, D.W. "Marking in College Physical Education Activities." *Research Quarterly*, 19 (October 1948), 178–184.

JACKSON, E.L. "The Improvement of Marking in College Physical Education." *The Physical Educator*, 14 (December 1957), 140–142.

JENSEN, CLAYNE. "Improve Your Marking System in Physical Education." *The Physical Educator*, 19 (October 1962), 97–98.

KIRBY, RONALD F. "Improvement: A Factor in Grading." *The Physical Educator*, 27 (December 1970), 150–151.

LIBA, MARIE R., and JOHN W. LOY. "Some Comments on Grading." *The Physical Educator,* 22 (December 1965), 158–160.

MARSH, RICHARD L. "Physically Educated—What it Will Mean for Tomorrow's High School Student." *Journal of Physical Education and Recreation*, 49 (January 1978), 50.

MASSEY, BENJAMIN H. "The Use of T-Scores in Physical Education." *The Physical Educator*, 10 (March 1953), 20–21.

McCRAW, LYNN W. "A Comparison of Methods of Measuring Improvement." *Research Quarterly*, 22 (May 1951), 191–200.

_____. "Principles and Practices for Assigning Grades in Physical Education." *Journal of Health, Physical Education, and Recreation*, 35 (February 1964), 24–25.

MELOGRANO, VINCENT J. "Evaluating Affective Objectives in Physical Education." *The Physical Educator*, 31 (March 1974), 8–12.

MILLER, K.D. "A Plea for the Standard Score in Physical Education." *The Physical Educator*, 8 (May 1951), 49.

MONTOYE, HENRY J. "A Plea for the Percentile Rank in Physical Education." *The Physical Educator*, 8 (December 1951), 112.

SMITH, B.C., and H.A. LERCH. "Contract Grading." *The Physical Educator.* 29 (May 1972), 80–82.

SOLLEY, W.H., H. FABRICIUS, and R.N. SINGER. "Grading Procedures in Physical Education." *Journal of Health, Physical Education, and Recreation*, 38 (May 1967), 34–39.

TRAVERS, R.M.W., and N.E. GRONLUND. "The Meaning of Marks." *Journal of Higher Education*, 21 (October 1950), 369.

TURNER, EDWARD T. "A Creative Evaluation Experiment." *Journal of Physical Education and Recreation*, 46 (November-December 1975), 24–25.

WAGLOW, I.F.   "Marking in Physical Education." *Journal of Health, Physical Education, and Recreation,* 25 (May 1954), 48.

——— and A.C. MOORE.   "The Comparison of Marks and Marking Systems." *The Physical Educator,* 13 (March 1956), 22.

——— and C.A. BOYD.   "Scoring Systems." *The Physical Educator,* 19 (March 1962), 15–16.

WATTAN, RICHARD, and JOHN R. MAGEL.   "Let the Students Grade the Course." *Journal of Health, Physical Education, and Recreation,* 42 (February 1971), 39–40.

WEBER, L.J. and T.L. PAUL.   "Approaches to Grading in Physical Education." *The Physical Educator,* 28 (May 1971), 59–62.

WICKSTROM, RALPH.   "Ruminations on Grading." *The Physical Educator,* 30 (October 1973), 118–121.

# APPENDIX A
# SAMPLE COMPUTER
# FORMS

## EXAMPLE OF A COMBINATION RESEARCH FORM AND CODING SHEET

Project:_____  Name of Coder: ___Lucas___  Col.

Subject Name: ___Sonya Smith___  Subject I.D. ___235___  **235**

Operation Date: ___1–10–80___                                 1-3
                                                              **01080**
                                                              4-9

### Body Part Injured

| | |
|---|---|
| 1) Hip . . . . . . . . . . . . . .( ) | 6) Foot. . . . . . . . . . . . . .( ) |
| 2) Thigh . . . . . . . . . . . . .( ) | 7) Head. . . . . . . . . . . . . .( ) **05** |
| 3) Knee . . . . . . . . . . . . .( ) | 8) Neck. . . . . . . . . . . . . .( ) 10-11 |
| 4) Foreleg. . . . . . . . . . . .( ) | 9) Chest . . . . . . . . . . . . .( ) |
| 5) Ankle. . . . . . . . . . . .(✓) | 10) Abdomen . . . . . . . . . .( ) |

### Tissue Involved

1) Muscle . . . . . . . . . . . .( )
2) Bone . . . . . . . . . . . . .( )                  **5**
3) Skin. . . . . . . . . . . . . .( )                 12
4) Tendon. . . . . . . . . . . .( )
5) Ligament. . . . . . . . . . .(✓)

### Type of Injury

1) Strain. . . . . . . . . . . . .(✓)
2) Bruise. . . . . . . . . . . . .( )                  **1**
3) Fracture . . . . . . . . . . .( )                  13
4) Dislocation . . . . . . . . .( )
5) Abrasion. . . . . . . . . . .( )

### Explanation

The data to be keypunched are organized in a column to the right of the form (handwritten numbers). Below each line appears the computer-card columns into which the handwritten numbers are to be keypunched. If, for example, body weight is to be recorded and can be either two digits (less than 100 pounds/kilograms) or three digits (more than 100 pounds/kilograms), three columns must be allowed for the number. Values less than 100 should either be written with a leading zero (e.g., 095) or right-justified, i.e., a blank followed by 95.

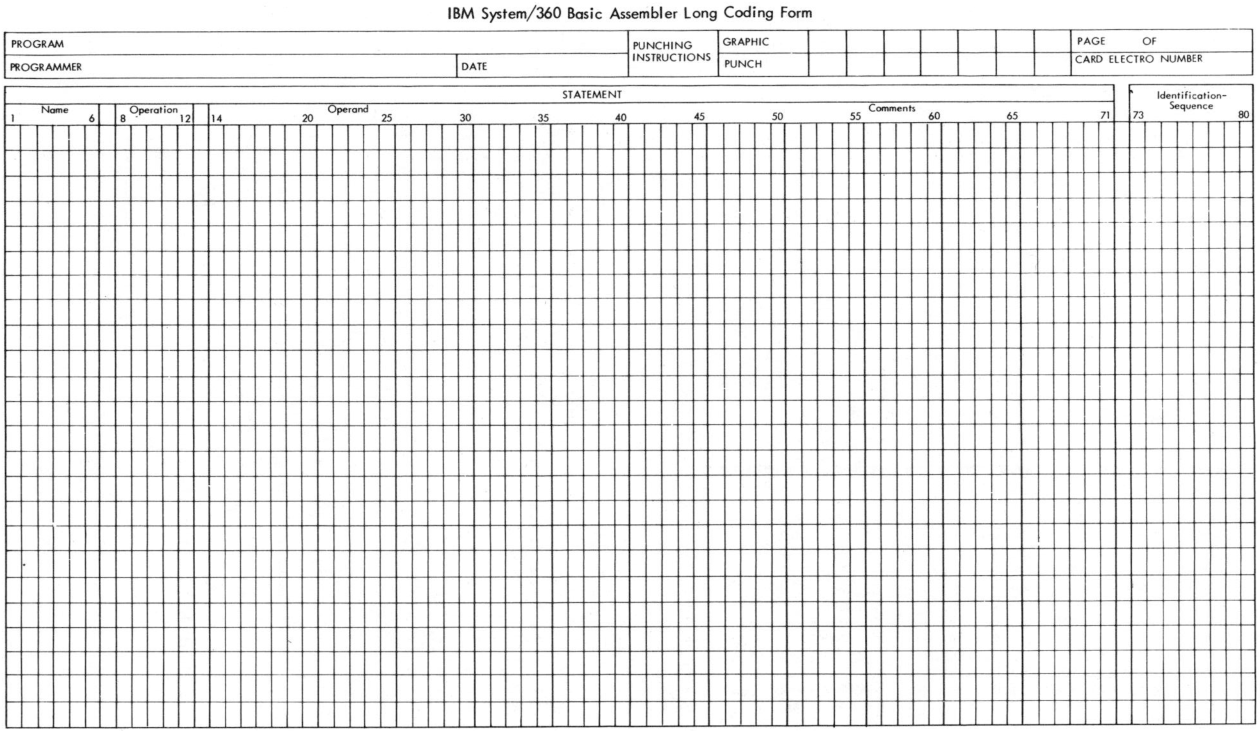

IBM System/360 Basic Assembler Long Coding Form

| PROGRAM | | PUNCHING INSTRUCTIONS | GRAPHIC | PAGE OF |
| --- | --- | --- | --- | --- |
| PROGRAMMER | DATE | | PUNCH | CARD ELECTRO NUMBER |

STATEMENT

Name 1 6 | Operation 8 12 | 14 20 Operand 25 30 35 40 45 50 55 Comments 60 65 71 | Identification-Sequence 73 80

**FIGURE A.1** Example of a Coding Sheet. This form contains lines divided into 80 columns; each column on the form represents one computer-card column. The values of each variable are recorded in a fixed position (set of columns on the form). Each line is to be keypunched as a computer card.

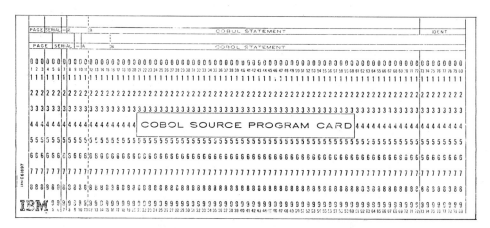

FIGURE A.2  Example of an Optical Scanner Form.

FIGURE A.3  Standard IBM Computer Punch Card.

336

# APPENDIX B
# OVERVIEW OF THE SPSS PROCESS

SPSS processes a sequence of user-prepared control cards. It is important that the user arrange the control cards in the appropriate sequence. The control cards must be prepared in a particular format so that the SPSS system will recognize them.

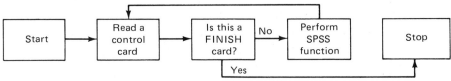

SPSS control cards serve two kinds of functions. They provide SPSS with descriptions of the information required for *processing* user data, or they instruct SPSS to *execute* the specified statistical computations.

All SPSS control cards consist of two fields. The *control* field, which is punched in card columns 1 to 15, consists of the control word or words that identify the card to the system. The *specification* field occupies card columns 16 to 80 of the first and all subsequent cards necessary to complete the parameters required by that particular control field.

*Names* are mnemonics supplied by the user. Names are used to refer to files, subfiles, and variables. Names are limited to eight characters, and the first character must be an alphabetic letter. They may be composed of letters and/or numbers.

A *codebook* is a document prepared by the user to describe each variable that occurs within the study. This description includes the meaning of the variable, the code used and its meaning, where the variable occurs in the record, and the name that is used to reference the variable.

## SEQUENCE OF CONTROL CARDS

### Variable List

Each variable in the SPSS file must be referred to by a unique variable name. The VARIABLE LIST control card enters the variable names into SPSS. The variables on this control card must be in the same order as the variables on the data card.

Format: VARIABLE LIST    list
           VARIABLE LIST    COMCODE, MEDSCH. . . . , PARTROLE
           VARIABLE LIST    VAR001 to VAR005

### Input Medium

The INPUT MEDIUM control card specifies the type of input from which the user's data will be entered (card, tape, disk, etc.).

Format: INPUT MEDIUM    type
           INPUT MEDIUM    CARD

### Input Format

Variables used by SPSS must be described to the system. The INPUT FOR-MAT control card specifies whether the data are organized in fixed-column or free-field format, whether the variables are numeric or alphanumeric, and the column location of each of the variables.

> Format: INPUT FORMAT    organization (format)
> INPUT FORMAT    FIXED (F3.0, F2.0, F4.1 . . . . 5F1.0)

### N of Cases

The N OF CASES card informs the SPSS system of the number of cases in the user's data file. If the data file is structured into subfiles, the number of cases in each subfile is placed in the specification field.

> Format: N OF CASES    number of cases
> N OF CASES    64

### Task-Definition Cards

The TASK DEFINITION cards allow the user to specify which calculations are to be performed by SPSS on the user's data.

> Format: control word    variables
> CODEBOOK    LIFE, TIME, NEWSWEEK, READDIG
> CODEBOOK    ALL

### Read Input Data

The READ INPUT DATA card instructs the system to begin reading the input data.

> Format: READ INPUT DATA    (this control card has no specification field)

### Finish

The FINISH card terminates the SPSS run.

> Format: FINISH    (this control card has no specification field)

## SYSTEM CARDS

This computer system requires certain system control cards in addition to the SPSS control cards. The following card-deck set up must be used when submitting an SPSS job. The first three lines represent the information to be punched on the three system control cards.

$JOB,acct.no,name
$RAT,841/2
$SPSS,c,v      c = number of cases;  v = number of variables
SPSS CONTROL CARDS (in sequence outlined above)
DATA CARDS
FINISH

## ADDITIONAL TASK
## DEFINITION CARDS

The following task definition cards are optional:

### Run Name

The RUN NAME card titles the printed output of the SPSS run.

Format: RUN NAME      label
          RUN NAME      SAMPLE SPSS RUN

### Var Label

SPSS permits the user to use an extended label for any or all of the variables
in the data file. The VAR LABEL control card is used to assign the variable label.

Format: VAR LABEL      variable name, variable label/variable name,
                        variable label/. . . , variable name, variable label

         VAR LABEL      COMCODE, COMMUNITY CODE? PARTROLE,
                        ACTUAL ROLE OF PARTIES ELEC HEAD

### Value Labels

The values associated with each variable may also be labeled. If the VALUE
LABELS control card is used, the variable values will automatically appear on the
printed output.

Format: VALUE LABELS      variable name (value$_1$)label$_1$ (value$_2$)label$_2$ . . .
                        (value$_n$)label$_n$/variable name(value)label

        VALUE LABELS      HRS WORK (1) LESS THAN 5 HRS (2)
                        6-10 hrs (3)11-20 HRS (4)21-30 HRS (5)
                        31-40 HRS (6)OVER 40 HOURS (7)MISSING
                        (8)INAPPLICABLE (9)NA

### Missing Values

If complete information is not available for all variables within all the cases, it might be beneficial to use the **MISSING VALUES** card in processing the data through **SPSS**. The user specifies the missing value for each variable.

Format: MISSING VALUES    variable name (missing values)
        MISSING VALUES    HRSWORK (7, 8, 9)
        MISSING VALUES    TEST SCORE (0)/MEDFIND, POP60,
                           POPLAT, SPISOL(0)

# APPENDIX C
# EQUIVALENT PERCENTILE AND STANDARD (Z) SCORES

| S.S. | %TILE | S.S. | %TILE | S.S. | %TILE | S.S. | %TILE |
|------|-------|------|-------|------|-------|------|-------|
| 100 | 99.86 | 70 | 88.49 | 40 | 27.43 | 10 | .82 |
| 99 | 99.84 | 69 | 87.29 | 39 | 25.46 | 9 | .69 |
| 98 | 99.80 | 68 | 85.99 | 38 | 23.58 | 8 | .59 |
| 97 | 99.76 | 67 | 84.61 | 37 | 21.77 | 7 | .49 |
| 96 | 99.71 | 66 | 83.15 | 36 | 20.05 | 6 | .41 |
| 95 | 99.65 | 65 | 81.59 | 35 | 18.41 | 5 | .35 |
| 94 | 99.59 | 64 | 79.95 | 34 | 16.85 | 4 | .29 |
| 93 | 99.51 | 63 | 77.23 | 33 | 15.39 | 3 | .24 |
| 92 | 99.41 | 62 | 76.42 | 32 | 14.01 | 2 | .20 |
| 91 | 99.31 | 61 | 74.54 | 31 | 12.71 | 1 | .16 |
| 90 | 99.18 | 60 | 72.57 | 30 | 11.51 | 0 | .14 |
| 89 | 99.04 | 59 | 70.54 | 29 | 10.38 | | |
| 88 | 98.87 | 58 | 68.44 | 28 | 9.34 | | |
| 87 | 98.68 | 57 | 66.28 | 27 | 8.38 | | |
| 86 | 98.46 | 56 | 64.06 | 26 | 7.49 | | |
| 85 | 98.21 | 55 | 61.79 | 25 | 6.68 | | |
| 84 | 97.93 | 54 | 59.48 | 24 | 5.94 | | |
| 83 | 97.61 | 53 | 57.14 | 23 | 5.26 | | |
| 82 | 97.26 | 52 | 54.78 | 22 | 4.65 | | |
| 81 | 96.86 | 51 | 52.39 | 21 | 4.09 | | |
| 80 | 96.41 | 50 | 50.00 | 20 | 3.59 | | |
| 79 | 95.91 | 49 | 47.61 | 19 | 3.14 | | |
| 78 | 95.25 | 48 | 45.22 | 18 | 2.74 | | |
| 77 | 94.74 | 47 | 42.86 | 17 | 2.39 | | |
| 76 | 94.06 | 46 | 40.52 | 16 | 2.07 | | |
| 75 | 93.32 | 45 | 38.21 | 15 | 1.79 | | |
| 74 | 92.51 | 44 | 35.94 | 14 | 1.54 | | |
| 73 | 91.62 | 43 | 33.72 | 13 | 1.32 | | |
| 72 | 90.66 | 42 | 31.56 | 12 | 1.13 | | |
| 71 | 89.62 | 41 | 29.46 | 11 | .96 | | |

# APPENDIX D
# SYMBOLS FOR READING TABLES IN CHAPTERS 8–10

SH = split-halves reliability method

T-R = test-retest reliability method

AV = analysis of variance reliability method

IVC = internal validity criterion used

EVC = external validity criterion used

lit. = the author did not compute realibility coefficients but, rather, accepted coefficients published by other authors.

log. = logic or content validity. The author felt no need to obtain statistical validity since the test or test item was to be used as an end in itself rather than as a predictor of a more complex performance.

# NOTES

## CHAPTER TWO

[1]H. Scheffé, "Statistical Inference in the Non-Parametrics Case," *Annals of Mathematical Statistics,* 14 (1943), 305–32.

[2]Herbert Simon, "Designing Organizations for an Information Rich World," in *Computers, Communications, and the Public Interest,* Martin Greenberger, ed. (Baltimore: The Johns Hopkins Press, 1971).

[3]Anderson R. Molnar, "The Next Great Crisis in American Education: Computer Literacy," *EDUCOM,* 14 (Spring 1979), 2–6.

[4]Roy J. Shephard, *Men at Work: Applications of Ergonomics to Performance and Design* (Springfield, IL: Charles C. Thomas, 1974).

[5]*Ibid.*

[6]S.S. Stevens, "On the Theory of Scales of Measurement," *Science,* 103 (June 1946), 677–80.

[7]*BMDP Biomedical Computer Programs, P Series,* W.J. Dixon, ed. (Berkeley: University of California Press, 1977), pp. 47–68. Note: Programs were developed at the Health Sciences Computing Facility–UCLA–sponsored by NIH Special Research Resources Grant RR-3.

[8]*Ibid.*

[9]*Ibid.*

[10]N. Nie et al., *SPSS, Statistical Package for the Social Sciences,* 2nd ed. (New York: McGraw-Hill, 1975).

## CHAPTER THREE

[1]For one example, see Paul Raffaele, "Chinese Train to be the World's Best Athletes," *Parade,* July 23, 1977, pp. 14, 16.

[2]William F. Gustafson, "The Graduate Record Examination and the Advanced Physical Education Test as Predictors of Success in a Master's Degree Program," *70th Proceedings, National College Physical Education Association for Men,* (1966), 96–98.

[3]Ted A. Baumgartner, "The Application of the Spearman-Brown Prophecy Formula When Applied to Physical Performance Tests," *Res. Quart.,* 39 (December 1968), 847–56.

[4]For analysis of the underlying theories upon which reliability formulas have been established, the reader is advised to consult Margaret J. Safrit, ed., *Reliability Theory* (Washington, D.C.: AAHPERD Publications, 1976).

## CHAPTER FOUR

[1]John Brock, Walter A. Cox and Erastus W. Pennock, "Motor Fitness," *Res. Quart.,* Supplement, 12 (May 1941), 407–15.

[2]Charles H. McCloy, *Tests and Measurements in Health and Physical Education* (New York: F.S. Crofts and Co., 1945), pp. 122–33.

[3]Thomas K. Cureton, *Physical Fitness Appraisal and Guidance* (St. Louis: C.V. Mosby Co., 1947), pp. 13–28.

[4]*Measurement and Evaluation Materials in Health, Physical Education and Recreation* (Washington, D.C.: AAHPERD Publications, 1950), pp. 53–54, 59.

[5]Edwin A. Fleishman, *The Structure and Measurement of Physical Fitness* (Englewood Cliffs, N.J.: Prentice-Hall, Inc., 1964), pp. 3–15.

[6]B. Fruchter, *Introduction to Factor Analysis* (Princeton, NJ: D. Van Nostrand Co., Inc., 1954).

[7]H. Harmon, *Modern Factor Analysis* (Chicago: University of Chicago Press, 1960).

[8]George B. Pearson and Jacqueline K. Whalin, *Reference Index of the Research Quar-*

*terly (1930-1960),* (San Diego, CA: All American Productions and Publishers, 1964), pp. 518-21.

[9]Cureton, *Appraisal and Guidance,* pp. 391-410.

[10]Darrel Latham, "Factor Analysis of the Illinois 14-Item Motor Fitness Screen Test," (unpublished master's thesis, University of Illinois, 1945).

[11]J.W. Seaver, *Anthropometry and Physical Education* (New Haven: A.O. Dorman Co., 1896), p. 205.

[12]J.F. Bovard and F.W. Cozens, *Tests and Measurements in Physical Education,* 2nd ed. (Philadelphia: W.B. Saunders Co., 1938), pp. 74-79.

[13]D.A. Sargent, "Intercollegiate Strength Tests," *American Physical Education Review,* 2 (December 1897), 216.

[14]D.A. Sargent, "Twenty Years of Progress in Efficiency Testing," *American Physical Education Review,* 18 (October 1918), 452.

[15]Frederick Rand Rogers, *Physical Capacity Tests in the Administration of Physical Education* (New York: Bureau of Publications, Teachers College, Columbia University, 1925), Contributions to Education, No. 173.

[16]Paul A. Hunsicker and Richard L. Donnelly, "Instruments to Measure Strength," *Res. Quart.,* 26 (December 1955), 408.

[17]H. Harrison Clarke and David H. Clarke, *Developmental and Adapted Physical Education* (Englewood Cliffs, N.J.: Prentice-Hall, Inc., 1963), pp. 73-96.

[18]H. Harrison Clarke, *Muscular Strength and Endurance in Man* (Englewood Cliffs, N.J.: Prentice-Hall, Inc., 1966), Chapter 2.

[19]Richard A. Berger, "Classification of Students on the Basis of Strength," *Res. Quart.,* 35 (December 1963), 514-15.

[20]Barry L. Johnson and Jack K. Nelson, *Practical Measurements for Evaluation in Physical Education* (Minneapolis, Minn.: Burgess Publishing Co., 1969), pp. 242-63.

[21]Helen Hislop and James J. Perrine, "The Isokinetic Concept of Exercise," *Jour. of the Amer. Phys. Ther. Assoc.,* 47 (February 1967), 114-17.

[22]Rogers, *Physical Capacity Tests.*

[23]Edgar W. Everts and Gordon J. Hathaway, "The Use of the Belt to Measure Leg Strength Improves the Administration of Physical Tests," *Res. Quart.,* 9 (October 1938), 62.

[24]Aileen Carpenter, "A Study of the Angles of Measurement of the Leg Lift," *Res. Quart.,* 9 (October 1938), 70-72.

[25]Rogers, *Physical Capacity Tests,* p. 32.

[26]Eleanor Metheny, "Breathing Capacity and Grip Strength of Pre-School Children," *University of Iowa Studies in Child Welfare,* 18 (1940), pp. 114-15.

[27]Thomas K. Cureton, "Improving the Physical Fitness of Youth," *Monographs of the Society for Research in Child Development,* Serial No. 95, 29, no. 4 (1964), p. 171.

[28]Edwin A. Fleishman, *Examiner's Manual for the Basic Fitness Tests* (Englewood Cliffs, N.J.: Prentice-Hall, Inc., 1964), p. 24.

[29]Cureton, *Appraisal and Guidance,* pp. 366-71.

[30]Thomas K. Cureton and Leonard A. Larson, "Strength as an Approach to Physical Fitness," *Res. Quart.,* Supplement, 12 (May 1941), 391-406.

[31]Fleishman, *Structure and Measurement of Physical Fitness,* p. 65.

[32]McCloy, *Tests and Measurement,* pp. 19-37.

[33]Cureton, *Appraisal and Guidance,* p. 385.

[34]Cureton, "Improving the Physical Fitness of Youth," pp. 183-86.

[35]Fleishman, *Examiner's Manual,* p. 53.

[36]Clarke and Clarke, *Developmental and Adapted Physical Education,* pp. 73-97.

[37]H. Harrison Clarke, "Objective Strength Tests of Affected Muscle Groups Involved in Orthopedic Disabilities," *Res. Quart.,* 19 (May 1948), 118-47.

[38]H. Harrison Clarke, *Cable Tension Strength Tests* (Springfield, Mass.: Stuart E. Murphy, 1953).

[39] Clarke, "Objective Strength Tests of Affected Muscle Groups Involved in Orthopedic Disabilities," pp. 118–47.

[40] H. Harrison Clarke, *Muscular Strength and Endurance in Man* (Englewood Cliffs, N.J.: Prentice-Hall, Inc., 1966), pp. 141–72.

[41] Rogers, *Physical Capacity Tests.*

[42] H. Harrison Clarke and Richard A. Munroe, *Test Manual: Oregon Cable-tension Strength Batteries for Boys and Girls from Fourth Grade Through College* (Eugene, OR: Microform Publications in Health, Physical Education and Recreation, University of Oregon, 1970).

[43] Richard A. Berger, "Determination of the Resistance Load for 1-Rm and 10-Rm," *Journ. of the Assoc. for Phys. and Mental Rehab.,* 15 (July-August 1961), 108–10 and 117.

[44] Richard A. Berger, "Classification of Students on the Basis of Strength," *Res. Quart.,* 34 (December 1963), 514–15.

[45] John P. O'Shea, *Scientific Principles and Methods of Strength Fitness* (Reading, Mass.: Addison-Wesley Publishing Co., 1969), p. 22.

[46] Barry L. Johnson and Jack K. Nelson, *Practical Measurements for Evaluation in Physical Education* (Minneapolis, Minn.: Burgess Publishing Co., 1969), pp. 242–55.

[47] Berger, "Classification of Students," pp. 514–15.

[48] Johnson and Nelson, *Practical Measurements for Evaluation,* pp. 242–55.

[49] Berger, "Determination of the Resistance Load," pp. 108–10 and 117.

[50] G. Lawrence Rarick, "An Analysis of the Speed Factor in Simple Athletic Activities," *Res. Quart.,* 8 (December 1937), 89–105.

[51] K.B. Start, R.K. Gray, D.J. Glencross and A. Walsh, "A Factorial Investigation of Power, Speed, Isometric Strength and Anthropometric Measures in the Lower Limb," *Res. Quart.,* 37 (December 1966), 553–59.

[52] Johnson and Nelson, *Practical Measurements for Evaluation,* p. 80.

[53] D.A. Sargent, "The Physical Test of Man," *American Physical Education Review,* 26 (April 1921), 188–94.

[54] L.W. Sargent, "Some Observations in the Sargent Test of Neuromuscular Efficiency," *American Phys. Ed. Rev.,* 29 (1924), 47–56.

[55] B.E. Phillips, "The JCR Test," *Res. Quart.,* 18 (March 1947), 12–19.

[56] Fleishman, *Structure and Measurement of Physical Fitness,* p. 48.

[57] D.B. Van Dalen, "New Studies in the Sargent Jump," *Res. Quart.,* 11 (May 1940), 112–15.

[58] Karl W. Bookwalter, "Test Manual for Indiana University Motor Fitness Indices for High School and College Men," *Res. Quart.,* 14 (December 1943), 356–65.

[59] D.J. Glencross, "The Nature of the Vertical Jump Test and the Standing Broad Jump," *Res. Quart.,* 37 (October 1966), 353–59.

[60] Fleishman, *Structure and Measurement of Physical Fitness,* p. 59.

[61] Cureton, "Improving the Physical Fitness of Youth," p. 172.

[62] McCloy, *Tests and Measurements,* pp. 59–61.

[63] Glencross, "The Nature of the Vertical Jump Test," pp. 353–59.

[64] D.J. Glencross, "The Power Lever: An Instrument for Measuring Muscle Power," *Res. Quart.,* 37 (May 1966), 202–10.

[65] N.P. Neilson and Frederick W. Cozens, *Achievement Scales in Physical Education Activities for Boys and Girls in Elementary and Junior High Schools* (Sacramento, CA: California State Department of Education, 1934), pp. 54–55; 118–19.

[66] Frederick W. Cozens, Hazel J. Cubberly and N.P. Neilson, *Achievement Scales in Physical Education Activities for Secondary School Girls and College Women* (Cranbury, NJ: A.S. Barnes and Co., 1939), p. 64.

[67] Cureton, "Improving the Physical Fitness of Youth," p. 193.

[68] Johnson and Nelson, *Practical Measurement for Evaluation,* p. 82.

[69] *AAHPER Youth Fitness Test Manual,* revised ed. (Washington, D.C.: AAHPERD Publications, 1976), p. 33.

[70] Glencross, "Nature of the Vertical Jump Test," pp. 353–59.

[71] Fleishman, *Structure and Measurement of Physical Fitness,* p. 48.

[72] Karl W. Bookwalter and Carolyn W. Bookwalter, "A Measure of Motor Fitness for College," *Bulletin of the School of Education,* Indiana University, 19, No. 2 (March 1943).

[73] Glencross, "The Power Lever," pp. 202–10.

[74] Elizabeth Powell and E.C. Howe, "Motor Ability Tests for High School Girls," *Res. Quart.,* 10 (December 1939), 81–88.

[75] Fleishman, *Structure and Measurement,* p. 116.

[76] *AAHPER Youth Fitness Test Manual,* pp. 41, 49.

[77] R.K. Gray, K.B. Start and D.J. Glencross, "A Test of Leg Power," *Res. Quart.,* 33 (March 1962), 44–50.

[78] Glencross, "The Power Lever," pp. 202–10.

[79] Johnson and Nelson, *Practical Measurements for Evaluation,* pp. 92–94.

[80] Barry L. Johnson, "Establishment of a Vertical Arm-Pull Test (Work)," *Res. Quart.,* 40 (March 1969), 237–39.

[81] Johnson and Nelson, *Practical Measurements for Evaluation,* pp. 89–90.

[82] Mary Ann Diridon, "A Study of Methods of Testing Arm and Shoulder Girdle Musculature Capacity with an Emphasis on the Bent-Knee Push-up and Bent-Arm Hang Tests for High School Girls," (unpublished student project, San Jose State College, 1967).

[83] R.T. DeWitt, "A Comparative Study of Three Types of Chinning Tests," *Res. Quart.,* 15 (October 1944), 240–48.

[84] *AAHPER Youth Fitness Test Manual,* p. 29.

[85] Thomas K. Cureton, *Endurance of Young Men* (Washington, D.C.: Society for Research in Child Development, National Research Council, 1945), p. 97.

[86] Cureton, "Improving the Physical Fitness of Youth," p. 173.

[87] Fleishman, *Structure and Measurement,* p. 59.

[88] Cureton, *Endurance of Young Men,* p. 271.

[89] Fleishman, *Structure and Measurement,* p. 64.

[90] L.A. Larson, "A Factor Analysis of Motor Ability Variables and Tests, with Tests for College Men," *Res. Quart.,* 12 (October 1941), 499–517.

[91] Cureton, *Endurance of Young Men,* p. 271.

[92] Cureton, "Improving the Physical Fitness of Youth," p. 192.

[93] *AAHPER Youth Fitness Test Manual,* p. 46.

[94] Fleishman, *Structure and Measurement,* p. 114.

[95] California State Department of Education, *The Physical Performance Test for California,* revised (Sacramento, CA: California State Department of Education, 1971), pp. 58, 64.

[96] *AAHPER Youth Fitness Test Manual,* p. 31.

[97] Cureton, *Endurance of Young Men,* p. 97.

[98] Fleishman, *Structure and Measurement,* p. 132.

[99] Johnson and Nelson, *Practical Measurements for Evaluation,* p. 278.

[100] Cureton, *Endurance of Young Men,* p. 156.

[101] Fleishman, *Structure and Measurement,* p. 64.

[102] Johnson and Nelson, *Practical Measurements for Evaluation,* p. 279.

[103] *AAHPER Youth Fitness Test Manual,* pp. 39, 47.

[104] AAHPERD *Health-Related Physical Fitness Test Manual* (Washington: AAHPERD Publications, 1980).

[105] Johnson and Nelson, *Practical Measurements for Evaluation,* p. 272.

[106] *AAHPER Youth Fitness Test Manual,* p. 30.

[107] Johnson and Nelson, *Practical Measurements for Evaluation,* p. 276.

[108] Fleishman, *Structure and Measurement,* p. 50.

[109] *Ibid.,* p. 64.

[110] Cureton, *Endurance of Young Men,* p. 156.

[111] *AAHPER Youth Fitness Test Manual,* p. 38.

[112] Cureton, *Endurance of Young Men,* p. 280.

[113] Fleishman, *Structure and Measurement,* p. 52.

[114] *Ibid.,* p. 59.

[115] *Ibid.,* p. 64.

## CHAPTER FIVE

[1] Margaret L. Moore, "The Measurement of Joint Motion: Introductory Review of the Literature," *Physical Therapy Review,* 29 (June 1949), 281.

[2] F.J. Wiechec and F.H. Krusen, "A New Method of Joint Measurement and a Review of the Literature," *Amer. Jour. of Surg.,* 43 (1939), 3.

[3] Jack R. Leighton, "An Instrument and Technic for the Measurement of Range of Joint Motion," *Archives of Phys. Med. and Rehab.,* 36 (September 1955), 571–78.

[4] P.V. Karpovich and G.P. Karpovich, "Electrogoniometer: A New Device for Study of Joints in Action," *Federation Proceedings,* Part 1, 18 (March 1959), 79.

[5] Peter V. Karpovich, *Physiology of Muscular Activity,* 6th ed. (Philadelphia: W.B. Saunders Co., 1967), pp. 37–39.

[6] Marlene Adrian, Charles W. Tipton and Peter V. Karpovich, *Electrogoniometer Manual* (Springfield, Mass.: Springfield College, 1965).

[7] Thomas K. Cureton, "Flexibility as an Aspect of Physical Fitness," *Res. Quart.,* Supplement, 12 (May 1941), 381–90.

[8] *Ibid.*

[9] Thomas K. Cureton, "Improving the Physical Fitness of Youth," *Monographs of the Society for Research in Child Development,* Serial No. 95, 29, no. 4 (1964), pp. 171–72.

[10] Cureton, "Flexibility as an Aspect of Physical Fitness," pp. 381–90.

[11] Thomas K. Cureton, *Physical Fitness Workbook* (St. Louis: The C.V. Mosby Co., 1947), p. 133.

[12] Cureton, "Improving the Physical Fitness of Youth," pp. 188–89.

[13] Barry L. Johnson and Jack K. Nelson, *Practical Measurements for Evaluation in Physical Education* (Minneapolis, Minn.: Burgess Publishing Co., 1969), pp. 204, 206, 212.

[14] Katharine F. Wells and Evelyn K. Dillon, "The Sit and Reach—A Test of Back and Leg Flexibility," *Res. Quart.,* 23 (March 1952), 115–18.

[15] M. Gladys Scott and Esther French, *Measurement and Evaluation in Physical Education* (Dubuque, Iowa: Wm. C. Brown Co., 1959), pp. 311–13.

[16] Johnson and Nelson, *Practical Measurements for Evaluation,* pp. 199–200.

[17] AAHPERD *Health-Related Physical Fitness Test Manual* (Washington: AAHPERD Publications, 1980).

[18] Edwin A. Fleishman, *The Structure and Measurement of Physical Fitness* (Englewood Cliffs, N.J.: Prentice-Hall, Inc., 1964), p. 78.

[19] *Ibid.,* p. 111.

[20] Leighton, "An Instrument and Technic for the Measurement of Range," pp. 571–78.

[21] Joseph M. Forbes, "Characteristics of Flexibility in Boys," (unpublished doctoral dissertation, University of Oregon, 1950).

[22] Clair Jennett, "An Investigation of Tests of Agility," (unpublished doctoral dissertation, State University of Iowa, 1959).

[23] Thomas K. Cureton, *Physical Fitness of Champion Athletes* (Urbana, IL: University of Illinois Press, 1951), p. 68.

[24]Leroy F. Sterling, "Effect of Badminton on Physical Fitness," (unpublished master's thesis, University of Illinois, 1955), p. 21.

[25]Mary F. O'Connor and T.K. Cureton, "Motor Fitness Tests for High School Girls," *Res. Quart.,* 16 (December 1945), 302–14.

[26]Cureton, "Improving the Physical Fitness of Youth," p. 172.

[27]Donald D. Gates and R.P. Sheffield, "Tests of Change of Direction as Measurements of Different Kinds of Motor Ability in Boys of the Seventh, Eighth and Ninth Grades," *Res. Quart.,* 11 (October 1940), 136–74.

[28]Thomas K. Cureton, *Physical Fitness Appraisal and Guidance* (St. Louis: C.V. Mosby Co., 1947), pp. 393–410.

[29]O'Connor and Cureton, "Motor Fitness Tests," pp. 302–14.

[30]Thomas K. Cureton, Lyle Welser and W.F. Huffman, "A Short Screen Test for Predicting Motor Fitness," *Res. Quart.,* 16 (May 1945), 106–19.

[31]Cureton, "Improving the Physical Fitness of Youth," p. 190.

[32]O'Connor and Cureton, "Motor Fitness Tests," pp. 302–14.

[33]C.H. McCloy and Norma D. Young, *Tests and Measurements in Health and Physical Education,* 3rd ed. (New York: Appleton-Century-Crofts, Inc., 1954), p. 80.

[34]Royal H. Burpee, "Differentiation in Physical Education," *Jour. of Phys. Ed.,* 18 (March 1931), 130–36.

[35]Royal H. Burpee, *Seven Quickly Administered Tests of Physical Capacity* (New York: Bureau of Publications, Columbia University, 1940).

[36]O'Connor and Cureton, "Motor Fitness Tests," pp. 302–14.

[37]Gates and Sheffield, "Tests of Change of Direction," pp. 136–74.

[38]McCloy and Young, *Tests and Measurements,* p. 76.

[39]O'Connor and Cureton, "Motor Fitness Tests," pp. 302–14.

[40]Johnson and Nelson, *Practical Measurements for Evaluation,* p. 102.

[41]Gates and Sheffield, "Tests of Change of Direction," pp. 136–74.

[42]*Ibid.*

[43]Frances Sierakowski, "A Study of Change-of-Direction Tests for High School Girls," (unpublished master's thesis, State University of Iowa, 1940).

[44]Johnson and Nelson, *Practical Measurements for Evaluation,* p. 110.

[45]Gates and Sheffield, "Tests of Change of Direction," pp. 136–74.

[46]Vivian D. Collins and Eugene C. Howe, "A Preliminary Selection of Tests of Fitness," *Amer. Phys. Ed. Rev.,* 29 (December 1924), 563–71.

[47]H. Hugh Mumby, "Kinesthetic Acuity and Balance Related to Wrestling Ability," *Res. Quart.,* 24 (October 1953), 327–34.

[48]Ruth I. Bass, "An Analysis of the Components of Tests of Semicircular Canal Function and of Static and Dynamic Balance," *Res. Quart.,* 10 (May 1939), 33–52.

[49]Fleishman, *Structure and Measurement of Physical Fitness,* p. 128.

[50]*Ibid.,* p. 96.

[51]Johnson and Nelson, *Practical Measurements for Evaluation,* p. 162.

[52]Fleishman, *Structure and Measurement of Physical Fitness,* p. 115.

[53]Johnson and Nelson, *Practical Measurements for Evaluation,* p. 158.

[54]Harold G. Seashore, "The Development of a Beam-Walking Test and Its Use in Measuring Development of Balance in Children," *Res. Quart.,* 18 (December 1947), 246–59.

[55]Bass, "Analysis of Components of Tests of Semicircular Canal Function," pp. 33–52.

[56]Johnson and Nelson, *Practical Measurements for Evaluation,* p. 169.

## CHAPTER SIX

[1]C.W. Crampton, "A Test of Condition: A Preliminary Report," *Medical News,* 87 (September 1905), 529–35.

[2] C.W. Crampton, "The Blood Ptosis Test and its Use in Experimental Work in Hygiene," *Proceedings of the Society for Experimental Biology and Medicine,* 12 (1915), 119.

[3] W.L. Foster, "A Test of Physical Efficiency," *Amer. Phys. Ed. Rev.,* 19 (December 1914), 632–36.

[4] E.C. Schneider, "A Cardiovascular Rating as a Measure of Physical Fitness and Efficiency," *Journ. of the Amer. Med. Assoc.,* 74 (May 1920), 1507.

[5] J.H. McCurdy, *Physiology of Exercise,* 1st ed. (Philadelphia: Lea and Febiger, 1924), p. 24.

[6] J.H. McCurdy and L.A. Larson, "Measurement of Organic Efficiency for Prediction of Physical Condition," *Res. Quart.,* Supplement, 6 (May 1935), 11–41.

[7] W.W. Tuttle and R.E. Dickinson, "A Simplification of the Pulse-Ratio Technique for Rating Physical Efficiency and Present Condition," *Res. Quart.,* 9 (May 1938), 73–81.

[8] Lucien Brouha, "The Step Test: A Simple Method of Measuring Physical Fitness for Muscular Work in Young Men," *Res. Quart.,* 14 (March 1943), 32–36.

[9] H.C. Carlson, "Fatigue Curve Test," *Res. Quart.,* 16 (October 1945), 169–75.

[10] Thomas K. Cureton, *Physical Fitness Appraisal and Guidance* (St. Louis: C.V. Mosby Co., 1947), pp. 162–231.

[11] Dorothy Mae Hart, "A History of Cardiovascular Testing of Normal Subjects," (unpublished master's thesis, University of Illinois, 1946).

[12] Thomas K. Cureton, *Physical Fitness of Champion Athletes* (Urbana, IL: University Of Illinois Press, 1951), pp. 314–50.

[13] Balke, B., "A Simple Test for the Assessment of Physical Fitness," in *CARI Report* (Oklahoma City: Civil Aeromedical Research Institute, Aviation Agency), p. 196.

[14] Irma Rhyming, "A Modified Harvard Step Test for the Evaluation of Physical Fitness," *Arbeitsphysiologie,* 15 (1954), 235–50.

[15] Charles E. Billings, J. Tomashefski, E.T. Carter and W. Ashe, "Measurement of Human Capacity for Aerobic Muscular Work," *Jour. Appl. Phys.,* 15 (1960), 1001–1006.

[16] Richard B. Alderman, "Reliability of Individual Differences in the 180 Heart Rate Response Test in Bicycle Ergometer Work," *Res. Quart.,* 37 (October 1966), 429–31.

[17] Jeanne T. Truett, Herbert Benson and Bruno Balke, "On the Practicability of Submaximal Exercise Testing," *Jour. Chronic Disease,* 19 (1966), 711–15.

[18] Schneider, "Cardiovascular Rating as a Measure," p. 1507.

[19] Thomas K. Cureton, Physical Fitness Research Laboratory Materials, University of Illinois.

[20] Thomas K. Cureton, *Endurance of Young Men* (Washington, D.C.: Society for Research in Child Development, National Research Council, 1945), p. 214.

[21] R.A. McFarland and J.H. Huddleston, "Neurocirculatory Reactions in the Psychoneuroses Studied by the Schneider Method," *Amer. Jour. Psych.,* 93 (November 1936), 567–99.

[22] Anna Espenschade, "A Study of the Factors of Physical Endurance," *Res. Quart.,* Supplement, 9 (March 1938), 11–12.

[23] F. Henry and W. Herbig, "The Correlations of Various Functional Tests of the Cardio-Circulatory System with Changes in Athletic Conditions of Distance Runners," *Res. Quart.,* 13 (May 1942), 185–200.

[24] Cureton, *Endurance of Young Men,* p. 233.

[25] *Ibid.,* p. 204.

[26] Thomas K. Cureton, "Improving the Physical Fitness of Youth," *Monographs of the Society for Research in Child Development,* Serial No. 95, 29, no. 4 (1964), pp. 196–98.

[27] E.L. Collis and M.S. Pembrey, "Observations Upon the Effects of Warm Humid Atmospheres in Man," *Jour. of Phys.,* 43 (1911), 11.

[28] J.M.H. Campbell, "The Pulse Rate after Exercise in Health and Disease," *Guy's Hospital Reports,* 77 (1917), 184–215.

[29] W.W. Tuttle, "The Use of the Pulse-Ratio Test for Rating Physical Efficiency," *Res. Quart.,* 2 (1931), 5–17.

[30] W.W. Tuttle and George Wells, "The Response of the Normal Heart to Exercises of Graded Intensity," *Arbeitsphysiologie*, 4 (1931), 519–26.

[31] Tuttle and Dickinson, "Simplification of the Pulse-Ratio Technique," pp. 73–81.

[32] Franklin M. Henry and Daniel Farmer, "Functional Tests II: The Reliability of the Pulse-Ratio Test," *Res. Quart.*, 9 (May 1938), 81–87.

[33] Marjorie Phillips, Eloise Ridder and Helen Yeakel, "Further Data on the Pulse-Ratio Test," *Res. Quart.*, 14 (December 1943), 425–29.

[34] K. Flanagan, "The Pulse-Ratio Test as a Measure of Athletic Endurance in Sprint Running," *Res. Quart.*, 6 (October 1935), 46–50.

[35] Franklin M. Henry and Frank L. Kleeberger, "The Validity of the Pulse-Ratio Test of Cardiac Efficiency," *Res. Quart.*, 9 (March 1938), 32–46.

[36] Cureton, *Appraisal and Guidance*, p. 190.

[37] Thomas K. Cureton, *The Physiological Effects of Exercise Programs on Adults* (Springfield, IL: Charles C. Thomas Co., 1969), pp. 104–5.

[38] Lucien Brouha, "The Step Test: A Simple Method of Measuring Physical Fitness for Muscular Work in Young Men," *Res. Quart.*, 14 (March 1943), 32–36.

[39] Cureton, *Endurance of Young Men*, pp. 94–97.

[40] Karl W. Bookwalter, "A Study of the Brouha Step Test," *The Physical Educator*, 5 (May 1948), 55.

[41] Cureton, *Endurance of Young Men*, pp. 188–89.

[42] Cureton, *Appraisal and Guidance*, p. 190.

[43] R.E. Johnson and S. Robinson, "Selection of Men for Physical Work in Hot Weather," *Appendix I, CMR, OSRD, Report 16* (Harvard Fatigue Laboratory, 1943).

[44] Donald K. Mathews, *Measurement in Physical Education*, 3rd ed. (Philadelphia: W.B. Saunders Co., 1968), p. 219.

[45] J.R. Gallagher and L. Brouha, "A Simple Method of Testing the Physical Fitness of Boys," *Res. Quart.*, 14 (March 1943), 23–30.

[46] H.L. Clarke, "A Functional Physical Fitness Test for College Women," *Jour. of Health and Phys. Ed.*, 14 (September 1943), 358–59.

[47] L. Brouha and M.V. Ball, *Canadian Red Cross Society's School Meal Study* (Toronto: University of Toronto Press, 1952), pp. 55–56.

[48] Vera Skubic and Jean Hodgkins, "Cardiovascular Efficiency Test for Girls and Women," *Res. Quart.*, 34 (May 1963), 191–98.

[49] Vera Skubic and Jean Hodgkins, "Cardiovascular Efficiency Test Scores for Junior and Senior High School Girls in the United States," *Res. Quart.*, 35 (May 1964), 184–92.

[50] Jean Hodgkins and Vera Skubic, "Cardiovascular Efficiency Test Scores for College Women in the United States," *Res. Quart.*, 34 (December 1963), 454–61.

[51] Cureton, *Appraisal and Guidance*, pp. 451–56.

[52] Cureton, *Fitness of Champion Athletes*, pp. 319–23.

[53] Stanley Brown, "Factors Influencing Improvement in the Oxygen Intake of Young Boys," (unpublished doctoral dissertation, University of Illinois, 1960), p. 60.

[54] Leroy F. Sterling, "A Factorial Analysis of Cardiovascular Variables," (unpublished doctoral dissertation, Univeristy of Illinois, 1960), pp. 91–93.

[55] Balke, "A Simple Test for the Assessment of Physical Fitness."

[56] Maxwell Howell and others, "Progressive Treadmill Test Norms for College Males," *Res. Quart.*, 35 (October 1964), 322–25.

[57] Richard Alderman, "Reliability of Individual Differences in the 180 Heart Rate Response Test in Bicycle Ergometer Work," *Res. Quart.*, 37 (October 1966), 429–31.

[58] F.W. Kasch and others, "Maximum Work Capacity in Middle-Aged Males by a Step Test Method," *Jour. Sports Med.*, 5 (December 1965), 198–202.

[59] F.W. Kasch and others, "A Comparison of Maximum Oxygen Uptake by Treadmill and Step Test," *Jour. Appl. Phys.*, 21 (July 1966), 1387–88.

[60] Billings and others, "Measurement of Human Capacity," pp. 231–38.

[61] P.O. Åstrand and Kaare Rodahl, *Textbook of Work Physiology* (New York: McGraw-Hill Book Co., 1970), pp. 618–27.

[62] Monark Bicycle Ergometer, Monark-Crescent AB, Varberg, Sweden.

[63] Robert L. Kurusz, "Construction of the Ohio State University Cardiovascular Fitness Test," (unpublished doctoral dissertation, The Ohio State University, 1967).

[64] Kenneth H. Cooper, *The Aerobics Way* (New York: M. Evans and Company, Inc., 1977).

[65] Balke, "A Simple Test."

[66] Andrew S. Jackson, "Technical Report 1: Normative Study of the Texas Physical Fitness–Motor Ability Test," mimeographed material from the Governor's Commission on Physical Fitness, Austin, 1974.

[67] Kenneth H. Cooper, "A Means of Assessing Maximum Oxygen Intake," *Jour. of Am. Med. Assoc.,* 203 (1968), 201–4.

[68] Kenneth H. Cooper, *The New Aerobics* (New York: Bantam Books, 1970).

[69] B. Gutin, R.K. Fogle and K. Stewart, "Relationship among Submaximal Heart Rate, Aerobic Power, and Running Performance in Children," *Res. Quart.,* 47 (1976), 536–39.

[70] R.L. Doolittle and Rollin Bigbee, "The Twelve-Minute Run-Walk: A Test of Cardiorespiratory Fitness of Adolescent Boys," *Res. Quart.,* 39 (1968), 491–95.

[71] Margaret J. Safrit, *Evaluation in Physical Education,* 2nd ed. (Englewood Cliffs, N.J.: Prentice-Hall, Inc., 1981), p. 226.

[72] George T. Jessup, Homer Tolson and James W. Terry, "Prediction of Maximal Oxygen Intake Capacity from Åstrand-Rhyming Test, 12-minute Run and Anthropometric Variables Using Stepwise Multiple Regression," paper read at AAHPER Convention, Minneapolis, 1973.

[73] Doolittle and Bigbee, "The Twelve-Minute Run-Walk."

[74] Cooper, "A Means of Assessing Maximum Oxygen Intake."

[75] Safrit, *Evaluation in Physical Education,* p. 226.

[76] *Ibid.,* p. 224.

[77] H. Harrison Clarke, *Application of Measurement to Health and Physical Education,* 5th ed. (Englewood Cliffs, N.J.: Prentice-Hall, Inc., 1976).

## CHAPTER SEVEN

[1] Robert H. McCollum and Richard B. McCorkle, *Measurement and Evaluation: A Laboratory Manual* (Boston: Allyn and Bacon, Inc., 1971), pp. 55–56.

[2] C.H. McCloy, "An Analytical Study of the Stunt Type Test as a Measure of Motor Educability," *Res. Quart.,* 8 (October 1937), 26–55.

[3] Eleanor Metheny, "Studies of the Johnson Test as a Test of Motor Educability," *Res. Quart.,* 9 (December 1938), 105–14.

[4] C.H. McCloy, *Tests and Measurements in Health and Physical Education* (New York: F.S. Crofts and Co., 1946), Chapter VII.

[5] Lucille Hatlestad, "Motor Educability Tests for Women College Students," *Res. Quart.,* 13 (March 1942), 10–15.

[6] Aileen Carpenter, "Strength Testing in the First Three Grades," *Res. Quart.,* 13 (October 1942), 328–35.

[7] Aileen Carpenter, "The Measurements of General Motor Capacity and General Motor Ability in the First Three Grades," *Res. Quart.,* 13 (December 1942), 444–65.

[8] McCloy, *Tests and Measurements,* p. 46.

[9] Thomas K. Cureton, *Endurance of Young Men* (Washington, D.C.: Society for Research in Child Development, National Research Council, 1945).

[10] Harold M. Barrow, "Test of Motor Ability for College Men," *Res. Quart.,* 25 (October 1954), 253–60.

[11] Edwin A. Fleishman, *The Structure and Measurement of Physical Fitness,* (Englewood Cliffs, N.J.: Prentice-Hall, Inc., 1964).

[12] Edwin A. Fleishman, *Examiner's Manual for the Basic Fitness Tests* (Englewood Cliffs, N.J.: Prentice-Hall, Inc., 1964).

[13] M. Gladys Scott, "The Assessment of Motor Abilities of College Women Through Objective Tests," *Res. Quart.,* 10 (October 1939), 63–83.

[14] M. Gladys Scott, "Motor Ability Tests for College Women," *Res. Quart.,* 14 (December 1943), 402–5.

[15] M. Gladys Scott and Esther French, *Measurement and Evaluation in Physical Education* (Dubuque, Iowa: Wm. C. Brown Co., 1959), Chapter 9.

[16] C.H. McCloy, "The Measurement of General Motor Capacity and General Motor Ability," *Res. Quart.,* Supplement, 5 (March 1934), 46–61.

[17] C.H. McCloy and Norma D. Young, *Tests and Measurement in Health and Physical Education,* 3rd ed. (New York: Appleton-Century-Crofts, Inc., 1954), Chapter 17.

[18] Scott and French, *Measurement and Evaluation,* pp. 351–57.

[19] Frederick Rand Rogers, *Physical Capacity Tests in the Administration of Physical Education* (New York: Bureau of Publications, Teachers College, Columbia University, 1926).

[20] H. Harrison Clarke, *Application of Measurement to Health and Physical Education,* 2nd ed. (New York: Prentice-Hall, Inc., 1950), pp. 155–91.

[21] Donald K. Mathews, *Measurement in Physical Education,* 3rd ed. (Philadelphia: W.B. Saunders Co., 1968), pp. 77–78.

[22] Clarke, *Application of Measurement,* pp. 174–80.

[23] Thomas K. Cureton, *Physical Fitness Appraisal and Guidance* (St. Louis: The C.V. Mosby Co., 1947), pp. 374–82.

[24] McCloy, *Tests and Measurements,* pp. 21–24.

[25] H. Harrison Clarke and Gavin H. Carter, "Oregon Simplifications of the Strength and Physical Fitness Indices for Upper Elementary, Junior High and Senior High School Boys," *Res. Quart.,* 30 (March 1959), 3–10.

[26] Emory W. Seymour, "Follow-up Study on Simplifications of the Strength and Physical Fitness Indices," *Res. Quart.,* Part I, 31 (May 1960), 208–16.

[27] B.E. Phillips, "The JCR Test," *Res. Quart.,* 18 (March 1947), 12–29.

[28] Leonard A. Larson, "Some Findings Resulting from the Army Air Forces Physical Training Program," *Res. Quart.,* 17 (May 1946), 144–64.

[29] Leonard A. Larson, "A Factor and Validity Analysis of Strength Variables and Tests with a Test Combination of Chinning, Dipping and Vertical Jump," *Res. Quart.,* 11 (December 1940), 82–96.

[30] Cureton, *Endurance of Young Men,* p. 94.

[31] D.J. Glencross, "The Nature of the Vertical Jump Test and the Standing Broad Jump," *Res. Quart.,* 37 (October 1966), 353–59.

[32] L.A. Larson and R.D. Yocom, *Measurement and Evaluation in Physical Education, Health and Recreation Education* (St. Louis: C.V. Mosby Co., 1951), p. 474.

[33] Thomas K. Cureton, *Physical Fitness of Champion Athletes* (Urbana, IL: University of Illinois Press, 1951), p. 66.

[34] K.W. Bookwalter, "Achievement Scales in Strength Tests for Secondary School Boys and College Men," *Physical Educator,* 11 (February 1942), 130–51.

[35] Elizabeth Powell and E.C. Howe, "Motor Ability Tests for High School Girls," *Res. Quart.,* 10 (December 1939), 81–88.

[36] "Wellesley College Studies in Hygiene and Physical Education," *Res. Quart.,* Supplement, 9 (March 1939), 49–56.

[37] *AAHPER Youth Fitness Test Manual,* revised ed. (Washington, D.C.: AAHPERD Publications, 1976).

[38] *Physical Fitness Motor Ability Test* (Austin, TX: Texas Governor's Commission on Physical Fitness, 1973).

## CHAPTER EIGHT

[1] Harold M. Barrow and Rosemary McGee, *Practical Approach to Measurement in Physical Education* (Philadelphia: Lea and Febiger, 1964).

[2] M. Gladys Scott and Esther French, *Measurement and Evaluation in Physical Education* (Dubuque, Iowa: Wm. C. Brown Co., 1959), pp. 18–19.

[3] Ibid., pp. 14–15.

[4] B.L. Johnson and J.K. Nelson, *Practical Measurements for Evaluation in Physical Education* (Minneapolis, Minn.: Burgess Publishing Company, 1969), pp. 49–50.

[5] Edith I. Hyde, "The Measure of Achievement in Archery," *Jour. of Ed. Res.,* 27 (May 1934), 673–86.

[6] Edith I. Hyde, "National Research Study in Archery," *Res. Quart.,* 7 (December 1936), 64–73.

[7] Edith I. Hyde, "An Achievement Scale in Archery," *Res. Quart.,* 8 (May 1937), 109–16.

[8] *AAHPER Skills Test Manual: Archery for Boys and Girls* (Washington, D.C.: AAHPERD Publications, 1967).

[9] Hyde, "National Research Study in Archery," pp. 64–73.

[10] *Ibid.,* p. 68.

[11] Robert M. Zabik and Andrew S. Jackson, "Reliability of Archery Achievement," *Res. Quart.,* 40 (March 1969), 254–55.

[12] Marjorie Phillips and Dean Summers, "Bowling Norms and Learning Curves for College Women," *Res. Quart.,* 21 (December 1950), 377–85.

[13] Joan Martin, "Bowling Norms for College Men and Women," *Res. Quart.,* 31 (March 1960), 113–16.

[14] Joan Martin and Jack Keogh, "Bowling Norms for College Students in Elective Physical Education Classes," *Res. Quart.,* 35 (October 1954), 325–27.

[15] Marie Liba and Janice K. Olsen, "A Device for Evaluating Spot Bowling Ability," *Res. Quart.,* 38 (May 1967), 193–201.

[16] Mary Jo Shelly, "Some Aspects of the Case For and Against Objective Testing of Dance in Education," *Res. Quart.,* 1 (October 1930), 119–24.

[17] Dudley Ashton, "A Gross Motor Rhythm Test," *Res. Quart.,* 24 (October 1953), 253–60.

[18] Ellen R. Vanderhoof, "Beginning Golf Achievement Tests," (unpublished master's thesis, State University of Iowa, 1956).

[19] Eugene Wettstone, "Tests for Predicting Potential Ability in Gymnastics and Tumbling," *Res. Quart.,* 9 (December 1938), 115–25.

[20] Vincent DiGiovanna, "The Relation of Structural and Functional Measures to Success in College Athletics," *Res. Quart.,* 14 (May 1943), 199–216.

[21] James S. Bosco, "The Physical and Personality Characteristics of Champion Male Gymnasts," (unpublished doctoral dissertation, University of Illinois, 1962).

[22] Margaret G. Fox, "Swimming Power Test," *Res. Quart.,* 28 (October 1957), 233–38.

[23] N.P. Neilson and Frederick Cozens, *Achievement Scales in Physical Education Activities for Boys and Girls in Elementary and Junior High Schools* (Sacramento, CA: California State Department of Education, 1934).

## CHAPTER NINE

[1] Esther French and Evelyn Stalter, "Study of Skill Tests in Badminton for College Women," *Res. Quart.,* 20 (October 1949), 257–72.

[2] Helen M. Eckert, *Practical Measurement of Physical Performance* (Philadelphia: Lea and Febiger, 1974), p. 74.

[3]H. Harrison Clarke, *Application of Measurement to Health and Physical Education,* 2nd ed. (New York: Prentice-Hall, Inc., 1950), p. 303.

[4]Aileene Lockhart and Frances A. McPherson, "The Development of a Test of Badminton Playing Ability," *Res. Quart.,* 20 (December 1949), 402-5.

[5]Eckert, *Practical Measurement,* pp. 72-73.

[6]Donald K. Mathews, *Measurement in Physical Education,* 3rd ed. (Philadelphia: W.B. Saunders Co., 1968), pp. 176-77.

[7]Patricia F. Kuhajda, "The Construction and Validation of a Skill Test for the Riposte Lunge in Fencing," (unpublished master's thesis, Southern Illinois University, 1970).

[8]Robert N. Singer, "Speed and Accuracy of Movement as Related to Fencing Success," *Res. Quart.,* 29 (December 1968), 1080-83.

[9]G. Gary Pennington and others, "A Measure of Handball Ability," *Res. Quart.,* 38 (May 1967), 247-53.

[10]Kenneth W. Tyson, "A Handball Skill Test for College Men," (unpublished master's thesis, University of Texas, 1970).

[11]Jack E. Hewitt, "Hewitt's Tennis Achievement Test," *Res. Quart.,* 39 (October 1968), 552-55.

[12]Joanna T. Dyer, "Revision of the Backboard Test of Tennis Ability," *Res. Quart.,* 9 (March 1938), 25-31.

[13]Harry L. Seavers, "The Measurement of Potential Wrestling Ability," (unpublished master's thesis, State University of Iowa, 1934).

[14]Barron J. Bremner, "Measurement of Potential Wrestling Ability," (unpublished master's thesis, State University of Iowa, 1964), p. 46.

## CHAPTER TEN

[1]*AAHPER Skills Test Manual—Softball for Boys* (Washington, AAHPERD Publications, 1966).

[2]*AAHPER Skills Test Manual—Softball for Girls* (Washington: AAHPERD Publications, 1966).

[3]*AAHPER Skills Test Manual—Softball for Boys.*

[4]*Ibid.,* p. 11.

[5]Avis L. Leilich, "The Primary Components of Selected Basketball Tests for College Women," (unpublished doctoral dissertation, Indiana University, 1952).

[6]*AAHPER Skills Test Manual—Basketball for Boys* (Washington: AAHPERD Publications, 1966).

[7]*AAHPER Skills Test Manual—Basketball for Girls* (Washington: AAHPERD Publications, 1966).

[8]Grace Hartley, "Motivating the Physical Education Program for High School Girls," *Amer. Phys. Ed. Rev.,* 34 (May-June-September 1929), 284, 344, 405.

[9]Margaret Schmithals and Esther French, "Achievement Tests in Field Hockey for College Women," *Res. Quart.,* 11 (October 1940), 84-92.

[10]*AAHPER Skills Test Manual: Football* (Washington: AAHPERD Publications, 1966).

[11]H.H. Merrifield and Gerald A. Walford, "Battery of Ice Hockey Skill Tests," *Res. Quart.,* 40 (March 1969), 146-52.

[12]Lloyd G. McDonald, "The Construction of a Kicking Skill Test as an Index of General Soccer Ability," (unpublished master's thesis, Springfield College, 1951).

[13]Joseph R. Johnson, "The Development of a Single-Item Test as a Measure of Soccer Skill," (unpublished master's thesis, University of British Columbia, 1962).

[14]Elinor A. Crawford, "The Development of Skill Test Batteries for Evaluating the Ability of Women Physical Education Major Students in Soccer and Speedball," (unpublished doctoral dissertation, University of Oregon, 1958).

[15] Phyllis Cunningham and Joan Garrison, "High Wall Volley Test for Women's Volleyball," *Res. Quart.,* 39 (October 1968), 486–90.

[16] *AAHPER Skills Test Manual–Volleyball for Boys and Girls* (Washington, D.C.: AAHPERD Publications, 1969).

[17] Arthur F. Lambert and Robert Gaughran, *The Technique of Water Polo* (Hollywood: Swimming World, 1969), p. 22.

[18] W.K. Anttila, *Water Polo Drills and Playing Hints* (Stockton: San Joaquin Delta College, 1963), p. 5.

[19] Lee A. Walton, "Water Polo Decathlon," *Water Polo Illustrated,* 1 (May 1966), 10–12.

[20] Louis J. Tully, "A Statistical Analysis of the Walton Water Polo Decathlon," (unpublished student project, San Jose State College, 1970).

## CHAPTER ELEVEN

[1] *AAHPER Cooperative Physical Education Tests* (Princeton: Educational Testing Service, 1970).

[2] *Handbook (for) The AAHPER Cooperative Physical Education Tests* (Princeton: Education Testing Service, 1971), pp. 27-29.

## CHAPTER TWELVE

[1] Charles C. Cowell, "The Contributions of Physical Activity to Social Development," *Res. Quart.,* 31 (May 1960), 286–306.

[2] Gerald S. Kenyon, "Sociological Considerations." *Jour. of Health, Phys. Ed. and Rec.,* 39 (November-December 1968), 31.

[3] *Ibid.,* p. 33.

[4] *Ibid.*

[5] Cowell, "Contributions of Physical Activity," p. 286.

[6] Amatai Etzioni, "Human Beings are not Very Easy to Change After All," *Saturday Review,* June, 1972, 45.

[7] *Ibid.*

[8] Christopher L. Stevenson, "Socialization Effects of Participation in Sport: A Critical Review of the Research," *Res. Quart.,* 46 (October 1975), 287.

[9] Bryant J. Cratty, *Social Dimensions of Physical Activity* (Englewood Cliffs, N.J.: Prentice-Hall, Inc., 1967), p. 108.

[10] *Ibid.,* p. 106.

[11] Carlos L. Wear, "The Evaluation of Attitude Toward Physical Education as an Activity Course," *Res. Quart.,* 22 (March 1951), 114–26.

[12] *Ibid.,* p. 114, citing Rensis Likert, "A Technique for the Measurement of Attitudes," *Archives of Psychology,* 22 (June 1932), 5–43.
A Likert Scale is one that restricts respondent to five options—e.g., strongly agree, agree, neutral, disagree, strongly disagree—or seven, by adding very strongly agree and very strongly disagree.

[13] C.L. Wear, "Construction of Equivalent Forms of an Attitude Scale," *Res. Quart.,* 26 (March 1955), 113–19.

[14] Marion R. Broer, "Evaluation of a Basic Skills Curriculum for Women Students of Low Motor Ability at the University of Washington," *Res. Quart.,* 26 (March 1955), 15–27.

[15] Janet A. Wessel and Richard Nelson, "Relationship Between Strength and Attitudes Toward Physical Education Activity Among College Women," *Res. Quart.,* 35 (December 1964), 562–69.

[16] Eveline E. Kappes, "Inventory to Determine Attitudes of College Women Toward Physical Education and Student Services of the Physical Education Department," *Res. Quart.,* 25 (December 1954), 429–38.

[17] R.S. Adams, "Two Scales for Measuring Attitude Toward Physical Education," *Res. Quart.*, 34 (March 1963), 91–94.

[18] L.L. Thurstone and E.J. Chave, *The Measurement of Attitude* (Chicago: University of Chicago Press, 1929).

[19] Nancy J. Mista, "Attitudes of College Women Toward Their High School Physical Education Programs," *Res. Quart.*, 39 (March 1968), 166–74.

[20] Charles W. Edgington, "Development of an Attitude Scale to Measure Attitudes of High School Freshman Boys Toward Physical Education," *Res. Quart.*, 39 (October 1968), 505–12.

[21] Charles E. Richardson, "Thurstone Scale for Measuring Attitudes of College Students Toward Physical Fitness and Exercise," *Res. Quart.*, 31 (December 1960), 638–43.

[22] B.D. McPherson and M.S. Yuhasz, "An Inventory for Assessing Men's Attitudes Toward Exercise and Physical Activity," *Res. Quart.*, 39 (March 1968), 218–20.

[23] Gerald S. Kenyon, "Six Scales for Assessing Attitude toward Physical Activity," *Res. Quart.*, 39 (October 1968), 566–74.

[24] Gerald S. Kenyon, "A Conceptual Model for Characterizing Physical Activity," *Res. Quart.*, 39 (March 1968), 96–105.

[25] Julie A. Simon and Frank L. Smoll, "An Instrument for Assessing Children's Attitudes toward Physical Activity," *Res. Quart.*, 45 (December 1974), 407–15.

[26] Linda B. Zaichkowsky, "Attitudinal Differences in Two Types of Physical Education Programs," *Res. Quart.*, 46 (October 1975), 364–70.

[27] Frank L. Smoll, Robert W. Schutz and Joan K. Keeney, "Relationships Among Children's Attitudes, Involvement, and Proficiency in Physical Activities," *Res. Quart.*, 47 (December 1976), 797–803.

[28] Fred M. Apgar, "Emphasis Placed on Winning in Athletics by Male High School Students," *Res. Quart.*, 48 (May 1977), 253–59.

[29] Daniel C. Neale, Robert J. Sonstroem and Kenneth F. Metz, "Physical Fitness, Self-Esteem, and Attitudes toward Physical Activity," *Res. Quart.*, 40 (December 1969), 743–49.

[30] Robert J. Sonstroem, "Attitude Testing Examining Certain Psychological Correlates of Physical Activity," *Res. Quart.*, 45 (May 1974), 93–103.

[31] Barbara L. Drinkwater, "Development of an Attitude Inventory to Measure the Attitude of High School Girls toward Physical Education as a Career for Women," *Res. Quart.*, 31 (December 1960), 575–80.

[32] Betty Foster McCue, "Constructing an Instrument for Evaluating Attitudes toward Intensive Competition in Team Games." *Res. Quart.*, 24 (May 1953), 205–9.

[33] Phebe Martha Scott, "Attitudes toward Athletic Competition in Elementary Schools," *Res. Quart.*, 24 (October 1953), 352–61.

[34] Rosemary McGee, "Comparison of Attitudes toward Intensive Competition for High School Girls," *Res. Quart.*, 27 (March 1956), 60–73.

[35] William L. Lakie, "Expressed Attitudes of Various Groups of Athletes toward Athletic Competition," *Res. Quart.*, 35 (December 1964), 497–503.

[36] Rosemary Selby and John H. Lewke, "Children's Attitudes toward Females in Sport: Their Relationship with Sex, Grade, and Sports Participation," *Res. Quart.*, 47 (October 1976), 453–63.

[37] Robert A. McAfee, "Sportsmanship Attitudes of Sixth, Seventh, and Eighth Grade Boys," *Res. Quart.*, 26 (March 1955), 120.

[38] Mary Jane Haskins, "Problem-Solving Test of Sportsmanship," *Res. Quart.*, 31 (December 1960), 601–6.

[39] Marion Lee Johnson, "Construction of Sportsmanship Attitude Scales," *Res. Quart.*, 40 (May 1969), 313.

[40] Marion Lee Johnson, citing Allen L. Edwards, *Techniques of Attitude Scale Construction* (New York: Appleton-Century-Crofts, 1957).

[41] *Ibid.*, pp. 312–16.

[42] Brian M. Petrie, "Statistical Analysis of Attitude Scale Scores," *Res. Quart.*, 40 (May 1969), 434–36.

[43]Wayne B. Brumbach, "A Response to Petrie's Note on Statistical Analysis of Attitude Scale Scores," *Res. Quart.,* 40 (May 1969), 436–37.

[44]E.G. Booth, Jr., "Personality Traits of Athletes as Measured by the MMPI," *Res. Quart.,* 29 (May 1958), 127–38.

[45]Jack Keogh, "Comments on the Selection of Data for Presentation," *Res. Quart.,* 31 (May 1960), 240.

[46]E.G. Booth, Jr., "Personality Traits of Athletes as Measured by the MMPI: A Rebuttal," *Res. Quart.,* 32 (October 1961), 421–23.

[47]Philip J. Rasch, M. Briggs Hunt and Port G. Robertson, "The Booth Scale as a Predictor of Competitive Behavior of College Wrestlers," *Res. Quart.,* 31 (March 1960), 117–18.

[48]Walter Kroll and Kay H. Petersen, "Cross-Validation of the Booth Scale," *Res. Quart.,* 37 (March 1966), 66–70.

[49]S.R. Hathaway and J.C. McKinley, *Minnesota Multiphasic Personality Inventory Manual* (New York: The Psychological Corporation, 1967), p. 8.

[50]*Ibid.*

[51]Harrison G. Gough, *California Psychological Inventory Manual* (Palo Alto, CA: Consulting Psychologist Press, Inc., 1969).

[52]Raymond B. Cattell and Herbert W. Eber, *Handbook for the Sixteen Personality Factor Questionnaire* (Champaign, IL: Institute for Personality and Ability Testing, 1964).

[53]Raymond B. Cattell, *Personality and Mood by Questionnaire* (San Francisco: Jossey-Bass Publishers, 1973), p. 309.

[54]Raymond B. Cattell and Mary D.L. Cattell, *Handbook for the Jr.-Sr. High School Personality Questionnaire* (Champaign, IL: Institute for Personality and Ability Testing, 1969).

[55]Walter Kroll and Kay H. Petersen, "Personality Factor Profiles of Collegiate Football Teams," *Res. Quart.,* 36 (December 1965), 433–40.

[56]Kenneth Tillman, "Relationship Between Physical Fitness and Selected Personality Traits," *Res. Quart.,* 36 (December 1965), 483–89.

[57]Elizabeth Yeckel Brown and Carl N. Shaw, "Effects of a Stressor on a Specific Motor Task on Individuals Displaying Selected Personality Factors," *Res. Quart.,* 46 (March 1975), 71–77.

[58]James H. Widdop and Valerie A. Widdop, "Comparison of the Personality Traits of Female Teacher Education and Physical Education Students," *Res. Quart.,* 46 (October 1975), 274–81.

[59]Thomas A. Tutko, Leland P. Lyon and Bruce C. Olgivie, *Athletic Motivation Inventory Manual* (San Jose, CA: The Institute of Athletic Motivation, 1975).

[60]Dennis Harry Fosdick, "The Relationship of the Athletic Motivation Inventory and the 16 Personality Factor Questionnaire as Measures of the Personality Characteristics of College Varsity Swimmers," unpublished master's thesis, San Jose State College, 1972).

[61]Linda L. Bain, "An Instrument for Identifying Implicit Values in Physical Education Programs," *Res. Quart.,* 47 (October 1976), 307–15.

[62]Linda L. Bain, citing Margaret J. Safrit, *Evaluation in Physical Education* (Englewood Cliffs, N.J.: Prentice-Hall, Inc., 1973), p. 99.

[63]Ronald E. Smith, Frank L. Smoll and Earl Hunt, "A System for the Behavioral Assessment of Athletic Coaches," *Res. Quart.,* 48 (May 1977), 401–7.

[64]Marie Weber, "Physical Education Teacher Role Identification Instrument," *Res. Quart.,* 48 (May 1977), 445–51.

[65]Charles D. Spielberger, ed., *Anxiety, Vol. 1* (New York: Academic Press, 1972), pp. 35–38.

[66]For specific reliability and validity data, readers are advised to consult C.D. Spielberger, R.L. Gorusch and R.E. Lushene, *Manual for the State-Trait Anxiety Inventory* (Palo Alto, CA: Consulting Psychologist Press, 1970).

[67]Marilyn L. Basler, A. Craig Fisher and Nancy L. Mumford, "Arousal and Anxiety Correlates of Gymnastic Performance," *Res. Quart.,* 47 (December 1976), 586–89.

[68] Rainer Martens, *Sport Competition Anxiety Test* (Champaign, IL: Human Kinetics Publishers, 1977).

[69] Tara Kost Scanlan, "The Effects of Success-Failure on the Perception of Threat in a Competitive Situation," *Res. Quart.,* 48 (March 1977), 144–53.

[70] Rainer Martens and Julie A. Simon, "Comparisons of Three Predictors of State Anxiety in Competitive Situations," *Res. Quart.,* 47 (October 1976), 381–87.

[71] Rainer Martens and Diane L. Gill, "State Anxiety Among Successful and Unsuccessful Competitors Who Differ in Competitive Trait Anxiety," *Res. Quart.,* 47 (December 1976), 698–708.

[72] Janet A. Taylor, "A Personality Scale of Manifest Anxiety," *Jour. of Abnormal and Social Psych.,* 48 (1953), 285–90.

[73] Barbara A. Nelson and Dorothy J. Allen, "Scale for the Appraisal of Movement Satisfaction," *Perceptual and Motor Skills,* 31 (1970), 795–800.

[74] Elsie Carter Burton, "Relationship Between Trait and State Anxiety, Movement Satisfaction, and Participation in Physical Education Activities," *Res. Quart.,* 47 (October 1976), 326–31.

[75] Rainer Martens, "Anxiety and Motor Behavior: A Review," *Jour. of Motor Behavior,* 3 (June 1971), 151–79.

[76] Albert V. Carron, "Reactions to 'Anxiety and Motor Behavior,'" *Jour. of Motor Behavior,* 3 (June 1971), 181–88.

[77] Ronald G. Marteniuk, "Two Factors to be Considered in the Design of Experiments in Anxiety and Motor Behavior," *Jour. of Motor Behavior,* 3 (June 1971), 189–92.

[78] Janet Taylor Spence, "What Can You Say About a Twenty-Year Old Theory That Won't Die?," *Jour. of Motor Behavior,* 3 (June 1971), 193–203.

[79] Charles D. Spielberger, "Trait-State Anxiety and Motor Behavior," *Jour. of Motor Behavior,* 3 (September 1971), 265–79.

[80] Sabina June Breck, "A Sociometric Measurement of Status in Physical Education Classes," *Res. Quart.,* 21 (May 1950), 75–82.

[81] See J.L. Moreno, "The Three Branches of Sociometry," *Sociometry Monographs,* No. 21 (New York: Beacon House, 1949), pp. 4–5, for a discussion of the historical development of sociometry.

[82] Patricia Whitaker Hale, "Proposed Method for Analyzing Sociometric Data," *Res. Quart.,* 27 (May 1956), 152–61.

[83] Jack K. Nelson and Barry L. Johnson, "Effects of Varied Techniques in Organizing Class Competition upon Changes in Sociometric Status," *Res. Quart.,* 39 (October 1968), 634–39.

[84] Eleanor C. Yukie, "Group Movement and Growth in a Physical Education Class," *Res. Quart.,* 26 (May 1955), 222–33.

[85] Eleanor C. Yukie, citing Hedley S. Dimock, *Rediscovering the Adolescent* (New York: Association Press, 1937).

[86] Elvera Skubic, "A Study in Acquaintanceship and Social Status in Physical Education Classes," *Res. Quart.,* 20 (March 1949), 80–87.

[87] Frances Todd, "Sociometry in Physical Education," *Jour. for Health, Phys. Ed. and Rec.,* 24 (May 1953), 23–24, 36.

[88] Charles C. Cowell, "Validating an Index of Social Adjustment for High School Use," *Res. Quart.,* 29 (March 1958), 7–18.

[89] Charles C. Cowell, citing William G. Trapp, "A Related Study of Social Integration in a College Football Squad," (unpublished minor research project, Purdue University, 1953).

## CHAPTER THIRTEEN

[1] Clifford A. Boyd, "A Philosophy of Assigning Grades in Physical Education Classes," *Phys. Educator,* 14 (May 1957), 64.

[2] Marion R. Broer, "Are Our Physical Education Grades Fair?," *Jour. of Health, Phys. Ed. and Rec.,* 30 (March 1959), 27.

[3] Charles A. Bucher, *Administration of School Health and Physical Education Programs,* 2nd ed. (St. Louis: C.V. Mosby Co., 1958), p. 345.

[4] Mary J. Moriarty, "How Shall We Grade Them?," *Jour. of Health, Phys. Ed. and Rec.,* 25 (January 1954), 27.

[5] Edward F. Voltmer and Arthur A. Esslinger, *The Organization and Administration of Physical Education,* 3rd ed. (New York: Appleton-Century-Crofts, Inc., 1958), p. 346.

[6] John B. Shea, "The Pass-Fail Option and Physical Education," *Jour. of Health, Phys. Ed. and Rec.,* 42 (May 1971), 19–20.

[7] *Webster's Collegiate Dictionary,* 5th ed. (Springfield, Mass.: G. and C. Merriam Co., 1945), p. 74.

[8] William F. Gustafson, "Are Grades Losing Their Significance?," *The Phys. Educator,* 15 (October 1958), 93–94.

[9] Edward L. Clark, "Reliability of Grade-Point Averages," *Jour. of Ed. Res.,* 57 (April 1964), 430.

[10] Warren P. Fraleigh and William F. Gustafson, "Can We Defend Required Programs?," *Jour. of Health, Phys. Ed. and Rec.,* 35 (February 1964), 32.

[11] William F. Gustafson, "A Look at Evaluative Criteria in Physical Education," *The Phys. Educator,* 20 (December 1963), 173.

[12] Amatai Etzioni, "Human Beings Are Not Very Easy to Change After All," *Saturday Review,* June 3, 1972, 45.

[13] William F. Gustafson, "A Look at Evaluative Criteria in Physical Education," pp. 172–73.

[14] Harry Bender, "From Anarchy Toward Order in Grading," *The Tower,* San Jose State College, 1 (Spring 1964), 33–53.

[15] Harold Ladas, "Grades: Standardizing the Unstandard Standard," *Phi Delta Kappan,* LVI (November 1974), 185–87.

[16] Richard C. Callahan, "Contract Grading and Student Performance," *Jour. of Instruct. Psych.,* 6 (Summer 1979), 3–7.

[17] Ronald L. Partin, "Multiple Option Grade Contracts," *The Clearing House,* 53 (November 1979), 133–35.

[18] Callahan, "Contract Grading," p. 6.

[19] Neil Postman, "A D+ for Mr. Ladas," *Phi Delta Kappan,* LVI (November 1974), 187–88.

[20] Ray Hull, "Fairness in Grading: Perceptions of Junior High School Students," *The Clearing House,* 53 (March 1980), 343.

[21] John Cheffers, "Teacher Behavior and Attitudes: Is Change Needed?," in *Briefings 1, Title IX: Moving Toward Implementation,* The National Association for the Physical Education of College Women and The National College Physical Education Association for Men, 1975.

# AUTHOR INDEX

# SUBJECT INDEX